D0145891

ABC-CLIO LITERARY COMPANION

Encyclopedia of Apocalyptic Literature

ABC-CLIO LITERARY COMPANION

Encyclopedia of Apocalyptic Literature

Valerie P. Zimbaro

ABC-CLIO

Santa Barbara, California
Denver, Colorado
Oxford, England

Library of Congress Cataloging-in-Publication Data

Zimbaro, Valerie P.
Encyclopedia of apocalyptic literature / Valerie P. Zimbaro.
p. cm. — (ABC-Clio literary companion)
Includes bibliographical references and index.
ISBN 0-87436-823-5 (alk. paper)
1. Apocalyptic literature—Encyclopedias. 2. Apocalyptic. literature—History and criticism. I. Title. II. Series.
PN56.A69Z56 1996
809′.9338—dc21 96-47123

02 01 00 99 98 97 96 95 10 9 8 7 6 5 4 3 2 1 (cloth)

ABC-CLIO, Inc.
130 Cremona Drive, P.O. Box 1911
Santa Barbara, California 93116-1911

This book is printed on acid-free paper ♾.
Manufactured in the United States of America

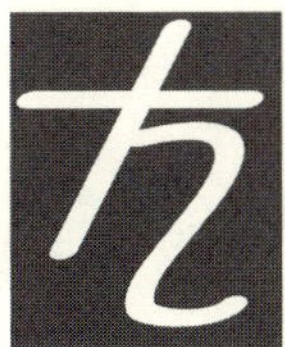

CONTENTS

ACKNOWLEDGMENTS

Preparing this work has been a labor of love. Many individuals contributed to making this text possible, but most did so out of their love for me, their love of literature, and their love of God. Among those who took part in this process are a number of friends, colleagues, students, and relatives without whom this book would not have been possible.

First, I wish to thank my friend and colleague, Mary Ellen Snodgrass, whose experiences as a scholar, writer, editor, and teacher have inspired my own literary career for nearly the past ten years. Next, a most grateful acknowledgment must go to my editors at ABC-CLIO, Suzanne Chance and Henry Rasof. Their patience, enthusiasm, and confidence in my work helped me reach my goals throughout each phase of this process. Further, I would also like to thank the following friends and colleagues for their suggestions, encouragement, and a mountain of borrowed books: Dr. Sylvia Holladay, Dr. Richard LaManna, Dr. Janice Buchanan, Dr. Betty Tutton, Evelyn Finklea, Barbara Wahking, Linda LaPointe, Gabriel Horn (White Deer of Autumn), and Nick Bekas.

I am also deeply grateful to the administrators and staff of the St. Petersburg Junior College Library. I am particularly indebted to Joyce Burkhart, Jayson Nestler, and Dr. Susan Anderson, whose professional assistance and insights proved most valuable to me throughout the completion of this project.

Finally, I wish to thank my entire family, particularly my husband, Ingmars Fridmanis, and my children, Todd and Tracy Pursel. Throughout the year during which I researched and wrote this book, each one provided me with sustaining love as well as continual food for thought, body, and spirit. To these and many more, I extend my deepest appreciation and affection.

INTRODUCTION

Write, therefore, what you have seen, what is now, and
what will take place later.
Revelation 1:19

I write, not to predict possible futures, but to prevent them. If we can learn from
these futures, maybe then we'll behave.
Ray Bradbury—Keynote address. Opening Session. NCTE Convention.
Los Angeles, November 1987

Because I could not stop for Death
He kindly stopped for me.
The Carriage held but just Ourselves—And Immortality.
Emily Dickinson

So we beat on, boats against the current, borne back ceaselessly into the past.
F. Scott Fitzgerald—The Great Gatsby

Things fall apart; the center cannot hold . . . . surely some revelation is at hand.
William Butler Yeats—"The Second Coming"

Take ye heed, watch and pray: for ye know not when the [end] time is.
Mark 13:33

At the time of this writing, the world is poised on the precipice of the year 2000—a monumental millennial milestone. Concurrently, we are also witnessing the final years of yet another century and—much like that which occurred during the *fin de siècle* movement of the late nineteenth century—a resurgent decadence with regard to sociological, ecological, and technological concerns is once again accompanied by an unsettling sense of closure to the prodigious period we've come to know as the twentieth century.

As history reveals, this sense of societal *dis-ease* that occurs while waiting within the silent abyss that links the old to the new corresponds to the sensations evoked by the sounding of the proverbial bell that tolls as a tribute to the final moments of life. As such, whether this bell tolls at the end of an individual life, at the end of a century, or as in the present case, at the end of a millennium, people's souls are, nonetheless, instinctively stirred. Such stirrings have long been evident in the remarkable efforts of the world's great artists, scientists, and visionaries whose works reflect a longing for the past, a strained tolerance for the present, and fantastic dreams for the future. Traditionally, however, many of these fantasies have been most notably recognized throughout the arts in the forms of painting, sculpture, architecture, and music, which have been inspired and celebrated by diverse cultures from around the world. But perhaps nowhere is this creative and curious compulsion about humanity's "endings" more thoroughly analyzed and more completely expressed than it is within the collective body of work known as *apocalyptic literature.* Therefore, this text, which is by no means inclusive of all of the world's apocalyptic writings, is intended both as an introduction to this timely literary genre as well as a tribute to the world's major authors whose prose and poetry reflect their respective hopes, dreams, and fears for the world's last days.

Before addressing the authors and works that *are* included within this volume, it is necessary to make note of a few omissions. For example, although this book is intended to address apocalyptic literature across cultures, readers will find that there is a significant dearth of material related to works by writers from Eastern cultures. This omission, hopefully, is an obvious one inasmuch as the concept of an apocalypse, or a singular cataclysmic ending, is essentially antithetical to most cyclical Eastern philosophies, with the notable exception of the catastrophic myth related to the *kali yuga,* or "evil age, [which is] the last of the four ages of the Indian cosmic cycle." (May 1972, 34) Nevertheless, in an attempt to analyze such apocalyptic themes of either non-Western, primitive, or preliterate cultures, a list of entries pertaining to significant apocalyptic myths, legends, and scriptures has been provided in appendix D to this volume.

Further, as is confirmed by the noted scholar Lois Parkinson Zamora in her study entitled *Writing the Apocalypse,* the following entries also reflect a "virtual absence of women writers . . . . [which] would seem to suggest that apocalyptic modes of conceiving history and narration are less attractive to women than to men." Nevertheless, although she admits that "such a generalization is problematic," she also proffers that there are notable exceptions which include such formidable works as *Frankenstein* by Mary Wollstonecraft Shelley, *The Violent Bear It Away* by Flannery O'Connor, and *The Almanac of the Dead* by Leslie Marmon Silko. (Zamora 7) Clearly, other critics of the genre, such as Joseph Dewey, agree with this observation about the relative lack of women apocalyptic writers, but he also suggests, conversely, that women are directly responsible for developing novels in 1970s and 1980s that have since become recognized as a subgenre of apocalyptic utopian fantasy that has "helped to introduce a sense of radical change, an appreciation of the global stage, and a sense of ministering to a community in crisis" (Dewey 1990, 42). Unfortunately, however, while utopian fiction is as extensive as it is fascinating, it would be impossible to include it in this single volume text. As such, readers who are interested in exploring this particular apocalyptic subgenre are directed to Mary Ellen Snodgrass's *Encyclopedia of Utopian Literature,* which treats both the authors and their works with the considerable depth and insight they deserve.

Nevertheless, returning to the text at hand, this particular book deals solely with the topic of apocalyptic literature. Therefore, the following analysis of such works must naturally commence with humanity's ubiquitous fascination with the world's "end times." In order to explain this fascination, which clearly resonates throughout a prodigious body of literature, Frank Kermode, a venerable scholar of literary apocalypse, produced a seminal study in 1966 entitled *The Sense of an Ending*. As readers will plainly see, his text has been a significant resource in the development of this *Encyclopedia of Apocalyptic Literature*. In his study, Kermode posits that, at its core, apocalyptic literature fulfills a basic human need. Furthermore, he observes that in the twentieth century, perhaps more than at any other time in history, "there is . . . a need to speak humanly of a life's importance . . . a need in the moment of existence to belong, to be related to a beginning and to an end." (Kermode 1967, 4) Ultimately, this need "to belong" and "to speak . . . of a life's importance" serves as the common thread between the works and authors that have been selected for this book. Hopefully, if readers will follow this thread as it weaves its intricate pattern throughout literary time and space, they will all gain a greater appreciation for the terrifying (albeit triumphant) tapestry that portrays the indomitable fabric of the human spirit.

Before examining the specific texts that are included in this work, it is advisable for readers first to become familiar with a few terms that may seem interchangeable but that actually have diverse and precise meanings. For example, the word *apocalyptic* originates from the Greek word *apokalypsis*, which literally means an unveiling, an uncovering, or a revealing of truths that were once withheld. While most cultures of the world still treasure their myths, legends, and moral revelations that have been passed down from generation to generation via oral traditions, students of the apocalypse should note that the first formal apocalyptic writings appeared during the Judeo-Christian period, beginning about 200 B.C. and flourishing through 350 A.D. Because much of this literature was both inspired by, as well as a reaction against, Greco-Roman and Persian religious and political tyranny, it is not surprising that the body of the earliest texts appear either in the forms of protests or prophesies of better times to come. Readers of such early documents should become familiar with another term known as *eschatology* or the study of "last things," a concept that is linked to, but not to be confused with, the actual unveiling of future events, which stands as the hallmark of apocalyptic literature.

While prophetic eschatology clearly led the way for the emergence of apocalyptic literature, considerable discussion of their intertwining meanings continues among scholars, theologians, and agnostics to the present. However, the first formal distinction between the two terms was proposed, in 1979, by the Apocalypse Group of the Society of Biblical Literature Genre's Project. As a result of their efforts, according to John J. Collins and the other members of the group project, the Greek translation of the word *apokalypsis*, and the one which serves as the heart of this text, refers to a particular literary genre that has been defined as follows:

> "Apocalypse" is a genre of revelatory literature with a narrative framework, in which a revelation is mediated by an otherworldly being to a human recipient, disclosing a transcendent reality which is both temporal, insofar as it envisages eschatological salvation, and spatial, insofar as it involves another, supernatural world. (Reddish 1990, 20)

Essentially, this definition of *apocalypse*, in its purest sense, was the working guideline that was originally employed as a means of selecting and categorizing the works that have been included in this book. However, after analyzing such fiction in a broader sense, the term *apocalypticism* seems a more appropriate lens through which to examine certain common elements that are found in most of the entries that readers will observe within the following encyclopedic text. According to Michael G. Reddish, the editor of a Judeo-Christian apocalyptic anthology, the term *apocalypticism* refers to "a pattern of thought or a world view [that is] dominated by the kinds of ideas and motifs found in apocalypses." (Reddish 1990, 23) Based on this premise, therefore, such ideas and motifs as the universal battle between good and evil; the instances of supernatural intervention, of either divine or demonic origins, and the ultimate judgment of humanity after death are all common elements that pervade the multicultural body of literature that has been selected for this text.

Clearly, while the works of Frank Kermode and Michael Reddish were invaluable in the development of this encyclopedia, there is one work, in particular, that provides the rubric or paradigm upon which all entries in this book have been based. The text that contains this paradigm is John R. May's classic study entitled *Toward a New Earth: Apocalypse in the American Novel* (1972). In this work, May (to whom I feel deeply indebted) has provided a list of the "constitutive elements" of various types of apocalypse, which include the following categories:

- Traditional: Primitive
- Traditional: Judeo-Christian
- Anti-Christian
- Secular: Apocalypse of Despair
- Secular: Humorous. (May 1972, 229)

While each of these categories contains specific apocalyptic elements, i.e., forms of judgment, catastrophic warnings, signs of end times, as well as possibilities for new life or regeneration, the following references to individual novels that are specifically covered within this book will best illustrate May's system for categorizing the various types of works that comprise the complete spectrum of the apocalyptic literary genre.

First, since much of the imagery and symbolism found in apocalyptic literature has been inspired by the Bible's final words in Revelation, it is appropriate that this work be identified as an archetype for May's category of Traditional: Judeo-Christian apocalypse. Within this category, May identifies essential elements that had previously been prophesied in such Old Testament texts as Daniel, which include a "Coming Kingdom," the "Last Loosing of Satan," a cataclysmic confrontation between good and evil, and a "linear" progression toward a feeling of "genuine hope." (Ibid.) Therefore, within this encyclopedia, readers will discover countless examples of this type of apocalypse. Most notable among such nonscriptural fictional adaptations are William Faulkner's two classic novels, *Absalom, Absalom!* and *As I Lay Dying;* Flannery O'Connor's *The Violent Bear It Away;* Fyodor Dostoyevsky's *The Brothers Karamazov;* Herman Melville's *Moby Dick;* C. S. Lewis's *Perelandra;* Dante's *The Divine Comedy;* and Walker Percy's *The Thanatos Syndrome,* to name only a few.

Unlike the Traditional Judeo-Christian apocalypse, the Traditional Primitive apocalypse, according to May, *begins* with an earthly paradise rather than the anticipation of a celestial realm. This paradise, however, is soon overtaken by an evil influence, which causes chaos to reign for a time. In spite of the damage caused by the demonic influence, however, the action in such fiction usually concludes with a cyclic return to a more somber reality. (Ibid.) Typical examples of primitive apocalyptic literature include Gabriel Garcia Marquez's *One Hundred Years of Solitude;* Herman Hesse's *Siddhartha;* Leslie Marmon Silko's *Almanac of the Dead;* Jamake Highwater's *Kill Hole,* Carlos Fuentes's *Terra Nostra,* and most notably, Nathaniel Hawthorne's archetypal novel, *The Blithedale Romance.*

Far removed from either of the aforementioned types of traditional apocalypse is a category known as Anti-Christian apocalypse. Based upon its classification, it is not surprisingly, therefore, that such fiction is identifiable by the conspicuous absence of any theocratic forms of guidance, but in their place reign the myriad heresies of a god-less world. Essentially, in such a world ruled by human heretical ideologies, major characters are completely vulnerable to the chaotic forces of both man and nature. Moreover, within such an environment, protagonists often find themselves trapped between their internal delusions, external forces, and societal deceptions, severe conflicts that usually result in death or other forms of disastrous consequence. Although some illusory promise of hope may glimmer for a brief moment near the end of each story within this apocalyptic category, the main characters in such novels, if they have a future at all, are forced to face it squarely with a sense of utter hopelessness. (May 1972, 229) Typical of the Anti-Christian apocalyptic works included in this text are James Baldwin's *Go Tell It on the Mountain;* Mark Twain's *The Mysterious Stranger;* and two poignant works by Nathanael West, *Miss Lonelyhearts* and *The Day of the Locust.*

While the category of Anti-Christian apocalypse represents a dim future in which there is little or no hope, the following two categories of secular apocalyptic literature, with which modern readers are most familiar, clearly reflect a more nefarious and potentially devastating alternative for the future of humanity. Clearly, the movement toward the secular apocalypse originated during the mid-nineteenth century, at about the same time as the optimism regarding the British Industrial Revolution began to spread to America and, later, throughout the world. Bolstered by the seemingly limitless potential of man in control of his newly developed machines, the nineteenth century world began to deify human ingenuity and thereby attempt to attain "the ultimate ideal of transformation without suffering—of progress without end. . . . " (May 1972, 38) This new world view, which was essentially egocentric and gravely ingenuous of any corresponding spiritual, moral, or ethical consequences, soon proved, however, to be devastating to the human spirit. Perhaps the earliest example of humanity's hubris in regard to its use of science and technology occurs in a famous apocalyptic work, which some consider the precursor for the popular genre of science fiction, entitled *Frankenstein, or the Modern Prometheus,* which was written by Mary Wollstonecraft Shelley in 1817. Throughout this regrettable chronicle of a monomaniacal iconoclast who foolishly reveres scientific discovery more than ethical responsibility, readers are vividly introduced to the realization of their futuristic fantasies; what they will find, however, is not a modern miracle but rather a howling, demanding, and tormented monster of technology that will never be appeased until its creator, as well as itself, are both destroyed. Specifically, the publication of this sensational novel opened a veritable Pandora's Box related to apocalyptic literature, which ironically revealed, much too late, that "the trigger for this new [type of secular] apocalypse would be humanity rather than God. . . . [and as such,] humans, it would seem, would [inevitably] plot, construct, and then execute their own demise." (Dewey 1990, 7)

Nevertheless, despite this staggering revelation, the fascination for science fiction, as a subset of secular apocalyptic literature, proliferated within the works of later authors such as H. G. Wells and Jules Verne, and it has continued, to date, in such novels as Mark Twain's *A Connecticut Yankee in King Arthur's Court*, C. S. Lewis's *Out of the Silent Planet*, Aldous Huxley's *Brave New World*, Ray Bradbury's *Fahrenheit 451*, and Pat Frank's *Alas, Babylon*.

Secular apocalypse is not, however, limited strictly to the genre of science fiction. In fact, more often than not, the *first* type of May's secular apocalypse specifically focuses on the internal conflicts of individuals as they struggle to survive amidst the oppressive societal changes that have come about as a result of science, technology, and industrialization. Specifically, in spite of the promise of greater productivity and abundance that was engendered by the early proponents of industrialization, the more sordid side of such an existence has historically been reflected in several novels May identifies in his category known as the Apocalypse of Despair. Within such novels, mankind creates his own gods. And whether these gods be money, licentiousness, or power, innocent people are often unwittingly sacrificed as human beings who carelessly victimize one another in an attempt to appease their personal icons.

Countless examples of this type of literature exist, particularly within the novels written in the late nineteenth and early twentieth centuries. One of the earliest illustrations of humanity's ruthless and predatory nature appears in a savage social satire, replete with apocalyptic imagery, entitled *The Confidence Man: His Masquerade*, the final work by the aging, world-weary cynic, Herman Melville, written in 1857. And just as the "con-men" of Melville's day freely take advantage of simple and guileless people, so too do many representatives of the dominant white culture continue to exploit countless African-Americans who reluctantly populate the seething urban jungles of such apocalyptic novels as Richard Wright's *Native Son*. Consequently, since this type of exploitation has become more evident, particularly within societal and bureaucratic systems, it is understandable how people might have begun to develop a growing sense of paranoia such as that in Thomas Pynchon's satirical novel of life in the modern world, *The Crying of Lot 49*. Consequently, as a result of this increasing pattern of corruption, oppression, and deception, literature that falls within this category clearly illustrates how individuals who confront indomitable forces that are beyond their control inevitably become crushed under the weight and ultimately have no choice but to succumb to utter despair.

While this sense of desperation continues to run throughout the extant body of popular literature, R. W. B. Lewis notes that these "perennial degenerative tendencies of human nature and . . . metaphors to gauge their enormity" have since engendered a new, and perhaps more ameliorative literary form which May categorizes as "Humorous apocalypse" (May 1972, 227). Essentially, this type of literature, which reflects many of the cultural values of the second half of the twentieth century, "recreates man's capacity to look with hope upon his history of mistakes" and urges him not only to use laughter to "relieve the tension" of modern life, but also to allow it to become "a passage to the future" (May 1972, 228). Specific novels that seem to reflect the modern paradox of anger mixed with laughter, or hope stained by despair include an impressive body of works by formidable authors such as Kurt Vonnegut, in both *Slaughter-House Five* and *Cat's Cradle;* John Barth, in *Giles Goat-Boy;* and Thomas Pynchon, in his magnum opus and what some consider to be the final word on the fate of modern man in the nuclear age, *Gravity's Rainbow.* In his last comments within the novel, Pynchon likens the modern world to a European war theater in which humanity—each person in his or her own way a fascinated student of the apocalypse—waits and watches a silent white screen and anticipates life's culminating event with such instinctive shouts as: "Come-*on! Start*-the *show!* (Pynchon 1973, 760). Nevertheless, in the last moments, his microcosmic universal audience is nearly blinded by a "luminous" star, perhaps "a bright angel of death" that fills the screen with "a film that we have not [completely] learned to see." (Ibid.)

But what we *can* eventually see, both as readers and viewers of this expansive apocalyptic screen is, as Pynchon states, "a close-up of the face, a face we all know." (Ibid. 760) Further, this face has an ancient voice that has always spoken to man throughout art and literature and continues to speak even now, as humanity waits within a darkened theater nearing the end of time. Ultimately, after reading this text, readers will become better able to recognize this venerable voice that has resonated throughout literary history, and as a result, will either be soothed or haunted by the words contained in the following apocalyptic promise: ". . . behold, I come quickly; and my reward is with me, to give every man according as his work shall be. I am the Alpha and Omega, the beginning and the end, the first and the last." (Revelation 22:12-13)

ABSALOM

The brief, proud, and rebellious life of Absalom and its consequences are recounted in the Old Testament book of 2 Samuel, chapters 13–20. As detailed in the scripture, Absalom was the third son of King David; handsome and headstrong, Absalom was able to engender support from the men of Israel to help him overthrow his father and become the new king. While King David and his army knew of this pending rebellion, the king gave orders for his soldiers not to harm his beloved son. Neverthless, the plans of both father and son were thwarted during the definitive battle at Ephraim. While riding into battle on a mule, Absalom's hair became entangled in the branches of an oak tree. Seizing this opportune moment to protect his master, King David's general, Joab, killed Absalom while the young man was suspended in the tree.

Upon learning that his son had been murdered in spite of his command, King David was overcome with grief and wailed this resounding lament: "O my son Absalom my son, my son Absalom! would I had died for thee, O Absalom, my son, my son!" (2 Samuel 18:35–37). The story of King David's tragic loss and the death of a son whose life held such promise has become a classic reference to the bottomless grief resulting from a parent's loss of a child. In addition, this story has served as the basis of many modern tales of rebellious progeny, deferred familial dreams, and parental despair (*Open Bible* 1975).

See also *Absalom, Absalom!;* Faulkner, William; Sutpen, Thomas.

ABSALOM, ABSALOM!

Absalom, Absalom! (1936) is William Faulkner's ninth and most critically acclaimed novel about the personal grief and societal loss that occurred throughout the nineteenth-century American South. Using a complex experimental style, Faulkner reveals the tragic entanglements of several families in Jefferson, Mississippi, by intermingling the narrative voices of witnesses and ancestors affected by the events surrounding a single demonic character, Thomas Sutpen.

According to the criteria established by critic of apocalyptic literature John R. May, this novel, as does most of Faulkner's fiction, represents a classical treatment of the Judeo-Christian apocalyptic tradition. According to this tradition, "it is the dark moment of truth for the individual that yields new life for those judged worthy of the kingdom" (May 1972, 205); such is the case for the narrators of the story *Absalom, Absalom!*, whose individual truths are memories born in water that are ultimately purified by the wrathful judgment of fire.

As established by various narrators, the "truth" was born in 1833 when a mysterious stranger, Thomas Sutpen, came to Jefferson in a furious entrance worthy of the Four Horsemen of the Apocalypse. According to one account, this "man-horse-demon" invaded the peaceful town with a "faint sulphur-reek still in hair clothes and beard," accompanied by a wild band of Haitian blacks, wagon loads of guns and tools, and an indentured French architect. Sutpen's intent, diabolical as well as mythical in proportion, was to wrest from the watery swamp a "hundred square miles of tranquil and astonished earth [and to] drag house and formal gardens violently out of the soundless Nothing . . ." (*Absalom* 4). This grand "design," which eventually becomes known as "Sutpen's Hundred," serves as the setting for the antagonist's destructive legacy of incest, miscegenation, misery, and murder.

The title of the novel comes directly from the tragic story of King David and his son Absalom, in 2 Samuel. In many ways, King David's fate, and the inevitable destruction of his family, resulted from his willful pursuit of his own wishes. Because of his overwhelming desire for another man's wife, King David abused his power, arranged for the murder of an innocent man (Uriah, the Hittite), and eventually took the man's widow as his wife. Although he hoped that theirs would be a fruitful union upon which to build his kingdom, their first son died, and much later, another beloved son, Absalom, rose up against the father and was also murdered, thereby thwarting the king's great plan.

Many similarities to this tale exist in Faulkner's work. Specifically, in order to fulfill his own grand design, Thomas Sutpen feels he is justified in using any means to gain his end result. His methods parallel those of King David in that he deserts one wife and child because of the secret of mixed blood in her line, cruelly exploits workers, lovelessly takes a second wife in order to become part of an established family, and then ruthlessly destroys anyone—family, friend, or foe—who dares threaten the success of his plan. Nevertheless, in spite of his elaborate efforts to create a paradise on earth in which he and his progeny would flourish, Thomas Sutpen's egoistic actions ironically result in his own violent death, the incendiary destruction of his prized plantation, and, with the singular exception of an idiot black descendent, the complete ruination of his entire family line.

Ultimately, the only thing that remains of Sutpen's efforts is the story itself that is passed from generation to generation, and eventually to an objective, non-Southern narrator. Clearly, the myth of Sutpen, in all of its cataclysmic detail, was intended by Faulkner to deliver an apocalyptic message. This view is supported by literary critic Lois Parkinson Zamora, who concludes that the destruction of Sutpen's Hundred in *Absalom, Absalom!* epitomizes literary apocalypse because it emphasizes "the irrefutability of the end" and "implies the death not only of an individual . . . , but of a people," specifically, the people and the traditions of the antebellum American South (Zamora 1989, 38).

See also Apocalypse: Traditional Judeo-Christian; Coldfield, Rosa; Compson, Quentin; Faulkner, William; Sutpen, Thomas.

ACHEBE, CHINUA

Born in 1930, Chinua Achebe is the distinguished Nigerian novelist, poet, essayist, and short-story writer who is best known for his work detailing the problems of assimilation for people living between the Western European and African cultures. His first novel, *Things Fall Apart* (1958), brought him critical acclaim as one of Africa's greatest writers. In this work, which is today considered a universal classic, Achebe reflects on the problems facing traditional Africans who struggle to maintain their ancient rituals, while at the same time attempting to assimilate some of the more attractive elements of the dominant Western culture. The author clearly addresses these themes of tribal versus colonial life in his subsequent books, *No Longer at Ease* (1960), *Arrow of God* (1964), and *Anthills of the Savannah* (1987), as well as in most of his notable short stories.

In addition to his own writing, Achebe has also edited the respected Nigerian literary journal for new writers, *Okike*, since 1971, and he has taught both English and African studies at numerous universities. Although Achebe continues his work, his life has been drastically changed as a result of a 1990 car accident that left him paralyzed from the waist down.

See also Apocalypse: Traditional Primitive; Eliot, T. S.; Entropy; *The Hollow Men; Things Fall Apart*.

Nigerian author Chinua Achebe, a visiting professor at Bard College in New York in 1988 when this photograph was taken, writes of the clash between tribal and Western European cultures in Africa.

AHAB

Ahab was one of the most pernicious kings of Israel whose torment of the Old Testament prophet Elijah is chronicled in 1 Kings 16–22. So objectional were his efforts that the name Ahab has long been considered synonymous with a narcissistic willfullness and a tendency toward depravity. Ahab's extreme nature was re-created most memorably in the modern literary classic by Herman Melville, *Moby-Dick* (1851). In this milestone of American literature, the character Ahab is Melville's antagonist whose myopic malevolence, as captain of the *Pequod,* is responsible for his own destruction as well as that of most of his crew.

In order to appreciate the intense determinism of Melville's Ahab, it is necessary first to become familiar with the biblical account of King Ahab and his corrupt wife, Jezebel, who were jointly responsible for encouraging the idolatrous worship of the false god Ba'al. While most of their related activities, including the recognition of countless false prophets, were offensive to the Lord God and to the prophet Elijah, Ahab's most egregious error in judgment was the establishment of an elaborate garden shrine wherein the ritual worship of Ba'al was conducted with regularity. Ultimately, as was prophesized by the Old Testament sage, King Ahab (much like Melville's character of the same name) was undermined and finally destroyed by his own interminable megalomania.

See also Ahab, Captain; Apocalypse: Traditional Judeo-Christian; *Moby-Dick.*

AHAB, CAPTAIN

Captain Ahab is the flawed fictional hero of Herman Melville's apocalyptic magnum opus, *Moby-Dick* (1851). Although prior to the beginning of the novel, Ahab is portrayed as having been a devoted family man as well as an intelligent and respected sailor whose exploits provided him with a wide range of adventures, his character within the novel is one of a tyrant who reigns as the vengeful captain of the whaling vessel the *Pequod.*

The event that transforms this once admirable man into a raging monomaniac occurs prior to the beginning of the story when a fierce white whale attacks Ahab's ship and malevolently bites off his leg. The trauma of this attack, on both his physical body as well as his pride, gradually disintegrates Ahab's humanity throughout the novel, turning him into a ruthless leader whose sole focus in life is to exact revenge by hunting and killing Moby-Dick, the great white whale.

Ahab's anger at the whale, however, is really representative of his anger toward the God of the universe, whom the captain blames for allowing such a senseless accident to ruin his life. Thus, the peg leg upon which Ahab perpetually paces the deck of the ship serves as a constant reminder of his wounded pride. It is this profound humiliation that propels him to re-create his own universe by destroying the force that he believes has destroyed his life. In the process, Ahab uses bribery, verbal abuse, and bodily harm to enlist members of his crew to disregard their initial whaling mission and to join him in his unholy quest for revenge.

Ahab's methods are persuasive, but even in the midst of his escalating treachery, some remnants of his former basic human kindness are apparent, par-

Captain Ahab, tangled in lines on the flank of the long-sought white whale Moby-Dick, drives home a harpoon. Herman Melville's 1851 novel about the monomaniacal Ahab was released as a movie in 1956 with Gregory Peck as Ahab.

ticularly his treatment of the idiot sailor, Pip. Such fleeting demonstrations provide cause for his crew's loyalty and evidence of the suffering that Ahab must have known before becoming the madman who eventually leads them to their collective doom.While this highly intelligent leader does not suffer fools well, and in some cases treats his less intelligent subordinates with contempt, Captain Ahab understands the importance of engendering a unity of purpose if he is ever to accomplish his mad albeit monomaniacal personal goal. As such, Ahab personifies the typical apocalyptic hero whose own will, intelligence, or intense pride causes him to retrace the steps of the archetypal Adam and pursue a cataclysmic course that will eventually lead to the annihilation of his or her world along with those who unwittingly inhabit it.

See also Ahab; Apocalypse: Traditional Judeo-Christian; Apocalyptic Literature; Archetype; Ishmael; *Moby-Dick.*

ALAS, BABYLON

This 1959 novel by Pat Frank (a.k.a. Harry Hart) contains traditional apocalyptic elements, including the theme of humanity's destruction as a result of society's reckless behavior and progressive state of moral decline. While the novel has enjoyed great popularity, critics still disagree about its literary merit. Some believe that the tale is a minor work that merely attempts to retell the story of Robinson Crusoe. Others disregard it as an optimistic fantasy that understates the gravity of a nuclear catastrophe. Still others, however, view the work as a commercial exploitation of society's fears of nuclear holocaust and dismiss it as a heavy-handed modern-day morality play that interprets a nuclear accident as the advent to the Christian Day of Judgment (Dewey 1990, 9).

Nevertheless, in spite of these negative critical opinions, *Alas, Babylon* remains popular among readers because it examines important issues concerning individual responsibility, the destructive potential of technology, and the pervasive ethical decay that threatens the survival of humankind. While these issues are indeed weighty and complex, the story itself is a simple one dealing with the effects of a national catastrophe on the lives of a few ordinary citizens in a small Southern town named, ironically, Fort Repose, Florida.

The insignificance of this sleepy town is demonstrated at the outset of the novel through the actions of the main characters. From the beginning, they move listlessly in and out of their daily routines that are punctuated only by the fleeting entertainment of local animal antics, televised news reports, and the steady stream of neighborhood gossip. One of the favorite topics of gossip is the novel's protagonist, Randy Bragg, a local attorney who is the playboy bachelor son of the deceased Judge Bragg and brother of the equally formidable Mark Bragg, an intelligence officer for the Strategic Air Command.

Because he has found it difficult to live up to his family's expectations, Randy becomes an underachiever and alcoholic. All of this changes, however, after he receives a Western Union telegram from his brother, Mark, who has shared the secret code, "Alas, Babylon," with Randy to warn him of impending disaster. This phrase, taken from the biblical book of Revelation, was one that the brothers had heard in a sermon of a zealous Baptist preacher during their youth. Recalling the profound impact of this fire and brimstone sermon, they agreed if Mark, in his high military position, were given warning of a nuclear attack, he would communicate this phrase to Randy, who would then have sufficient time to save both himself and his brother's family. As such, when Randy reads his brother's telegram, he knows that he can no longer remain irresponsibly inert.

Essentially, this telegram marks the pivotal point in the plot of the novel wherein the news of an accidental nuclear attack sends the town into a frenzy. While Randy discovers his true nature and emerges as a community leader, other citizens take advantage of the chaotic situation and resort to looting, suicide, and murder. Although the bomb blast kills most of the people in the country, a small group of survivors decides to band together as Randy's paramilitary "Bragg troop," using their remaining natural resources to forge a new society. Ironically, the book ends with the Phoenixlike group's having succeeded in literally fighting fire with fire, i.e., with the destructive forces of technology being consumed by the regenerative forces of intellect, hope, and the indomitable human spirit (Frank 1959, 1983).

See also Apocalypse: Traditional Judeo-Christian; Babylon; Phoenix; Revelation, Book of; Science Fiction.

ALLEGORY

Allegory is a type of figurative language used in fictional narratives to convey multiple levels of meaning. The types of allegory that are most recognizable include fables, such as those of Aesop, and parables, such as those that appear in both the Old and New Testaments of the Bible. In regard to the use of allegory in literature, however, writers often attempt to convey complex experiences or abstract ideas in terms of actual characters, behaviors, or material objects.

One of the more popular allegories of all time is John Bunyan's two-part religious allegory entitled *The Pilgrim's Progress.* In this work, the author uses specific characters to personify human traits. For example, Faithful, Hopeful, and Evangelist are actual characters, but their names also clearly inform the readers of their respective roles within a story that, when read on a literal level, is merely a tale of a man's journey through life. However, when the work is interpreted on a figurative level, this one man's journey and the characters he meets can also represent the challenges and triumphs of the spiritual pilgrimage that is common to the universal human experience.

In addition to the traditional allegory is an alternate form of the technique known as symbolic allegory. Within this form, not only is a character a representation of some abstract concept or idea, but he or she is also a real and often identifiable person. For example, Dante Alighieri uses symbolic allegory in his apocalyptic masterpiece, *The Divine Comedy,* in which the protagonist's guide through hell and purgatory is the revered Roman poet Virgil. In a figurative sense, Virgil represents the qualities of intellectual choice based upon reason, but as the author of the poetic narrative *The Aeneid,* he also brings historical significance as it relates to his function in Dante's work.

While allegory, as a means of literary expression, was a favorite literary form employed by ancient authors, it has also served as a valuable tool for modern writers as well. One of the more popular and widely read modern allegories that deals with the issue of politics is George Orwell's 1945 novel entitled *Animal Farm.* In this work, the animals on the farm join forces to overthrow the corrupt farmer who seems insensitive to their daily tribulations. While they succeed in doing so, it is not long before the animals themselves split into factions, demonstrating similar callousness in regard to the oppression they place on members of rival factions. This story, when read on the literal level, is an entertaining moral fable; its deeper meaning, and one that was deliberately intended by the author, relates how the Russian people, who had supported the Bolshevik Revolution, were disappointed when Russia's new form of government proved to be even more oppressive than its former system of rule.

While allegory has always functioned as a means of literary expression, it was not always held in high regard, particularly by those who, in the nineteenth century, found it difficult to delineate between the opposing forces of reason and imagination. Nevertheless, as a result of the psychoanalytical dream interpretations of Sigmund Freud, the theory of the collective unconscious promoted by Carl Jung, the father of psychological archetypes, and the mythological studies of James Frazer in *The Golden Bough,* allegory has reemerged as a significant factor in the development of modern literature. Consequently, this technique has been skillfully used by such renowned authors as James Joyce, William Golding, William Faulkner, Franz Kafka, and D. H. Lawrence. And as a result of their successful application of the device, allegory is certain to remain a prominent technique in the development of novels in the future.

See also *Absalom, Absalom!;* Apocalyptic Literature; Archetype; Freud, Sigmund; Jung, Carl Gustav; *Lord of the Flies;* Myth; Revelation, Book of; Symbol.

ALMANAC OF THE DEAD

Almanac of the Dead (1991) is the voluminous apocalyptic novel by Leslie Marmon Silko, who has been hailed as one of the most significant Native American authors of the twentieth century. As the title implies, the "Almanac" refers to an actual set of ancient codicils, or historical manuscripts, that recorded the behaviors and beliefs of the Mayan Indian people so that their culture would not be forgotten after the imminent destruction of their civilization. Although fragments of these documents actually exist and are located in Mexico City, Madrid, Paris, and Dresden, the premise of Silko's novel involves the fictional existence of a fifth almanac that has found its way into the hands of the central characters within the novel.

By relying upon the metaphor of an almanac, which deals with traditions of the past, present, and future, Silko creates a powerful apocalyptic narrative that recounts the brutal obliteration of a culture in the name of developing a white American civilization. She does so by introducing Yoeme, a previously persecuted woman from the Yaqui tribe, who possesses fragments of a fifth almanac manuscript. Believing in the limitless power within the words of the historical document, Yoeme presents it as a gift to her twin granddaughters, Lecha and Zeta, who set out to decode the enigmatic text. During the process of decoding the almanac, Silko reveals details about the violence experienced by Lecha and Zeta as well as the collective despair of nearly seventy other characters whose daily lives have driven them, in some cases, to the edge of madness. Through the interlacing of various narrative tales written from the Native American perspective, *Almanac of the Dead* constructs an apocalyptic prophecy in which the vengeful spirits of decimated tribal nations join forces in retaliation against the dominant white culture to reclaim North America at the end of the millennium.

See also Apocalypse: Traditional Primitive; Apocalyptic Literature; *Kill Hole;* Silko, Leslie Marmon.

ANATOMY OF CRITICISM: FOUR ESSAYS

This work by respected writer and critic Northrop Frye, published in 1957, is a seminal reference of stylistic elements found in various literary genres. Essentially, this text is a reader's companion that explains the basic principles of literary theory. Within the four essays of the text, Frye examines the criteria used to conduct critical analysis of literary works: rhetorical modes, symbols, myths, and literary genres. Moreover, Frye examines specific works of Western literature according to historical references and significance, ethical treatment of subject matter, specifically chosen archetypal patterns with universally understood meanings, and the rhetorical style through which particular authors express their creativity. While Frye's text is considered a primary resource for literary scholars, he is generous in his acknowledgments of other researchers, and their valuable resources, who contributed to his critical approach, such as Carl Jung (theory of archetypes) and James Frazer (treatise on folklore, religion, and myth entitled *The Golden Bough*) (Frye 1971).

See also Apocalyptic Literature; Apocalypticism; Archetype; Freud, Sigmund; *The Golden Bough: A Study in Magic and Religion;* Jung, Carl Gustav; Myth; Symbol.

ANTICHRIST

According to 1 John 2:22, the Antichrist is "He that denieth the Father and the Son." Another description of this apocalyptic archetype is recorded in 2 Thessalonians 2:1–17, which warns believers not to fall prey to the deceptions that "the man of sin, the son of perdition" (v. 3, KJV) will employ to delude the faithful and thereby keep them from attaining eternal salvation. The Bible, particularly in the New Testament book of Revelation, is filled with prophesies pertaining to the destruction caused by the Antichrist. Other sources originating in Babylonian myth and later supported in Judaic literature reveal legends about Satan's minion and formidable enemy of God who is scheduled to arrive prior to the Second Coming of Christ in a desperate effort to delude the faithful and lead them to ultimate damnation upon the Last Judgment. The reason that the Antichrist will have such influence is indicated throughout the scriptures. For example, according to Revelation 13:3, the Antichrist will become a celebrated miracle worker. Also in Revelation, the Antichrist has some identifiable characteristics that include bestial traits of multiple heads and horns with ominous references to the number 666.

Although the Antichrist is expected to arrive at a time near the end of the world when apostasy and faithlessness are pervasive, some have linked his historical appearance with specific tyrannical and corrupt leaders such as the Roman emperors Nero and Caligula; this suspicion of early Christians is also recorded in Revelation 17:9–10. Believers should be vigilant in their study of the scriptures so that they will be able to recognize the charismatic leader who will become a false prophet—the nefarious enemy of righteousness who will seduce unwitting followers with the promise to restore the holy city of Jerusalem. According to prophecy, however, deluded believers will realize they have fallen into his trap but will be helpless and spiritually lost as the Antichrist prepares for the final battle with the church in which he will be vanquished by the omnipotent forces of God.

See also Allegory; Apocalypse: Traditional Judeo-Christian; Apocalyptic Literature; Dante Alighieri; God; Hell; Mephistophiles; Revelation, Book of; Satan.

The top register of this mid–thirteenth century English manuscript shows the Antichrist sitting on a throne, right, his tail draped with his robes. A soldier, left, sword raised, threatens four priests. The bottom register shows Christ toppling the Antichrist from the throne while two devils hold his hands.

APOCALYPSE: ANTI-CHRISTIAN

One type of apocalyptic fiction, containing heretical elements that run counter to those of the traditional Judeo-Christian form of apocalypse as found in the book of Revelation, is anti-Christian apocalypse. According to John R. May's framework of apocalyptic fiction, the anti-Christian apocalypse is characterized by the absence of theocratic forms of justice in favor of the secular mores of a corrupt human system. As such, given the absence of traditional spiritual wisdom as a guide for human behavior, the world is ripe for the tyrannical intrusion of a demonic force that brings chaos to an already rudderless world.

Using biblical terms to describe this diabolical reign of terror, May introduces the apocalyptic concept of the "Last Loosing" of Satan, or more appropriately, the autocratic influence of a ruthless antagonist whose evil and self-serving actions result in either the literal or figurative death of a protagonist, a sacrificial archetype, or a previously held system of belief (May 1972, 229). Although for a time, within an anti-Christian apocalypse, the characters are either numbed or completely deluded by the negative force in their lives, any attempt to escape the antagonist or avoid the inevitable consequences of his actions results in a sense of hopelessness, loss, and waste.

See also Baldwin, James; *The Day of the Locust; Go Tell It on the Mountain; Miss Lonelyhearts; The Mysterious Stranger;* Shrike; Simpson, Homer.

APOCALYPSE: BUDDHIST

The myth of Maitreya (c. 500–600 B.C.) is based upon an account included within the Mahayana Buddhist writings, or a collection of sacred texts that "have their origins in ancient Indian thought, particularly in the *Bhagavad Gita*" (Feibleman 41–42). This form of Buddhism, which initially proliferated throughout Tibet, Korea, Japan, and Mongolia, promises that if individuals live their lives according to Dharma, or "the rule of law which determines one's duties and according to which there is no distinction between the laws of nature and those of human society (5–6), then it is possible to enter into the eternal state of heavenly bliss known as Nirvana.

The myth of Maitreya is not one that deals directly with elements of apocalypse; rather, it deals more with the completion of a human and spiritual cycle that can be predicted by events that will take place at some time in the remote future. At that time, significant changes will be noted within the world. In regard to geography, the partial evaporation of the oceans will enable Asia to reclaim land for its growing population and will make it easier for people to travel. In addition, human hostility will subside, and this will lead to greater longevity, a diminution of sickness, and the elimination of war. At that time, the earth will be under the rulership of a Buddha named Shankha who will spread his Dharma, or way of enlightenment, throughout the people of the world. During his reign, he will also prepare the world for the coming of the final Buddha, named Maitreya, whose birth will "announce that this is [Buddha's] last [incarnation]," thereby leaving Nirvana or "the supreme enlightenment" as his final destination (Bierlein 246).

During the reign of Maitreya, he "will contemplate the nature of things and see the illusory aspect of mortal life." Maitreya, and his huge number of followers, will be directly addressed from the heavens by "Brahma, the Eternal God, [who] will announce the truth of the Dharma out of heaven in his own voice." Upon hearing the word of Brahma, people will rearrange their priorities. Essentially, they will focus more on achieving enlightenment than on acquiring material possessions. Celibacy will be a common practice; there will be no need to continue procreation since humans will live very long lives. In their midst, "Maitreya himself will preach for over sixty thousand years in this environment of perfect harmony, after which he will leave the earth to go to his Nirvana, absolute union with God." In regard to those remaining on the earth, the Dharma, or eternal law, will be practiced by all people for another period lasting ten thousand years, after which "all humans will achieve Nirvana." At the end of this period, and after pain, oppression, and confusion disappear from the earth, "Brahma himself will teach the universal truth directly to humankind, revealing things concealed even from the Buddhas" (246).

See also Apocalypse: Traditional Primitive; Apocalypticism; Eschatology; God; Myth.

APOCALYPSE: HINDU

In the Myth of Rudra (c. 2000–1000 B.C.), Rudra is the storm god or "destroyer of all things" who emerges from the form of Vishnu at the end of the last of the Four Ages, or yugas, according to the Hindu account of the apocalypse. Although the concept of one final apocalypse is antithetical to most Eastern religions, the concept of triadic cycles, i.e., creation (Brahma), sustenance (Vishnu), and destruction (Shiva), is common to Hindu apocalyptic myth.

Essentially, after the final yuga has been completed, the myth indicates that the earth will be "completely exhausted of its resources." At such time, Rudra will cause a 100-year drought that will eliminate all forms of life on earth. Upon completion of this phase, Rudra will then enter the sun and will dry up all the waters of the earth; "the ancient teachers called this 'the sucking of the waters by Rudra.'" Once all the planet's moisture has been removed, the sun's heat will burn and thereby purify the planet until Rudra, breathing thunderbolts and clouds, will cause it to rain for at least one thousand years until the fires of the earth are smothered. Eventually, however, when the waters reach "the realm of the seven sages, far above the surface of the earth," then Brahma will generate a wind to absorb some of the moisture leaving the earth amidst "a watery chaos" that will serve as the "primordial" site for the creation of a new world (Bierlein 1994, 238).

See also Apocalypse: Traditional Primitive; Apocalypticism; God; Myth.

APOCALYPSE: ISLAMIC

Islamic apocalypse is based upon the scripture known as the Qu'ran, Quran, or the Koran, which Muslims believe consists of revelations presented directly to Muhammad by God, Allah, as an expression of the eternal truth. The Qu'ran is considered by Muslims to be the ultimate authority in regard to righteous behavior, requirements of faith, and spiritual practice in preparation for the end times.

As in most eschatological accounts, the Islamic apocalypse will be heralded by earthquakes and the leveling of mountains across the surface of the earth. At that time, humanity will appear before Allah and be separated into three groups: the blessed will stand to the right, the damned will stand to the left, and the righteous, consisting of great souls from the past, will stand to the fore of the crowd and "shall be brought near to their Lord in the gardens of delight" (Bierlein 1994, 242). The rewards to the righteous will consist of opulence and the fulfillment of all of their desires. They will "recline on jeweled couches," be served the finest wines and the most sumptuous fruits and fowl, and be presented with beautiful dark-eyed women who will eagerly fulfill their sensual desires (242). As for the blessed, or those on the right hand of Allah, they too will enjoy the opulence and fulfillment of their desires although it will be to a lesser extent than will be experienced by the righteous. The damned, or those on the left hand of Allah, will "dwell amidst scorching winds and seething water; in the shade of pitch black smoke, neither cool nor refreshing" (242). And in spite of their efforts to convince the blessed to share some of their eternal rewards, their requests will be denied, as symbolized by a great wall with a gate that will eternally separate the factions. "Inside shall be mercy, and out, to the fore, the scourge of hell" (243). At this point, the damned will know that they had been deceived during their wretched lives on earth, and for eternity they will suffer with the knowledge that there will be "no ransom . . . accepted" for the remission of their sins (243).

The Hadith is an Islamic text that contains fragments of the oral traditions historically associated with Muhammad's prophesies. In the Hadith, Muhammad explains which signs will herald the end of the world. First, the prophet asserts that people will stop studying the Qu'ran. This will come as a result of their relentless pursuit of material wealth and sensual pleasure on earth. They will be shaken from their complacency and immorality, however, by a series of cataclysmic events including epidemics, famines, plagues, thunderstorms, floods, the invasion of murderous bandits, and the appearance of the Dajjal—the Antichrist who will conduct a reign of terror for forty days until Jesus arrives to do battle with the Beast. In spite of the rampant fear that will reign over the earth, a number of believers will assist Jesus in his defeat of the Dajjal, but the Dajjal will not be killed; instead, God will cause his feet to be "fixed firmly to the earth" while Jesus prepares to "administer the fatal blow" (244).

After the destruction of the Dajjal, Jesus will bring forth a reign of peace over the earth for a period of eighty-seven years, after which his soul will be taken back to heaven. Within the following week, however, "the monstrous Gog and Magog, . . . who had been imprisoned by Alexander [Iskandar] the Great, will break free, ruining civilization. In response to this, God will send two angels to the earth. The first, Azrail, also known as the angel of death, will gently call the righteous to eternal rest, after which, he will savagely tear the souls out of the bodies of the wicked (244). The second angel, Israfil, will then "blo[w] the trumpet of the last day." At that time, those still left on the earth will suffer terrestrial cataclysms. A second blast of the trumpet will herald the reunion of the bodies and souls of the righteous dead, and the third trumpet blast will herald the return of Muhammad, who brings with him the "great scales of judgment" in order to determine who will be saved and who will be damned. Further, according to scripture, this "Judgment will last only one hour." In the end, everyone, both the righteous and the damned, "will cross the bridge into Paradise, which is as thin as a hair" (245). Therefore, according to plan, the righteous will cross easily into their eternal reward, whereas the damned will fall from the bridge to suffer perpetual torment in hell.

See also: Apocalypticism; Eschatology; God; Gog and Magog; Myth.

APOCALYPSE: NORSE

The Myth of Ragnarok (c. A.D. 800) is only one of the ancient Norse myths concerning the end of the world, which will usher in a golden age that is referred to as the "Twilight of the Gods" (Bierlein 1994, 246). Essentially, doomsday will involve the ultimate battle wherein Loki, the "Evil One" or the god of chaos, will cause earthquakes, floods, and famine to destroy all the other gods as well as the mortals who inhabit the earth. Also, as in other myths, on that fateful day "the sun will no longer shine, and the stars will fall from heaven" (247).

Following the complete destruction of the earth, Alfadur, also known as "All Father, the great and only eternal God," will be the only deity to remain in existence, and he will begin again to re-create a new earth. He will populate the earth with new creatures by restoring Lif (female life force) and Lifthrasir (male life force), enabling them to "start the human race anew" (248).

See also Apocalypse: Traditional Primitive; Apocalypticism; Eschatology; Myth.

APOCALYPSE: PERSIAN

The Persian apocalypse is based on the Iranian religion known as Zoroastrianism. The *Gathas* (c. 630–550 B.C.) or the seventeen religious poems that are embedded within the scripture, the *Avesta*, were written by Zoroaster, the founder of the ancient doctrine. As revealed within this scriptural document, Zoroaster's vision of the end of the world has striking similarities with Greek, Jewish, and early Christian eschatological doctrines.

According to the myth, Zoroaster, as a representative "Believer of the True Faith," directs several questions to Ormazd, also known as "the Wise Lord," regarding the ultimate fate that will befall both the righteous and the wicked at the Last Judgment. Further, he asks what a righteous person could do in order to prepare for Judgment Day. In response, Ormazd warns the supplicant against listening to "the followers of the Evil One." Although believers might be influenced by the dreadful power of the Evil One and his followers during the end times, true believers are urged to "[f]ight them with all [their] might!" By doing so, the righteous will "be saved from destruction and darkness," they will be "granted the joy of divine fellowship," and they will experience "the fulness of health, immortality, just and power. . . ." Conversely, however, the "wicked ones" are warned to "beware" because as a result of their evil deeds, they will be scourged with "foul food and the worst curses at the time of the end days" (Bierlein 1994, 239–240).

In order for the righteous to be prepared for the end times, the Wise Lord presents a series of events or signs that will foreshadow the Day of Judgment. First, he states that "[t]here will be three saviors sent to earth . . . before the final, inevitable battle that will result in the ultimate triumph of good over evil, the Last Judgment, and the resurrection of the dead" (240). Specifically, the birth of the first savior and "champion of the faithful" will be named Anshedar. He will come following a time referred to as "the Period of Iron" during which demons will have attacked the earth and tormented its inhabitants. In a supernatural response to the demonic devastation, the sun and the moon will be dimmed, and then "a shower of stars will occur to herald" Anshedar's birth. He will be born to a fifteen-year-old virgin "who will bathe in a sacred lake in Iran that has been miraculously impregnated with the sperm of the prophet Zoroaster" (240).

Although this savior will settle the earth for a time, "suffering, disease, war, and hunger" will herald the birth of a second savior, Aushedarmah, who will be conceived in the same way as his predecessor. In the days of Aushedarmah's reign, "evil will be subdued, but not entirely conquered." In addition, the people of the world will become vegetarians in order to limit the aggression intrinsic to carnivorous human behavior. The more frightening aspect of Aushedarmah's reign, however, is that an "evil dragon, Azhidahaka," will rise from his long sleep, will emerge from his primordial cave, and will begin to kill "one third of all humans and animals." In order to subdue the beast, an ancient Persian hero, Keresaspa, "will be resurrected by the Lord" and will slay the beast allowing good to reign temporarily over evil (241).

Within the next thousand-year period, Saoshyant, the third and final savior, also originating from a virgin birth in the same manner as his precursors, "will herald the final judgment of the living and the dead." Upon his arrival, the wicked people upon the earth will be consumed by a flood of molten metal; although this flood will cover the earth, only the wicked will suffer great pain while to the righteous, the flood will seem like a "refreshing warm bath" (241).

At this point, the souls of the dead as well as those of the living will be joined for final judgment. Saoshyant will preside over the event that will result in the Evil One being sent to hell for eternity; the cessation of all death, disease, and suffering; and the restoration of a "new Paradise" on earth wherein the "blessed will enjoy immortality . . . and [will] live in hope!" (241).

See also Apocalypse: Traditional Judeo-Christian; Apocalypticism; Eschatology; Zoroaster.

APOCALYPSE: SECULAR

Secular apocalypse refers to the type of fiction in which secular or worldly explanations "attac[k] the roots of religious faith" by eliminating its symbols and creating its own bifurcated apocalyptic framework (May 227). Specifically, without the promise of eternal salvation or the threats of eternal damnation to motivate characters, the inherent randomness of the universe drives them either to despair of their pitiable circumstances or to laugh in the face of life's inexplicable ironies.

According to R. W. B. Lewis, the apocalypse of despair "concentrates on 'the perennial degenerative tendencies of human nature and . . . [the concomitant] metaphors [that] gauge their enormity'" (qtd. in May 1972, 277). Within this type of apocalypse, secularism, or the natural morality of humanity rather than that which has been imposed by a supernatural entity, causes an instinctive alienation between the individual and others within the world. Because there are no rules in such a world wherein each person follows his or her own sense of ethics, characters are easily swayed by the charismatic influence of the archetypal trickster or deceiver who arrives in their midst. Such is the case in Herman Melville's apocalyptic work *The Confidence-Man: His Masquerade.* Within this novel, Melville mocks the gullibility of a society so influenced by the philosophy of self-reliance that it fails to recognize the myriad disguises of "a secular Satan" (74). Similarly, in Richard Wright's powerful novel *Native Son,* the protagonist, a young black murderer named Bigger Thomas, is duped by a system represented by a white, Communist defense attorney, Boris A. Max. Believing Max's claims that only "the Party" can protect him from the injustices of racism, he unwittingly allows himself to be used as a symbol by an organization that is more concerned with furthering its own cause than in defending Thomas. The end result is either resignation, as occurs in Melville's work, or despair, as depicted by Wright in *Native Son.* However, these two reactions are not the only ways in which to view the fate of a God-less world.

Another type of secular apocalypse, according to John R. May, is one in which humanity survives certain catastrophe by laughing at the absurdities of life. Such is the case with Kurt Vonnegut's *Cat's Cradle* and Ralph Ellison's *Invisible Man.* Vonnegut is a master of identifying life's absurdities. Within his novel, science is the deceiver, pride is the flaw, and the entire human race is the victim of a cruel joke of nature. Ellison's message, while less jocular in tone, is equally incongruous with the protagonist's expectations. Throughout Ellison's novel, the character who is only known as the invisible man is really a black man trying to find his individual identity in an amoral and chaotic world. What he learns, ironically, is that only by disguising himself, and literally losing his identity, will he ever be free to pursue his life's goals without societal intrusion. Unlike the apocalypse of despair, however, these novels end with a theme of psychological hope in which life is affirmed, if only by a marginal prospect of a more promising future (229).

See also Apocalyptic Literature; *Cat's Cradle; The Confidence-Man: His Masquerade; Gravity's Rainbow; The Invisible Man.*

APOCALYPSE: TRADITIONAL JUDEO-CHRISTIAN

The most predominant form of apocalyptic literature is traditional Judeo-Christian apocalypse. Its original archetype, the Book of Revelation, set the pattern for the genre. This archetype is so pervasive in Western literature that it is easier to discern which works deviate from the form than to identify all of the

Michelangelo decorated the Vatican's Sistine Chapel with *The Last Judgement,* a visual summary of the Book of Revelation.

works within the category. The majority of the apocalyptic novels cited within this volume fall within John R. May's category of the traditional Judeo-Christian apocalypse, at least to some degree or another.

The pattern, according to May, involves the promise of a "Coming Kingdom," the inevitable "Last Loosing of Satan," which leads to death and/or cataclysm, followed by a linear progression toward a sentiment of genuine hope (May 1972, 229). He identifies two authors whose works conform to this archetypal pattern, William Faulkner and Flannery O'Connor, both of whom, ironically, are identified as Southern novelists. In the case of William Faulkner, two of his novels, *As I Lay Dying* and *Absalom, Absalom!*, epitomize the Judeo-Christian apocalyptic tradition. In *As I Lay Dying*, Addie Bundren, the dissatisfied wife and weary matriarch, finds that her only reward for her earthly toil will be eternity in heaven and burial in her home city of Jefferson, Mississippi. Although this might seem a reasonable expectation from a woman who has lived Addie's life, her intent is to punish her cruel and selfish husband, Anse, by making him promise to take her body on its perilous journey home. As the entire family attempts to fulfill her dying wish, literally "all hell breaks loose," in the forms of storms, floods, and fire, until the deed is done, and the action draws to an ironic and undramatic conclusion. Events, however, are even more tumultuous in *Absalom, Absalom!* in which the monomaniacal Thomas Sutpen attempts to create his own earthly paradise by manipulating, stealing, and terrorizing his way to his ultimate goal. Through the course of the novel, however, as the following generations evolve from Sutpen's corrupt origins, he becomes decimated by cataclysmic events, illustrating that through his sin of pride, he has evoked the wrath of God. The other Southern novelist who wrote in this tradition is Flannery O'Connor in her riveting work *The Violent Bear It Away.* In this novel the traditional battle between good and evil is fought over the life of a young boy. While he initially sides with the fundamentalist beliefs of his elder relative, he learns, through a series of horrid experiences, that violence is the only gateway through which his personal truth will be revealed.

See also *Absalom, Absalom!*; Allegory; Apocalyptic Literature; *As I Lay Dying; Love in the Ruins: The Adventures of a Bad Catholic at a Time Near the End of the World;* Revelation, Book of; *The Thanatos Syndrome.*

APOCALYPSE: TRADITIONAL PRIMITIVE

The term used by John R. May to categorize fiction that attempts to "resolv[e] the tension between the ideal and the real, between the pursuit of reform and the tyranny of history, [or] between the desire for happiness and human existence as it is experienced" is *traditional primitive apocalypse* (May 1972, 43). Unlike the traditional Judeo-Christian apocalypse, which relies on the prophetic symbolism in the New Testament book of Revelation for the resolution of such tensions, the primitive apocalypse is less structured. May identifies Nathaniel Hawthorne's novel *The Blithedale Romance* as a representative work of primitive apocalyptic fiction.

Whereas the Judeo-Christian apocalypse begins with the hopeful anticipation of a glorious kingdom, the primitive apocalypse begins amidst a paradise on earth. Such is the case of the Blithedale experiment, which was based upon the author's real-life observations of the Transcendentalist experimental society known as Brook Farm. Accordingly, the Blithedale community begins much in the same way: it is based upon the idealistic illusions of seemingly altruistic individuals who have more sinister ulterior motives. With such deception in their midst, it is not long before the beauty of nature, the serenity of silence, and the familial fellowship are shattered by the emergence of individual pride. In the case of Hawthorne's novel, two of the key characters, the flamboyant Zenobia Moodie and the charismatic and convincing Hollingsworth, sense that their goals are no longer shared and set into motion sinister plans wherein each plots to destroy the other. In the end, Zenobia, realizing that she has been manipulated, kills herself in shame and despair, whereas Hollingsworth, having won the victory, is so haunted by her suicide and by the failure of his communal dream that he lives the rest of his life as a diminished self. In each case, the idealism that launched the experiment proved too lofty a goal for intrinsically flawed humans. The survivors of the experiment emerge with a sobering knowledge or a "contact with reality" (229) that will hopefully prevent them from succumbing to such future folly.

See also Allegory; Apocalyptic Literature; Archetype; *The Blithedale Romance;* Hollingsworth; Moodie, Zenobia.

APOCALYPTIC LITERATURE

The term *apocalyptic literature* originates from the Greek word *apokalypsis*, which means literally an "uncovering" or a "revelation." This literary genre is believed to have flourished from approximately 200 B.C. to A.D. 200 with a proliferation of works within the traditions of Judaism and Christianity. An acceptable definition of the apocalyptic literary genre comes from the members of the Apocalypse Group of the Society of Biblical Literature's Genre Project whose findings are quoted in an apocalyptic anthology:

> "Apocalypse" is a genre of revelatory literature with a narrative framework in which a revelation is mediated by an otherworldly being to a human recipient, disclosing a transcendent reality which is both temporal insofar as it envisages eschatological salvation, and spatial insofar as it involves another, supernatural world (Reddish 1990, 20).

In more accessible terms, the apocalyptic genre contains symbolism intended to provide hope for oppressed people who need to know that the forces of good will eventually overcome the forces of evil. According to apocalyptic scholar and teacher Michael G. Reddish, special criteria exist to determine whether or not a work may be included in this particular genre. The primary criterion requires that an author (or character) experience a divine revelation. This character is usually a hero of the past, such as Daniel, Adam, Enoch, or one who demonstrates heroic traits. The next component of literary apocalypse is an interest in an afterlife, including a final divine judgment that will reward those who are righteous and punish those who are evil. Such literature also features descriptions of otherworldly symbols such as angels, demons, heaven, and hell. Overall, the main purpose of apocalyptic literature is to encourage the faithful to endure their worldly suffering, at least for a time, until, at the Final Judgment,

God intervenes to judge individuals with either eternal salvation or eternal damnation (21–23).

Although apocalyptic literature thrived nearly two thousand years ago, it has experienced a significant resurgence in modern literature. Because of the existence of nuclear power, modern malaise, and recurrent millenarian movements, the thematic components of apocalyptic literature continue to thrive, both in the mainstream milieu as well as in more imaginative works within the science fiction genre.

The following list includes a summary of Old and New Testament references upon which modern apocalyptic treatments have been based. In the Old Testament, the most noted apocalyptic scriptural references include Isaiah 24–27, Ezekiel 38–39, Joel 2–3, as well as the book of Daniel, considered by many to be one of the finest apocalyptic presentations. In addition, other noncanonical Jewish apocalypses, including 1 Enoch, 2 Enoch, 2 Baruch, and 3 Baruch, reveal similar characteristics.

Much like the Jewish noncanonical literature, Christian apocalyptic literature also includes relevant pseudonymous works with apocalyptic themes such as *The Apocalypse of Peter*, *The Revelations of St. Bartholomew*, *The Apocalypse of Paul*, *The Shepherd of Hermas*, and *The Christian Sibylline Oracles*. Within the canonical body of the New Testament, several specific passages in Mark 13 and 2 Thessalonians 2 deal with the Parousia, or the Second Coming of Christ. Nevertheless, the book that is most responsible for the symbolism, imagery, and thematic concerns reflected in the apocalyptic literary genre is the Book of Revelation, the concluding book of the New Testament.

See also Apocalypse: Traditional Judeo-Christian; Apocalypticism; Daniel, Book of; Eschatology; Millennialism; Revelation, Book of; Science Fiction.

APOCALYPTICISM

The term that describes movements or ideological perspectives focusing on eschatological or end-time conditions is *apocalypticism*. While it is commonly believed that apocalyptic literature originated with Zoroastrianism, the sixth-century B.C. Iranian religion, its symbols appear throughout early Judaic and Christian literature.

Apocalypticism as a movement concerns enigmatic prophesies, the upheavals caused by unexpected cataclysms, and the climactic intervention of a supreme being in the affairs of humanity. This intervention, occurring presumably at the end of the world, will separate the righteous from the damned, destroy God's enemies, and enthrone the elect, under the leadership of God, in a renewed heaven and earth (Reddish 1990).

See also Apocalypse: Traditional Judeo-Christian; Daniel, Book of; Eschatology; Millennialism; Revelation, Book of; Science Fiction; Zoroaster.

ARCHETYPE

Archetype is a term used to determine meaning in the areas of both psychology and literary criticism. Literally meaning a pattern or model from which copies are created, an archetype is a recurrent representation that reveals common traits shared by characters or situations that have been recorded in humanity's "collective unconscious." The ability to draw upon these unconscious patterns in order to find meaning is an area that was explored extensively by psychoanalyst Carl Jung. According to Jung's findings, the collective memories of human beings contain primordial or prelogical images that have their origins in myth, history, and religion. Jung contends that these unconscious images are somehow stored and encoded in the minds of past, present, and future generations.

While the psychological significance of archetypes is readily apparent, Jung's work has also provided valuable insights into how literature continues to convey universal meaning to readers who live in different times than those in which the works were created. Two influential scholars who have based their studies on Jung's findings and furthered the understanding of archetypes are James G. Frazer and Northrop Frye. Frazer is best known for his seminal work entitled *The Golden Bough,* in which he examines the archetypal relationships between the world's myths, religions, rituals, and folklore. By examining both Jung's psychological studies and Frazer's mythological inferences, renowned literary critic Northrop Frye developed an extensive system of archetypal study in his classic literary reference, *Anatomy of Criticism.* The combined efforts of these formidable theorists have provided a broader understanding of the powerful elements and general themes that unifies the majority of Western literary forms.

Specifically, some of the more common archetypal themes that recur throughout literature include those that define the human experience, i.e., birth, death, initiation, love, sin, revelation, judgment, redemption, and fate versus free will. In addition to these themes, various archetypal characters also permeate literature through a complex, albeit unified, catalog of fictional representations. Some of the more common archetypal characters represented in literature include the hero, the virginal heroine, the martyr, the rebel, the fool, the wise elder, and most significantly, the myriad representations of both God and the devil as well as heaven and hell. While most authors rely on archetypal situations or characters to convey meaning, others prefer the more ambitious technique of applying archetypal symbolism.

Since a symbol is traditionally defined as anything that represents its singular self as well as a meaning that is larger than itself, countless archetypal symbols have also become commonplace among the world's greatest literary works. The most common archetypal symbols include creatures such as eagles, doves, lions, lambs, whales, and serpents. In addition, authors also rely heavily upon various forms of vegetative symbolism, such as flowers, gardens, and laurel or olive branches. Color symbolism is employed as a powerful method of conveying human emotion, such as the use of the color red to represent anger, lust, or other powerful urges; white for purity; black for obscurity or occultism, and purple for righteous judgment. Perhaps the most common archetypal symbols used throughout the history of literature involve the representation of various natural forces that have an impact on humanity such as storms, earthquakes, floods, fire, and ice.

See also *Anatomy of Criticism: Four Essays;* Apocalypse: Traditional Judeo-Christian; Freud, Sigmund; *The Golden Bough: A Study in Magic and Religion;* Great Chain of Being; Jung, Carl Gustav; Myth; Revelation, Book of.

ARIEL

Ariel is the name of the beneficent "spirit of the air" or magical sprite, a common device used in Italian pastoral romances, whose enchanting personality and magical ways propel the plot in William Shakespeare's apocalyptic tragicomedy *The Tempest* (c. 1611). Ariel is an inhabitant of the island upon which the play's protagonist, Prospero, the wrongly exiled Duke of Milan, lands with his three-year-old daughter, Miranda, some twelve years prior to the action of the story. While Ariel and Prospero have developed a mature and generally congenial relationship early in the play, Ariel's service to Prospero bears a note of reluctance. This sentiment is not without reason. It was Prospero who had freed Ariel from imprisonment in a pine tree by Sycorax, the former wicked witch of the island, who meant to punish Ariel for being too gentle a spirit to do her evil bidding. But the price of Ariel's freedom was service to Prospero.

For the twelve years during which Prospero and his daughter inhabit the island, Ariel assists the deposed duke in both the study and practice of white magic. Prospero is interested in magic as a means to avenge the injustice done to him as well as to Miranda. At the beginning of the play Ariel grows impatient for release from his servitude because he knows that the end is near. He has accomplished the ultimate task of causing a great storm, or tempest, to toss the ship carrying Prospero's enemies onto the shore of his own island kingdom. Ariel is pleased with the result of his effort; the ship has run aground and not a soul has been lost, but he must then assist Prospero in righting the wrong before he can become truly free.

In this action, Ariel seems omnipresent. Through his magic spells, people appear and disappear at the most opportune times. He causes them to be overcome with sleep as he goes about his business of enchantment, and most importantly, he delights in bringing about the fortuitous meeting of the two most beautiful and innocent people on the island, Prospero's daughter, Miranda, and the son of the King of Naples, Ferdinand. Their union is a happy accident of Prospero's plan. Ariel is most effective in using his powers to arrange for the ultimate meeting between Prospero and his enemies. Through Ariel's intervention, Prospero's enemies admit their unjust actions to the wronged duke, the marriage of Miranda and Ferdinand is blessed, and Prospero, having been influenced by the happiness of his daughter, forgives his enemies and releases Ariel from his earthbound duty.

See also Apocalypse: Traditional Judeo-Christian; Apocalypticism; Caliban; Ferdinand; Miranda; Prospero; Shakespeare, William; *The Tempest*.

ARMAGEDDON

As revealed in the New Testament, Armageddon is the name of the location for the final battle between good and evil that will occur on Judgment Day (Revelation 16:16). This name, which in some texts is written as *Harmagedon*, is said to have originated from a famous hill named Megiddo, on the plain of Esdraelon in Galilee, whereupon the most significant Israelite battles were fought. The following description chronicles specific events that occurred on Megiddo as recorded in various Old Testament accounts:

> Megiddo was the scene of the defeat of the Canaanite kings (Judges 5:19) and the tragic death of King Josiah, who was slain by the Pharaoh (2 Chronicles 35:22–25; 2 Kings 23:29). Thus, the Megiddo pass, which commanded control of northern Palestine, became a symbol of disaster. [According to the Greek translation of the word *Har Mo-ed,* or] "the meeting place". . . . [it is also known as] the mountain mentioned in Isaiah 14:13 . . . on which the deities assemble and which the arrogant king of Babylon attempts to mount with his blasphemous pride. Thus Armageddon would be the demonic counterpart of the Mount of God. . . .[and as such, it is [where] the final battle will take place (*Anchor Bible* 1975, 274).

Because of its import as the scene for the final apocalyptic conflagration, Armageddon has also come to bear symbolic reference in various works of literature that deal with the conflicting forces of good and evil.

See also Apocalypse: Traditional Judeo-Christian; Apocalyptic Literature; Apocalypticism; Archetype; Revelation, Book of; Science Fiction.

ARTHUR, KING

King Arthur is the legendary monarch of sixth-century Britain whose chivalric ideals are chronicled in numerous sources related to medieval romance. Speculation still exists on whether the fictional character was based on the life of an actual king. Two specific works, *Historia Brittonum* and *Annales Cambriae,* created respectively during the ninth and tenth centuries, contain detailed accounts of the battles and victories of a military professional who was also respected as a national leader.

According to the ninth-century Welsh chronicler Nennius, Arthur was most likely responsible for leading the resistance against the invasion of Germanic tribes as well as for executing the famous British victory at Mount Badon. Other scholars, however, such as R. G. Collingwood, who wrote *Roman Britain and the English Settlements* (1936), suggest that Arthur may have descended from Roman ancestry and was therefore instrumental in leading a British cavalry, which had been trained on Roman soil, to defeat the wandering Saxon invaders. Regardless of the speculative views pertaining to Arthur's historical counterpart, the fictional legend of the noble son and heir to British King Uther Pendragon's throne is presented in glorious detail throughout the body of Western literature.

The fictional representation of King Arthur is based upon the following tenets of lore. First, he was a fierce warrior whose love for the land matched his love for life. Second, he was initially reluctant to accept the role as Britain's monarch, but with the continual assistance of his famous friend, adviser, and magician, Merlin, he became a great and honorable king. Third, he was the unwitting casualty of an adulterous relationship between his beloved wife, Queen Guinevere, and his favorite and most sterling knight, Sir Lancelot. Fourth, after the serious misfortunes that resulted from this royal scandal, King Arthur initiated the quest for the Holy Grail, the chalice said to have been used by Christ at the Last Supper, in the hopes of restoring the greatness of his kingdom. Finally, and most importantly, King Arthur was creator of the flourishing kingdom of Camelot. During the kingdom's finest hour, King Arthur ruled, with the help of the world's finest knights, at his famed Round Table. King Arthur and his Knights of the Round Table have become synonymous with the equanimity, grandeur, and honor that embodies the chivalric tradition immortalized in Western literature, theater, and film.

See also Apocalypse: Secular; Apocalypse: Traditional Judeo-Christian; *A Connecticut Yankee in King Arthur's Court*; *The Faerie Queene*; Merlin; Morgan, Hank; *Le Morte d'Arthur.*

AS I LAY DYING

Written by the renowned Southern author William Faulkner, *As I Lay Dying* (1930) deals with the death of a character named Addie Bundren and the odyssey that ensues as her husband and children fulfill her last wish to return to Jefferson, Mississippi, for a proper burial. The thematic construct of the novel reflects an apocalypticism found in several of Faulkner's works, most notably *Absalom, Absalom!* This work also uses Faulkner's signature techniques of stream of consciousness and interior monologue to address the impact of the journey from the point of view of several of the main characters, including Anse, Addie's husband, as well as her children, Cash, Jewel, Darl, Vardaman, and Dewey Dell.

As the plot of the novel unravels through the narrative, the tenuous relationships between Addie, her husband, and her children is revealed. It seems preposterous, under the circumstances, that the survivors would agree to grant the final wish of a woman whose intent was revenge upon them. During the course of their journey, the family faces a series of overwhelming upheavals including a disastrous river crossing, during which the mules are drowned, Cash breaks his leg, and Addie's coffin is overturned. Following the flood, the group faces yet another ordeal, a fire set by Darl to end the journey and consume the decaying body of his mother in the flames of a burning farmhouse. Nevertheless, in spite of the cataclysmic occurrences that threaten to thwart their mission, Addie's body is eventually interred in Jefferson. Later, Darl, the fire-setting son, is declared insane and Addie's insensitive husband, Anse, acquires a new wife.

See also *Absalom, Absalom!*; Apocalypse: Traditional Judeo-Christian; Apocalyptic Literature; Bundren, Addie; Bundren, Anse; Bundren, Darl; Bundren, Jewel.

AZAZEL

According to Leviticus 16:1–28, Azazel is the name of a demon who lived in the most desolate part of the Syrian desert, i.e., the wilderness of Judea, located to the south of the city of Jerusalem. The story of Azazel, which involves a blood sacrifice on the Day of Atonement, is part of Hebrew and Canaanite tradition. Although specific details of the original event have been modified throughout history, remnants of the ritual still exist in the contemporary religious practice of Yom Kippur. The scriptural ritual recalls God's concern for the sins committed by his chosen people. In a merciful gesture to expiate the impurities that had run rampant throughout the Israelite community, God ordered Moses to tell his brother, Aaron, to select two unblemished goats for the purpose of ritual sacrifice. He further ordered them to draw lots deciding which one would serve as the "scapegoat" or the beast who would carry the weight of the sins of Israel and be sacrificed to Yahweh for the spiritual cleansing of his people. The remaining goat was sent out into the desert to serve as a sacrifice for the demon, Azazel, whose prideful disobedience separated him eternally from God's forgiveness.

Similar details of this primitive ritual also appear in the pseudepigraphic book of *Enoch* as well as in Muslim accounts. The lesson of this ritual is often included as a metaphorical warning in contemporary apocalyptic novels such as Walker Percy's *The Thanatos Syndrome* (1987). In this novel, a diabolically destructive force threatens the moral fabric of the modern world. The author acknowledges that while righteousness will ultimately triumph, earthly sacrifices are often required to appease earthly demons that hold sinners in their thrall. The primary reason for noting this particular modern literary parallel lies in the novel's gripping explanation of the Azazel myth:

> Mohammedans believe that Azazel is a jinn [or spirit] of the desert, formerly an angel. When God commanded the angels to worship Adam, Azazel replied, "Why should a son of fire fall down before a son of clay?" Whereupon God threw him out of heaven and down into the Syrian desert, a hell on earth. At that very moment his name was changed from Azazel to Eblis, which means despair. [And Percy adds the final note that another author,] Milton [,] made Azazel [famous as] the standard-bearer of all the rebel angels (*TS* 69).

See also Apocalypse: Traditional Judeo-Christian; Mephistophiles; *Paradise Lost; The Thanatos Syndrome.*

BABYLON

Babylon was one of the first great cities of the world. Bearing the name of Bab-Ilu, or "gate of the gods," this city was located atop the desert plain of Babylonia. Because of its proximity to the Euphrates River, and partially because of the successes of Sumerian irrigation and civilization, Babylon became a populous city well known as a thriving merchant seaport, the source of highly skilled tradesmen, and the hub of culture and learning. In about 1800 B.C., Babylon attained its greatest recognition when King Hammurabi inscribed a code of law on a grand pillar displayed in the city. This code, enforced by the judges and governors of the land, reflects the class system and economic conditions of Hammurabi's time. It was also under his leadership that Marduk, the creator god of Babylon, and Ishtar, the goddess of fertility, were elevated as objects of worship.

Over the next several centuries, various tribes fought for control of Babylon. Among the tribes that seized the capital were the Aramaeans, the Assyrians, and the Chaldeans. Within the Assyrian territory was the tiny kingdom of Judah, located a few miles above Jerusalem. Judah was the home of the Israelites, God's "Chosen People," descendents of such great kings as David and Solomon who had struggled to suppress idolatry, to claim the law of God in the land, and to restore the kingdom of Israel. The fulfillment of this promise seemed possible under the capable leadership of Josiah, one of Judah's last great kings.

However, after thirty-one years of leadership, Josiah learned that Egyptian armies were planning to join the Assyrians (who had long been hated by Josiah's people) in an effort to thwart the invasion of Babylonian armies. Because Josiah wanted to prevent the union of the Assyrian and Egyptian armies, he gathered a small army of his own to warn the two groups against such a union, but Josiah was killed in the process. His death marked the beginning of the end for the kingdom of Judah, and it also foreshadowed the eventual fall of Nineveh, the Assyrian capital, at the hands of Babylon's imperial ruler, Nebuchadnezzar II.

At the beginning of Nebuchadnezzar's reign, the people of Jerusalem were left in peace; they agreed to pay tribute to Babylon for several years. During that time, however, the Israelites became complacent and many began to fall away from the word of God by participating in the various idolatrous rites of Babylon.

These events are chronicled, along with a sustained apocalyptic warning, in Jeremiah 4:14: "O Jerusalem, wash thine heart from wickedness, that thou mayest be saved." Jeremiah laments over his people's foolishness, perversity, indolence, adultery, idolatry, civil disobedience, and spiritual corruption. Further, he prophesies the coming captivity of the Israelites, the horrid details of their bondage, and the promise that although the Lord will still have his hand upon them, he will "doubly repay their iniquity and their sin, because they have polluted [his] land with the carcasses of their detestable idols, and have filled my inheritance with their abominations" (Jeremiah 16:18).

This prophesy was soon fulfilled when Jerusalem came under siege. The last king of Judah, the weak-willed and exhausted Zedekiah, was captured by Nebuchadnezzar. He was shamefully dragged through the streets of the city, tried and condemned, forced to watch the murder of each of his sons, cruelly blinded, and then was thrown into prison to await his death. Ultimately, as Jeremiah prophesied, the holy city of Jerusalem was laid to waste for the next fifty years, the kingdom of Judah came to an end, and the Israelites became lost amidst the chaos of a pagan world.

While, for a time, life seemed dismal for the followers of the Kingdom of God, the followers of the kingdom of man thrived in Nebuchadnezzar's Babylon, with its impressive roadways, awe-inspiring temples and palaces, and the famous Hanging Gardens, which eventually became known as one of the seven ancient wonders of the world. Also in this city, near Procession Street, which spanned from the exquisite Gate of Ishtar to the formidable Temple of Marduk, stood one of many multiterraced towers. This particular tower, also known as a *ziggurat* or holy mountain, is believed to be the original Tower of Babel, the source of chaos that is first described in the biblical book of Genesis; the story and its land are revisited in great and glorious detail in the final book of the New Testament, the apocalyptic Revelation. Therefore, when considered in its entirety, the city of Babylon, in its greatest hour, represented the finest efforts of humankind that were, unfortunately, inspired by humanity's worst possible motives: pride, greed, and lust.

Throughout apocalyptic literature, the city of Babylon is used as a metaphor for humanity's intrinsic penchant for corruption. It has been referred to directly and indirectly in several apocalyptic novels such as Pat Frank's *Alas, Babylon* and William Faulkner's *Absalom, Absalom!*. It is also featured prominently in William Blake's *Jerusalem* and Stephen Benet's popular short story "By the Waters of Babylon." Less specifically, Babylon, or simply the "city," is depicted throughout literature as a place where chaos reigns and corruption rules. Twentieth-century novelists are widely known for their referral to city life as a vehicle for humanity's or society's moral as well as physical decline. Nathanael West, in particular, uses the Hollywood-as-Babylon motif in his novel *The Day of the Locust* and refers to the despair of city life in *Miss Lonelyhearts*. The work of the Southern gothic writer Flannery O'Connor also vilifies the contagious corruption of the city in her novel *The Violent Bear It Away*. Many writers of the Harlem Renaissance, specifically Richard Wright and James Baldwin, depict the apocalyptic consequences of life in the city in their novels *Native Son, Black Boy,* and *Go Tell It on the Mountain*.

See also *Absalom, Absalom!; Alas, Babylon;* Apocalypse: Traditional Judeo-Christian; *The Day of the Locust; Go Tell It on the Mountain; Miss Lonelyhearts; Native Son;* Revelation, Book of; *The Violent Bear It Away.*

BALDWIN, JAMES

Novelist, essayist, and dramatist, James Baldwin (1924–1987) is perhaps best known for his first novel, *Go Tell It on the Mountain* (1953), which recounts his own childhood experiences, most notably his religious awakening at fourteen years of age in the ghettos of Harlem. The novel vividly describes Baldwin's life with his rigid father, who was both a factory worker and part-time fundamentalist lay preacher. Young James was torn between the power of his father's religious zeal and his own yearning for more worldly concerns. However, at age fourteen, James, like his fictional counterpart, began a three-year ministry in a storefront church. Family crises intervened to cause Baldwin to reject religion, mostly as an overt rejection of his father's values. This traumatic experience provided Baldwin with the artistic spark necessary to develop both his first novel and his first play.

In 1942, soon after his graduation from De Witt Clinton High School, the aspiring author left his childhood home and attempted to launch his writing career. However, because his expectations for success were initially not met, he decided, like many expatriate artists before him, to move to Paris in 1948, where he wrote most prolifically until his return to America in 1957. Among the successful works he completed during his time abroad were *Go Tell It on the Mountain* (1953) and *Giovanni's Room* (1956). Other fictional works by Baldwin include *Another Country* (1962), *Tell Me How Long the Train's Been Gone* (1968), and *If Beale Street Could Talk* (1974). These, like most of his works, contain the themes of racism, social injustice as experienced by African Americans, and prophetic, often apocalyptic, visions of divine punishment for racial injustice in America, as perpetuated in its laws and institutions.

Although his fictional works strongly convey these themes, they are stated perhaps even more stridently in his works of nonfiction. For example, his essay collections entitled *Notes of a Native Son* (1955), *Nobody Knows My Name* (1961), and *The Fire Next Time* (1963) serve as radical indictments against the widespread cultural inequities tolerated within predominantly white American society.

Baldwin's literary versatility and tendency toward stylistic experimentation enabled him to also write plays, including *The Amen Corner* (1955), *Blues for Mr. Charlie* (1964), and *One Day, When I Was Lost* (1973), which was based on the *Autobiography of Malcolm X*. Baldwin eventually returned to writing a sixth novel entitled *Just above My Head* (1979). He also published several nonfiction collections such as *The Price of the Ticket* (1985) and *Evidence of Things Not Seen* (1986).

As a result of this prodigious body of work, James Baldwin is considered one of the most important contributors to American fiction, in general, and to African-American fiction, in particular. His timeless themes, which include humanity's ongoing search for individual, artistic, social, sexual, and, most importantly, spiritual identity, have placed him in a position somewhere between conflict and celebrity. In spite of his death in 1987, James Baldwin continues to

James Baldwin

be recognized as one of the most important modern naturalist and urban regionalist writers of his time (May 1972).

See also Apocalypse: Anti-Christian; *Go Tell It on the Mountain;* Harlem Renaissance; Naturalism.

BARTH, JOHN

Contemporary American novelist John Barth (1930–) is best known for his stinging satire as well as his profound psychological explorations. Born in Cambridge, Maryland, Barth first studied jazz at the Julliard School of Music in New York but later pursued his literary studies and ultimately earned both his B.A. and M.A. degrees at Johns Hopkins University in Maryland. Although he has taught English at a variety of higher educational institutions, including Johns Hopkins and Pennsylvania State universities as well as the State University of New York in Buffalo, Barth is still recognized primarily for his writing.

While he readily experiments with nontraditional literary techniques, acknowledging the influence of both Franz Kafka and James Joyce on his writing style, his works mask their serious themes through the use of surrealistic situations, whimsical fantasy, and occasionally bawdy humor. His early fictional works include two novels, *The Floating Opera* (1956) and *The End of the Road* (1958), as well as a historical farce set in the early days of the state of Maryland, *The Sot-Weed Factor* (1960). But his most significant work, according to critical opinion, is *Giles Goat-Boy,* which was published in 1966.

Barth followed these works with more experimental forms such as his collection of childhood tales entitled *Lost in the Funhouse* (1968) and his three-volume novella entitled *Chimera,* published in 1972. Barth wrote yet another experimental novel, *Letters* (1979), but has since returned to a more traditional style, as is evident in his two latest works to date, *Sabbatical* (1982) and *The Tidewater Tales* (1987).

See also: Apocalypse: Secular; Apocalypticism, *Giles Goat-Boy; or The Revised New Syllabus.*

BEATRICE

Beatrice is the beloved object of worship and inspiration in the epic allegorical poem by Dante Alighieri entitled *The Divine Comedy* (1321). According to Dante's biographical information, as well as poetic revelations about this woman in his collection of verse entitled *La Vita Nuova,* the Beatrice of literary legend was most likely a young woman named Beatrice Portinari, whom Dante had met when he was only nine years old and she was only eight.

Apparently, Dante was immediately stricken by Beatrice's beauty and grace when he was first introduced to the enigmatic child clad in a crimson gown during a May Day celebration in his father's home. And although he only saw her infrequently thereafter, she became the focus of his obsessive thoughts and evolved into something of a symbolic figure of all that is good and divinely inspired in the universe. Dante's arranged marriage to another woman, Gemma Donati, and Beatrice's marriage to a wealthy banker, Simone de' Bardi, only heightened her inspirational effect on his work, which reflects

John Barth

a reverence for the perfect albeit unattainable love as represented in the medieval chivalric tradition.

Dante's strong feelings for Beatrice were given full expression, however, following the young woman's early death in 1290, when she was just twenty years old. For Dante, Beatrice's death elevated her to the level of a saint. Unable to be idolized as a living person, she became the inspiration for most of his works. As such, he dedicated to Beatrice his magnum opus on the spiritual condition of humanity, its fall, and its promise of redemption. Consequently, Dante's glorified representations of her character have been immortalized forever in one of the most significant apocalyptic works of Western literature, *The Divine Comedy.*

See also Apocalypse: Traditional Judeo-Christian; Apocalyptic Literature; Archetype; Dante Alighieri; *The Divine Comedy;* God; Heaven; Hell; Myth; Satan; Virgil.

BLACK RAIN

Black Rain (1969) is a novel written by the award-winning Japanese author Masuji Ibuse about the aftermath of the atomic bombing of Hiroshima at the conclusion of World War II. Although it is based on real-life diaries and interviews with survivors, a technique similar to that used by the American author John Hersey in his journalistic novel entitled *Hiroshima* (1946), Ibuse's work focuses less on the massive and graphic devastation and more on the personal impact of the blast on families, friends, and communities.

While Hersey maintains an objective, journalistic tone, Ibuse, in contrast, almost understates the horror of the event by emphasizing nuances of individual personalities, often using his customary dry humor in an attempt to reveal the follies and flaws demonstrated by real-life people as they recover from a real-life nightmare. While the art of *Black Rain* can only be appreciated by a quiet reading of the novel itself and a gradual familiarity with its characters, perhaps the most cogent overview of the work has been provided by John Bester, the translator of the novel, who describes it as follows:

> *Black Rain* is a portrait of a group of human beings; of the death of a great city; of a nation crumbling into defeat. It is a picture of the Japanese mind that tells more than many sociological studies. Yet more than this, it is a statement of a philosophy. Although that philosophy, in its essence, is neither pessimistic nor optimistic, it seems to me to be life-affirming. Dealing with the grimmest of subjects, the work is not, in the end, depressing, for the author is ultimately concerned with life rather than with death, and with an overall beauty that transcends ugliness of detail (*BR* 8).

See also Allegory; Apocalypse: Secular; Apocalyptic Literature; *Hiroshima;* Ibuse, Masuji.

BLAKE, WILLIAM

William Blake (1757–1827) was one of England's most imaginative and versatile artists of the seventeenth-century Romantic period. His creative genius and preoccupation with the mystical became evident at the age of four when he alarmed his parents with a scream asserting that he had experienced a vision of the head of God. This initial incident was followed by others in which he also claimed to have seen visions of both angels and the prophet Ezekiel. Concerned about his child's volatile temperament and ability to withstand the discipline of school, Blake's father provided him with an elementary-level education. However, at age ten, Blake demonstrated unusual drawing ability and soon became an artist's apprentice. While he continued to pursue this form of expression, Blake simultaneously began an intensive self-study of the great philosophers and poets. This combination of artistic and literary interests encouraged him to embark on a formal apprenticeship, at age fourteen, as an engraver of books under James Basire. In the following years, Blake's skill in drawing and poetry made him quite marketable, and he gained enough commissions from booksellers to assert himself professionally.

At age twenty-four, Blake met and married a calm and pleasant, albeit illiterate, young woman, Catherine Boucher. In exchange for her tolerance of his visionary temperament and her innate tranquility that soothed his soul, Blake taught his wife to read, write, sketch, and paint well enough to serve as his assistant in his work. His income, however, was sporadic; in 1800, the Blakes accepted an offer to work under the artistic patronage of William Hayley. Hayley, who lived in the Sussex seacoast town of Felpham, dedicated himself to making Blake a capable breadwinner. However, Blake's rebellious nature soon caused him to resent the man whose practicality violated the artist's mystical sensibilities.

While in Felpham, another more significant event occurred that had an indelible impact on the life and work of Blake. It began with an argument between Blake and a private in the Royal Dragoons, John Schofield. Later, Schofield accused Blake of making rebellious statements against both his king and country. This accusation led to Blake's incarceration and eventually to a trial in which Blake was acquitted. Nevertheless, the memory of private Schofield and his military cohorts continued to haunt Blake for the rest of his life, with their threats growing to demonic proportions in his subsequent prophetic works. In the aftermath Blake became even more preoccupied with dangerous forces that seemed to impinge upon humankind at every turn.

Blake's meditation on human duality was best presented in the 1794 publication of his earlier works entitled *Songs of Innocence and Experience,* from which some of his best-known poems, *The Tyger* and *London,* originated. In an effort to explore the complexities of the human and spiritual worlds in highly metaphorical and symbolic language, Blake departed from literary convention by developing a population of "Giant Forms" who served as the basis for the artist's own unique mythology. This mythology, an amalgam of his fascination with humanity's creation and fall as well as the exaltation and freedom of the human senses, was developed in a body of major and minor prophetic books that culminated in 1820 with the completion of his greatest poems, *The Four Zoas, Milton,* and *Jerusalem.*

After having mastered the poetic art, Blake devoted himself to drawing, painting, and engraving. Among his best works in these areas are his epic

Artist, poet, and mystic William Blake, portrayed here in 1807, illustrated Dante's *Divine Comedy*.

pictorial representations of the *Canterbury Tales* pilgrims, the book of Job, and Dante's *Divine Comedy*. From all accounts, Blake was productively and contentedly working on these ambitious endeavors at the time of his death on August 12, 1827.

See also Apocalypse: Traditional Judeo-Christian; Dante Alighieri; *The Divine Comedy;* Romanticism.

BLEDSOE, DR.

Dr. Bledsoe is the hypocritical administrator of a state college for Negroes in Ralph Ellison's apocalyptic novel *The Invisible Man* (1952). Bledsoe epitomizes human duplicity in that he is willing to say or do anything as long as it supports his personal cause of gaining unparalleled wealth and power. His quest for power, however, is even more perverse because he has obtained the respected position of a college president not by his own merit but by an obsequious fidelity to the most powerful and wealthy white men within his community.

Although he recognizes his role as a "token" black American success story, he uses this dubious status, as well as his high visibility, to his personal advantage. His position and fund-raising skill earns him the respect of the academic community and fulfills his dream of becoming one of America's most prestigious educators. In spite of his success and his seamless integration into white society, however, he is angry, retaliatory, and intentionally cruel.

Each of these characteristics is revealed in the novel during scenes in which Dr. Bledsoe interacts with the narrator known only as the Invisible Man. During an interview with a student, Bledsoe discloses his deceitful methods for manipulating the white man and reveals that false humility and subservient displays are necessary if blacks are ever to gain social, political, and financial advantage within a predominantly white society. While the Invisible Man is shocked by this deceit, he is further offended that Bledsoe, in his attempt to scale the ladder of success in the white man's world, is also directly insulting his own race by implying that blacks are intrinsically inferior.

When the protagonist deliberately disobeys Bledsoe's orders to refuse the wishes of a white contributor to the college, Bledsoe uses his skills as a hypocrite and a liar to undermine the student's academic future. When the Invisible Man is censured for his actions and Bledsoe recommends that the student leave the college for one semester, the student agrees. He does so, however, after Bledsoe promises to write him several glowing letters of recommendation with which he can find suitable employment. Bledsoe's true nature is revealed when the Invisible Man learns that the president has taken advantage of his ingenuous integrity; i.e., he has not opened the letters of recommendation that are, in reality, filled with lies and derision intended to thwart the student's future success. Ultimately, when his prospective employer reveals the contents of the condemning letter, the Invisible Man learns for himself that Bledsoe's duplicity is not restricted to members of the white race; it is, in fact, a weapon that he uses to destroy anyone who challenges his position, even if it results in the betrayal of a member of his own race.

See also Apocalypse: Secular; Archetype; Ellison, Ralph; *The Invisible Man;* Satan; Symbol.

THE BLITHEDALE ROMANCE

The Blithedale Romance (1852) is the story of a small community's disillusionment with its attempt to re-create the Judeo-Christian ideal of Eden. The natural, somewhat primitive setting of "Blithedale," the name of the experimental community, is at the center of this novel by Nathaniel Hawthorne, who was inspired to write this story from his personal experience at Brook Farm, the mid-nineteenth-century utopian community begun by the Transcendentalists in West Roxbury, Massachusetts.

One of the principal characters in the novel is Miles Coverdale, who, as some critics suggest, may be the voice of Hawthorne himself, the detached observer of an ingenuous attempt at societal reform (May 44). While many of Coverdale's actions compromise his intended detachment, he nevertheless diligently chronicles the activities of the community upon his arrival at Blithedale. The community arrives in April, when it is expected that the farm should be budding with new life, but the sobering reality of a relentless spring snowstorm portends the future for the characters who are, as yet, unaware of the volatility of nature's myriad forces.

In spite of the snowstorm, Coverdale is greeted and introduced to his new world by a creature whose visage is the antithesis of the wintry setting. The vibrant, worldly, and renowned magazine writer who welcomes Coverdale is Zenobia. Although not her birth name, her self-selected moniker heralds her cause of women's rights and is reminiscent of the powerfully ambitious Queen of Palmyra whose goal was to take control the entire Eastern Empire from Rome. Such lofty ambitions were obviously admired by this woman. Zenobia's bold sensuality is symbolized by the exotic wildflower with which she adorns her hair each day.

An equally compelling character in this novel is Hollingsworth. Revered as a social reformer and a generous philanthropist, Hollingsworth immediately takes charge of the small community by his enthusiasm, physical presence, and unwavering self-determination. While early in the novel Hollingsworth seems to share the group's common cause, he hides a personal agenda. In short, he hopes someday to become known as the creator of a center for criminal reform that will provide a permanent cure for crime, one of society's greatest ills. Without sharing his specific plan with the community at the outset of the novel, however, his private intention is somewhat megalomaniacal; if all goes as planned, the Blithedale experiment will inevitably turn his personal dream into a celebrated communal reality.

Although Hollingsworth's arrival is significant, he does not come to Blithedale alone. In response to a request by a rustic character, Old Moodie, Hollingsworth agrees to bring a plain, strange young woman named Priscilla to the new community. Upon their arrival at Blithedale, Priscilla, for some unknown reason, is transfixed by Zenobia; this unusual relationship propels the action in the novel.

Soon after the community's initial meeting, which had been filled with idealistic visions of a new and more perfect world, the reality of life at Blithedale takes its toll on each of the characters. First, Coverdale loses some of his melancholic detachment and is transformed physically and, to some extent, emotionally by daily physical labor. Hollingsworth, conversely, begins to reveal his obsessive compulsion to reform all of society's criminals and ne'er-do-wells by teaching them how to live productively and thereby avoid eternal damnation. While Coverdale finds Hollingsworth's increasing fervor exceedingly tedious, Zenobia and Priscilla begin to fall deeply in love with him.

Although the original intent of the Blithedale experiment was to create a haven for equality and equanimity between all participants, a palpable intensity of feeling begins to charge the atmosphere between Priscilla, Zenobia, and Hollingsworth with a dangerous electricity. Although Priscilla is completely and mysteriously devoted to Zenobia, the once pallid waif begins to bloom, mentally and physically, amidst the wild natural setting of Blithedale. And while Zenobia had originally been amused by Priscilla's unwavering admiration and loyalty, Priscilla's developing maturity makes Zenobia less vibrant, less generous, and less accessible to the younger woman, who has unwittingly become her rival for Hollingsworth's affections.

While Hollingsworth seems to thrive under the glow of his ambition and the two women's admiration, Coverdale begins to doubt the validity of their social experiment, believing it has had a negative impact on his own life as an artist. Always a careful observer, he begins to notice changes taking place within each person in his group. Particularly disturbing to him is the enmity that Zenobia shows toward Priscilla. He has grown fond of Priscilla and fears that Zenobia might eliminate this young rival.

At this point in the story, an odious character named Professor Westervelt arrives at Blithedale, seemingly concerned about the relationship between Zenobia and Priscilla. Although neither character says as much, Coverdale suspects Zenobia and Westervelt have known each other in the past. Later, Coverdale becomes convinced that Westervelt has had a powerful relationship with Zenobia after overhearing a conversation between the two during which they treat each other with a combination of familiarity and disdain.

Not long after this encounter, several things happen. Zenobia becomes blindly and somewhat frantically devoted to Hollingsworth, so much so that she agrees to finance his utopian dream. Tiring of his activities at Blithedale, Coverdale decides to go into town for a while, but is shocked to find that Zenobia, Westervelt, and Priscilla have also gone into town. It is during a meeting with the three that Coverdale suspects Priscilla will be the victim in a plot between the desperate Zenobia and the nefarious Westervelt.

Coverdale decides to question Old Moodie, who was responsible for Priscilla's presence at Blithedale. The truth is devastatingly simple. In his youth, Old Moodie had been a respectable member of society and a man of considerable wealth. Bad decisions and injudicious actions caused him to lose his money and his reputation; in shame, he left his wife and his beautiful daughter, Zenobia. Zenobia went to live with her wealthy uncle and became self-centered, headstrong, and rich through the inheritance of her uncle's money upon his death. There were also rumors that she had married a man of ill repute, but her money and her charismatic ways kept her respectable. As a result of his financial ruin, Old Moodie's life had become a downward spiral of poverty and despair. He wandered this way through many years, during which his first wife died, but eventually married again. This second marriage produced another daughter, Priscilla, who seemed the reflection of Moodie's broken spirit and the polar opposite of her half-sister, Zenobia.

Coverdale's discovery of the natural bond between the two women explained Priscilla's curious devotion to Zenobia. And although Old Moodie had urged Zenobia to be kind to Priscilla, it becomes apparent that she will ultimately do the younger woman some harm because of their rivalry for Hollingsworth's affections. Zenobia's plot against Priscilla is revealed to Coverdale during his visit to a magic show in a village near Blithedale. In the audience, he sees Hollingsworth; on the stage, he sees the odious magician Westervelt, and he observes the mysterious "Veiled Lady" who seems to be under Westervelt's control. In a gallant gesture, Hollingsworth demands that the ethereal figure on the stage remove her veil and reveal herself. In response, the wraith transforms into Priscilla, and she runs to him as though he has saved her from death and eternal damnation.

Once Zenobia learns of Hollingsworth's decision to be with Priscilla, she rails against him, calling him heartless and evil for having exploited her for her money and affection. She warns Priscilla of Hollingsworth's selfishness. Stripped of her finances and her dignity, Zenobia decides to end her pain by drowning herself in a nearby river.

Blithedale, and all of its potential, seems to wither after Zenobia's suicide. Coverdale decides to leave the estate, return to the city, and continue his work. Priscilla and Hollingsworth continue their lives together, but after Zenobia's death, Hollingsworth loses all interest in reforming society. Instead, he commits himself to reforming just one sinner—himself. His guilt over Zenobia's death has killed his spirit and his dreams. While Priscilla remains devoted to him, Hollingsworth, as always, is too self-absorbed to return her due. The sense of waste is complete with Coverdale's almost ridiculous and untimely admission, in his later years, that he too had been in love with Priscilla.

Hawthorne's tale is an important literary work and a fine example of traditional primitive apocalypse, as defined by May (May 1972, 229). The story begins with the idealistic vision of a perfect world. This vision, however, is soon clouded by the insidious persistence of evil—a paradise lost—demonstrated by Hollingsworth, Zenobia, and Westervelt. This failure of their noble social experiment is compounded by the chaotic degeneration of their relationships. Hawthorne's *Blithedale Romance* teaches a somber lesson about humankind's recurrent pursuit of paradise and the hubris that destroys such plans.

See also Apocalypse: Traditional Primitive; Brook Farm; Hawthorne, Nathaniel; Hollingsworth; Moodie, Priscilla; Moodie, Zenobia; Romanticism; Transcendentalism.

BONALI, VINCE

A disgruntled former mine worker appointed as the leader of an organization known as "The Common Sense Committee," Vince Bonali is the character who fights a zealous millenarian movement in Robert Coover's apocalyptic novel *The Origin of the Brunists* (1966). One of the only realistic characters in Coover's metafiction, Bonali is imperfect and truly human. From the outset, he resists the seductive wave of apocalypticism that overtakes his small town after a devastating mining disaster. All around him, people try frantically to find mystical explanations for the event that has shattered West Condon, Pennsylvania. But all Bonali can see are the grim realities of his own life. His faith in God has been shaken because of the mining accident. Even before the accident, he has acknowledged that his town is dying—jobs are few, and the young people have begun moving out of the community. Further, his marriage to an overweight, overly sensitive, and simple woman has become tedious. He is also aware that, as an older man who is unskilled for any other type of labor, his job prospects diminish with each passing day.

To escape such moments of painful clarity, he seeks solace in the companionship of his drinking buddies, who include other unemployed miners and disbelievers of the "Brunist" movement, dim-witted "good ole boys," and sadistic bullies. They appoint him as the head of their ad hoc "Common Sense Committee." While at first Vince finds new hope in leading this committee, he learns that their efforts are futile against the contagious apocalyptic fervor of a town that believes in the imminent end of the world. And although he secretly dreams that this leadership role might eventually propel him to higher political positions, such as that of mayor of West Condon, his delusions of grandeur fade, as does the security of his marriage, when he and other members of the committee are arrested for the drunken molestation of a local woman with whom he has had a previous illicit sexual relationship.

While others in the town attempt to escape the world in which they live, either through religious fanaticism or carnal pleasures, "Vince resolves to carry on. He is the ideal metafictionist hero, resisting patterns and roles, engaging history without script or clever repartee, with only the will to keep going" (Dewey 1990, 109). Even though at the end of the novel he has lost his job, damaged his marriage, and discarded his dreams, Bonali seems to survive his own personal apocalypse and is redeemed by his commitment to reality and renewed faith in his personal God. For Vince Bonali, it is not the end of the world; in spite of everything that has happened, he continues to believe that life will go on.

See also Apocalypse: Traditional Judeo-Christian; Apocalyptic Literature; Millennialism; Miller, Justin ("Tiger"); Naturalism; *The Origin of the Brunists.*

BRADBURY, RAY

Ray Bradbury (1920–) is well known as one of the best writers of American science fiction. As a writer of novels, short stories, screenplays, poems, and children's literature, Bradbury's prolific body of work has been widely anthologized and has been televised in dramatic segments of *Alfred Hitchcock Presents, The Twilight Zone,* and *The Ray Bradbury Theater.*

Born into a family of established publishers and editors, Bradbury often publishes his work using familial pseudonyms, such as his father's name, Leonard Spaulding or Douglas Spaulding. While Bradbury is best known as a science fiction writer, he considers himself a visionary and a moralist who writes "not to predict possible futures, but to prevent them."

Born in Waukegan, Illinois, on August 22, 1920, Bradbury has made his life in Los Angeles, California, where his family moved in 1934. Several incidents in his young life would permanently influence the direction of his writing career. One compelling incident occurred during the family's move to California when he witnessed the carnage caused by a violent automobile accident. This event traumatized the boy and instilled in him a lifelong concern with the destructive potential of technology. (To date, he still refuses to drive a car.) Humankind's inability to handle the unwieldy forces of technology is a recurrent theme in much of his fiction. Other life events reflected in his fiction include his introduction to horror movies at the age of three; his discovery of a compelling science fiction magazine, *Amazing Stories;* his early exposure to magicians at local fairs; and his voracious reading of the fantastic and illusory exploits depicted in *Buck Rogers* and *Flash Gordon* comics.

Bradbury began his writing career at twelve years old when he wrote his first story on a roll of butcher paper. It was eventually published in his hometown newspaper, an event that encouraged him to continue writing. During his high school years, Bradbury wrote and mimeographed his own quarterly magazine entitled *Futuria Fantasia.*

After graduating from Los Angeles High School in 1938, he sold newspapers. He enrolled in night school in 1943 to take classes in short-story writing; it was during this time that Bradbury met the formidable science fiction writer Robert A. Heinlein.

In the years that followed, Bradbury wrote countless stories and published many of them in pulp and mainstream magazines. Although his short fiction appears frequently in literary anthologies, and he is recognized for penning the screenplay for the film version of *Moby-Dick,* Bradbury is best known as the author of *The Martian Chronicles* (1950) and *Fahrenheit 451* (1953). In both of these books, readers can see through his antitechnology chimera to the real meaning of his work. Essentially, he believes that humanity's only hope for the future lies in the genius of intuition, the sanctity of personal freedom, the preservation of traditional values, and the ethical application of technical knowledge in the pursuit of a better world.

See also Apocalypse: Traditional Judeo-Christian; *Fahrenheit 451;* McClellan, Clarisse; *Moby-Dick;* Montag, Guy; Phoenix.

BRAVE NEW WORLD

Brave New World is the futuristic satire, replete with apocalyptic elements, written by English author Aldous Huxley in 1932. Contemporary readers of this work are often fascinated with the author's vision, particularly its representation of genetic engineering as a means of creating a utopian society. This story of a strange, highly mechanized society, set sometime in the future during the year of 632 A.F. (After Ford), tells of its concerted effort to eliminate all disruptive human variables, such as individuality, creativity, marriage, and family, in order to streamline productivity in the workplace and maintain uniform pacivity in a scientifically balanced world.

Within this society, human reproduction is a highly controlled industry, which involves the harvesting of female eggs, their artificial fertilization, and the genetic manipulation of embryos by teams of skilled technicians in order to mass-produce clones for specified tasks. Among the classes in this world of efficiency are the higher-order thinkers, known as Alphas, who are designated as the world leaders of the future. Betas are next in line in intelligence and aptitude. Below these are the bestial Deltas and the semimoronic Epsilons. Because of a sophisticated process of behavior modification conducted in the Infant Nurseries and the Neo-Pavlovian Conditioning Rooms (Huxley 12), people are, for the most part, satisfied and proud to have been selected as members of their designated caste.

While great pains are taken to keep everyone happy and satisfied with their societal roles, even greater efforts are undertaken to distract individuals from thinking, remembering, or emoting. In order to control these intrinsic human traits, the government manufactures, distributes, and encourages the use of a euphoria-inducing drug called *soma.* The effect of this drug renders the user completely submissive to the pursuit of sensory pleasures; all worry vanishes in such a dream state. Amidst this controlled, sterile, and mechanical society is a "savage" named John who was taken from his New Mexican Indian reservation that serves as an observatory for monitoring primitive behaviors.

John is a light-haired, light-skinned "savage" whose communication skills suggest he is not an original member of a reservation clan. In truth, he is the product of a sexual union between a high-ranking government official and a former Beta worker named Linda. Ashamed that she had gotten pregnant and had borne a child in such an uncivilized way, the father, who was actually the director of the Central London Hatchery and Conditioning Center, abandons Linda and the child at the reservation. Although Linda, who had been previously conditioned in her former life, hates the reservation and desperately misses her daily dose of *soma,* her son, John, lives happily on the reservation amidst the magic, the primitive rituals, the unchecked emotion, and the free-thinking environment. There he is allowed to read the drama of William Shakespeare. (Incidentally, the term *brave new world* originated in Shakespeare's apocalyptic play *The Tempest.*) In spite of his satisfaction with the reservation, John feels compelled to visit the "Other Place," about which his mother had described with such enthusiasm. He was eager when given the opportunity to go there, unaware that he would be subjected to further experimentation.

Soon after their arrival in the "Other Place," however, John's mother becomes heavily addicted to *soma.* John is disturbed when he sees her in a drug-induced delirium. Although "in the chaos of grief and remorse that filled his mind. . . . [all he could say was] 'Oh, God, God, God . . . .' " (141); he feels no connection with the creative force as he stands amidst this ruinous scene. John watches helplessly as his mother fades in and out of consciousness, and when he excitedly runs for help, he is chastised for being a bad example to the highly conditioned children of the embryo hatchery.

Overwhelmed by the tragedy of his mother's overdose, John rebels against the dehumanizing forces at work, stirs a massive revolt against the system, but ultimately, despairs of the human condition and finally kills himself, unable to live in a mechanical world.

See also Apocalypse: Secular; Apocalypse: Traditional Primitive; Huxley, Aldous Leonard; Science Fiction.

BROOK FARM

Brook Farm was the experimental community, conceived by George Ripley in 1841, located on a two-hundred-acre farm in West Roxbury, Massachusetts. Ripley, along with his wife, Sophia, Bronson Alcott, and Margaret Fuller, felt strongly about establishing a utopian center for communal living where families would work together, produce their own food, build their own homes, share the profits of their agricultural endeavors, and engage in intellectual pursuits. Although Ripley had the dream, he did not, however, have the finances with which to establish it.

He and his cohorts began to ask others to invest in the community. Several people expressed an interest in the experiment, such as Albert Brisbane, William Henry Channing, Charles A. Dana, and G. W. Curtis. A great effort was made to interest the wealthy and formidable Transcendentalist Ralph Waldo Emerson in the enterprise. But from the outset Emerson was skeptical of the success of communal living; he objected for a number of reasons, not the least of which was that the concept ran counter to his personal philosophy of "self-reliance." In spite of George Ripley's detailed letters explaining the academic possibilities of such a community, and in spite of the considerable efforts of the dynamic Margaret Fuller to obtain his support, Emerson ultimately declined the invitation to invest in the community.

One of his contemporaries, however, was convinced of the potential of the community. Nathaniel Hawthorne became interested in the possibilities of Brook Farm as an opportunity to combine physical and intellectual labor and to provide an economical home for himself and his new wife. He invested one thousand dollars toward the enterprise that he hoped would allow him to live inexpensively and to write freely in a natural setting. Hawthorne's idealistic vision, however, did not come to pass at Brook Farm. In a short time, he found the rigors of sustaining an agricultural community so physically draining that he was unable to generate the creative energy necessary for his writing. Hawthorne's wife was equally disillusioned with the social experiment; consequently, they moved from Brook Farm. The essence of their experiment in communal living at Brook Farm is captured in his novel *The Blithedale Romance.* Because of disagreements among the participants and recurrent misfortunes, such as a fire that burned down one of the major meeting halls, the community finally dissolved in 1846.

See also *The Blithedale Romance;* Emerson, Ralph Waldo; Hawthorne, Nathaniel; Transcendentalism.

BROTHER JACK

Brother Jack is the ideological leader of a powerful labor organization advocating racial equality known as "The Brotherhood" in Ralph Ellison's apocalyptic novel *The Invisible Man* (1952). At first glance, Brother Jack is a symbolic savior for the Invisible Man as he suffers through harsh working conditions at the Liberty Paint Factory. Although the narrator of the novel distrusts Jack because he is a white man, Jack wins him over with a seemingly judicious and genuine concern for the welfare of all members of his organization. Initially, Brother Jack is a kind of Christ-figure whom the Invisible Man willingly follows in the belief that he will be an inspirational figure for the protagonist.

These expectations are dashed, however, when the narrator observes Jack's irrational fanaticism in regard to his organization. Anyone who attempts to place individual concerns above those of the collective cause is in direct defiance of Jack's ideal mission for the organization. In one particularly symbolic scene, Jack becomes so enraged during a meeting that his glass eye accidentally pops out of its socket. While this incident, which suggests Jack's moral blindness, disturbs the narrator of the story, it reveals Jack as a demonic force with whom the protagonist is now forced to contend.

After witnessing Brother Jack's nefarious transformation, as well as learning of his intention to cause widespread destruction during a riot, the Invisible Man sees Jack for what he really is. He is no longer seen as a Christ-figure, but rather more like the archetypal betrayer, Judas Iscariot, who seduces, manipulates, and destroys for personal gain. His true personality is revealed when it is uncovered that Brother Jack, the defender of equality, had actually been the author of a racist letter to the Invisible Man. In this letter he suggests that the Invisible Man remember that he is living in a "white man's world," and that the best way to further the Negro cause is to remain anonymous, that is, "invisible."

See also Apocalypse: Secular; Apocalypticism; Archetype; Bledsoe, Dr.; *The Invisible Man;* Rinehart.

THE BROTHERS KARAMAZOV

Written by the great Russian novelist Fyodor Dostoyevsky, *The Brothers Karamazov* (c. 1879–1880) is a philosophical drama, a sophisticated murder mystery, and an apocalyptic vision. It is considered by many to be one of the most significant novels in world literature. In this work, an elderly and licentious landowner, Fyodor Pavlovich Karamazov, is the focal point of Dostoyevsky's moral revelation. The other primary characters within the novel include his children: Dmitri, a lustful yet noble son; Alyosha, the young and pure-hearted novice studying under a zealous monk; Ivan, a tormented intellectual with suppressed rage toward his father; and Smerdyakov, Fyodor's bastard epileptic child who is both impressionable and dangerously impulsive.

Dostoyevsky intended for the three legitimate sons to represent the three aspects of humanity: body (Dmitri), mind (Ivan), and spirit (Alyosha). As such, their conflicts with one another, as well as with their father, are meant to illustrate the psychological complexities intrinsic to human nature. Two of the strongest human impulses, sexuality and greed, are aroused by the local temptress named Grushenka, who has been the mistress of Fyodor but who is powerfully attracted to his son, Dmitri. In order to have her, however, Dmitri must secure his inheritance, which his father has thoughtlessly squandered over the years on vodka and women. When Fyodor is found murdered, suspicion falls on Dmitri, who has both a motive and an opportunity. After a lengthy trial, Dmitri is convicted, yet he is actually innocent of the crime.

All parties involved are affected by the murder. Ivan, the avowed atheist whose thoughtless rhetoric inadvertently inspires the illegitimate son, Smerdyakov, to kill his father, becomes mentally deranged. Alyosha, the fervent student of the religious leader Zosima, decides to serve God in a secular rather than clerical capacity. And finally, Dmitri, the son who is most like his dead father, is unjustly punished by socialist reforms that, in the author's opinion, violate the sanctity of human freedom.

Ultimately, while this work does not fall into any specific category of apocalyptic literature, it does contain elements of apocalypticism. Literary critic Harold Bloom notes that this work is considered by many to be "Dostoyevsky's apocalypse." Bloom believes that novel should be categorized as "scripture" rather than tragedy, chronicle, or saga. Specifically, Bloom contends that the novel contains the collective human experience as presented in the Bible. He describes the scope of the work, in regard to specific life lessons, as ranging from "Genesis to Revelation, with the Book of Job and the Gospel of John as the [moral] centers" revealed within the novel (Bloom 1988, 1). Another apocalyptic aspect of the novel comes in the scene where Alyosha asks Father Zosima to bless his brothers. Because the monk has the supernatural gift of discernment, he offers a blessing upon Ivan, well aware that he will "undergo spiritual punishment" for his egoistic sins. When Zosima approaches Dmitri, he says nothing to the man but "bows down low" before him, because he knows that Dmitri's punishment "is to be both spiritual and temporal; he is to suffer not only from the consciousness of his own guilt, but is also to be cut off like an infected limb by the mechanical justice of the State" who will sentence him to exile in Siberia (Peace 1988, 22). Realizing that Dmitri will be unfairly punished for the murder of his father, Zosima makes a gesture that illustrates that God's mercy is superior to man's justice. The fallibility of human justice is, perhaps, one brief summation of the message in Dostoyevsky's majestic work. *The Brothers Karamazov* is a masterful portrayal of the social, ethical, religious, and psychological aspects of human nature, in general, and of both Dostoyevsky's life as well as Russian society, in particular.

See also Apocalypse: Traditional Judeo-Christian; Apocalypticism; Karamazov, Alyosha Fyodorovich; Karamazov, Dmitri Fyodorovich; Karamazov, Fyodor Pavlovich; Karamazov, Ivan Fyodorovich.

BRUNO, GIOVANNI

Giovanni Bruno is the immigrant Italian miner who becomes the unwitting messianic figure of a millenarian cult in Robert Coover's naturalistic novel *The Origin of the Brunists* (1966). A tragic mining accident in a squalid town called West Condon, Pennsylvania, kills ninety-seven men. The only one to survive is Giovanni Bruno. Prior to the cataclysmic event, Bruno was not considered particularly bright nor was he particularly beloved by his coworkers. Yet, his survival in the mines elevates him to mythical, if not divine, status in a town that is traumatized and desperately searching for a hopeful sign amidst its inexplicable loss.

Immediately following the mining disaster, Bruno is hospitalized in a coma from carbon monoxide poisoning and psychological trauma. During the time he is comatose, several individuals within the town, beginning with the evangelistic widow of another dead miner, Ely Collins, begin to gather scraps of circumstantial evidence, including a cryptic note from Collins, a former preacher, that indicates, at least to those who are dazed and disoriented by grief, that the accident is some kind of warning to the town that "*God's final judgment is near. . . .*" (106).

Although Bruno recovers physically, he has sustained some brain damage as a result of oxygen depravation. His family, especially his virginal and devout Catholic sister, Marcella, and a number of widows in the town, wait for a revelation from the accident's sole survivor. It comes soon after Bruno recovers from his coma when he announces that he has had "*a visitation by. . . . the Holy Virgin during his entombment* [, and that]. . . . [s]he had appeared to him . . . in the form of a . . . white bird" (145).

His declaration validates the suspicions of those in the town who believe Judgment Day is near. The message, however, is of particular interest to Eleanor Norton, a peculiar local woman who has been having a lifelong mental dialogue with a higher force she refers to as Domiron. Convinced that Domiron's prophesies correspond directly with Ely Collins's message, Bruno's fragmented revelation, and the predictions of a obsessive accountant who develops a complex system of apocalyptic numerology, Norton forms a millenarian movement that sweeps the town with its increasingly ritualized preparations for the end of the world.

For the most part, Bruno is detached from the activities that surround him. Nevertheless, he is appointed the titular head of a group known as "The Brunists," named in his honor. Throughout the remainder of the novel, Bruno himself appears only occasionally because he is merely the catalyst for a movement that seems an inevitable development for a town devoid of hope and awash in misery.

By the end of the novel, a cataclysmic event is orchestrated by the group, and although it permanently alters the lives of the townspeople, it does not precipitate in the end of the world. Giovanni Bruno, in the end, does not deliver them from the evils of this world; instead, the disillusioned group splits into several factions while Bruno, his true mental condition ultimately revealed, is admitted to a psychiatric hospital.

See also Apocalypse: Traditional Judeo-Christian; Apocalyptic Literature; Bonali, Vince; Millennialism; Miller, Justin ("Tiger"); Naturalism; *The Origin of the Brunists.*

BUCHANAN, DAISY

Daisy Buchanan is the fictional re-creation of Zelda Sayre, the wife of author F. Scott Fitzgerald, who was immortalized in the apocalyptic romance of the Jazz Age, *The Great Gatsby* (1925). Daisy, the beautiful yet shallow Southern belle, is the object of desire for the obsessive and ambitious protagonist of the novel, Jay Gatsby. In every way, Daisy epitomizes the frivolity and underlying decadence of upper-class society in America during the "Roaring Twenties."

Prior to the beginning of the novel, Daisy, herself a youthful delicate flower, has captivated the attention of the young, handsome, but impoverished James Gatz. Their young love is thwarted by Daisy's refusal to accept him due to her prevailing materialism. The memory of her wistful yet unattainable countenance inspires Gatz to re-create himself, by whatever means possible, into the wealthy and powerful racketeer, Jay Gatsby, so that he will be worthy of her devotion. Although Daisy is lovely, what Gatsby and others remember most about this alluring young woman is her lyrical voice, which invites her audience to share her elusive dream world. Her cousin, and narrator of the novel, Nick Carraway considers the magical spell she weaves: "[Daisy's voice] was full of money—that was the inexhaustible charm that rose and fell in it, the jingle of it, the cymbals' song of it . . . High in a white palace the king's daughter, the golden girl. . . ." It was precisely this siren's song that captured the heart of Gatsby, but he fails to realize that her voice and dream world are neither exclusive to him nor enough to sustain a mature and lasting love.

After the pretentious nouveau-riche Gatsby returns to claim Daisy, he is undaunted by the fact that, in his absence, she has married a wealthy and vulgar former football hero, Tom Buchanan. In spite of her marital status, however, Daisy eagerly encourages Gatsby's attentions, partly because she wishes to remain in a state of perpetual youth and partly because she is disillusioned by her husband's infidelities and lack of sensitivity. While Daisy engages in an escalating flirtation, Gatsby is determined to possess her and thereby attain what he views as the ultimate success, regardless of the cost.

The illusion Daisy hopes to sustain is, however, marred by the reality of her inevitable adulterous relationship with Gatsby. And because the world of reality is an inhospitable environment for such a self-centered adolescent as Daisy, she ultimately destroys Gatsby with her reckless behavior and her refusal to accept responsibility for any of her actions. With his dream shattered and his reputation compromised by the consequences of their flagrant affair, Gatsby is ultimately murdered. Although Daisy is not directly responsible for his death, Gatsby is, nonetheless, sacrificed and emotionally abandoned by the one woman in the world whom he had truly loved. Daisy's reaction to Gatsby's death is devoid of any genuine emotion. After Gatsby's death, Daisy is eager to retreat into her own dream life, where she feels safe and can exist within the wealthy womb of a world forever sheltered by her indifference and her husband's money.

See also Apocalypse: Secular; Apocalyptic Literature; Carraway, Nick; Gatsby, Jay; *The Great Gatsby.*

BUNDREN, ADDIE

Addie Bundren is the central character of an apocalyptic novel written by Southern author William Faulkner entitled *As I Lay Dying* (1930). She incites the action of the narrative, which is told from various points of view, by making a last wish on her deathbed that her family return her body to Jefferson, Mississippi, for an appropriate burial. In making this request, Addie, who has spent the majority of her years burdened by a loveless marriage and continual childbearing, secretly plans to avenge her harsh life by inflicting physical hardships on her family, particularly her husband.

After her death, the family sets out for Jefferson unaware that they will suffer a series of catastrophes somehow arranged by the dying woman. Addie feels entitled to her vengeance because she has been deprived of the passion and fulfillment that she had expected from her marriage. Her willful nature as well as her justification for revenge is revealed in the novel through a brief affair with a local preacher, Whitfield. Addie's relationship with Whitfield, which is a silent and genuine expression of love, is set in sharp contrast to the empty and vociferous relationship between her and her mean-spirited husband.

See also *Absalom, Absalom!;* Apocalypse: Traditional Judeo-Christian; Apocalyptic Literature; *As I Lay Dying;* Bundren, Anse; Bundren, Darl; Bundren, Jewel.

BUNDREN, ANSE

Anse Bundren is the husband of Addie Bundren, the protagonist, in William Faulkner's apocalyptic novel *As I Lay Dying* (1930). Although Anse maintains a consistent level of personal strength throughout the novel, his actions and attitudes make him the most despicable character within the work. In spite of his hunched stature and downcast personality, he is neither a victim nor a villain. He is portrayed throughout the novel as a self-serving egoist who is a disgraceful husband, a hollow man as illustrated by his empty words, and a greedy individual whose sole interest in life is that of his own survival.

See also *Absalom, Absalom!;* Apocalypse: Traditional Judeo-Christian; Apocalyptic Literature; *As I Lay Dying;* Bundren, Addie; Bundren, Darl; Bundren, Jewel.

BUNDREN, DARL

Darl Bundren is the second son of Addie and Anse Bundren in William Faulkner's apocalyptic odyssey entitled *As I Lay Dying* (1930). As a sensitive and intensely contemplative adolescent, Darl is perhaps the one most affected by the death of his mother. Grieving her loss takes a serious toll on the boy as he and his family endure a series of catastrophic events during the trip to return her body for burial in Jefferson, Mississippi.

Even though he feels obliged to honor her wish for burial in Jefferson, he is horrified by the journey, during which the wagon carrying his mother's coffin is overturned in a flood thereby revealing her putrefied corpse. In an attempt to bring an end to the senseless task, as well as to honor his mother's remains, he sets fire to the farmhouse where her corpse has been stored. Darl is eventually driven mad by this ordeal. Ultimately, he becomes so withdrawn and obsessed that he is committed to a state-run insane asylum.

See also *Absalom, Absalom!;* Apocalypse: Traditional Judeo-Christian; Apocalyptic Literature; *As I Lay Dying;* Bundren, Addie; Bundren, Anse; Bundren, Jewel.

BUNDREN, JEWEL

Jewel Bundren is the illegitimate offspring of an adulterous liaison between the protagonist, Addie Bundren, and a local preacher named Whitfield in William Faulkner's novel *As I Lay Dying* (1930). Throughout the novel, Jewel's physical attributes as well as his emotional countenance are very different from the other children in the Bundren household. He is, most particularly, the direct opposite of his mean-spirited "father," Anse Bundren, in that he is sensitive, relatively silent, and genuinely loving toward his mother.

These characteristics are extensively drawn by Faulkner to emphasize that Jewel is the natural son of Whitfield rather than Anse Bundren. They also explain Addie's favoritism toward Jewel and her implicit trust that he will guard her corpse until it reaches its final burial place in Jefferson, Mississippi.

See also *Absalom, Absalom!;* Apocalypse: Traditional Judeo-Christian; Apocalyptic Literature; *As I Lay Dying;* Bundren, Addie; Bundren, Anse; Bundren, Darl.

BUNYAN, JOHN

John Bunyan (1628–1688) was the zealous Christian writer and part-time preacher who wrote *The Pilgrim's Progress,* one of the most popular apocalyptic allegories of all time. As the son of a tinker from Bedforshire, England, Bunyan continued in his father's humble line of work until his service in the parliamentary army from 1644 to 1646. Following this period, Bunyan married a woman who would forever change the course of his life.

His wife's dowry included two texts of devotional literature. After reading them, Bunyan began to contemplate spiritual matters. In spite of a willingness to accept Christian doctrine, Bunyan found himself wrestling with the issues of sin, forgiveness, and redemption. He eventually resolved these inner conflicts and joined the congregation of a local Baptist church. As a result of his personal study as well as the influence of his church, Bunyan also took it upon himself to become a lay preacher. This decision, however, directly contradicted royal laws forbidding lay preaching.

Although he was warned by authorities to cease his extemporaneous sermons, which were most often delivered at nonliturgical locations, Bunyan refused to obey and was sentenced to a harsh imprisonment for twelve years.

Fueled by religious conviction, Bunyan used the twelve years of incarceration to meditate on the Bible, to study such works as Foxe's *Book of Martyrs,* and, more importantly, to write several of his own books, including an autobiography entitled *Grace Abounding to the Chief of Sinners.*

Following the completion of his prison sentence, Bunyan renewed his commitment to preaching the word of God by becoming a minister in the Bedford Nonconformist Church. In 1675, after he was caught preaching outside of the church, he was briefly put in prison again. During this imprisonment he worked on a two-part Christian allegory entitled *The Pilgrim's Progress,* later recognized as the second most popular book next to the Bible. It chronicles one man's journey through life, replete with obstacles and temptations that caused him to choose the path to eternal salvation rather than to damnation and infernal torment.

The popularity of this work was due to its relevance to the everyday lives and concerns of his contemporaries. As a writer, Bunyan is known for his masterful use of figurative language, concrete imagery, and a sincere simplicity that places him in the company of a few authors who have the talent and conviction to express the complexities of the human experience through the power of pure art.

See also Allegory; Apocalypse: Traditional Judeo-Christian; Apocalypticism; Myth; Symbol.

CALIBAN

Caliban is the fishlike monster, the type of wicked spirit that is common to the Italian pastoral romance, who appears in William Shakespeare's apocalyptic tragicomedy entitled *The Tempest* (c. 1611). According to lore, Caliban is the son of a union between the devil and Sycorax, the wicked witch of an uninhabited island. While Caliban is essentially a soulless being, he has a natural intelligence that makes him valuable as a servant to the exiled Duke of Milan, Prospero, who washes upon the shore of the deserted island twelve years prior to the action of the play.

During the twelve years of their acquaintance, the noble duke never attempts to reform the diabolical creature because he understands that Caliban is "a devil, a born devil, on whose nature/Nurture can never stick" (4.I. 188–189). In spite of his lack of morality, however, Prospero finds Caliban capable of learning tasks that can assist the exiled duke in the furtherance of his plans. Although Caliban is obviously disgusting and generally reprehensible, he does elicit some sympathy as the poor ill-conceived creature who will never be able to fulfill the love he has for Prospero's beautiful and innocent fifteen-year-old daughter, Miranda.

In spite of his resentment of Prospero for twelve years of enslavement, Caliban is briefly allowed to enjoy himself in the comic scenes where he shares the company of other fools, Stephano and Trinculo, who provide him with wood alcohol. He serves them in the hopes that they will fulfill their promise of setting him free.

See also Apocalypse: Traditional Judeo-Christian; Apocalypticism; Ariel; Ferdinand; Prospero; *The Tempest.*

CARRAWAY, NICK

Nick Carraway is the narrator of F. Scott Fitzgerald's apocalyptic romance entitled *The Great Gatsby* (1925). Born to a wealthy Midwestern family, Nick lives a comfortable life in which he enjoys the security of a stable community with heartland values. He attends Princeton University and prepares to become a bonds broker in New York City. While looking for a place to live that is removed from the chaos of the city, Nick gets an opportunity to rent a small residence in

Caliban, a fishlike monster and wicked spirit in William Shakespeare's play *The Tempest,* was portrayed by George Selway in a 1962 production at the Old Vic in London.

the Long Island community called West Egg, which is just across the way from the more fashionable community of East Egg.

While making these arrangements, he learns that he will live in close proximity to a distant cousin, Daisy Buchanan, and her husband, Tom. They renew their relationship, and Nick becomes unwittingly involved in Daisy's personal drama that serves as the core of the novel. He learns that Daisy, once a highly regarded Southern debutante, is unhappily married to her coarse and philandering husband. The couple's money and lavish lifestyle seems to be the link that binds them in spite of their obvious incompatibility.

As Nick becomes more familiar with the residents of the community, particularly one of his cousin's friends, Jordan Baker, with whom he later becomes romantically involved, he uncovers the details regarding the mysterious exploits of his millionaire neighbor, Jay Gatsby, who is famous for throwing lavish parties. Nick also learns from Jordan that Daisy, in her youth, had dated a poor young man named James Gatz (Gatsby) but decided instead to marry Tom for the security he could offer her. Nick remains understandably curious about both Gatsby and Daisy, and eventually he finds himself seduced by each of their individual charms.

Although she is his cousin, Daisy often teases and flirts with Nick; in turn, he is captivated by her vivacity and the lyrical resonance of her magical voice. Similarly, after developing a friendship with his neighbor, Nick finds Gatsby equally compelling. While pondering Gatsby's magnetism, Nick concludes that "[I]f personality is an unbroken series of successful gestures, then there was something gorgeous about him, some heightened sensitivity to the promises of life. . . ." (Fitzgerald 2). Captivated by these two volatile and self-indulgent personalities, Nick inevitably serves as a mediator for a reunion of the former lovers.

In the meantime, however, Nick himself becomes absorbed, at least temporarily, in Gatsby's extravagant lifestyle. While he dislikes the vulgar displays of these wealthy revelers, he is envious of the ease and indifference with which they seem to live their lives. One particular incident that reflects the upper-class disregard for basic morality occurs during a golfing date with Jordan Baker. Although he had previously been attracted to her, the fact that she blatantly cheats at golf appalls him and sours their romantic relationship. Thereafter, they are only casual acquaintances.

Nick also finds it unsettling that his two friends, Daisy and Gatsby, subtlely manipulate him until he agrees to invite the two to his home for an afternoon tea. At this reunion, he forgives their indiscretions because he senses the powerful emotions behind their strained formality. Having served as the facilitator of this meeting, Nick is both relieved yet troubled when Gatsby later invites Daisy to visit his mansion. Daisy is unaware that Gatsby has amassed a considerable fortune and all of its lavish accoutrements in the hopes of winning her heart. She is giddy with excitement as she sorts through his clothes, his furniture, and his artistic treasures that offer her the promise of a more fulfilling life.

Ultimately, Nick's mediation is no longer required; Daisy and Gatsby consummate their relationship, thereby changing the dynamics of their friendship with Nick. Soon after, Nick notices their innocent flirtation has given away to clandestine couplings, which he finds almost as unsettling as Tom Buchanan's ongoing affair with a tawdry housewife, Myrtle Wilson. For the duration of the novel, Nick is caught in the middle. He later witnesses the decline and fall of Gatsby's hard-earned American Dream at the reckless hands of Daisy.

When all is said and done, Nick realizes that the chaotic indulgences of Daisy and Gatsby are only hollow imitations of lives, devoid of emotional and spiritual fulfillment. In their world, everyone is spiritually and morally dead. (He acknowledges this disturbing truth after Gatsby's murder.) Gatsby, the once-popular party host, is virtually abandoned by the throng of partyers who had once taken advantage of his generosity. Another of Nick's revelations is that Daisy's affection is both false and fleeting, particularly after she chooses to withdraw from Gatsby, the devoted man who later dies on her account, in favor of her boorish husband who has nothing to offer her but money and status.

As such, on the day of Gatsby's funeral, Nick realizes that he had been Gatsby's only friend in the world. His despair over this tragedy is heightened by the appearance of Gatsby's father, who knew nothing of his son's exploits but eagerly accepts the consoling remarks of his son's true friend. In the aftermath, Nick resolves to return to his Midwestern roots. But as he prepares to leave, he is haunted by Gatsby's dream and understands that he will remain forever changed by having shared it with his friend for a brief but glorious time.

See also Apocalypse: Secular; Apocalyptic Literature; Buchanan, Daisy; Gatsby, Jay; *The Great Gatsby*.

CAT'S CRADLE

Cat's Cradle (1963) is an important twentieth-century apocalyptic novel, written by Kurt Vonnegut, Jr., that employs elements of science fiction and black comedy to satirize technology, religion, and human folly in the modern world. In the novel, the protagonist, symbolically identified as Jonah-John, is a writer who sets out to gather information for a book he plans to call *The Day the World Ended.* "The [intended] book [which never actually gets written] was to be an account of what important Americans had done on the day when the first atomic bomb was dropped on Hiroshima, Japan" (Vonnegut CC 1). In his search for material, Jonah-John comes in contact with the youngest son of a Nobel Prize–winning physicist, Dr. Felix Hoenikker, who relates his father's direct involvement in the development of the bomb.

What Jonah-John learns, via letters and meetings with the other two children of the deceased scientist, is that before his death Dr. Hoenikker had been working on a molecular structure intended to help soldiers fight more effectively in boggy and wet environments. According to all accounts, what the physicist discovered as a result of his experimentation was a creation called "ice-nine," which would stack and freeze atoms immediately in order to create a hard surface. Anything that would come in contact with this crystalline substance would immediately solidify and remain so unless it were exposed to a torrid Fahrenheit temperature, or "a melting point of one-hundred-and-thirty degrees" (21). Hoenikker realized the devastating potential of his discovery: if ice-nine were to be misappropriated, even the rain would "freeze into hard little hobnails

. . . and that would be the end of the world!" (23). Before he could announce to the world the nativity of his apocalyptic "beast," Dr. Hoenikker died on December 24, Christmas Eve, while on vacation with his children. Prior to his death, however, he told his three children (two not very "wise" men and a woman) about ice-nine; moreover, they witnessed firsthand, via the accidental freezing of their family dog, the devastating impact of his deadly new creation. Aware of the potential power and profit that might result from their father's invention, the children divided the substance that their father had taken to their vacation cottage, and they kept secret the existence of ice-nine until it became advantageous for each of them to share the information for personal gain.

Inspired by the story told by Hoenikker's youngest son, Newt, Jonah-John embarks on a pilgrimage that leads him to Dr. Hoenikker's eldest son, Franklin, who has used the influence of his father's work to gain the position of "Major General . . . and *Minister of Science and Progress in the Republic of San Lorenzo* [italics in original]" (37), a mythical nation located somewhere in South America. Upon his arrival in San Lorenzo, Jonah learns of another invention that is spiritual rather than scientific in nature; it is the man-made religion known as Bokononism, which the protagonist describes by citing the first sentence in *The Book of Bokonon,* which asserts that "[a]ll of the true things I [Bokonon] am about to tell you are shameless lies." This religion, admittedly based upon lies, consists of riddles, rituals, rules for relationships, and the relentless pursuit of health and general happiness. The absurdity behind this so-called religion is presented in its founder's utopian vision, cited in *The Seventh Book of Bokonon:*

> The hand that stocks the drug stores rules the world. Let us start our Republic with a chain of drug stores, a chain of grocery stores, a chain of gas chambers, and a national game. After that, we can write our Constitution (189–190).

Vonnegut uses the cynicism, cruelty, and commercialism of Bokononism to comment on religious dogmas as they are practiced within the spiritual vacuum of our modern world.

Ironically, this widely practiced religion is officially forbidden by the San Lorenzo government. For San Lorenzians, church and state must remain separate entities; anyone observed practicing Bokononism is sentenced to die by being impaled upon "the Hook," a medieval device designed solely for the purpose of public executions. In spite of such dire consequences, the citizens of San Lorenzo, compelled by the perversities of human nature, secretly practice Bokononism because it, like most formal religions, seems to offer a modicum of order in an otherwise chaotic world.

Although the chronicle of the characters and their absurd circumstances are presented in Vonnegut's irreverent and colloquial style, the issues surrounding scientific experimentation, ethical leadership, and spiritual belief are seriously addressed in the body of apocalyptic literature. There are many similarities between *Cat's Cradle* and another apocalyptic classic, Herman Melville's *Moby-Dick.* One specific parallel is found in the opening line of *Cat's Cradle* in which the narrator says "Call me Jonah," reminiscent of the narrator's introduction in *Moby-Dick,* "Call me Ishmael." In each book, the protagonists are observers, participants, and chroniclers of events in their individual worlds. Similarly, each novel revolves around a terrifyingly powerful icon that serves as the major obsession of deluded, idealistic leaders. Whereas Melville's Captain Ahab tries to control his world by killing the great white whale, "Papa" Monzano, San Lorenzo's leader, attempts to control the world by harnessing the power of Felix Hoenikker's ice-nine. In the end, however, human folly is exposed when the whale destroys both *The Pequod* and those who participate in Ahab's revenge. In *Cat's Cradle,* it is the leviathan of science, manifested by the tiny molecules of ice-nine, that inevitably destroys San Lorenzo and its childlike leaders, and the entire world. Critical opinion suggests that the narrators of these apocalypses survive primarily because of their unwillingness to surrender completely to the iconoclastic pursuits of either world (either the hunt for the whale or the worship of science). Furthermore, both Jonah's and Ishmael's experiences compel them to retell their tales to warn others of the destruction caused by the relentless hubris of humanity.

The cataclysmic consequences of humanity's defiance of the universal plan, or more specifically, of God's design, is a theme as old as one of the most apocalyptic books of the Old Testament, the book of Jonah. Like Vonnegut's Jonah and Melville's Ishmael, Jonah, the biblical archetype of the reluctant prophet, carries the same message to the modern world. He is ordered to warn the city of Nineveh to stop its wicked ways lest it suffer the wrath of God. At first, Jonah ignores God's orders by traveling instead to Tarshish, "away from the presence of the Lord" (Jonah 1:3). His disobedience is divinely punished when he is tossed into a raging sea where he is swallowed by a great whale, remaining there to reconsider his decision for three days and nights. After he is expelled from the belly of the whale, he obeys his orders and travels to Nineveh, where the people repent and God's will is accomplished. Unlike Captain Ahab who is blinded by revenge, and "Papa" Monzano whose judgment is blurred by the power of science, Jonah survives having learned a valuable lesson about mercy, justice, and the insignificance of humanity against the creative forces of the universe. Jonah, the Old Testament scribe, serves as a model for countless prophets whose warnings are heard, but most often unheeded, throughout the body of apocalyptic fiction.

See also Apocalypse: Secular; Apocalypse: Traditional Judeo-Christian; Apocalyptic Literature; Hoenikker, Felix; Ice-Nine; Jonah, Book of; Jonah-John; Leviathan; *Moby-Dick*, Vonnegut, Kurt, Jr.

COLDFIELD, ROSA

In William Faulkner's tale of the decadence of the antebellum South, *Absalom, Absalom!* (1936), Rosa Coldfield is the sister-in-law of the demonic character, Thomas Sutpen. She is the oldest witness to the events within the novel. Although she is committed to telling the unvarnished truth to another narrator, a young Harvard student, Quentin Compson, Rosa's account is marred by both her age and her violent prejudice against the obsessive Thomas Sutpen, who had married her sister, Ellen Coldfield, and who had, either directly or indirectly, influenced the downfall, death, and emotional destruction of all of his descendents.

Rosa Coldfield's lack of objectivity in her recounting of events is perhaps related to her overt romanticism, fostered by sheltered childhood. This romanticism may also have been inherited from the general nature of the Coldfield clan. In any case, Rosa's heightened sense of guilt and need to cast blame colors her view of Thomas Sutpen. She holds Sutpen wholly responsible for the destruction of her family for a number of reasons. First, even though he had married her sister and had provided sufficiently for her needs, his personal nature and relentless egoism brought shame to the Coldfield name. Such self-serving actions would clearly violate the essence of the Southern aristocratic tradition carried by Rosa's family. Secondly, and perhaps most significantly, Sutpen's actions to prevent the marriage of his mixed-blood son, Charles Bon, and his half-sister, Judith (Sutpen's daughter by Ellen), convinced Rosa of Sutpen's completely evil nature. The sad truth was that Rosa's hopes for a marriage between Charles and Judith had revived her own romantic inclinations. Thus, Sutpen's involvement in Bon's murder, and the exile of his step-brother, Henry, caused Rosa's hatred of her brother-in-law to deepen dramatically. The final event that confirmed her hostility toward Sutpen was his suggestion, much later in life, that they she and he mate (not marry) in order to produce a male heir for Sutpen's Hundred, thus fulfilling his grand design.

This proposal was an incomprehensible abomination to Rosa's romantic nature and for the remainder of her days, she contemplates the nature of evil, as personified by Thomas Sutpen. Ultimately, Rosa concludes that she, much like humankind, in general, and the South, in particular, are doomed to be victims of the diabolical, irrational, and enigmatic forces that have always threatened the universe.

See also *Absalom, Absalom!*; Apocalypse: Anti-Christian; Archetype; Compson, Quentin; Satan.

COMPSON, QUENTIN

Quentin Compson is one of the major narrators in William Faulkner's 1936 apocalyptic novel, *Absalom, Absalom!* At the beginning of the novel, Quentin has been selected to receive the fatalistic tale of Thomas Sutpen, an archetypal villain, from an aging Southern spinster, Miss Rosa Coldfield.

Quentin, a student at Harvard University and himself the grandson of a contemporary of Thomas Sutpen, is the standard bearer for the antebellum South and its eventual decline. Although there are other narrators within the novel, Quentin distinguishes himself with his intelligence, sensitivity, and fervent interest in his rich Southern heritage. His natural curiosity, coupled with his determined objectivity, propels him in his investigation of the truth that he shares with his college roommate, a Northerner named Shreve McCannon.

Through this investigation, Quentin examines his own relationship to the past as well as the actions and consequences surrounding the life of the main character in the novel, Thomas Sutpen. Ultimately, Quentin suffers a personal dilemma in which he is torn between familial loyalty and his morality. At the end of the novel, although he vehemently denies that he hates the South, he is tormented by the historical fact that much of the South, its cultural traditions, and his own personal heritage have been based on the cruel and inequitable exploitation of one segment of humanity at the hands of the ruthless determination of another.

See also *Absalom, Absalom!;* Apocalypse: Anti-Christian; Archetype; Coldfield, Rosa.

THE CONFIDENCE-MAN: HIS MASQUERADE

The Confidence-Man (1857) is a bitter social satire on the gullibility and cynicism of the human race. Set onboard a Mississippi riverboat, ironically named the *Fidele,* on April Fools' Day, *The Confidence-Man* is Herman Melville's last piece of full-length fiction. Unlike his earlier novels, in which he draws multidimensional characters, vividly describes dramatic action, and microscopically explores the complexities of human nature, *The Confidence-Man* portrays characters superficially and is notably devoid of significant action. Melville only hints at the psychological motivations of the human condition of the early nineteenth century, which he believed to be rotten to the core. John R. May, in his insightful criticism of Melville's text, believes that it was the author's intention to focus on the surface of things, and thereby manipulate both the structure and imagery within the novel in order establish its undeniably apocalyptic tone (May 1972, 61).

As is the case with many American novels, *The Confidence-Man* was inspired by a newspaper article, written in July of 1849, entitled "Arrest of the Confidence Man"; the article began:

> For the last few months a man has been traveling about the city, known as the "Confidence Man"; that is, he would go up to a perfect stranger in the street, and being a man of genteel appearance, would easily command an interview. Upon this interview he would say, after some little conversation, "have you confidence in me to trust me with your watch until tomorrow"; the stranger, at this novel request, supposing him to be some old acquaintance, not at the moment recollected, allows him to take the watch, thus placing "confidence" in the honesty of the stranger, who walks off laughing, and the other, supposing it to be a joke, allows him so to do. In this way many have been duped . . . (Tanner xii).

Given this framework, readers can better understand the diabolical motives of the central character of Melville's novel, who attempts to dupe a series of people, each of whom represents a "'type' of the Fall of Man" (Hoffman 1962, 126). Melville's literary skill methodically employs features used in a variety of world narratives, such as classical mythology, religious symbolism, and cultural folklore, in which the archetypal devil, "trickster," or "shape-shifter" gleefully confounds a series of unwitting prey (Tanner xiii).

The character of the chameleonlike con-man serves as the filter through which various flawed characters are examined. While this technique was unusual, particularly in regard to the literary tastes of the period, some of Melville's contemporaries complained bitterly, as did a reviewer of the work in the *Literary Gazette,* who said that the interlacing of various narrative threads caused him to experience "an uncomfortable sensation of dizziness in the head." Further, the reviewer failed to accept that *The Confidence-Man* was even an acceptable representation of the novel form, "unless a novel means forty-five conversations . . . conducted by personages who might pass for the errata of creation" (Hoffman 129).

The proliferation of such "errata of creation," however, is precisely the author's point. In fact, Melville made a concerted effort to show how the enthusiasm of America's early settlers was being slowly undermined by an evolving society in which "the old, well-proven, conservative crust of religion, government, family, and even common respect for age, education and experience was rapidly melting away, and was indeed already broken into fragments, swept about by the seething mass of scum ever rising in greater quantities to the surface" (Tanner xiv). *The Confidence-Man* can be read as an allegory in which each character represents both himself as well as a trait within human nature.

There is still considerable debate on this topic. For example, some critics believe that the deaf-mute, clothed in cream-colored clothing and writing verses from 1 Corinthians while begging for alms, symbolizes Jesus Christ, whose message of love was disregarded and mocked, like the beggar in Melville's novel. Other critics, however, challenge this view and regard the beggar as yet another diabolical disguise used by the confidence-man to extort money from unsuspecting travelers. While this debate remains unresolved, there is no doubt among critics about the symbolic meaning of the old man who appears in the apocalyptic conclusion of the novel.

John R. May describes the closing scenes of the novel as Melville's attempt to "fram[e] his fantasy of the last loosing of Satan within the primary numerical symbol of the Book of Revelation" (May 66). May argues that Melville, as an avid Bible scholar, would have been well aware of the significance of the number seven. The confidence-man dons seven disguises throughout the novel, and seven, being the biblical number of completion, portends the "end of the American world of the *Fidele*" as well as the end of the world in general. This view is supported in the last chapter of the work in which the old man sits alone and reads by the singular light of a solar lamp. When the confidence-man encounters the "robed man with the halo [who] could be any Christian saint," the scene "almost certainly refers to the popular but traditional association of the John of Revelation with St. John the apostle and evangelist" (67). When the confidence-man extinguishes the lamp and leads the unsuspecting man into the impenetrable darkness, it is clear that Melville intended the reader to appreciate the apocalyptic "irony of an aged Simeon waiting to bless his savior and instead being led off into the darkness by Satan himself—in sheep's clothing, of course" (68).

See also Allegory; Apocalypse: Secular; Apocalyptic Literature; Archetype; *Moby-Dick; The Mysterious Stranger;* Myth; Symbol.

A CONNECTICUT YANKEE IN KING ARTHUR'S COURT

Connecticut Yankee (1889) is the social satire by Mark Twain that chronicles the farcical, albeit serious, events that occur to a nineteenth-century Connecticut Yankee when he is mysteriously transported back to the life and times of King Arthur's sixth-century feudal England. The story begins with a tale revealed to an omniscient narrator, M. T. (assumed to be Mark Twain). This revelation or, more specifically, this historical account, is delivered by a stranger with whom M. T. becomes acquainted while visiting Warwick castle. This stranger, named Hank Morgan (Morgan LeFay), is a disoriented former superintendent of an arms factory in Hartford, Connecticut. He relates a saga to M. T. that supposedly began after being accidentally hit on the head with a crowbar by a coworker in a factory brawl. According to his account, when he awoke from this astonishing blow, which had actually occurred during the nineteenth century, he found himself in the remarkable predicament of facing the point of a spear wielded by Sir Kay, a knight of King Arthur's Round Table.

After an amicable resolution to their initial encounter, Hank followed the knight back to the glorious medieval kingdom known as Camelot. Although Hank still believed he was delusional from the recent blow to the head, the specifics of the displaced Yankee's predicament were provided by a young page named Clarence, who confirmed the time traveler's arrival at the court in the month of June in the year A.D. 528. Having no choice in the matter, Hank listened curiously to the boastful stories presented by Arthur's knights. Accordingly, following Sir Kay's articulation of his initial discovery and capture of his prisoner, Merlin, the famed magician of Arthurian lore, suggested that the stranger be imprisoned in the dungeon until June 21, the day upon which he would be burned at the stake.

Meditating on such troubling events, after having been stripped of his foreign clothing and thrown into a rat-infested cell, the Yankee conceived a plan, based upon his nineteenth-century knowledge, to confound the kingdom and thereby neutralize Merlin's power as well as other prevailing superstitious forces. Having knowledge about a coming total eclipse, he told Clarence to announce to the court that on the day of his planned execution the sun would become dark and that the kingdom would be destroyed upon his death. As predicted, at the moment when the prisoner was about to be burned, the sky went dark; consequently, the king ordered his immediate release from the stake, and Merlin's credibility as a sorcerer was viewed by the people as subordinate to Hank Morgan's magic.

Awed by this demonstration, the king's court required further proof of the Yankee's necromantic abilities. Hank enlisted Clarence's services once again to mystify the people. He used his vocational experience as a mechanic of firearms to construct makeshift explosives, telling the people that he could prove his superior power by destroying Merlin's tower. When the tower predictably exploded into ruins, the discredited Merlin was immediately imprisoned, and Hank was appointed the official magician of the court.

Inspired by his new position, Hank began to consider his new environs, as they compared with those of nineteenth-century New England, and became troubled by the kingdom's general lack of education and dearth of labor-saving mechanical devices. So Hank decided to initiate a plan to save the common people from their mechanical ignorance and continued feudal injustices. The people began referring to him as "the Boss," and he eagerly accepted this role by preparing the kingdom for the great wonders of the modern world.

Hank set about his plan to disempower the cruel nobility in the following ways. First, he would free the commoners from their slavery by secretly setting up schools across the country, counteracting the superstitious mandates of the local church. Next, he initiated an elaborate training program to promote mechanical skill and the manufacture of useful materials. His belief in a free press led him to teach Clarence the trade of journalism. Finally, convinced that communication between the various hamlets was a necessity, he installed crude telephone wires throughout the kingdom.

Hank's power was soon questioned by Sir Sagramor, who challenged him to a duel. Because he had never participated in such an event, he reluctantly followed the king's suggestion to embark upon a mission in preparation for the battle. His assignment involved the safe transport of a maiden named Alisande (whom he subsequently called Sandy) to her castle, where a harem of forty-five princesses were currently being held captive by three hideous ogres. Even though he was less than thrilled by the assignment, Hank set forth on his mission, but his reluctance was ameliorated by Sandy's cheerful and incessant stories as they travel the countryside. Throughout their travels, however, the Yankee became appalled by the suffering of the commoners under feudal conditions. In an effort to help them escape continued tyranny, he decides to create a community of skilled leaders; each time he met someone who was particularly talented or intelligent, he sent that individual back to Camelot to receive valuable instruction from his apprentice, Clarence, who was in charge of the newly created "Man Factory" (Twain *CY* 66). In the meantime, whenever possible, Hank stops at the many castles he encounters on his journey and releases any prisoners who have been mercilessly cast into dungeons.

Feeling encouraged by his mounting victories, Hank meets his next challenge in a place known as the Valley of Holiness. Upon his arrival, he learns that the town's sacred well was dried up because someone had befouled it by bathing in it. Earlier, Merlin had been summoned by the holy abbot to release the well from its apparent curse. The magician, of course, welcomed the opportunity to demonstrate his power, but in spite of his considerable efforts he could not restore the fountain, claiming that if he couldn't do it, then no mortal could. Once again, Hank is given another opportunity to enhance his reputation by challenging Merlin's power. Upon close inspection, he discovers that the failure of the well was not the result of an evil spell but simply from a leak in its foundation. He sends for the necessary supplies and a cadre of recently trained tradesmen to assist in providing the town with an extravagant miracle. In short, the Boss and his men repair the leak, then wait until the water has risen to an appropriate level to insert a pump to restore the former flourish of the fountain. In addition, Hank decides to take advantage of the gullible townspeople by staging a dramatic prelude to the well's restoration, consisting of fireworks accompanied by a series of nonsensical incantations. When the crowd has reached its peak of expectation, Hank's men engage the pump and the fountain gushes its miraculous stream among the appreciative faithful. And once again, Merlin slips away from the spectacular scene overwhelmed by shame, consternation, and rage.

Soon after he completes his well miracle, Hank visits one of the caves in which a telephone had been installed. Upon placing a call to Clarence to inform him of his triumph, Hank learns that the king has already left Camelot to witness the miracle firsthand. Following the call, Hank returns to the town only to overhear another less impressive magician claim the ability to divine the whereabouts of any living person. Disgusted by this claim, he decides to impress the crowds once again by asking the magician about King Arthur's present status. When the magician ceremoniously asserts that the king is presently asleep at Camelot, Hank counters with his well-informed prediction that Arthur is, in fact, not in his castle at all but rather is already on his way to the fountain. This entertaining debate is settled when the king arrived on the scene, leaving the townspeople, once again, amazed by the Yankee's incredible power.

In a subsequent conversation with the king, Hank takes advantage of the monarch's magnanimity by suggesting that together they embark on a journey throughout the countryside disguised as common folk; this suggestion arises from Hank's belief that the king is basically kind and has been kept uninformed of the great suffering endured by his lowly subjects. Moved by the occasion of his request, the king agrees to Hank's proposal; but soon after they set forth on this journey, they are accosted by a local earl and sold into slavery in London because they are unable to verify their true identities.

Even in this dire circumstance, the Yankee uses his mechanical ingenuity to spring the lock of his cell and escape. Upon learning of his flight, the earl condemns all imprisoned slaves to death by hanging. Fearing for the life of King Arthur, Hank uses a telephone to alert Clarence to the problem, thereby initiating the invasion of the prison by Sir Lancelot and his army with the intent of saving their beloved king.

Because of his skill and courage, Hank receives a hero's welcome upon his return to Camelot. In spite of his successful exploits throughout the countryside, Hank must keep his word to participate in the duel with Sir Sagramor. While ready to accept this challenge, he is unaware that the challenge of Sir Sagramor is really a ruse by which Merlin can exact his revenge. Merlin has told the knight that he will be rendered invisible during the duel, thereby ensuring a victory over his opponent. Although Sir Sagramor is clearly visible during the duel, he believes the ancient sorcerer and fights with confidence in his invincibility. In the meantime, Hank, who fights without armor, exhausts Sagramor by repeatedly dodging his advances. Sensing the knight's vulnerability, Hank succeeds in roping Sagramor and dismounting him from his steed. Undaunted by this humiliation, the knight eventually returns to the forum, but this time Hank's strategy is thwarted by Merlin's theft of the lasso. Hank has no other choice but to shoot the charging knight with his gun. After Arthur's court reacts strongly against this power, Hank shoots to death eleven knights and forces the retreat of the remaining court. Having thereby established his supremacy, he finally feels free to develop all the aspects of modern civilization.

The novel continues after a three-year lapse. The chivalric code has been abolished. Hank's technology continues to proliferate; he has married Sandy and they have a daughter. During this time, Hank was planning, with Clarence's help, the details of the modernized republic they would oversee following the death of King Arthur. Hank's plans are interrupted, however, by the illness of his daughter, which requires an immediate stay at the seashore for her recovery. Upon his return to Camelot, Hank is shocked to learn that much has happened in his absence. Essentially, the kingdom has collapsed after a series of events stemming from the disastrous love triangle that developed between King Arthur, his wife, Queen Guinevere, and his most beloved knight, Sir Lancelot. Clarence, having remained to inform his master of the devastating events, reveals to the incredulous Yankee that after King Arthur's death, the church had issued an interdict that would give them control over the kingdom as well as the authority to destroy all of Hank's innovations.

Fearing for their safety amidst the church's resurgent superstition, Hank and Clarence seal themselves within a fortress that had been surrounded by an electrified boundary. In spite of this barrier, the remaining knights storm the fortress, in what became known as the Battle of the Sand Belt. Ultimately, the medieval warriors are no match against the cumulative forces of technology and skill as demonstrated by Hank and Clarence. However, after the battle, while attempting to assist the wounded, Hank responds to the plea of a wounded knight who, upon recognizing his foe, smites the unwary Yankee with his sword.

The faithful Clarence carries his fallen leader to a cave where he attends his wounds. A few days pass, during which they ponder their dilemma: they can neither stay nor go if they wish to survive. Their deliberations are interrupted by the arrival of a "simple old peasant goodwife" (271), who offers to nurse the recovering hero. Ultimately, they learn that Merlin decides to exact his revenge on Hank by disguising himself as the nurse and casting a spell on his unsuspecting rival that would cause him to sleep for the next thirteen centuries, or until the time of Hank's initial fight in the factory had occurred.

It is suggested in the conclusion of the story that the faithful Clarence had hidden Hank's sleeping body, as well as the journals detailing his adventures, safely within the recesses of a cave. The written record of these events and Hank himself had survived to the nineteenth century, at which time the wandering stranger meets M. T. at Warwick castle. In Hank's final delusional outpouring, however, the fragile time traveler rambles in his sleep to the attentive M. T. about the medieval dream he had endured for so long. As he dies, however, he says he never understood why the technological society he had planned to conquer the superstitions of the king's court was, in reality, no match for his ultimate vanquisher.

An explanation to Hank's eternal question is provided in a formidable critical analysis by noted author Douglas Robinson, who identifies the conqueror of the deluded modern man and thereby reveals the final outcome of Mark Twain's convoluted apocalypse. Based on the thematic continuity of the novel, Robinson explains the protagonist's personal apocalyptic message:

> Superstition (Merlin's tool) is *in* [society], and Hank fails to educate it *out;* the Church's threat of eternal damnation, the substance of the Interdict, remains for the Britons a most powerful presence, God's judgmental presence. [As such,] the *divine* threat wielded by the Church remains sovereign . . . [a lesson that both Hank, as well as his modern day fictional counterparts, unfortunately fail to learn] (Robinson 1985, 82).

See also Apocalypse: Secular; Apocalypse: Traditional Judeo-Christian; Arthur, King; *The Faerie Queene*; Merlin; Morgan, Hank; *Le Morte d'Arthur; The Mysterious Stranger;* Twain, Mark.

CONRAD, JOSEPH

Joseph Conrad (1857–1924) was the Polish-born novelist and seafaring adventurer whose fictionalized physical as well as psychological experiences served as the basis for some of the most powerfully written literature of the European modernist period. Conrad, born Jozef Teodor Konrad Nalecz Korzeniowski, came from a long line of patriotic Polish literati. The author's father, a poet by avocation and a translator of English and French by vocation, was a revolutionary against the oppressive Russian regime. In 1862, Conrad's family was forced into exile in Volgoda, a harsh city in northern Russia. Because of the emotional and physical burdens of their exile, both of Conrad's parents died, within just a few years of one another, leaving their young twelve-year-old orphan to be placed in the custody of an uncle who still lived in Poland.

Understandably, the humiliation of exile, the devastating loss of his parents, and his involuntary placement with a distant relative culminated in Conrad's turning inward for psychological healing and escape from a dreary existence. Conrad's means of escape came in the form of literature; he became a voracious reader of swashbuckling sea travelogues. Conrad nurtured these fantasies until the age of sixteen, unfettered by traditional bonds of family responsibility, when he turned his daydreams into realities by joining the French Merchant Marines, an organization that provided the young idealist with the opportunity to complete his first three sea journeys.

In 1878, Conrad's interests and exploits led him to England, where he decided to anglicize his name and become a subject of the British throne. Although Conrad had not spoken the English language until the age of twenty, he was diligently self-taught, and soon, he not only excelled in the language, but he also became a commander of British ships that traveled both to the Orient as well as to the Congo. These experiences, particularly his visit to the Congo in 1890, led to the development of several works, including *The Nigger of the Narcissus* (1897), *Lord Jim* (1900), and *Heart of Darkness,* one of literature's most masterful apocalyptic works, which was published within a larger work entitled *Youth* in 1902.

While all of his tales are, on a literal level, adventure stories about his forays into South America, Asia, and Africa, they are also, on a more sophisticated

Joseph Conrad aboard a ship, 1 May 1923

and critical level, explorations into the hearts and minds of modern men who exploited foreign lands in the name of progress and for personal gain. The psychological complexity of his works reflect the foundational influence of other writers such as H. G. Wells, Henry James, Ford Madox Ford, and the naturalist Stephen Crane. But it was Conrad's own romantic proclivity, combined with a profound moral intensity and commitment to his craft, that led him to compose a body of work that will be remembered for a poetic reflection of the beauty and the savagery that is, at once, both frighteningly real and essentially human.

See also Apocalypse: Secular; Apocalypse: Traditional Judeo-Christian; Apocalyptic Literature; *Heart of Darkness; The Invisible Man;* Kurtz, Mr.; Marlow, Charles.

COOVER, ROBERT

Born in 1932, the critically acclaimed novelist and short-story writer Robert Lowell Coover was influenced early in his life by his family's move to Herrin, Illinois. Perhaps the first notable influence on Coover's fiction came from exposure to the small-town newspaper that his father managed. This newspaper provided detailed coverage of a local mining disaster, an event that served, in many ways, as the inspiration for his first apocalyptic novel, *The Origin of the Brunists* (1966).

Although Coover was raised in a small town, he became fascinated by the journalistic process and the opportunities offered through travel. He began his higher education at a local college, Southern Illinois University, but later moved away to complete his studies at Indiana University, earning a B.A. in 1953. Upon graduation, Coover joined the United States Naval Reserve and distinguished himself in the rank of lieutenant. During his service overseas he met and, in 1959, married a Spanish woman named Marie del Pilar San-Mallafre.

Although Coover had had modest success with the reception of his short story "Blackdamp," upon which the novel *Origin* was based, he had difficulty supporting his family solely through his writing career. He and his wife returned to the United States, where he pursued and accepted various teaching positions at Bard College, the University of Iowa, Princeton University, Columbia University, and Washington University, among others.

While Coover's works appeal to a relatively narrow readership, perhaps because of their experimental nature, academic critics recognize the author for his innovative and courageous approach to fiction. Among the various awards he has earned for his work are the William Faulkner Award for best first novel (1966), two Guggenheim fellowships (1971 and 1974), as well as a National Book Award nomination for his controversial novel *The Public Burning* (1977).

Currently, Coover lives in Providence, Rhode Island, and continues teaching and writing on a variety of topics as a film and writing instructor at Brown University. While he maintains an avid interest in American popular culture, his work at present revolves around film and the art of detective fiction.

See also Apocalypse: Traditional Primitive; Bruno, Giovanni; Millennialism; Miller, Justin ("Tiger"); *The Origin of the Brunists.*

CORDELIA

Cordelia is the devoted daughter of an aging monarch in William Shakespeare's apocalyptic tragedy *King Lear* (1605). She is the youngest of three sisters and the favorite of her father. In almost every way, Shakespeare portrays this character as one who is beyond reproach. Her sweet and humble nature are presented in direct contrast with the self-serving and vindictive personalities of her older sisters, Goneril and Regan.

Even though the play takes place in pre-Christian Britain, Cordelia has Christ-like qualities that merge with those of Christ's earthly mother, Mary. Cordelia's first action in the play confirms that honesty is one of her primary virtues. While this trait is certainly honorable in an ideal world, the tragic world of the play inverts Cordelia's best intentions and punishes her for her honesty. Most notable is the scene wherein the weary Lear decides to retain his authority as king of Britain but announces his plan to divide his kingdom among his three daughters. His method for distributing this land, however, places Cordelia in a precarious position because Lear's intent is to give the largest portion of land to whichever daughter presents the greatest public display of affection for him.

As the eldest daughter, the shrewd Goneril proceeds with a florid declaration filled with meaningless superlatives. She is the most avaricious of the sisters. Not to be outdone, Regan, the middle and ultimately the most cruel daughter of the three, follows with similar hypocritical platitudes and attempts to ingratiate herself to the monarch with an apology for her lack of verbal effusion in comparison with Goneril's.

Upon hearing their speeches, Cordelia becomes concerned, stating, "I am sure my love's / More ponderous than my tongue." At this early point in the play, Cordelia loves her father dearly, in fact, much more than do her two sisters. Nevertheless, in Act 1, Scene 1, when Lear asks Cordelia, ". . . what can you say to draw / A third more opulent than your sisters?," her response is simple, "Nothing." To convey both her reverence and affection for her father, Cordelia feels compelled to honor him with the unvarnished truth: "Unhappy that I am, I cannot heave / My heart into my mouth. I love your Majesty / According to my bond, no more nor less."

Through this simple statement, she implies the depth of her affection for him, but she remains true in her spoken words. Although the king should respect Cordelia's forthrightness, he instead goads her to inflate her speech with ritual hyperbole. Her refusal to do so disappoints and enrages him. Consequently, his injured pride causes him to disinherit her and marry her off to the king of France.

Even after she has suffered because of her father's willful pride, Cordelia persists in her love and loyalty to him; in fact, she goes a step further by showing pity for the misguided king. In a pointed illustration of her devotion before she leaves for her new home in France, Cordelia begs her sisters to take care of their father. She is worried because she knows her sisters well and justly has concerns about Lear's future happiness. She expresses both her pity for him and her sadness that, as a result of her honesty (and perhaps an inherited sense of pride), she is no longer in a position to take care of him in his retirement, a preference of the king himself.

Nevertheless, even in her absence from her father, Cordelia does what she can to care for him. When she learns that Lear has been treated harshly by both Goneril and Regan, and that he has fled in desperation into a raging storm, Cordelia urges her new husband to gather an army to help Lear return to Britain to reclaim his throne. Her efforts do not go unnoticed by other characters who are equally devoted to the king (i.e., Kent and the Fool). Cordelia's attempt to restore her father to his throne is for naught when Goneril and Regan combine forces to capture both Lear and Cordelia. They mean to prevent Lear from reclaiming the kingdom and seeking retribution for their treachery.

What the sisters intend as punishment, however, turns into a special regenerative opportunity for Lear and Cordelia. During their brief reunion, Lear realizes that his demands for a public display of affection were foolish, and Cordelia realizes the importance of setting aside pride in order to express genuine affection for loved ones. It is amidst the sweetness of their time together, however, that the greatest loss in the play occurs when Lear, delirious with grief, carries the dead body of his beloved Cordelia into the court after finding her hanged by orders of her jealous sisters.

Although the play ends with her sacrificial death, as well as the deaths of her evil sisters, Lear himself, and other characters, Cordelia's grace has a lasting impact upon all who remain. Because they have witnessed how her faithfulness had briefly restored the nobility and sanity of her formerly deranged father, her death ultimately is a legacy of honor upon which, under the leadership of the equally respected Edgar, they may begin to build a better kingdom.

See also Apocalypse: Traditional Primitive; Edgar; Edmund; Gloucester (Earl of); Goneril; Great Chain of Being; *King Lear;* Lear, King; Regan.

COVERDALE, MILES

Miles Coverdale is the main character and sometimes unreliable narrator of Nathaniel Hawthorne's apocalyptic novel *The Blithedale Romance* (1852). Coverdale most closely resembles the author himself; nevertheless, Hawthorne insisted that Coverdale, like the other characters within the novel, is nothing more than a fictional creation. Miles Coverdale, like Hawthorne himself, is a writer—a minor poet of his time. Sharing the popular Transcendental fascination with physical labor and communal living, Coverdale joins a rural community known as Blithedale. It is the hope of all participants of Blithesdale, Coverdale included, that they will be able to enjoy a better way of life through a closer relationship between humanity and nature, thereby establishing an improved world order. Not all participants, however, have the same degree of commitment to the success of the experiment.

Like Coverdale at Blithedale, Hawthorne himself participated briefly in the Transcendental utopian society in Concord, Massachusetts, known as Brook Farm. Coverdale, also like Hawthorne, becomes involved with a utopian experiment for practical more than idealistic reasons. Hawthorne joined Brook Farm with the hope of earning enough money to get married, while Coverdale joins

Blithedale primarily out of boredom, curiosity, and the veiled intent of gathering interesting insights and material for his work. Both Coverdale and Hawthorne pursued communal living for only a brief time and with more of a detached curiosity than a genuine interest in furthering the cause of Transcendentalism.

Like Hawthorne, Coverdale is a vigilant observer of human nature. Hawthorne places Coverdale directly in the midst of all of the key scenes within the story. He is present at the outset of the Blithedale experiment and introduces one of the novel's most riveting characters, Zenobia. His descriptions of this sensual and self-serving character present her as the epitome of woman: sexual, mysterious, capable, and complex. He is also present when the egocentric Hollingsworth enters the scene, with his grandiose scheme for social reform, accompanied by the pallid and obsequious foil to Zenobia, a character who is later revealed as Zenobia's half-sister, Priscilla. From the outset of the novel, Coverdale observes the machinations of this doomed love triangle, as well as the intervention of some nefarious secondary characters, and ultimately witnesses the decline of their collective dream, the death of their idealism, and the dissolution of their individual life plans.

See also Apocalypse: Traditional Primitive; *The Blithedale Romance;* Brook Farm; Hawthorne, Nathaniel; Hollingsworth; Moodie, Priscilla; Moodie, Zenobia; Romanticism; Transcendentalism; Westervelt.

DANIEL, BOOK OF

The book of Daniel (c. 165 B.C.) is considered to be one of the most significant books of the Old Testament, as well as one of the most profound apocalyptic prophesies within the Jewish scriptures. However, as is the case with much of the Old Testament, the book of Daniel's historical perspective has long been a matter of debate. Nevertheless, a majority of scholars agree that the book was written originally as a form of protest. During the time in which the work was composed, Palestine was being torn by Egyptian and Syrian rulership. In 167 B.C., when a Syrian ruler named Antiochus demanded that the Jews abandon their religious practices in favor of the Greek state religion, the book of Daniel was composed to help the Jews recall a hero who had remained faithful to God's laws in spite of similar persecution. Daniel shares with other apocalyptic works an intent to help a persecuted people sustain their hopes of imminent divine intervention that will conquer the oppressive forces that threaten their lives.

In the first six chapters, Daniel, along with his fellow scribes at a Babylonian school, distinguish themselves among the other students. While their accomplishments are acknowledged, the elders are unaware that their excellent performance is related to a strict adherence to dietary laws. God rewards them, particularly Daniel, with the unique ability to interpret visions and dreams. King Nebuchadnezzar sends for Daniel and his peers because he has heard that they are "ten times better than all the magicians and astrologers that were in all his realm" (Daniel 1:20).

During the following year, the king begins to experience troubled sleep and violent dreams, which leads him to draw upon his arsenal of visionaries and interpreters to help him understand their meaning. Because the impatient king threatens the lives of the wise men of the city who are either unable or unwilling to help him, Daniel volunteers to interpret Nebuchadnezzar's dreams. One of the king's dreams involves a formidable statue—featuring a golden head, silver chest and arms, bronze thighs and torso, iron calves, and feet of iron and clay—that has fallen and disintegrated. Daniel's interpretation reveals that the statue represents the successive empires that will attempt to rule the land of Judah, but which will be destroyed by the Jews, thereby ending their subjugation to foreign rule.

Humbled by this interpretation, Nebuchadnezzar honors Daniel by placing him in charge of Babylon's wise men. Daniel urges the king to place his friends, Shadrach, Meshach, and Abednego, in similar positions throughout the king's provinces. While Daniel and his friends are in the king's favor at this time, a conflict arises that sets them at odds with the ruler. Nebuchadnezzar, who has ordered that his image be cast in gold, commands all of his subjects to worship this idol or be cast into a fiery furnace as punishment. Because Daniel and his three friends refuse to obey this command out of loyalty to their God, the king becomes infuriated and orders Shadrach, Meshach, and Abednego into the fiery furnace, which he has made even hotter to show his wrath at their rebellion. When he learns that the three survive the fiery ordeal unscathed, he acknowledges the great power of their God.

Other demonstrations of God's power cause the prideful king to be humbled. The most famous of these tales is Daniel's survival after having been cast into the lion's den for defying the king's order to worship him. While these early chapters establish Daniel as a respected visionary within Nebuchadnezzar's court, their primary function is to urge the Jews to stand fast in their faith because their God has repeatedly proven Himself more powerful than even the most formidable kings on earth.

In chapters 7 through 12, Daniel is no longer interpreting another's dreams but is receiving the dreams himself. With the assistance of an angel, Daniel presents his dreams using an allegorical method by which to analyze four separate visions that all share the same theme: the Lord of the Jews will avenge the injustices of his people and will eventually free them from the tyranny of faithless rulership. The first allegorical vision features four predatory beasts representing four oppressive empires, the last of which is that of Antiochus, the most virulent of the beasts. These beasts, however, are eventually subdued by the Lord, who is portrayed as an omnipotent king; he not only vanquishes the beasts but restores the rule of Judah to its original people: ". . . his dominion is an everlasting dominion that shall not pass away, and his kingship is one that shall never be destroyed" (*Open Bible* 1975, Daniel 7:14). This Old Testament prophecy is fulfilled according to the New Testament story of the Great White Throne Judgment, found in Revelation (5:11; 20:4).

Daniel's second apocalyptic vision (8:1–27) describes a final battle between a he-goat and a ram. The ram represents the kings of Media and Persia and the he-goat represents the king of Greece; they will be destroyed when their empires collide. The third apocalyptic vision (9:1–27) recalls the prophet Jeremiah's prediction that the persecution of the Jews would last for a period of seventy years (approximately the projected duration of Babylonian rule.) While Daniel humbly accepts this period of subjugation as God's just punishment for his people's transgressions, he also begs God to forgive the people of Jerusalem and show them mercy by restoring their kingdom as soon as possible. In the midst of his plea, the angel Gabriel appears to Daniel and provides an interpretation of his most recent vision. Essentially, the core of the interpretation remains the same; however, in the later chapters, Daniel's dreams concentrate on issues related to his recent past, provide insights for the near future, and ultimately provide him with a lucid description of what humanity can expect as it enters its final days.

See also Apocalypse: Traditional Judeo-Christian; Apocalyptic Literature; Apocalypticism; Revelation, Book of; Symbol.

DANTE ALIGHIERI

Dante Alighieri (1265–1321) is best known for *The Divine Comedy,* his masterful apocalyptic allegory completed in 1320, approximately one year prior to his death. This work reflects the corruption and beauty of the world in which the author lived; it focuses on the prevailing philosophies, science, theology, and politics in which the author was embroiled during the writing of his magnum opus.

Little is known about the early life of Dante. Most scholars agree that he descended from a formerly wealthy lineage of Florentine nobility but was raised in modest surroundings. Details of his early education are equally sparse. He spent at least a year at the University of Bologna studying the formal curriculum, which included the *trivium* (grammar, logic, and rhetoric) and the *quadrivium* (geometry, astronomy, arithmetic, and music). In addition to his formal studies, he also learned much from his relationship with a fellow poet, Guido Cavalcanti, and to a lesser extent, from his relationship with the querulous poet Forese Donati.

In addition to his studies, Dante was diligent in his adherence to duty, both traditional and civil. When Dante was only twelve years old, his family and that of Gemma Donati sealed their children's fates by following the long-standing tradition of arranging their future marriage. Records indicate that Gemma's dowry was determined in 1277, thereby requiring them to honor the promised union when they reached an appropriate age. The couple married and had four children, three sons—Pietro, Jacopo, and Giovanni (sometimes referred to as Johannes)—and a daughter, Antonia, who later joined a convent. According to another tradition, Dante also fulfilled his family's expectations by serving briefly in the military as a mounted soldier. Because his family was connected with the Guelphs, the papal party that opposed the intrusion of the Ghibelline imperialists, Dante dutifully participated in the Guelph campaign to defeat the Aretines in 1289, during their battle at Campaldino.

These biographical details do not, however, provide insight into the major inspirational force for his art. At the young age of nine, during a May Day festival in his home, Dante was introduced to a stunning eight-year-old beauty in a bright red gown named Beatrice. He was so moved by her beauty and grace that for the remainder of his career, and in spite of his marriage to another woman, he continued to dedicate his writings to Beatrice.

Beatrice and Dante never really enjoyed a formal relationship; they had brief and often silent encounters that occurred sporadically over a period of years. While this was a frustrating situation and an impractical obsession, it was precisely these barriers of time, distance, and idealistic longing (i.e., the unattainable love of the medieval chivalric tradition) that fueled Dante's imagination and inspired the sweet yearning for spiritual completion that pervades his work.

His devotion to Beatrice remained undaunted, even after she married another man, a successful banker named Simone de' Bardi, in 1287. Her marriage to

Italian artist Domenico de Michelino shows Dante Alighieri, center, as a part of a depiction of *The Divine Comedy.*

another man and untimely death in 1290 at just twenty years of age helped to elevate her even more as Dante's inspiration. He continued to write poems about his love for her, some of which are included in his work entitled *Vita Nuova* (1292), and her influence on his work is most apparent in his dedication of *The Divine Comedy* to her memory.

In addition to Beatrice's death, Dante was influenced by other factors in his young life. As a dedicated student and practitioner of the liberal arts, he was encouraged to examine the great philosophical issues of the day, as expressed in the works of Aristotle and Thomas Aquinas; the influence of these two philosophers is found throughout *The Divine Comedy* as well as in his other works.

In the years following his formal study and his philosophical apprenticeship, Dante settled into married life, which enabled him to pursue his growing interest in the area of politics. He was elected in 1300 to the high position of prior to the city of Florence, serving for a period of only two months. This was a time of growing tensions between church and state. As a result of the intrusion of the pope in secular matters, a schism developed between the blacks, or the Guelphs, who were known as papal sympathizers, and the whites, who opposed the influence of the papacy in regard to civil politics. Initially, Dante supported the forced exile of the leaders of both factions, one of whom was his lifelong friend, Guido Calvacanti. But later, Dante became a white sympathizer.

Because of his sympathies, Dante was later banished from Florence, a sentence that carried over to his sons at the age of accountability. He remained an exile from his homeland for the following twenty-five years.

Although Dante's political efforts were, for the most part, ineffectual, his ideas, his hopes, and his spiritual beliefs are immortalized in his apocalyptic treatise, *The Divine Comedy.* Throughout this epic allegorical poem, the author uses his beloved Beatrice to represent all that is good and right in the world. It is through her guidance, as well as that of the wise philosopher Virgil, that Dante vividly portrays a journey through the deepest levels of hell, a visit to purgatory, and an ascension to paradise in an attempt to help humanity seek the path of righteousness and thereby live according to the divine laws established by the creator of the universe. Dante's apocalyptic legacy to the world was completed just prior to his death from malaria in 1321. His majestic epic continues to serve as an archetype for apocalyptic literature throughout the ages.

See also Apocalypse: Traditional Judeo-Christian; Apocalyptic Literature; Archetype; Beatrice; *The Divine Comedy;* God; Heaven; Hell; Myth; Satan; Virgil.

THE DAY OF DOOM

The Day of Doom (1662) is the graphic apocalyptic poem expressing the extreme Calvinistic beliefs of an American Puritan colonist, Michael Wigglesworth. It became known officially as "the first American best seller" (Lewicki 1984, 8). With at least one in every twenty New Englanders purchasing the compelling text, the work went through countless editions throughout the eighteenth century and made a significant impact upon the collective moral conscience of the early American colonists.

The work borrows liberally from the frightening imagery found in biblical apocalyptic canons. It gave assurance to those who remained faithful to its dictates that they would be spared the horrors of Judgment Day. Various themes in the work served as significant motivators for righteousness. The first theme presented in the poem emphasizes the immediacy and unexpectedness of the Day of Judgment. Arguing for spiritual readiness, the text presents scenes in the following manner:

> So at the last, whilst men sleep fast
> in their security,
> Surpris'd they are in such a snare
> As cometh suddenly, (qtd. in Lewicki 8).

Regarding the widespread panic and natural disasters that will overtake observers of Christ's return, Wigglesworth states:

> The wild Beasts flee into the sea,
> so soon as he draws near, . . .
> Amazeth Nature, and every Creature,
> doth more than terrify (qtd. in Lewicki 9).

Perhaps the most disturbing theme in the work is the cruel treatment of sinners, as their earthly wrongs are divinely punished and witnessed by those who have become saints. Wigglesworth condones such cruelty by projecting God's impatience with humanity's depravity:

It's now high time that ev'ry Crime
be brought to punishment;
Wrath long contain'd and oft restrain'd,
at last must have a vent.
Justice severe cannot forbear
to plague sin any longer,
But must inflict with hand most strict
mischief upon the wronger (qtd. in Lewicki 10).

A close reading of just these verses provides good examples of this bold and vividly detailed work that became a staple of learning within each American Puritan household. Moreover, it helped to influence American culture in a way that would ensure the continual reexamination of its apocalyptic themes. Michael Wigglesworth's *The Day of Doom* must be considered one of the most significant contributions to American apocalyptic literature, not only because the work "presents a very gloomy and frightening picture of the end of the world," but because it also provides hope that "'devastation would be a preliminary to [eventual spiritual] regeneration'" (Lewicki 11).

See also Apocalypse: Traditional Judeo-Christian; Apocalyptic Literature; Edwards, Jonathan; Revelation, Book of; Wigglesworth, Michael.

THE DAY OF THE LOCUST

The Day of the Locust (1939) is a short novel by Nathanael West that darkly satirizes Hollywood in its heyday. The protagonist, a young painter named Tod Hackett, is drawn to California with the dream of becoming a great artist. In the meantime, however, he serves as costume and set designer for a Hollywood movie studio. Like other characters in the novel, Tod represents the wave of people who moved to the American West in the 1920s and 1930s with hopes of finding fame and fortune in a sun-kissed promised land. However, he is stunned by the harsh realities of life.

What Tod finds in Los Angeles is an entire city of people yearning for some type of fulfillment, but as he later learns, the city offers nothing to satisfy them—no fulfillment, only frustrated desire. Some have come to California, after "slav[ing] at some kind of dull, heavy labor," with the hope of having their lives redeemed by the promise of "sunshine and oranges." Afterward, they "discover that sunshine isn't enough, [and] they get tired of oranges, even of avocado pears and passion fruit" (West 177). Others yearn for relaxation and pleasure, but they too find disappointment because "[t]hey don't know what to do with their time [, and t]hey haven't the mental equipment for leisure, the money nor the physical equipment for pleasure" (178). Ultimately, Tod concludes that "[t]heir boredom becomes more and more terrible. They realize that they've been tricked and burn with resentment" (178). Their only possible hope lies in the excitement that comes by reading the newspapers or watching movies. But this "daily diet" of "lynchings, murder, sex crimes, explosions, wrecks, love nests, fires, miracles, revolutions, [and] wars" (178) fail to sate them. As such, they feel a collective sense of betrayal and anguish. This failure to fulfill their desires or to attain what Douglas Robinson calls "the ritual icon" (220) only feeds their frenzy of frustration, which must eventually be released. It is this awareness that fuels the fiery portrait that burns in his imagination, an artistic vision reflecting the psychological state of city life entitled "The Burning of Los Angeles."

The completion of this masterpiece is Tod's "ritual icon," and the details of this painting consume Tod; they reflect the passion, escalating violence, and pervasive sense of despair that he sees in the lives of those around him. Faye Greener is a hard-hearted bleached blonde who is sustained by her dependence on hapless men and her delusions of Hollywood grandeur. In many ways, Faye is "paradise achieved. . . . California itself, the Promised Land of sun and oranges" (220). While Faye is complacent, her being causes violent reactions to her indomitable stasis. For example, in spite of her childlike selfishness, Tod is physically attracted to her and convinces himself that he is in love with her. He is later disabused of this notion by Faye's insensitive proclamation that she could never become involved with a man, like Tod, who could do nothing to advance her career. This revelation, however, only encourages Tod to take her by force.

Nowhere in the novel is the gulf between desire and fulfillment more pronounced as it is in the character of Homer Simpson. Like Tod, Homer, too, feels that he is in love with Faye. But his shy personality and simple Midwestern values are of no interest to Faye; these only make him vulnerable to exploitation by Faye and other characters. Homer's sympathetic/opportunistic reaction to Faye's misfortune—he invites her to live with him in a "business arrangement"—leads to his undoing. Although Homer intends for this invitation to lead to a more substantial relationship, this daily proximity, however, only serves to subject him to Faye's continued acts of cruelty and other humiliation at the hands of her friends and lovers. Her rejection of Homer's comforts reflect the angry frustration of the crowds who have moved to California only to end up feeling cheated.

As the situation becomes more grotesque, foreshadowing an escalating violence, Tod Hackett's artistic sensibilities are stirred to the point where he becomes obsessed with the completion of his masterpiece, "The Burning of Los Angeles." Featured among the lurid details of this painting is a hysterical torch-bearing mob. The mob represents California's disillusioned retirees, geographical transplants, and would-be movie stars who seem driven to avenge their wasted lives by ruining the city whose harsh reality has destroyed their dreams. Tod's vision becomes horrifyingly real in the climax of the novel, which takes place during a typical Hollywood movie premiere.

During this premiere, the streets are filled with desperate people; Homer Simpson, the shy neighbor whom Faye has callously deserted, is among them. In a state of confusion, haphazardly dressed, and carrying his suitcase, Homer mutters something about returning to his hometown as he ambles his way through the teeming throng. From a distance, Tod witnesses Homer's agitated state and general disorientation, but the crowds prevent his attempts to assist and comfort his neighbor, and he fears the inevitably "rapid proliferation of violence" (Robinson 221).

Later, in a gruesome scene, while Homer sits on a bench in disoriented reflection, he is driven to the brink of madness by the taunting of a cruel local boy, Adore, who represents, like Faye, the frustrating stasis of California life. After tormenting Homer, Adore tries to flee the scene but trips and falls amid the crowd. In front of thousands of horrified witnesses, including Tod Hackett, Homer Simpson unleashes his madness, brought about by his loss of Faye, by deliberately, mechanically, and ritualistically stomping Adore (Faye's counterpart) to death.

The scene is the pitifully ironic realization of Hackett's horrifying artistic vision. As though they have found a scapegoat for all of their disillusioned rage, the crowd "grab[s] and rend[s]" Homer (222). The mob collectively lifts its sacrificial victim, Homer Simpson, into the air and then proceeds to descend upon him, in a violent apocalypse of biblical proportions, as the plague of locusts descended upon Egypt during the exodus. Robinson concludes, "Non-ritual repetition of sacrifice escalates violence, and the apocalypse becomes reality" (222).

The novel concludes from the singular point of view of the tortured artist. Tod Hackett has witnessed the proverbial "last loosing of Satan" in the city. And because this ritualistic event accurately reflects the violent rage that has colored his imaginary portrait, "The Burning of Los Angeles," Tod is doomed to survive as a tormented messenger of truth. Tod's inability to accept this entropic reality is expressed, as he is driven away, in open-mouthed horror, simulating the maddening scream of the police car's interminable siren.

See also Apocalypse: Anti-Christian; Babylon; Greener, Faye; Hackett, Tod; Satan; Simpson, Homer; West, Nathanael.

DELITO

Delito is the name of the diabolical character who is a prominent member of an Indian tribe set on destroying the deluded Native American protagonist of Jamake Highwater's apocalyptic tale entitled *Kill Hole* (1992). Delito is a primitive version of the demonic archetype; he is sadistic, unfair, and relentlessly deceitful. Although he believes that his motives are honorable (i.e., he wants to protect his clan from "evil spirits" that may contaminate the purity of the children in his camp), he proves himself to be monomaniacal, dangerously prideful, and fueled by venomous hatred. He ends up killing the very children he has vowed to protect in revenge against his primary target, the accidental invader of his territory, the disillusioned Native American artist named Sitko Ghost Horse.

Delito's arrivals and departures within the novel are often marked with the stench of biblical fire and brimstone. Whenever he is present, the air smells stale and charred, he leaves a trail of ashes in his wake, and a small dark shadow seems to follow the short demonic character whenever he leaves a room. In one scene he torments his captor, Sitko, by making him believe that his leg has been broken. Instead of helping the young man, Delito uses Sitko's vulnerability to fill him with images of fear and dread. When he has satisfactorily broken Sitko into a reluctant promise of allegiance, Delito returns the young man's misplaced faith by attempting to poison him with a venomous spittle that he binds into Sitko's mutilated leg.

The only person in the novel who seems to have any control over Delito and his demonic dealings is Patu, the "strong woman" of the tribe who has been given the role of Sitko's nurse and guardian. In the presence of this powerful, dedicated, and essentially self-sacrificing woman, Delito has no choice but to dismiss himself. Patu and Delito represent the archetypal and eternal battle between good and evil as they war over the ultimate possession of humanity's collective body and soul.

In spite of Delito's deception, Patu helps Sitko realize the dangerous consequences of consorting with him. She also helps Sitko realize that the only power that Delito (or any demonic force) has over him is when he succumbs to fear rather than fighting for righteousness. Although Delito's scenes are few within the novel, his destruction is as devastating as his demonic potential. As in many works of apocalyptic literature, whether a traditional Judeo-Christian or a traditional primitive myth, the forces of good ultimately win over the forces of evil, and at least for the moment, chaos is calmed and there is hope for the future.

See also Apocalypse: Traditional Primitive; Apocalypticism; Ghost Horse, Sitko; Highwater, Jamake; *Kill Hole;* Patu.

DICKINSON, EMILY

Emily Dickinson (1830–1886) is considered by many literary critics to be one of America's greatest poets. Born in Amherst, Massachusetts, Dickinson was the second of three children born into the family of Edward Dickinson, who was well known as a lawyer and a treasurer of Amherst College. Emily received her education at both Amherst Institute and Mount Holyoke Female Seminary. Upon finishing her education, she retired to her home where she stayed until her death. Because of her penchant for dressing in white and avoiding strangers, Dickinson was considered somewhat of a recluse by her contemporaries. Her self-imposed isolation was meant to conserve her artistic energy. This discipline allowed her to write on average one poem per day during her adult years, and she produced a prodigious body of work consisting of nearly two thousand poems, only seven of which had been published in her lifetime.

Although she was strongly influenced by her Calvinist father and a number of other powerful men, she rejected binding commitments to any of them, preferring to remain faithful to her singular self and her art. Her work reflects the intense simplicity of her life. Although a prolific poet, she was less than a voracious reader of others poetry. The works she was most familiar with were Shakespeare's drama, the Bible, classical mythology, and the literature of her contemporary, Ralph Waldo Emerson; they all had an undeniable influence on much of her work.

Her poems are identifiable by their brevity, usually stanzas consisting of four lines; their simple proverbial style; and, most notably, their depth of emotion. They fearlessly probe the darkest recesses of the human spirit. The prevailing themes of Dickinson's poetry are nature, love, friendship, and immortality (also the concerns of the Transcendental movement). Her treatment of these themes varied greatly from the work of her contemporaries in that her poems addressed the mysteries of life in deep paradoxes through an inimitable experimental style.

Emily Dickinson

Although Dickinson was reticent to publish her work during her lifetime, she had friends and patrons who were committed to revealing her art to the world. In 1890, four years after her death, two family friends named Mabel Loomis Todd and Thomas Wentworth Higginson edited and published the first collection of Dickinson's poems.

See also Apocalypse: Traditional Judeo-Christian; Emerson, Ralph Waldo; Transcendentalism.

THE DIVINE COMEDY

The Divine Comedy (c. 1310–1314) is the name of the epic apocalyptic poem by Italian author Dante Alighieri. This magnum opus, which consists of three separate divisions—*Inferno, Purgatorio,* and *Paradiso*—is considered by many to be the most significant work of Western literature. It tells of the collective human journey that begins with the darkness of sin, leads toward divine revelation through repentance and restitution, and ends with the promised gift of eternal salvation.

In Dante's comprehensive apocalyptic vision, he presents a simple story through a complex poetic form, *terza rima* (i.e., aba, bcb, cdc), to tell of one man's journey through hell, purgatory, and paradise. Assisting him in his journey through hell and purgatory is the renowned Roman poet Virgil. The protagonist's journey through paradise, however, is led by an angelic form known simply as Beatrice, who is the fictional embodiment of an innocent and unrequited love of the author's young life. The journey occurs over a three-day period, from Good Friday evening, in 1300, through Easter Sunday. While this work portrays the saga of the fall of humanity, it retains a historical significance for the author who was exiled from his own country for his political and philosophical beliefs. The work is about reconciliation, not only for the author in particular, but also for humanity in general.

The poem consists of over 14,000 lines, written in triple rhyme, and one-hundred cantos containing 142 lines apiece. The numerical structure, particularly in regard to the one-hundred cantos, reflects the mythological significance of one-hundred as the numerological equivalent of perfection. Each canto describes in vivid detail the various levels of hell, the supplicant anticipation of purgatory, and the humble elation of paradise.

In hell, the levels of sin correspond to God's laws. For example, the first level of hell is for those souls who succumb to the temptations of lust, gluttony, and greed. The circles correspond to levels of violent behavior, with appropriate punishments for souls who have been violent toward their neighbors, toward themselves, and toward God. This area is divided into two groups related to the sin of fraudulence. Those who have defrauded humanity in general are punished according to their due, while those who have betrayed their relatives, friends, and political allies are punished more severely. At the frozen center of hell is the most nefarious sinner of them all—Lucifer, Satan, or Dis. This creature, who is imprisoned in ice from the chest down, has three faces—one red, one black, and one yellow. In order to maintain the frozen temperature of hell's icy prison, the creature's wings flap continually; this motion freezes the tears in the six eyes of the three-headed demon. While Dante is horrified by this vision, he is even more disturbed by the fate of the three most abominable traitors. While the mouth of the red face is rapaciously chewing on the head of Judas Iscariot (Christ's betrayer) and Satan's talons are tearing at his flesh, the mouth of the black face torments Brutus (the traitor of Julius Caesar), and the mouth of the yellow face destroys his wicked partner in tyranny, Cassius. Having witnessed the eternal torment of the frozen pit of hell, Dante is guided by Virgil out of the infernal region and is directed toward the earth to continue his journey.

Within the next thirty-three cantos, Dante describes his travels through purgatory, known to Roman Catholics as heaven's waiting room. Throughout this portion of the poem, Dante explores a seven-terraced mountain, with each terrace corresponding to the restitution for the seven deadly sins of pride, envy, wrath, sloth, avarice, gluttony, and lust. While the torment he witnesses on these levels is certainly less severe than what he observed in hell, Dante feels pity for those whose actions on earth keep them temporarily from attaining the highest level of Mount Purgatory, which is the earthly paradise of the Garden of Eden.

At this point, Virgil departs as Dante's guide, and he is greeted by his ideal of beauty and virtue, Beatrice, who introduces the poet to the realm of *Paradiso,* consisting of nine concentric circles that are surrounded by the Empyrean, otherwise known as the highest realm of heaven, where God and his angels reside. During this phase, Dante journeys to the planets beneath the sun, the sun itself, and those planets that exist above the sun. Atop these planetary levels, rests the Empyrean or realm of God. The planetary levels through which Dante travels correspond to the ascending levels of spiritual values, the highest of which, according to Catholic theology, are Faith, Hope, and Charity.

Besides being a poem with a message about morality, *The Divine Comedy* can be studied as a historical document that uses specific literary, political, and cultural references to illustrate the crises existing in Dante's country during the time of the poem's composition. Students of mythology will be fascinated with the countless classical allusions found in the rich narrative texture of the work. Dante's *Divine Comedy* is one of the most important literary works of all time because of its masterful amalgam of Judeo-Christian values, political concerns, and classical mythology. In it, Dante captures the essence of the human condition and unifies both the earthly and the eternal experience shared by the collective family of humankind.

See also Allegory; Apocalypse: Traditional Judeo-Christian; Apocalyptic Literature; Archetype; Beatrice; Dante Alighieri, God; Heaven; Hell; Satan; Virgil.

DOKTOR FAUSTUS

Doktor Faustus (1947; trans. 1948) is an apocalyptic novel written by the intense and insightful German author Thomas Mann. While on a basic level it is a modern retelling of the familiar Faust legend, in which demonic forces threaten to pervert and ultimately destroy ambitious intellectuals, scientists, and artists,

Doktor Faustus is also a political treatise portraying Germany's downfall during World War II as a specific illustration of the Faustian legend.

The narrator, named Serenus Zeitblom, recounts the rise and fall of a renowned musical composer, Adrian Leverkuhn, who is the protagonist of the story as well as a symbol of the inspirational force that music had on Nazism during the Third Reich.

As is the case within Goethe's archetypal *Faust* and Marlowe's *Dr. Faustus,* the protagonist, Leverkuhn, demonstrates how easily hubris can delude an inspired individual into obtaining short-term personal gain for the price of supporting a demonic enterprise. In addition, Mann also illustrates how artistic isolation, when combined with a lack of appropriate expressive outlets, can pervert the gift of creative energy and thereby channel it into a diabolical force capable of degrading the human spirit.

See also Apocalypse: Secular; Apocalypse: Traditional Judeo-Christian; Apocalypticism; Archetype; *Dr. Faustus; Faust;* Immelmann, Art; Leverkuhn, Adrian; *Love in the Ruins: The Adventures of a Bad Catholic at a Time Near the End of the World;* Mann, Thomas; Mephistophiles; More, Tom (Dr.); Satan; Thanatos; *The Thanatos Syndrome;* Zeitblom, Serenus.

DOSTOYEVSKY, FYODOR MIKHAILOVICH

Fyodor Dostoyevsky (1821–1881), also known as Fedor or Fiodor Dostoevski, is the great Russian novelist whose penetrating insights into the human mind and spirit have made him one of the world's most significant authors. Born in Moscow on November 11, 1821, Dostoyevsky was the second of seven children in an austere, middle-class family. Because his father, a physician, had been the son of an Orthodox priest, Dostoyevsky and his siblings were provided with a limited education, focusing primarily on the Bible. When he turned seventeen, he and his brother were sent to the College of Military Engineering; he graduated with a degree but later abandoned engineering as a career when he discovered his love for literature and his desire to write.

In 1839, a devastating personal event occurred that would shape the future of the young author's life as well as his work: his father was murdered by the disgruntled serfs who had worked on the family estate. This tragic loss of his father caused him psychological conflicts and may have been responsible for his development of epilepsy, which would plague him for the remainder of his life. Although these details have long been a matter of speculation, the themes of parricide, psychological guilt, and the scourge of epilepsy play a significant role throughout the development of Dostoyevsky's masterpiece, *The Brothers Karamazov* (1879–1880).

After his father's death and his formal schooling, Dostoyevsky spent two years in the service of the Russian army. At the completion of his commission, he resumed his writing in earnest and published his first work, *Poor Folk,* in 1846, which received popular and critical praise. But the same cannot be said about several of his subsequent works. Nevertheless, because of the acclaim received from *Poor Folk,* Dostoyevsky was invited to join a distinguished group of

Russian novelist Fyodor Dostoyevsky

Russian literati who believed that the salvation of Russia lay in the adoption of more modern European ideas.

Also during this period, he joined a group of socialistic radicals, known as the Petrashevsky Circle, whose goal it was to overturn the rule of the autocratic czar, Nicholas I. However, in 1849, its members were arrested, put on trial, and convicted; the sentence was death by a firing squad. Just before the sentence was to be carried out, Dostoyevsky and his co-conspirators were spared; instead, they were sentenced to four years in Siberian exile. During this exile, Dostoyevsky experienced a significant change of heart. His radical ways soon dissipated because of his isolation and his reintroduction to the Bible, the only book he was allowed to read. As a result, the author experienced a period of significant spiritual growth as well as a renewed reverence for his native Russian. These changes are described in a fictionalized account of his prison experience entitled *The House of the Dead,* which was published in 1861. After his release from prison, Dostoyevsky completed the remaining part of his sentence, another commission of army service; during that time he met and married Marya Isaev, a widow with a child. The marriage became an unhappy one.

Dostoyevsky returned to St. Petersburg in 1859, and he found the country very much changed. Amidst the new spirit of optimism, he and his brother founded a magazine known as *The Times,* wherein he published several of his stories that were modestly successful. He began to be curious about European cultures and later visited several western European countries. During these visits he also learned much about himself, about his nationalism, and about his repressed passions. He was accompanied on this trip by a woman named Polina Suslova (the basis for Grushenka in *The Brothers Karamazov*), with whom he was madly in love.

Upon his return, the political climate in Russia had changed for the worse. The government had begun to censor the works published in his magazine, and the brothers decided to end its publication and develop an underground tabloid. But these plans for the future were dashed by his brother's death and the death of his wife. Dostoyevsky found himself near financial ruin, unable to support his brother's family as well as his adopted son. He tried to earn enough money by returning to Europe on a gambling excursion, but fortune was not with him. Later, he was forced to sign a contract with a publisher who threatened to seize all of the copyrights to Dostoyevsky's works unless he delivered a new manuscript within six months.

Given the circumstances of his personal and professional life, Dostoyevsky was bereft. He attempted to meet the challenge by hiring a stenographer, Anna Snitkina, who not only helped him complete *The Gambler* (1866) according to contract, but who became the author's devoted companion and, later, his wife. Their happy union enabled him to resolve his financial indebtedness by writing several works for which he is best known—*Crime and Punishment* (1866), *The Idiot* (1869), *The Possessed* (1871), *A Raw Youth* (1875), and his magnum opus, *The Brothers Karamazov* (1879–1880). Dostoyevsky died from tuberculosis soon after the completion of his final work. Today, he is regarded as one of the greatest Russian novelists and perhaps the most important literary figure ever.

See also Allegory; Apocalypse: Traditional Judeo-Christian; Apocalyptic Literature; *The Brothers Karamazov;* Karamazov; Alyosha Fyodorovich; Karamazov, Dmitri Fyodorovich; Karamozov, Fyodor Pavlovich; Karamazov, Ivan Fyodorovich; Revelation, Book of.

DR. FAUSTUS

Also known as *The Tragical History of Dr. Faustus, Dr. Faustus* is the first dramatic portrayal of events surrounding a legendary sixteenth-century necromancer, Johann Faust, as represented by the rebellious Renaissance writer Christopher Marlowe. While this version of the legend differs in significant ways from the masterpiece later produced by Goethe, Marlowe's apocalyptic vision of the unrepentant egotist has served as a model for many works that warn against the pride and intellectual arrogance of those whose self-serving efforts defy divine authority and thereby threaten to unravel the modern world.

In Marlowe's tale, the basic nature of Faustus remains unchanged. At the beginning of the story, he expresses his frustration with the limits of man's knowledge, in spite of the fact that he has studied extensively in the areas of law, theology, and medicine. Faustus calls upon his servant Wagner to engage the services of two experts, Valdes and Cornelius, who are famous for their skills in the practice of magic. After receiving preliminary instructions from the two, Faustus experiments with an incantation that brings forth the horrific visage of Mephistopheles. Oddly, because of his inherent pride, Faustus has no real fear of the demon. He bids Mesphistopheles to change his diabolical form into that of a friar in order to make the spirit's appearance more acceptable.

Although Faustus becomes complacent with his incantational powers, he later learns that it isn't magic that draws forth the demon but the act of cursing the Holy Trinity, which makes humanity vulnerable to the temptations of the devil. As he ponders this situation as well as its infinite possibilities, he boldly orders Mephistopheles to return to hell and make a pact with the devil. In this pact, Faustus proposes to sell his eternal soul to Lucifer in exchange for twenty-four years of unlimited knowledge, power, and supernatural assistance from Mephistopheles. Angels, both good and bad, appear to the scientist to counsel him for or against this proposition. Mephistopheles later returns from hell urging Faustus to sign the infernal contract with his own blood.

After signing this fateful contract, Faustus begins to doubt his decision. He is particularly concerned when he asks Mephistopheles for a wife to fulfill his physical lusts, but the request is denied because he is no longer in a spiritual state that can sustain the sacrament of Holy Matrimony. Feeling cheated by this and other denials, Faustus tries to repent his decision, an act that causes Mephistopheles to distract him with an impressive comedic display in which he personifies the seven deadly sins. Although Faustus seems pacified by the performance, Mephistopheles offers to take him to Rome to meet the Pope. The spiritual decline of Faustus is readily apparent in this scene; whereas in the past he might have engaged the pope in a theological discussion of considerable import, he now is merely satisfied to torment the pontiff with a series of tawdry humiliations. This scene, intended to poke fun at the Catholic Church, is of little importance in relation to the weightier theme of the story. Marlowe's own prurient interests and occasional taste for low comedy were satisfied in this scene, which was intended to amuse his less sophisticated audiences.

The next locale in which Faustus demonstrates his supernatural powers, as well as his increasing baseness, is in the German court of Emperor Carolus. Once again, Faustus is in a position to learn much and to contribute much; however, he succumbs to the emperor's request to conjure the images of Alexander the Great and his lover. During this scene, a skeptical knight challenges Faustus's magical abilities, but he is later forced to acknowledge that the visages of Alexander and his paramour are genuine. Further, this admission happens before the court, who also see a pair of horns that Faustus has conjured for the querulous knight's head. Although the scene ends when the spell is rescinded and all of the emperor's entertainment requests have been satisfied, Faustus's integrity sinks rapidly with his preoccupation with trivial displays of power.

In the considerable time that passes thereafter, Faustus spends his remaining days preoccupied with impressive but inconsequential magic tricks. Realizing that his days are numbered, he prepares for death by distributing his worldly goods among his servants. But he seems genuinely unaware that he will have to pay the final price for his contract with Lucifer. When his colleagues, a group of respected scholars, request that he call forth the image of Helen of Troy, the most beautiful woman who had ever lived, Faustus does so without realizing that it will be his final necromantic demonstration. These scholars are pleased with the demonstration and thank him for his efforts, but finally they leave him alone.

Following the departure of the scholars, an old and physically debilitated man appears on the scene to serve as a dramatic foil to Faustus. This old man, with his faith in a God who will soon relieve him of his earthly woes, is presented in direct contrast with the physically sound but spiritually withered Faustus. The contrast is even more stark in that the old man, who is actually about Faustus's age, is anticipating death, whereas Faustus, unmoved by his counterpart's piety, sets his sights upon a new goal in his earthly life. Realizing that it is no longer unlimited power that he wants, Faustus states his desire to possess the magnificent Helen of Troy. To that end, he even ponders the possibility of renewing his contract with the devil in order to satisfy his lust and live forever in an earthly paradise with the coveted mythical beauty.

Even the old man's admission that he too has suffered temptation, but has been able to overcome it through his faith, fails to convince Faustus of his chance to repent. Only the striking of the clock brings Faustus to his senses; it indicates that he has only one more hour to live. In this horrific moment, terrified by the realization of the inevitable, Faust laments his circumstance and begs for more time:

> Stand still, you ever-moving spheres of heaven,
> That time may cease and midnight never come;
> Fair Nature's eye, rise, rise again, and make

Perpetual day; or let this hour be but
A year, a month, a week, a natural day,
That Faustus may repent and save his soul!

His pleadings, however, are for naught. In the remaining moments, he ponders his choices in life; he poses challenging theological questions to himself, and he even tries to bargain with the devil in an effort to convince him to take his body but leave his immortal soul. After a lifetime of self-delusion and egotistic self-indulgence, the answer to his feeble request is silence, confirming what he already knows to be true: he could have repented at any time, but he repeatedly refused to do so as a conscious act of will. The play ends as his frightened and futile plea for forgiveness is subsumed by the damnable chaos of thunder and lightening, heralding the arrival of the legion of demons who surround the screaming Faustus and resolutely escort him to suffer the eternal fires of hell.

See also Apocalypse: Secular; Apocalyptic Literature; *Doktor Faustus; Faust;* Immelmann, Art; *Love in the Ruins: The Adventures of a Bad Catholic at a Time Near the End of the World;* Marlowe, Christopher; Mephistophiles; More, Tom (Dr.); Satan; Thanatos; *The Thanatos Syndrome.*

EDGAR

Edgar is the eldest son of the Earl of Gloucester in Shakespeare's apocalyptic drama *King Lear* (1605). In the play, one of the recurring themes is the contrast between good and evil children and their impact on ingenuous parents. Edgar is the good son who cares for his father's needs, whereas Edmund, the bitter, illegitimate son, is ruthless and self-serving until the last moments of the play.

Intended as a dramatic parallel to King Lear's beloved daughter, Cordelia, Edgar too is devoted albeit somewhat naive about the forces of evil that threaten him. Also like Cordelia, Edgar believes that the gods who preside over pre-Christian Britain are basically beneficent. Nevertheless, both Edgar and Cordelia learn to use their resources more wisely throughout the course of the play. Edgar learns that by disguising himself as the deranged beggar, Tom o' Bedlam, he can both watch over his father as well as survive the destructive machinations of his evil half-brother, Edmund. In this manner, Edgar is also able to look after the suffering Lear for a time, proving his innate kind and selfless nature.

Like both Lear and Gloucester, Edgar learns how to recognize the presence of evil, to avoid judging people superficially, to act in a timely manner, and finally, after his duel with Edmund, to become a strong, wise, and capable leader for strife-torn Britain.

See also Apocalypse: Traditional Primitive; Cordelia; Edmund; Gloucester (Earl of); Goneril; Great Chain of Being; *King Lear;* Lear, King; Regan.

EDMUND 

Edmund is the younger illegitimate son of the Earl of Gloucester in Shakespeare's tragedy *King Lear* (1605). Unlike his legitimate half-brother, Edgar, Edmund depends on his natural abilities rather than on the generous intervention of beneficent gods. Whereas Edgar is devoted to the care of his aging father, Edmund is egocentric, manipulative, and free of any moral or ethical constraints that might make him feel responsible for his father.

While it is understandable that Edmund, as Gloucester's bastard son, greatly resents his lack of an honorable name and his concomitant lack of property, his bitterness and malice lead to his betrayal of Gloucester and his attempt to seize his half-brother Edgar's rightful inheritance.

He is also callous and opportunistic in his dealings with King Lear's diabolical daughters, Goneril and Regan. Since Edmund is Shakespeare's literary parallel to Lear's "unnatural" offspring, it is fitting that they become embroiled in a deadly triangle of lust and ambition that inevitably serves to destroy them all. For example, Edmund assists Goneril in her scheme to poison her husband, Albany, and he does nothing to stem the growing jealousy she feels toward Regan, whom she eventually poisons in order to have Edmund to herself.

By most standards, Edmund is a villainous character. However, the circumstances of his birth and upbringing make readers more willing to accept his last-minute change of heart that restores his goodness at the end of the play. Nevertheless, his good intentions come too late. Before his death at Edgar's hands, Edmund readily accepts his role in the destruction of the kingdom and admits, albeit cynically, some regret about the outcome of his relationships with the dead siblings Goneril and Regan. With his one heroic effort, his last-minute attempt to save Lear and Cordelia from death, Edmund provides a glimpse of the kind of man he might have become under better, more loving circumstances. Shakespeare shows some sympathy for Edmund, whose greatest flaw is his inability to understand that the perpetuation of evil can only lead to one's ultimate self-destruction.

See also Apocalypse: Traditional Primitive; Cordelia; Edgar; Gloucester (Earl of); Great Chain of Being; *King Lear;* Lear, King; Regan.

EDWARDS, JONATHAN

Jonathan Edwards (1703–1758) was an influential scholar, philosopher, and Calvinist theologian whose life's work made a significant moral impact on American literature. Born in East Windsor, Connecticut, to Reverend Timothy Edwards and Esther Stoddard Edwards, the daughter of Reverend Solomon Stoddard, Jonathan was destined for a clerical career. His early ability as an avid reader, writer, and thinker enabled him to be admitted to Yale College at the age of thirteen where he pursued his studies in theology.

In 1729, after the death of his maternal grandfather, Edwards was named to follow him as pastor of the Northampton church. For two decades he preached and authored important books, and each effort was met with equal success. Several events resulted in a marked change in Edwards's messages and motivation. Partly due to his intense conversion experience, based upon strict Christian doctrines, and partly because of the empirical philosophies of John Locke, Edwards's preaching became more fervent, more judgmental, and more offensive to his parishioners.

In an effort to deepen the spiritual commitment of his flock, Edwards began to identify backsliders in his congregation and deny them communion. This attitude was not well received by his parishioners. In 1750, his congregation of nearly 250 people recommended, by a nearly unanimous vote, Edwards's removal from the pulpit.

Although this ouster was devastating, Edwards soon redirected his evangelistic mission toward a group of Indians in Stockbridge, Massachusetts. While he practiced in Stockbridge as a missionary, Edwards received one last profes-

Jonathan Edwards

sional invitation; he was asked to preside over the College of New Jersey, which later became known as Princeton. After only three months as college president, he died of smallpox.

See also Apocalypse: Traditional Judeo-Christian; *Sinners in the Hands of an Angry God.*

ELIOT, T. S.

Thomas Stearns Eliot (1888–1965) is the British-American poet, critic, and playwright whose landmark works, specifically *The Waste Land* (1922) and *The Hollow*

Men (1925), defined the modernist movement in poetry and significantly influenced literature written after World War I. Eliot was born into a wealthy and traditional family from St. Louis, Missouri. Although physically frail, Eliot pursued vigorous study of philosophy, literature, and religion at Harvard University, where he received his master's degree in 1910.

From 1911 to 1914, he continued his graduate study briefly at Oxford, but eventually attended the Sorbonne, in Paris, where he was greatly influenced by the French philosopher Henri Bergson. His studies were interrupted by the outbreak of World War I, when Eliot moved to England. From 1915 through 1925, Eliot was an instructor at an all boys' school, and later he worked at Lloyd's Bank while completing his doctoral dissertation on the English philosopher F. H. Bradley. During that time, Eliot distinguished himself as an editor for a literary magazine entitled *The Egoist*, and later he founded a publication featuring literary reviews entitled *The Criterion*.

As a writer, he had also begun to develop a voice that represented the sentiments of spiritual malaise and alienation that was typical of his postwar generation. Eliot's poetic style was influenced by Dante, the Elizabethan dramatists, and the French symbolists. The work that best illustrates these influences is his poem entitled *The Love Song of J. Alfred Prufrock* (1910–1911). As he broadened his interests to include the experimental works of Ezra Pound and James Joyce (*Ulysses*, in particular), Eliot's poetry began to take on new dimensions that merged images of memory, myth, and mysticism.

Because he was extremely interested in human consciousness, human sexuality, and humanity's place in history, Eliot was able to develop an innovative amalgam of these themes in his epic poem, *The Waste Land*. His later writing focused more on individual alienation and the spiritual emptiness of the modern world, as seen in his highly symbolic and influential poem, *The Hollow Men*, a work that he dedicated to his editor and mentor, Ezra Pound.

In addition to achieving critical acclaim as an innovative modern poet, Eliot continued his experimentation in literature by extending his talents to the dramatic form. The results of these efforts were equally successful and produced such notable works as *Murder in the Cathedral* (1935), *The Family Reunion* (1939), *The Cocktail Party* (1949), *The Confidential Clerk* (1953), and his final full-length play, *The Elder Statesman* (1959).

See also Apocalypse: Secular; Apocalyptic Literature; Apocalypticism; Archetype; Freud, Sigmund; *Heart of Darkness; The Hollow Men;* Jung, Carl Gustav; Myth; *The Second Coming;* Symbol; *The Waste Land.*

ELLISON, RALPH

Ralph Waldo Ellison (1914–1994) is considered one of America's greatest naturalistic novelists. It is rare that a lifetime of critical acclaim rests on the publication of a single novel. Such is the case for Ellison, who is best known for his award-winning novel about African-American isolation and alienation, *The Invisible Man*, which was published in 1952.

Born on March 1, 1914, in Oklahoma, Ellison was the son of a construction worker, who named him after the famous American writer Ralph Waldo Emerson;

Ralph Ellison in 1964

his mother was a domestic who was known for her socialist leanings. Ellison's father died when he was only three years old. Under his mother's influence, and in the state of Oklahoma, which had been spared many of the ravages of slavery, he grew up with a feeling of freedom and possibility, in spite of his race.

In an environment that encouraged personal expression, Ellison explored many avenues of creativity in his young life. For example, he played trumpet in the high school band and developed a fondness for Southwestern jazz. From 1933 to 1936, Ellison pursued his studies in classical music at Alabama's Tuskegee Institute. Also during this time he was introduced to the works of Hemingway, T. S. Eliot, Stein, Joyce, Pound, and Stendhal.

In 1936, after a move to New York City to study sculpture, Ellison met two influential writers of the Harlem Renaissance, Langston Hughes and Richard Wright. Through his association with these formidable authors, Ellison was led to the works of Marx, Freud, and Dostoyevsky.

From 1939 to 1942, Ellison contributed to a publication known as *The New Masses,* and during the following year he served as the managing editor for a publication entitled *Negro Quarterly.* His efforts in these two publications reflected his growing interest in the Communist movement, which was supported by African-American intellectuals such as Richard Wright during that time. However, during his years of military service in World War II in the Merchant Marine, Ellison began to see the limitations of the Marxist movement. At the conclusion of the war in 1945, he renewed his commitment to art and received a Rosenwald Fellowship, which enabled him to work on *The Invisible Man.*

In 1953, the year following its publication, *The Invisible Man* won the National Book Award. During the years that followed, Ellison worked on several projects, one a collaborative project with Karl Shapiro appearing in 1964 entitled *The Writer's Experience,* and later in the same year a book of his own essays entitled *Shadow and Act.* Until the end of his life in 1994, Ellison continued his work as a writer, a professor of writing at Yale University, and a sought-after speaker on the literary lecture circuit.

See also Apocalypse: Secular; Harlem Renaissance; *The Invisible Man.*

EMERSON, RALPH WALDO

Ralph Waldo Emerson (1803–1882) is the poet, lecturer, and essayist whose name is synonymous with the Transcendental movement of the mid-nineteenth century. In both his life and his work, Emerson inspired other writers, such as Herman Melville, Nathaniel Hawthorne, Walt Whitman, Margaret Fuller, and Henry David Thoreau, to produce a body of literature that collectively reflects the period known as the American Renaissance.

Born on May 25, 1803, in Boston, Massachusetts, Emerson was the son of the pastor of the First Church of Boston. His father died young, leaving a wife and six children behind. Emerson lived a frugal material life but a rich intellectual one. He was admitted to Harvard University at fourteen and graduated at age eighteen. After graduation, Emerson was employed as a schoolteacher for three years. This work enabled him to finance his theological education at the Harvard Divinity School, where he received his licensure as a Unitarian

Ralph Waldo Emerson

minister in 1826. In 1829, he was ordained as the pastor of the Second Church of Boston. In that same year, he married his first wife, Ellen Louisa Tucker, pursued family life, and distinguished himself in his fledgling ministry by delivering stirring sermons that had the power to move even the most cynical audience.

In the next few years, Emerson suffered a series of personal losses. In 1831, his nineteen-year-old bride died. This tragedy was soon followed by the devastating loss of two of his brothers, Charles and Edward. Emerson himself became ill, and during that time he struggled through a personal darkness that led him to question many of his beliefs.

During this reflective period, Emerson pursued a regimen of personal study that led to his decision to resign as pastor of his church in 1832. He came to believe that the routine of the "Lord's Supper" ran counter to Christ's design for the sacrament. Because his conscience would no longer allow him to participate in communion, he resigned his post, thereby disappointing many of his devoted followers.

In an effort to find himself, he traveled to Europe and stayed there through 1833; during his stay, he became restored emotionally and creatively through his association with other writers such as Wordsworth, Landor, Carlyle, and Coleridge, whose work had a lasting influence on him. Upon his return to America, Emerson began a lyceum movement wherein he could lecture to large audiences on a series of broad philosophical issues.

Following this plan, Emerson was able to settle into a home in Concord, and a year later, in 1835, he married his second wife, Lydia (Lidian) Jackson. His career was launched in earnest with the publication of his essay *Nature* in 1836. This idealistic tome criticized America's unhealthy pursuit of materialism and its lack of moral and spiritual convictions. In 1837, he was invited to lecture at Harvard, where he delivered another controversial address entitled *The American Scholar*. In this work, he urged scholars and writers to break free of the stagnant and pedantic literary patterns of England's writers and to develop both a message and a style that was more intuitive and original.

It was also during this time that Emerson developed the concept of the "Over Soul," that which unites God with all of creation. In his definitive work, *Self-Reliance*, Emerson brought to fruition the Transcendental ideas about individuality and creativity that were inspired by Coleridge. His career and his personal life continued to thrive, with the great exception of the death of his son, Waldo. This loss resulted in a period of depression and internalization of grief. On July 24, 1872, Emerson's beloved home accidentally burned down. Neighbors and friends had worked feverishly to recover his books and manuscripts. In the aftermath, Emerson became listless, enervated, and depressed. To help him recover from this loss, his daughter Ellen accompanied him on an extended trip throughout Europe and to Egypt, a place Emerson found fascinating.

During this trip, Ellen realized her father's mental faculties were beginning to fail. While giving brief speeches or informal talks, he frequently forgot words or repeated himself. The concern for his health, and their weariness from travel, led Emerson and his worried daughter home.

Their homecoming was a testament to the love and loyalty that the Concord community had for its literary legend. As Emerson and Ellen disembarked from the ship, they were greeted at the dock by a cheering group of townspeople. This festive parade led Emerson to witness a miracle of human kindness: in his absence, several local merchants, tradesmen, and neighbors had combined their resources to rebuild the Emerson home. Emerson was delighted when he found his home completely restored, including the books and manuscripts in his study. According to his wife, this generosity did much to lift his depression and to renew his faith in God and humanity.

Although Emerson's senile dementia had begun to deteriorate his memory, thereby rendering him unable to continue lecturing, he spent his latter days either studying in solitude, visiting with friends, or enjoying his lifelong habit of taking long nature walks. During one of these walks, however, Emerson forgot to wear his raincoat. As a result of wandering through a downpour, Emerson caught a virulent cold that developed into pneumonia. Emerson died on April 27, 1882, and was buried, among other formidable literary cohorts, under a tree in the famed Sleepy Hollow Cemetery.

See also Brook Farm; Hawthorne, Nathaniel; Melville, Herman; Transcendentalism.

ENTROPY

Entropy is a term related to the level of randomness or chaos in a physical or an informational system. Entropy was first coined as a term in 1865 by Rudolf Clausius, a German physicist. His studies were augmented, in 1873, by an American physicist, J. Willard Gibbs, who examined the original theory in regard to a variety of natural processes. Their discoveries made a considerable contribution to the areas of physical and natural sciences, the theory of entropy, and powerful forces of its random and chaotic energy. Entropy also became an area of significant interest to authors of this period who were grappling with the complexities of human nature.

The theme of entropy has become synonymous with several modern and most postmodern writers. One of the first to examine this theory in connection with the chaotic nature of human beings was the Polish-born writer Joseph Conrad, author of the novella *Heart of Darkness* (1910), which features the "hollow" or soulless character of Kurtz, who also serves as a reference in several works of the following decade. Two other authors whose works also relate a direct understanding of this theoretical concept as it applies to humanity were William Butler Yeats, who wrote his entropic and apocalyptic poem entitled *The Second Coming*, (1920), and T. S. Eliot, whose poems *The Waste Land* (1922) and *The Hollow Men* (1925) not only paid tribute to Conrad's paradigmatic Kurtz but also inspired a legion of literati to experiment with this form. Among the authors who were clearly affected by this theory, as well as by Eliot's interpretation of the concept, was F. Scott Fitzgerald, who had personally witnessed the chaotic energy of the "roaring twenties" that caused his characters to run morally out of control in his symbolic novel *The Great Gatsby* (1925). Similarly, in 1933 and again in 1939, Nathanael West examined such issues in his novels *Miss Lonelyhearts* and *The Day of the Locust*.

Nevertheless, while this theory remained a popular literary theme within specific circles, it became a predominant force in the development of post–World War II fiction. Readers of this period had suddenly become familiar with the devastation of the atomic bomb; as a result, they could actually conceptualize for the first time the utter annihilation of a nation or even the entire human race. This awareness, however, was not limited to European literature; in fact, the fear of human destruction and cultural devastation was also apparent in 1959, when the Nigerian author Chinua Achebe examined the entropic forces of colonialism on African nationalism in his apocalyptic novel *Things Fall Apart*.

In writings of a later period, however, writers had begun to draw parallels between the devaluation of the human spirit as a result of its contact with such heartless and complex materialistic bureaucracies as industry, politics, and technology. In his novels *The Crying of Lot 49* (1966) and, to a larger extent, *Gravity's Rainbow* (1973), Thomas Pynchon attempts to warn humanity of the entropic threats of the universe. Southern satirist Walker Percy has presented the theory of entropy in two of his novels, *Love in the Ruins* (1971) and *The Thanatos Syndrome* (1987). While the list of authors who rely on entropic theory as a central metaphor for their works is sorely limited by the length of this particular text, it is certain that entropy, as the physical and natural theory of change within a system, will always remain a constant as long as it is applied to the dynamic construct of humanity.

See also Allegory; Apocalypse: Secular; Apocalypse: Traditional Judeo-Christian; Archetype; *The Great Gatsby; Heart of Darkness; The Hollow Men; Love in the Ruins: The Adventures of a Bad Catholic at a Time Near the End of the World; The Second Coming;* Symbol; *The Thanatos Syndrome; Things Fall Apart; The Waste Land.*

ESCHATOLOGY

Eschatology is a term originating in the Islamic and Zoroastrian religions and that was later included in Judeo-Christian doctrine pertaining to the "last things," or events that will occur before the end of the world. While Eastern religions and other nonliterate cultures share similar belief systems, some components of various world religions are fairly consistent, while others remain widely divergent. The essence of most eschatological doctrines, however, involves the ultimate struggle between order and chaos in the cosmos. According to such doctrines, whether they be mythical in nature or canons of formalized religions, at the end of history, all earthly disorder—wars, famines, social injustice, etc.—will be eliminated from the world. Order will finally be restored to the universe. Most important to eschatological views, however, is a belief that those who are evil will be punished and those who are righteous will be rewarded.

Within traditional Judeo-Christian eschatology is the belief that humankind's disobedience to God's laws has repeatedly resulted in catastrophic events reflecting God's disappointment and wrath. According to the Old Testament, human suffering and destruction will continue on the earth until the people conform to God's will. The purpose of this pattern is to fulfill the promises made to the Israelites, God's "chosen people." Thus, compliance with Judaic law will ultimately result in the reclamation of the Holy City and restoration of the persecuted race to a position of honor. By example, this restoration will serve as an example to gentiles and will eventually inspire eternal salvation for the rest of the people in the world.

While Judaism's eschatological position is based on messianic events that will occur sometime in the distant future, the New Testament doctrines of the end times reflect a belief that the fulfillment of prophesy has already begun through the birth, death, and resurrection of Jesus Christ. In Christianity, Jesus is the Messiah who, as both God and man, was sent to earth as a living example for humanity. During his life on earth, Jesus performed miracles, taught the ignorant, loved the unlovable, healed the sick, and raised the dead. As both God and man, Jesus knew that he would endure thirty-three years of life on this earth. Yet, out of obedience to God the Father, and because of his love for humanity, he willingly suffered the humiliation of an unjust persecution, by his own people, that ended with a violent and merciless death on the cross. Christians believe, therefore, that through the spilling of his sacrificial blood, Jesus ultimately redeemed the sins of humanity. Moreover, through the glory of his resurrection, Jesus promised that eternal salvation, through his grace, would be available for all who believe that he is the Son of God and the promised Messiah who came to earth to provide humanity with a glimpse of the eternal Kingdom of God.

While Judeo-Christian views tend to dominate Western thought, other diverse eschatological views exist in Eastern cultures. In contrast to Western philosophy, Buddhists believe that the end times will result in the end of all earthly suffering by the souls experiencing a series of periodic and cyclic rebirths. The form into which creatures are reborn depends upon the moral and behavioral actions that an individual demonstrated in a past life. Accordingly, souls must travel through various cycles of rebirth, daily living, and inevitable suffering until all of their individual spiritual lessons have been learned. When the soul no longer needs the body for understanding, and it finally achieves the highest level of enlightenment or "bliss," then its cycle will be complete through the attainment of eternal peace, a condition known to Buddhists as nirvana.

See also Apocalypse: Traditional Judeo-Christian; Apocalypse: Traditional Primitive; Apocalyptic Literature; Revelation, Book of.

EZEKIEL, BOOK OF

Ezekiel (written 593–571 B.C.) is the third book of the Hebrew Bible or Old Testament Bible that features a writer who is considered one of its major prophets. In its entirety, the book pertains to the thoughts, actions, and prophesies of a man named Ezekiel, the son of Buzi, who eventually became a priest and then a prophet of the Jews who were exiled to Babylonia. While the first section of the book (chapters 1–24), denounces Judah and predicts the fall of Jerusalem, and the second section (chapters 25–32) relates prophetic oracles against foreign nations, it is the third section of the book that holds the greatest apocalyptic significance. Chapters 33 through 48 present God's plan for the restoration of

Raphael's *Vision of Ezekiel* is housed by the Pitti Palace in Florence.

Israel, the reconstruction of its fallen Temple, and the reestablishment of the Temple as the center of worship. The chapters that most clearly reflect the apocalyptic themes featured in this encyclopedia are chapters 38 and 39, which present the final battle of Gog and Magog whereby God will retaliate against the forces that plan to prey upon Israel in the last days of the world.

At the beginning of chapter 38, Ezekiel proclaims that God told him to warn the armies of Gog and Magog, as well as their supporting armies from Persia, Ethiopia, and Libya, that he is aware of their diabolical intention to attack the unwalled villages of Jerusalem with the intent of killing Israelites in their sleep and taking many of them as slaves. God warns Ezekiel, however, to tell these potential attackers that he will avenge his people furiously with great earthquakes, the crumbling of mountains, and showers of "overflowing rain, and great hailstones, fire, and brimstone." Moreover, as if to seal his promise, God adds: "Thus will I magnify myself, and sanctify myself; and I will be known in the eyes of many nations, and they shall know that I *am* the Lord" (Ezekiel 38:19–23, KJV).

In chapter 39, the prophecy continues and provides details about God's plan to "smite" the warriors against his people, to "give [them] unto the ravenous birds of every sort, and to the beasts of the field to be devoured," and to "send a fire on Magog" that will convince them of his wrath (39:1–6). After the Lord tells Ezekiel about his own plans for the destruction of his enemies, he also assures the prophet that the Jewish people will then be given the opportunity to burn all of the opposing armies' weapons, throw their rotting corpses into open graves until they have completely decayed, and then fill in the graves with dirt, after which they will "cleanse" and "glorify" the land by renaming the city Hamonah (39:9–16). As a result of this apocalyptic conflagration and the promised victory that precedes the coming of the Messiah, God promises through Ezekiel that "all the heathen shall see my judgment that I have executed, and my hand that I have laid upon them. So the house of Israel shall know that I *am* the Lord their God from that day and forward" (39:21–22).

See also Apocalypse: Traditional Judeo-Christian; Apocalyptic Literature; Daniel, Book of; Gog and Magog; Isaiah, Book of; Joel, Book of; Revelation, Book of; Zechariah, Book of.

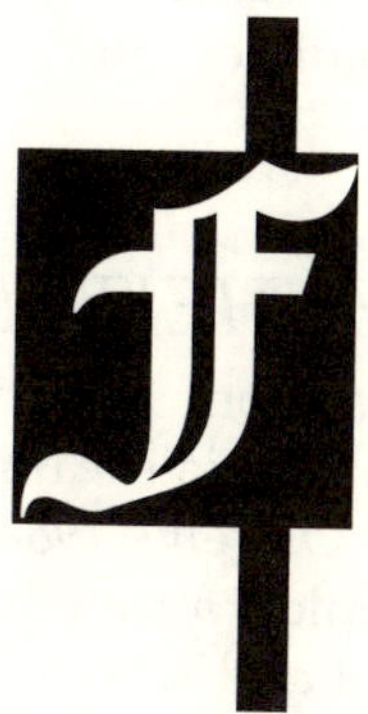

THE FAERIE QUEENE

The Fairie Queene (c. 1590–1609) is the title of an allegorical epic poem composed by Edmund Spenser, in honor of Queen Elizabeth I, that exalts Protestant nationalism, decries the papacy, and honors Prince Arthur as the paragon of knighthood. Written according to the form of the Italian romantic epic, *The Faerie Queene* consists of six books, although the original plan called for twelve books to correspond with the fictional exploits depicting the moral virtues of the twelve knights in Queen Gloriana's court.

Within the body of the work, Arthur is the central figure who unites the tales as he seeks to serve his queen and be found worthy of her admiration. As in most political or religious allegories, things do not go smoothly for the knights within any of the six books. As representative of the quest or grail motif, each knight must pit his particular moral virtue against the trials and temptations that threaten his eternal salvation. While this motif is carried throughout the six books of the poem, the apocalyptic elements of the work are emphasized within the first book entitled "The Legend of the Red Crosse Knight, or of Holiness."

According to one scholar of the work, "The Legend of Holiness is patterned . . . on the Apocalypse of John and is thus an 'apocalyptic' poem" (Sandler 149). And although the moral allegory presented within the poem deals with the necessary preparation for the coming of God's kingdom, it was written within a vernacular and historical perspective that would enable Elizabethan audiences to enjoy the poem, at least on its most basic, literal level.

Figuratively speaking, however, "The Red Crosse Knight, the hero of the legend, is introduced as one 'Faithful and True' (cf. Rev. 19:11) who must yet endure temptations and oppressions, the equivalent of the Apocalypse's plagues and tyrannies that try and winnow the just on the earth" (150). Among his trials, he must avoid the delusion of the False Prophet, the seduction of the Whore of Babylon, and must contend with a symbolic enemy, the Dragon, who engages him in battle for a period of three days. Fortunately, he is protected by his shield of faith and sustained by both the Well and the Tree of Life. Ultimately, as a reward for his faithfulness and his endurance under oppression, he is rewarded by receiving his bride, the virtuous and loving Una, who represents the eternal reward as is presented in the final chapter of the book of Revelation.

See also Allegory; Apocalypse: Traditional Judeo-Christian; Arthur, King; The Fisher King; Gloriana; The Grail (or Holy Grail); Revelation, Book of; Spenser, Edmund.

FAHRENHEIT 451

Fahrenheit 451 (1953) is the short apocalyptic novel written by Ray Bradbury that received the Commonwealth of California's Annual Gold Medal in 1954. Its message is similar to that of George Orwell's *1984* (1949) and Aldous Huxley's *Brave New World* (1932) in that it depicts a time in the near future where individualism is repressed and punished and where government has the power to control and destroy individuals or societies at will.

The story begins with the introduction of Guy Montag, the zealous veteran fireman of the future, who, in a time when houses have all been fireproofed, has been given the new task of suppressing societal rebellion by burning books. Bearing the symbolic number 451 on his uniform, the Fahrenheit temperature at which paper catches fire, Montag reeks of the "perfume" of kerosene, which is the staple of his trade. Although at the beginning of the novel, Montag is proudly complacent about his life and his work, he soon comes to question both after meeting his winsome young neighbor, Clarisse McClellan, during an impromptu evening stroll. This meeting marks the beginning of Montag's transformation; Clarisse causes him to think, perhaps for the first time, that his life might not be as meaningful as he had previously believed.

Clarisse's vivacity is in direct contrast with the character of Mildred, Montag's perpetually anesthetized wife. If Clarisse questions the status quo, Mildred represents the status quo. She willingly submits to society's myriad distractions, such as wall-to-wall interactive television, the constant pursuit of physical pleasure, and the wide availability of euphoric drugs, while never questioning governmental decisions to invade personal privacy or wage continual wars.

As a result of meeting Clarisse and experiencing her life-affirming presence, Montag is compelled to investigate the forbidden world that he had sworn to destroy. In the process, he questions his supervisor, veteran fire chief Beatty, who explains how things had been in the past and rationalizes that people are better off without the provocative insights of books that inevitably lead to a state of societal unrest. Montag, however, is unconvinced and later becomes committed to finding a way to help the world stop making the same devastating mistakes.

Recalling a strange man whom he had once observed in a park, Montag searches for him to become his mentor in the world of books. This character, named Faber, will alter Montag's future forever. As a retired English professor, Faber reveals the mysterious and universal power of the written word to Montag, and under his influence, Montag joins an underground movement to gather and illegally reprint the world's great books. Together, the two also devise a plan to undermine the credibility of the fire department by planting contraband texts in the firemen's homes. During the course of their relationship, however, Montag feels compelled to disregard Faber's instructions, as well as his own former caution, by shocking a gathering of his wife's vacuous guests with a reading of Matthew Arnold's poem of despair in the modern world entitled "Dover Beach."

This action sets the conclusion of the story into motion. Montag is thereafter identified as a subversive. In fear of her own future, his wife turns him over to the authorities. Although Beatty arrives to taunt and arrest him, Montag escapes by setting fire to both Beatty and his vicious mechanical tracking hound. In his flight from the scene, which contains all remnants of his past life, Montag again enlists the aid of Faber, who helps him to locate the itinerant community of "Book People." This nomadic society of fellow book lovers eventually accepts his presence and begins to teach him their ways. Although they are considered fugitives in their world, they hope that through the preservation of individual thought and the memorization of great literature, there will eventually come another time and place where the essence of the human spirit will rise from the ashes of humanity's destructive impulses and, once again, revel in the glory of the written word.

See also Apocalypse: Traditional Judeo-Christian; Bradbury, Ray; McClellan, Clarisse; Montag, Guy; Phoenix; Science Fiction.

FAULKNER, WILLIAM

William Faulkner (1897–1962), one of America's greatest writers, was born in New Albany, Mississippi, but lived most of his life in Oxford, Mississippi, the town that he fictionalized as Jefferson, Yoknapatawpha County. At the heart of Faulkner's mythology are several families—the Compsons, the Sartorises, and the Snopses—whose dramas reenact the social, racial, mental, and emotional conflicts experienced in the American South during and after the Civil War. While Faulkner's predominant themes involve the death of Southern aristocracy at the hands of Northern progress, his characters remain contemporary inasmuch as they capture the pride, alienation, sense of loss, and eventual regeneration that inevitably occurs in the human spirit during times of intrusive and relentless change.

These themes were most familiar to Faulkner in that they reflected elements of his family's past, and in many ways served as models for the tragic, and sometimes grotesque, events that unfolded in the body of his work. For example, the violent death of his great-grandfather, Col. William Culbert Falkner (the author later changed the spelling of his family name upon publication), inspired two novels, *Sartoris* and *The Unvanquished;* furthermore, Col. Falkner inspired the personality of the fictional Col. John Sartoris, a formidable character in the Southern tradition who appears throughout Faulkner's long and short fictions.

Many of the traits typified in Faulkner's fictional characters came from his early experiences as a member of a distinguished family that included the aforementioned Confederate colonel, who had served in both the Mexican and Civil Wars; respected businessmen; and even a Mississippi governor. In 1918, Faulkner himself was preparing to serve in the Royal Canadian Air Force; however, World War I ended before he saw any military action. Instead, Faulkner worked at odd jobs and briefly attended the University of Mississippi in order to continue writing his first work, which was a collection of verse entitled *The Marble*

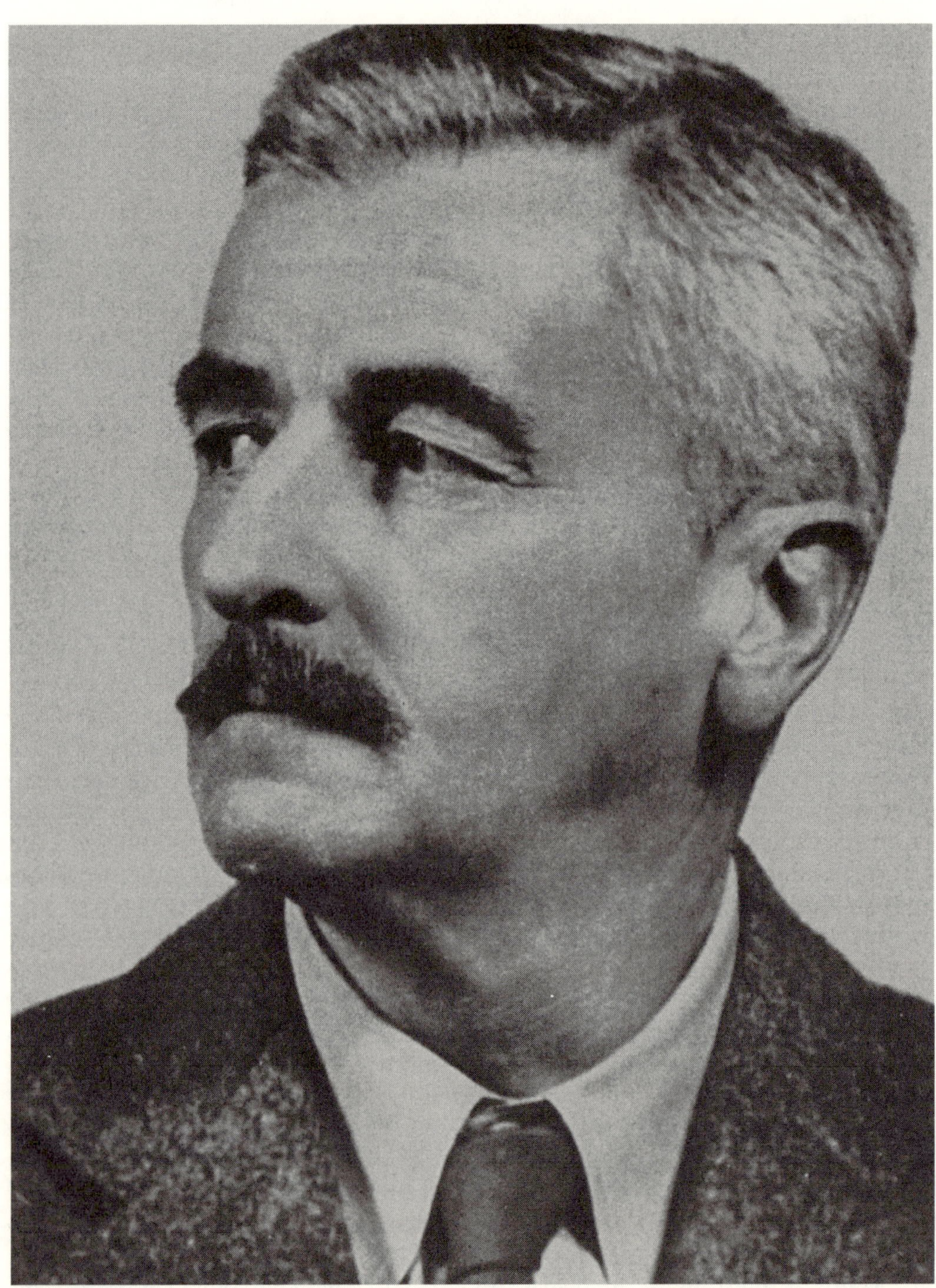

William Faulkner

Faun (1924). Faulkner later became acquainted with a fellow writer, Sherwood Anderson, who was instrumental in helping him publish his first novel entitled *Soldier's Pay* in 1926.

Faulkner married a woman named Estelle Oldham and they had one child, a daughter named Jill. These responsibilities, combined with other familial obligations, caused Faulkner to work ceaselessly, but most comfortably, in Oxford, Mississippi, where many of his prototypical characters were reborn within the fictional confines of Yoknapatawpha County. It was from this vantage point that Faulkner wrote his third book, *Sartoris* (1929), and in the same year replicated James Joyce's experimental stream-of-consciousness style in *The Sound and the Fury*. In *As I Lay Dying*, Faulkner continued to develop the theme of the death of the old Southern aristocracy. His work found popularity with the publication of the controversial novel *Sanctuary* in 1931.

Faulkner broke from the novel format with his next work, a collection of short stories entitled *These Thirteen*, but he returned to it in 1933 with the provocative tale of Joe Christmas in *Light in August*. While Faulkner continued to work on another collection of verse, *The Green Bough*, he completed his greatest critical accomplishment with the apocalyptic novel *Absalom, Absalom!*, in which he ties together a chronicle of events related to ill-fated characters and familiar locales that had previously appeared in six of his earlier novels.

Faulkner's prolific literary output included nearly twenty novels, two poetry collections, and miscellaneous essays, stories, and articles, some of which included *The Unvanquished* and *The Wild Palms* in 1939; *The Hamlet; The Town; The Mansion; Go Down, Moses; Intruder in the Dust; Knight's Gambit;* and *Requiem for a Nun*. Although Faulkner found acclaim somewhat late in his career, he worked ceaselessly and was honored in 1949 with a Nobel Prize in Literature. He later received a Pulitzer Prize for *A Fable* (1954) and *The Reivers* (1962).

Much of his writing focused on humanity's psychological and moral dilemmas as seen through the eyes of a small Southern county. These problems, however, were not unrelated to the author. Unfortunately, his personal struggles drove him to overwork and alcoholism, which may have led to decline and death in 1962. Nevertheless, Faulkner's message of hope amidst despair has made him one of the world's most influential writers. His work continues to influence writers in United States, Japan, and Latin America, where several renowned authors have imitated his style, re-created generational sagas, and perpetuated his epic themes of struggle, death, and regeneration of the human spirit.

See also *Absalom, Absalom!*; Apocalypse: Traditional Judeo-Christian; Archetype; *As I Lay Dying;* Coldfield, Rosa; Compson, Quentin; Satan; Sutpen, Thomas.

FAUST

Faust (Part I 1808; Part II 1832) is the name of the two-part work written by Johann Wolfgang von Goethe. This work, which is considered Germany's greatest contribution to Western literature, is based on a collection of tales known as the *Faustbuch* (1587). Although there is some controversy as to the exact identity of the historical Faust, most scholars agree that Goethe's work is based primarily on the famous legend of the evil German magician, astrologer, visionary, and alchemist, Dr. Johann Faust, who received a degree in natural science at Heidelberg in 1509 and, after a life of sodomitic revelry and sorcery, was allegedly destroyed by the devil while staying at a country inn at Wurttemberg.

According to Part I of Goethe's interpretation of the legend, the ambitious Dr. Faust is frustrated and dejected because in spite of his myriad intellectual, mystical, or religious pursuits he knows he will never enjoy the ecstasy of complete satisfaction. In response to his prideful musings, Mephistopheles, a cynical and insidious fallen angel, heeds the scientist's call. In fact, he is astounded by Dr. Faust, whose fearless egotism is reflected in his address to Mephistopheles: "My name is Faust, in everything thy equal" (17). Amused by such human hubris, Mephistopheles ultimately accepts Faust's challenge to make a pact with the devil in order to fulfill all of his earthly desires. To seal the pact, Mephistopheles tempts Faust with a promise:

> This hour, my friend, shall stir your senses, more
> Than any pleasures you have known before. . . .
> Ay, and the lovely sights they bring you,
> Are something more than magic's empty show.
> Your palate shall be satisfied,
> Your sense of fragrance gratified,
> And all your subtle feelings set aglow (Part I 78).

What follows this promise is the immediate fulfillment of Faust's overreaching desires. Most notable is Faust's apparent emotional rejuvenation through his love for the fair and ingenuous Margareta (a.k.a. Gretchen). In his eagerness to taste this forbidden fruit, Faust forgets Mephistopheles's claim that his spectral essence is that of the Spirit of Negation, an embodiment of evil that he announces to Faust during their first meeting:

> The spirit I, that endlessly denies. / And rightly, too; for all that comes to birth / Is fit for overthrow, as nothing worth; / Wherefore the world were better sterilized; / Thus all that's here as Evil recognized is gain to me, and downfall, ruin, sin/ The very element I prosper in (75).

Nevertheless, Faust is blinded by the limitless possibilities presented to him, and so he forgets the fact that although he will obtain fulfillment, he will never be able to sustain it. This reality becomes painfully obvious to him in his seemingly idyllic relationship with Margareta. Two tragic events occur that prevent their future happiness. First, he unintentionally slays a man in a duel whom he later learns is Margareta's brother. Disturbed by this revelation, he selfishly deserts his lover. In the second disaster, Faust's desertion compels the pregnant and desperate Margareta to drown their illegitimate child.

Although the remainder of the tale reflects other circumstances revealing Mephistopheles's manipulation of Faust, the drama concludes with the ultimate fulfillment of the terms of the diabolical pact. In spite of his last-minute redemptive effort to save Margareta, who has been sentenced to death for her crime, she resists his help, shrinking from his evil nature, preferring to die in atonement for her sins than to be damned along with Faust. Realizing the consequences of his pact, Faust laments that he was ever born, particularly when, in the end, her appeal for God's forgiveness is heard, and a heavenly voice confirms her eternal salvation. Part I ends with a temporary victory for Mephistopheles, Faust's loss of his earthly love, and a chastened spirit that paves the way for his gradual transformation in the second part of the work.

Although Goethe apparently began his work on Part II sometime between 1800 and 1831, he requested that the manuscript remain sealed until his death, which occurred in 1832, a year after he had finished it. In Part II, Faust has been sobered and spiritually inspired by Margareta's faithful death, and thereafter determines to reform his life by using his gifts for more noble causes. He has no difficulty using the wiles of Mephistopheles to fulfill this purpose. This intention is once again thwarted, however, by Mephistopheles, who allows Faust to be placed in a high position in the German emperor's court, contending that Faust has the power to restore the court's financial instability. Nevertheless, Faust's efforts fail because he has become valued in the court more for his ability to perform cheap magic tricks and otherwise entertain the court rather than for his financial counsel. Both his necromancy and his resolve are sorely tested in this venue when he conjures images of the magnificent Helen of Troy and her paramour, Paris. But finding himself smitten with Helen, Faust attempts to intervene in history by preventing Paris from claiming her. Once again, Faust's illusions dissipate as his physical intervention results literally in the explosion of the two figures, a visage so horrifying that he falls into a state of unconsciousness.

Later, Faust gets another opportunity to rescue Helen from her husband's wrath. At this point, the story resembles a Greek tragedy. Helen marries Faust and they bear a beautiful and talented son called Euphorion. As is always the case, however, Faust's marital and parental bliss is short-lived; their son is eventually killed, and the disconsolate Helen leaves Faust forever.

What follows is another series of situations in which Faust attempts, with the help of Mephistopheles, to quench the rebellious flames of society and to establish a more effective sense of order in his world. These efforts succeed, and Faust thereafter becomes known for his fame, his fortune, and his power. Deluded by his perceived power, and becoming bored with his righteous state, he demonstrates a lapse in judgment and finds himself embroiled in a Mephistophelan situation in which several innocent people are unjustly killed by his demonic minions. When he realizes that he too is part of this diabolical force, Faust attempts to renounce magic. In return for his lack of gratitude, he is blinded, but he still vows to fulfill his promise to redeem society and thereby grow closer to God.

Ultimately, Faust is killed through his redemptive efforts. At this moment, Mephistopheles tries to reclaim Faust's soul, but the demon's efforts fail. Because of Faust's humility, a legion of angels carries his soul to heaven. In the end, Faust is reunited with his beloved Margareta, and together they embark on a victorious ascent to a higher spiritual plane, thereby confirming Goethe's premise that humanity's faith in God, and in causes more important than oneself, can restore even the earth's most irredeemable sinner.

See also Apocalypse: Secular; Apocalyptic Literature; *Doktor Faustus; Dr. Faustus*; Freud, Sigmund; Immelmann, Art; *Love in the Ruins: The Adventures of a Bad Catholic at a Time Near the End of the World;* Mephistophiles; Satan; Smith, Father Rinaldo; Thanatos; *The Thanatos Syndrome.*

FERDINAND

Ferdinand is the handsome and just son of the King of Naples in William Shakespeare's apocalyptic tragicomedy *The Tempest.* Ferdinand's father, Alonso, is responsible for the exile of Prospero, the ousted Duke of Milan, an event that occurred twelve years prior to the action of the story. This event results in Ferdinand's presence on board a ship that becomes wrecked upon the shores of a deserted island. Ferdinand does not know, however, that Prospero has used magic to bring this ship, and its inhabitants, most of whom were responsible for his banishment, to the island.

While he is attempting to get his bearings on the island and locate any other survivors of the shipwreck, Ferdinand encounters one of the most beautiful young women he has ever seen. Miranda is her name, and true to its literal meaning, she seems a "wonder" to him because of her peerless beauty and her astonishing innocence. He learns, in a very short time, that she and her father, Prospero, had been cast into the ocean because of a plot devised by her wicked and ambitious uncle, Antonio, and his own father. None of these details matter much to either of them because they have fallen in love at first sight.

Although Ferdinand is initially startled by Miranda's candor in asking him whether or not he is in love with her, he realizes that her upbringing on the island has kept her free from the corrupt and deceitful influences of civilized society. As such, he is aware that she is a rare treasure, and in response to her question, he admits that he is in love with her and asks her to marry him. Miranda responds positively to his proposal, but makes the provision that she will only do so if her father approves of their union. From this moment on, Ferdinand becomes a willing slave to the whims of both Miranda and Prospero in the hopes of winning her for his wife.

Ultimately, the beauty of their innocent love softens the heart of Prospero, who had originally arranged for the crew to be shipwrecked in order to exact revenge upon his enemies. But when he witnesses the power of their love, he is moved to forgive his enemies, give up his interest in magic, and return happily to his rightful role as Duke of Milan knowing that his future will be blessed by the union of such a pure couple as Ferdinand and Miranda.

See also Apocalypse: Traditional Judeo-Christian; Apocalypticism; Ariel; Caliban; Miranda; Prospero; *The Tempest.*

THE FISHER KING

The Fisher King is the monarch most closely related to the ancient legend of the grail. According to Marx, in *Nouvelles Recherches sur la Litterature Arthurienne* [New Research on the Arthurian Legend], "this role of the mythical monarch relates him to the apostles or fishermen of the Sea of Galilee." Given this interpretation, the act of fishing not only relates to the apostolic purpose of "fishing for men," but it also involves either an internal or external quest in order to find the meaning of life (Cirlot 1971, 107–108).

The Fisher King legend dates back to the literature of Greek and Egyptian literature, which refer to ancient fertility rituals involving the sexual maiming or death of a god. When this ancient perspective was translated through the lens of Christian interpretation, the death of a god and the vitality of a people could be restored by the intervention of a grail hero. Such is certainly the case regarding the story of Christ's death and resurrection for the purpose of bringing men into the Kingdom of God. In the medieval romances, heroes such as Galahad must find the grail, and symbolically search for the truth, in order to restore the wasted land and nobility of a dying monarch.

The legend of the Fisher King pervades much of Western literature. Malory's *Morte d'Arthur,* Conrad's *Heart of Darkness,* and Eliot's *The Waste Land* are examples in which the Fisher King plays a dominant symbolic role in examining the vulnerability of the human condition.

See also Allegory; Apocalypse: Secular; Apocalypse: Traditional Judeo-Christian; Arthur, King; The Grail (or Holy Grail); *Heart of Darkness; The Waste Land.*

FITZGERALD, F. SCOTT

Francis Scott Key Fitzgerald (1896–1940) is the novelist and short-story writer who is perhaps best known for his portrayals of American decadence and disillusionment during the 1920s. He was born in St. Paul, Minnesota, to middle-class parents. Fitzgerald's early life was similar to that of many of his fictional characters who have humble origins but strive for wealth in order to transform their hopeless lives. With the financial support of an aunt, Fitzgerald received his early formal education at a Catholic boarding school, and in 1913, the aspiring writer/socialite entered Princeton University.

At Princeton, Fitzgerald became acutely aware of the subtle differences between himself and his wealthier classmates. One of his earliest disappointments resulted from his inability to make the school's renowned football team; nevertheless, he was an active participant in many of the college's extracurricular activities, specifically those related to literature and drama, where he befriended artists and intellectuals such as Edmund Wilson, who would remain a friend and literary advocate of Fitzgerald throughout his life. These activities were more important than his studies, and the budding writer was forced to leave the college because of poor academic performance.

Later in the same year, Fitzgerald joined the U.S. Army, and in 1918, while he was stationed in Montgomery, Alabama, he met the woman who would have a lasting impact over his life and work: Zelda Sayre. Although he was immediately smitten by her and was successful in dating her on a few occasions, this daughter of a Supreme Court justice later ended the relationship because he was of a lower social status. It was this rejection that ignited Fitzgerald's already smoldering desire both for Zelda as well as the lifestyle to which he had always aspired. In an effort to prove himself worthy of her affection, Fitzgerald proceeded to rewrite a novel entitled *This Side of Paradise* (1920), a work he had begun while at Princeton. It became a contemporary best-seller, earning him both money and celebrity at the young age of twenty-four. Zelda was impressed by his creative potential and agreed to marry her eminent suitor just one week following the novel's publication.

At this point, Fitzgerald had reached the pinnacle of his personal life. He had won the love of Zelda and was a rising star among the new American literati. Following the publication of his first novel, Fitzgerald was flooded with offers to write for such prestigious literary magazines as *Scribner's* as well as for the more mainstream and better paying periodicals such as *The Saturday Evening Post*. Typical of the short stories that were included in these publications was his fictional account of the young, rich, and beautiful of the "Roaring Twenties" entitled "The Diamond as Big as the Ritz." This story, as well as others with similar themes, were included in two literary collections, *Flappers and Philosophers* (1921) and *Tales of the Jazz Age* (1922) as well as in his second novel, *The Beautiful and the Damned* (1922).

By this time, Fitzgerald and his wife were completely engaged in an extravagant lifestyle. In 1924, the couple eagerly joined the cynical social circle of American literary expatriates by moving to the French Riviera. The exploits of this elite society were captured in Fitzgerald's last completed novel, *Tender Is the Night* (1934). Paradoxically, however, the couple fell prey to the decadence, vulgarity, and boredom that the novelist portrays in his masterpiece about the illusion of the American Dream, *The Great Gatsby*, published in 1925.

Much like the characters in the novel, on the surface the Fitzgeralds seemed to have it all, but the reality was a predictable downward spiral of alcoholism for him and recurrent mental illness for her. Nevertheless, while they were still considered favorably within literary and social circles, it became increasingly evident that their ability to spend Fitzgerald's fortune greatly exceeded his ability to replenish it. As such, ennui eventually led to despair, particularly for Zelda, who had severe mental breakdowns, both in 1930 and 1932, during which she was institutionalized and from which she never recovered. In an effort to find successful treatment for his wife and revive his flagging career, Fitzgerald returned from Europe in 1931 and reestablished himself near the hospital in Baltimore where Zelda would go for treatment. Upon their return, however, Fitzgerald was disappointed to learn that the Great Depression had taken such a toll on the country that the themes of his fiction were now unpopular. The devastating downturn of their lives is portrayed in his posthumously published chronicle entitled *The Crack-Up* (1945), which also details the nervous breakdown that preceded Zelda's death in 1947.

Fitzgerald, destitute and weakened by chronic alcoholism, struggled to earn a living and pay for his wife's medical care by working as a screenwriter in Hollywood. While in California, he met a gossip columnist, Sheilah Graham, with whom he developed a cohabitational relationship for the remainder of his life. Feeling encouraged by the resurgent stability in his life and work, Fitzgerald decided to use his Hollywood experiences as the backdrop for his final novel, *The Last Tycoon* (1941). Fitzgerald was unable to complete this novel because at the relatively young age of forty-four he died of a heart attack. Nevertheless, his longtime friend and advocate, Edmund Wilson, honored his colleague by completing and publishing the author's two unfinished works. In doing so, Wilson revealed the posthumous legacy of the literary icon who both created and was destroyed by the American Dream.

See also Apocalypse: Secular; Apocalyptic Literature; Buchanan, Daisy; Carraway, Nick; Gatsby, Jay; *The Great Gatsby.*

FRANKENSTEIN, OR THE MODERN PROMETHEUS

Frankenstein (1818) is the apocalyptic novel written by Mary Wollstonecraft Shelley. It uses elements of both gothic romance and science fiction to explore the ethical, moral, scientific, and psychological consequences of humanity's attempt to play God. The book was written at the suggestion of Lord Byron, a friend of Mary Shelley and her husband, the renowned romantic poet Percy Bysshe Shelley. During one of their routine literary discussions, Byron challenged each member of his group to create a horror story. Mary Shelley was at first puzzled as to what she would write; her inspiration came to her later in a nightmare. Her imaginative dream, in all of its vivid detail, serves as the core of *Frankenstein, or the Modern Prometheus.*

The novel itself is presented in a simple narrative structure that employs the epistolary form, or letter-writing mode, to develop its characters and to unravel its plot. The story begins when an English explorer named Robert Walton writes letters to his sister describing the adventures he encounters on his voyage. Within one of his letters he reveals his curious observation of a dog-drawn sled speeding across the northern ice that was led by "a being which had the shape of a man, but apparently of gigantic stature" (40). Later that same evening, when a dog, a sled, and a man floated toward his ship, Walton eagerly anticipated meeting the strange creature he had seen earlier in the day. However, much to his consternation, this person was a starving, frozen, dispirited man named Victor Frankenstein.

Although Frankenstein was near death, his rescue from the ice float, as well as the warmth, the food, and the fellowship provided by Walton, the captain of the vessel, revived the ragged wanderer to the point where he was willing to share his bizarre and painful tale. Having come from a respectable lineage from Geneva, his parents, concerned about the youngster's solitude, arranged for the arrival of a playmate who would become Victor's foster sister, Elizabeth. Soon after Elizabeth's arrival, his younger brother, William, was also born. In addition to the comfort of family, he had also been given a number of opportunities that helped him to develop his talent for the natural sciences. After pursuing a rigorous self-study throughout his youth, he eventually entered the University of Ingolstadt where he mastered the natural sciences.

Still hungry for more knowledge, however, Frankenstein's unorthodox research caused him to discover the dangerous secret of creating life. Undaunted by the moral implications and possible consequences of employing such knowledge, Frankenstein succeeded in creating an eight-foot-tall monster by using an amalgam of body parts recovered from medical dissecting rooms and local butcher shops.

It was not until the night of the monster's birth, however, that the scientist began to doubt the wisdom of his experiment. At the moment when the hideous monster awoke him from his restless sleep, Victor Frankenstein realized his horrible mistake, cried out at his creation, and sent the frightened creature fleeing aimlessly into the night. The experience so traumatized Frankenstein that he developed a "brain fever," not unlike a nervous breakdown, during which he was nurtured back to health by his best friend from Geneva, Henry Clerval.

In spite of Clerval's generosity, however, Frankenstein found it impossible to confide the terrible discovery he had made through his application of his unnatural science. The inability to clear his conscience of this terrible burden caused the scientist to become more pallid, reclusive, and eventually maddened by his diabolical deed. This torment was further exacerbated by the news that his younger brother, William, had been strangled while walking in a park. Returning to Geneva to investigate his brother's murder, Victor learned that the family servant, Justine, had been accused of the murder, but after hearing her story, both Victor and his sister, Elizabeth, were convinced that she was innocent of the crime. In spite of their confidence in her, however, circumstantial evidence led the authorities to condemn her for William's murder.

Obviously, the loss of his brother as well as a beloved family servant sent the unstable scientist to collect his thoughts during a solitary hike across the mountains. His solitude was abruptly halted by his sighting of a familiar disfigured creature, who, as he had feared, turned out to be his abominable creation. Frankenstein was forced to face the consequences of his hubris as the monster unraveled his ghastly tale. On the evening when Victor screamed with fright after seeing his creation, the monster fled throughout the countryside in search of solace and shelter. Although he was eager to make a personal connection, each attempt sent people running from him in a panic. As such, he wandered aimlessly, tormented by fear and isolation, until he discovered a hovel located nearby a country cottage.

During his hiding, the monster scavenged for food and observed, with great bitterness, the cruelty of strangers. As such, any shred of gentleness was gradually eliminated from his nature; he acted out his pain by strangling a young boy who was playing in a park. To Victor's horror, he realized that this young boy had been his brother, William. This horror became intensified when the monster threatened to continue killing unless Victor would end his loneliness by making him a mate. Victor, of course, found this request an unimaginable one; nevertheless, when the monster promised that he would stop killing and disappear forever with his mate, the scientist agreed to play God just one more time.

Eagerly awaiting his mate, the monster watched as the apprehensive scientist poised over his next terrible creation. However, just before he was to animate his new creature, he decided to destroy it, realizing the immorality of unleashing a species of monsters who would propagate and prowl the world. As such, when the monster witnessed the scientist's devastating act, he barged into the room, threatened Victor, and then killed Victor's friend and confidant, Henry Clerval, before fleeing once again into the gloom.

Victor was briefly held accountable for Henry's death; the charges, however, were later dropped. In order to find some peace, Victor returned to his home in Geneva and married his childhood sweetheart and foster sister, Elizabeth. On his wedding night, Victor prepared himself in the event of the monster's return; nonetheless, his efforts were for naught when he realized, too late, that his bride had been strangled in their room. Although the frenzied scientist attempted to kill the monster as he fled, the creature again managed to escape, thereby leaving Frankenstein to commit himself to tracking and killing his creation, even if such a quest would take the rest of his life.

It was in the pursuit of this mission that Frankenstein had been discovered by the seafaring vessel whose captain was the audience for his tale. With the release of his terrible story, the life soon drained from the scientist's grief-stricken and exhausted body. And so he died. His death, however, was soon attended by one last appearance of his horrid creature. At the end of the novel, the demonic being confronts Captain Walton to present his point of view before disappearing forever. In his pitiable account of alienation and despair, he acknowledges that although he has "murdered the lovely and the helpless," his wretchedness is still less than that of his thoughtless creator who, for his own sake, would doom a living being to a miserable and unfulfilled existence in which he must wait for death, forever "alone" (188).

See also Apocalypse: Traditional Primitive; Apocalypticism; *Dr. Faustus; Faust*; Gothic Fiction; Prometheus; Romanticism; Science Fiction; Shelley, Mary Wollstonecraft.

FRANKENSTEIN, VICTOR

Victor Frankenstein is the name of the protagonist and tormented scientist in Mary Wollstonecraft Shelley's gothic novel entitled *Frankenstein, or the Modern Prometheus* (1818). As the son of a wealthy couple living in Geneva, Italy, Victor lacked for nothing in regard to material goods. He was, however, an only child, and so his parents, eager to provide him with a companion, agreed to raise the impoverished and abandoned daughter of a Milanese nobleman whose wife had died in childbirth. This beautiful golden-haired child became Victor's lifelong companion, someone he considered as his alone "to protect, love, and cherish" (31). Later, their joy was complete with the birth of a younger brother, William.

In addition to health, wealth, and love, Victor also had an insatiable intelligence in the area of science. Primarily self-taught, Victor's enthusiasm for the laws of electricity emerged when a visitor to their home acquainted the boy with the natural laws that had caused a large tree in their yard to be shattered by lightening. This meeting changed the course of Victor's life; from that point, he put away his former studies and began his quest for knowledge in the areas of mathematics and natural science. His father sent him to study at the University of Ingolstadt. During his subsequent studies and ceaseless experimentation, Frankenstein experienced an epiphany that enabled him to bring an amorphous amalgam of flesh and bone to life.

This unabated pride in his newfound knowledge leads him down the same destructive path as many of his literary counterparts, many of whom are the archetypal gothic "mad scientists," such as Goethe's monomaniacal necromancer, Faust. Although some readers may be willing to forgive both Faust and Frankenstein as little more than misguided dreamers, literary scholars suggest that their egoistic dreams lack a specific "moral content."

> He [Frankenstein] creates without considering the full consequences. His monster remains unnamed, unmated, lacking everything that the maker himself seems to consider important for human life. Not only has the creator overreached himself, he has also demonstrated the moral void in his own plans, even while he considers himself the most moral of men (Karl 1974, 267).

Dr. Frankenstein learns that in attempting to play God, he has committed a demonic act. His creation, also referred to as Frankenstein, inevitably grows bitter and enraged, both by his disturbing appearance and the fear and isolation that comes about as a result of it. Consequently, having been deprived of the basic human need for nurturing, understanding, and love, the scientist's creature becomes a diabolical monster who wreaks havoc upon the countryside in retaliation against his maker. Although the monstrous being promises to do no more harm if the scientist creates a mate for him, Frankenstein, now aware of his folly, destroys the fabricated female just moments before bringing her to life. This act leads to the ultimate revenge—the enraged monster proceeds to murder many of Victor's loved ones.

The loss of his younger brother, William, his friend Henry Clerval, and most significantly, his beloved companion-sister-bride, Elizabeth, causes Frankenstein to realize, much too late (also like Faust), that a life without love and peace is no life at all. He spends the remainder of his wretched days stalking and trying to kill his creation, but dies of exhaustion, feeling damned, both by his un-avenged loved ones as well as by the life that still breathes within his ill-conceived and tormented creature.

See also Apocalypse: Traditional Primitive; Apocalypticism; *Dr. Faustus; Faust; Frankenstein, or the Modern Prometheus;* Goethe, Johann Wolfgang von; Gothic Fiction; Marlowe, Christopher; Prometheus; Romanticism; Science Fiction; Shelley, Mary Wollstonecraft.

FRAZER, SIR JAMES GEORGE

James Frazer (1854–1941) is the widely respected British anthropologist who authored the multivolume masterpiece of worldwide folklore, ritual, and myth entitled *The Golden Bough: A Study in Magic and Religion* (1914). Born in Glasgow, Scotland, and educated at Trinity College in Cambridge, England, Frazer was a reclusive scholar and teacher who spent the majority of his life teaching and researching in the field of anthropology.

He conducted most of the research for this monumental treatise while at home. He was able to gather significant data by mailing questionnaires to missionaries who were working among primitive cultures. Frazer's theory about human psychic belief focuses on three main evolutionary phases through which humanity has attempted to impose order on the natural world.

The first phase involves the use of magic, or supernatural rituals, within primitive societies to control the random and powerful forces of nature. He identifies countless examples of ancient myths that personify and even deify nature's basic elements, such as fire, water, air, and earth, in a futile attempt to impose control over them. According to Frazer, the influence of the supernatural was translated into the application of religion as a means of making sense of a chaotic world. Frazer notes that religion has slowly been supplanted by science and technology as the means through which humanity attempts to control the environment. The portrait of a dauntless human spirit and its vivid forms of expression make *The Golden Bough* an indispensable sociological, anthropological, and literary reference work.

See also Allegory; Archetype; *The Golden Bough: A Study in Magic and Religion;* Jung, Carl Gustav; Myth; Symbol.

FREUD, SIGMUND

Sigmund Freud (1856–1939) was the Austrian neurologist, physician, and psychiatrist who is recognized as the founder of psychoanalysis. Born on May 6, 1856, Freud was of middle-class Jewish descent. His family moved from Moravia, when Freud was three years old, to Vienna, where he later received training as a medical doctor at the University of Vienna. Although Freud never actually practiced internal medicine, his research reflects an early fascination with neuropathology and hypnotherapy. Although he received great satisfaction and recognition for his foundational work in neuron theory, his work in the area of hypnotism and its use as treatment for hysteria were less fulfilling.

During his work in hypnotism, Freud began to notice shared patterns and symbols in his patients' dreams. Such observations led him to develop a theory of free association, which became the hallmark of his psychoanalytical approach. Through his study of dreams, Freud claimed that individuals often repress their subconscious urges and emotions—many of which are of an aggressive or sexual nature. Convinced that these urges need expression, at least in some form, he concluded that recurrent repression of strong emotions caused neurotic behaviors.

According to Freud's theory, the human psyche consists of three powerful forces that govern its actions. The first life force, which Freud identified as the id, represents the instinctual drives of the human animal. Although the id is responsible for humanity's darker urges, it represents the powerful unconscious, albeit uncontrollable, drives that lead people toward gratification of such impulses. Freud identified the second facet of the psychic landscape as the ego, or the internal force that regulates impulses and helps the individual to respond appropriately to the demands of society. The ego is often referred to as the basis of an individual's concept of self. Freud identified a third level of psychological management, a governing entity he referred to as the superego, or the idealistic moral conscience that seeks to suppress the disruptive intrusion of the id and to keep the ego within the norms of acceptable social and moral behavior. These findings were first published in his landmark work entitled *The Interpretation of*

Dreams (1900) and were later expanded in his most popular book, *The Psychopathology of Everyday Life* (1904).

In the subsequent years following his earliest works, Freud's research began to lean toward an interest in the sexual impulses of children. At this point, a considerable body of detractors began to denounce his efforts, particularly those findings related to the Oedipus and Electra complexes in which Freud suggests that children have a natural sexual attraction for the parent of the opposite sex and an unconscious desire to eliminate the rival parent of the same sex. His studies in the area of eros, i.e., the libido or "life force," in opposition with thanatos, or the force known as the "death wish," served as fertile ground for what is still an ongoing psychological debate.

As a result of his research in these controversial areas, several of his earlier followers, such as Alfred Adler and Carl Jung, rejected Freud's later work. Nevertheless, while many of his earlier theories have since been discredited or at least viewed with greater skepticism, the fact is that the body of his work provided the medical community with a foundation for future work in the field of psychoanalysis.

In addition, aspects of his research led others, outside of the medical field, to pursue various experiments in the area of artistic expression. One of the arts most greatly influenced by his findings is that of literature. Specifically, his work is directly reflected in the writings of many prominent Western authors including D. H. Lawrence, Thomas Mann, and James Joyce, as well as the major apocalyptic writings of fellow psychiatrist and twentieth-century novelist Walker Percy.

Freud's work was disrupted by two events. He was diagnosed with cancer in his upper jaw, which led to a succession of operations and periods of painful nonproductivity. Later, Nazi persecution led to the confiscation of his work in 1938. Freud's longtime devotee and fellow writer Ernest Jones encouraged him to escape further persecution by moving to England, which he did in June of 1938. Unfortunately, however, this move did not prevent the final invasion that ultimately affected his life: the virulent recurrence of his cancer. In Freud's final days he was surrounded by visitors and friends, and he continued his writing up to just one month prior to his death on September 23, 1939.

See also Apocalypse: Traditional Judeo-Christian; *Love in the Ruins: The Adventures of a Bad Catholic at a Time Near the End of the World;* More, Dr. Tom; Smith, Father Rinaldo; *The Thanatos Syndrome.*

FUENTES, CARLOS

Carlos Fuentes (1928–) is the Mexican novelist, playwright, and international diplomat whose vivid and experimental style has earned him a worldwide reputation as a significant author. His work examines the "problems of Mexican identity—what it mean[s] to be Mexican—in an international context" (Faris 1983, 1). He became interested in the international perspective of his native country after extensive travel during his youth. As a son of a diplomat, Fuentes spent much of his childhood traveling abroad and lived in Switzerland, Argentina, Chile, and the United States. Moreover, his exposure to various educational systems made him sensitive to the political motivations intrinsic to this branch of bureaucracy, which caused him to become suspicious of the motives behind several of the military-based schools. For a time, Fuentes pursued an independent course of study by reading many of the world's so-called great books as well as becoming a voracious consumer of modern cinema. Among Fuentes's most significant early literary influences were such writers as Cervantes and Dante. Fuentes was also fascinated by the surrealistic art of the Spanish filmmaker Luis Bunuel.

Consequently, this early exposure to the world's myths, religions, literary classics, and experimental cinematic techniques caused the artist to claim writing as his vocation at an unusually young age. After his independent studies, he felt secure enough to continue his public education and graduated from a high school in Mexico City. Convinced that he would follow in his father's footsteps as a diplomat, Fuentes attended both the National University as well as the Geneva Institute for International Studies from 1950 to 1952. After his return to Mexico, he worked in a variety of editorial and administrative positions at the country's National University; he also briefly served as head of the Department of Cultural Relations at the Ministry of Foreign Affairs.

Although international diplomacy was his primary focus during these early years, Fuentes simultaneously immersed himself in literature, particularly French literature and criticism. Through these readings, he began to examine the influence of literature through a European perspective, which helped him to understand the importance of presenting one's own cultural heritage to the world. As such, he established and edited a number of periodicals, one of which included the *Mexican Review of Literature (Revista Mexicana de literatura)* from 1954 to 1958. Fuentes also published several stories within a 1954 collection of work entitled *The Masked Days* or *Los dias enmascarados,* which illustrated his early fascination with the combined elements of both fantasy and literary realism; this combination was the hallmark of his later works. The first work to bring him to national attention, however, was his 1958 novel entitled *Where the Air Is Clear,* a work in which he chided his country for its corruption.

Fuentes continued this theme, albeit more maturely and forgivingly, in his subsequent novel entitled *The Good Conscience (Las buenas conciencias),* which was published in 1959. His next novel, entitled *Aura,* published in 1962, featured a controlled fusion of reality and fantasy that would finally come to full fruition in his most popular work to date, *The Death of Artemio Cruz* (1962), a sweeping novel that finally established Fuentes as a major international writer. In two of his following works, *A Change of Skin* (1967) and *The New Hispano-American Novel* (1969), Fuentes examined the myths of Mexico. The novel that most effectively displays Fuentes's vast knowledge of myth, religion, history, philosophy, psychology, and archetypal symbolism is his apocalyptic magnum opus, appropriately titled *Terra Nostra,* literally translated as "our world," which was published in 1975. Within this work, Fuentes applies techniques he had admired in the works of James Joyce, William Faulkner, T. S. Eliot, Ezra Pound, and D. H. Lawrence. Guided by their experimental work, Fuentes learned to fuse historical, realistic, and mythical images of Mexican culture in an attempt to help his readers prepare for a better future by examining the country's errors, which had stultified its cultural and political development.

During his work on *Terra Nostra,* Fuentes became fascinated by the Jungian concept of the double, the shadow, the mask, mirror images, and the duality of human nature as illustrated in several of his later novels, including *The Hydra Head* (1978), *Distant Relations* (1980), *The Old Gringo* (1985), and *Christopher Unborn* (1987). His most recent publication, which was simultaneously published both in English and Spanish in 1992, is a book-length essay entitled *The Buried Mirror.* Perhaps the most precise explanation of Fuentes's art was made by fellow author and a longtime friend of Fuentes, Octavio Paz. In a speech honoring Fuentes, Paz summarized the substance of Fuentes's fiction by its focus on the extremes of "eroticism and politics" as well as its fascination with "desire and power, love and revolution" (qtd. in Faris 14).

See also Apocalypse: Traditional Judeo-Christian; Apocalypse: Traditional Primitive; Apocalypticism; Archetype; Symbol; *Terra Nostra.*

GARCÍA MÁRQUEZ, GABRIEL

Gabriel García Márquez (1928–), winner of the Nobel Prize in Literature in 1982, is the Colombian author whose seminal apocalyptic work, *One Hundred Years of Solitude* (1967), brought him to the attention of international audiences and established him as a leader within the Latin-American literary movement known as "magical realism."

García Márquez was born on Colombia's Caribbean coast. He was influenced by the fantastic tales told to him by his grandmother and inspired by the triumphs of his country's military heroes as related to him by his grandfather. He received his formal education in a Jesuit high school, where he graduated in 1946, and thereafter he studied both law and journalism, which led to his first job as a journalist beginning in 1948. In addition to being a traveling correspondent whose travels took him throughout Latin America as well as throughout Europe, he also worked as a screenwriter and publicist before settling in Mexico in the 1970s.

While García Márquez had written several major publications during these years, it was not until 1968, during his stay in Mexico, that he wrote his most critically acclaimed novel, *One Hundred Years of Solitude.* Within this work, he shows the influence of the American novelist William Faulkner, particularly his apocalyptic multigenerational sagas *As I Lay Dying* and *Absalom, Absalom!*, in the account of the Buendia family who founds the enchanting and terrifying village of Macondo.

While *One Hundred Years of Solitude* remains his best-known work, García Márquez continued within the fictional genre with the publication of *The Autumn of the Patriarch* (1975), *Chronicle of a Death Foretold* (1981), and his next most popular work, *Love in the Time of Cholera* (1985). He continued this narrative form in his subsequent novel, *The General in His Labyrinth* (1989), and has since produced a collection of twelve short stories published in Spanish in 1992 entitled *Doce cuentos peregrinos.*

See also *Absalom, Absalom!;* Allegory; Apocalypse: Traditional Primitive; Archetype; *As I Lay Dying;* Myth; *One Hundred Years of Solitude;* Symbol; *Terra Nostra.*

Gabriel García Márquez in Bogotá, Colombia, in 1982

GATSBY, JAY

Jay Gatsby is the romantic idealist and self-made millionaire who is the protagonist of F. Scott Fitzgerald's apocalyptic novel, *The Great Gatsby* (1925). Gatsby, born James Gatz, the son of a poor Midwestern family, dreamed that he would someday achieve a level of greatness in his life. Even as a child, he kept scrupulous records of his goals and accomplishments, an early discipline that motivated him in later years.

Although Gatsby was something of a drifter during his early years, he found a new identity as a soldier in World War I. As a dashingly handsome and confident young man in uniform, he was understandably attractive to a young woman, named Daisy Buchanan, who was a wealthy Southern belle. He truly fell in love with this wistful and delicate creature. But Daisy was only interested in a life of luxury and status. Gatsby, a poor soldier, could not provide for her. In spite of her deep feelings for him, Daisy rejected her true love and instead married a crass but wealthy former football hero, Tom Buchanan. Devastated by the loss of his "golden girl," Gatsby thereafter dedicated his life to winning her away from Tom.

His earlier idealism and diligence, however, slowly diminish as he feels the passage of time. As such, he becomes involved with a suspicious racketeer who shows him the way to financial success by exploiting the rules of society. This behavior helps the egoistic young man to excel in his efforts, particularly during a time in which Prohibition provided a profitable return for his valuable services. In spite of his underworld connections, however, in regard to Daisy, his idealism remains untouched. Consequently, as soon as he is able to do so, Gatsby exhibits the behaviors of the newly rich by purchasing an extravagant mansion in West Egg, Long Island, so that he can be close to his beloved Daisy, who lives in East Egg. His residence, however, is more of a showplace than a home, and he has specifically furnished it to impress and thereby win Daisy as his wife. His basic unfamiliarity with matters of taste are found questionable:

> [His home] was a colossal affair by any standard—it was a factual imitation of some Hotel de Ville in Normandy, with a tower on one side, spanking new under a thin beard of raw ivy, and a marble swimming pool, and more than forty acres of lawn and garden. It was Gatsby's mansion (Fitzgerald 5).

As one literary critic suggests, Gatsby, in his effort to achieve his goal, is unaware that he "*sees* only his dreams, his imaginative recreation of reality, relegating alien reality to the status of illusion and elevating dream to the reality that must displace illusion" (Robinson 84).

This is certainly true in regard to the elaborate plans he makes to convince his neighbor, and Daisy's cousin, Nick, to arrange a reunion between himself and his former lover. During this reunion, Gatsby sees the imminent fulfillment of his dreams, while Daisy sees only a temporary escape from her unhappy marriage. She needs Gatsby only in that he can make her feel like a carefree ingenue again. It is his blind obsession with her that causes him to risk everything for the chance of possessing her forever. And the risks he takes are great. First, he compromises his own integrity and defiles Daisy's marital vows in their impulsive sexual reunion. Next, believing that it is only a matter of time before she leaves her husband, Gatsby closes down his palatial estate, once the site of the island's most extravagant parties, in order to wait quietly until Daisy decides to visit him. Gatsby becomes impatient and disrespectful to her husband, thereby initiating a heated confrontation. Gatsby himself does not realize that Daisy does not wish to be inconvenienced by the unpleasantness of their circumstances. Furthermore, she does not want to be forced into making a choice.

After his altercation with Tom, Daisy wishes to escape the chaotic conditions she has created in her life, and as such, she drives away from the scene to flee her disturbing reality. However, because she is both distraught and an inexperienced driver, Daisy accidentally runs over a woman who approaches the car.

The woman is none other than her husband's mistress, Myrtle Wilson, who is killed upon impact.

While these events, under normal circumstances, should draw the lovers together, they instead pull them apart. Gatsby fails to realize that Daisy has deliberately distanced herself from him. Moreover, not only is she willing to have him take the blame for the accident, since it was his car, but Gatsby himself is also willing to sacrifice himself in the hopes of attaining his ultimate goal.

His efforts, however, are futile. As he waits alone in the night and watches her through windows, he doesn't understand that Daisy will never return to him. Gatsby is murdered, as a result of the accident, never knowing that his beloved would choose to abandon him in death as she had already done in life. As such, like the archetypal apocalyptic hero, Gatsby is judged harshly for his sins. Nevertheless, the ceaseless hope in his heart reflects a restorative innocence that will forever shape the future of his friend, and the narrator of the story, Nick Carraway.

See also Apocalypse: Secular; Apocalyptic Literature; Buchanan, Daisy; Carraway, Nick; *The Great Gatsby.*

GHOST HORSE, SITKO

Ghost Horse is the name of the Native American protagonist of Jamake Highwater's apocalyptic novel entitled *Kill Hole* (1992), a work that also contains autobiographical elements.

Essentially, Sitko is a Native American man whose life has been derailed by a series of tragedies. He is ill equipped to cope with them because of his lack of personal identity. He admits throughout the novel that he does not know much about his past. What he does know, however, is that he is out of touch with the strength that his Native American culture could provide for him. He is one of the many disenfranchised and relatively rootless people who function well enough to exist amidst the chaos of the modern world but who lack the personal freedom necessary to help them live meaningful lives. It is not until Sitko is forced to face death squarely and without fear that he is able to live as a free man in his world.

The beginning of Sitko's world is marred from the outset. According to a litany that he repeats several times throughout the novel, Sitko is the grandson of Amana, a strong Native American woman, and her beloved late spouse, Far Away Son. Apparently, sometime after her husband's death, Amana had a sexual encounter with a stranger, which lead to the birth of a daughter of mixed Anglo and Indian blood named Jemina Bonneville. Jemina eventually became pregnant by her handsome albeit hapless lover, Jamie Ghost Horse, who was an alcoholic aerialist in a circus, and together they bore two sons, Sitko and his older brother, Reno. After their father abandoned the family, Jemina was unable to raise the children herself and placed them in an orphanage; however, when she married an established Jewish man, named Alexander Milas-Miller, she urged the boys to live with them in their indisputably white, middle-class environment.

The loss of both his father and his culture caused Reno, the oldest son, to become rebellious and relentlessly enraged. Sitko reluctantly accepted the circumstances and even took the name Seymour or Sy Miller, thereby demonstrating the suppression of his cultural heritage. Sitko later rediscovered something of his true self in the world of art. All of his repressed frustrations and observations of the modern world flowed from his heart, through his paints, and onto his canvas. His artistic temperament, as well as the progressive environment in which he lived, led him to become involved in a loving homosexual relationship with Eric, a beautiful black man and artist who was also of mixed blood. Together they shared their lives in an artist's loft; Sy (Sitko) painted, Eric wrote, and although neither had experienced any level of financial success, they considered themselves fortunate and happy.

Their fortunes changed, however, when Sy reasserted his Native American identity by presenting his paintings as those of Sitko Ghost Horse. His work suddenly became the object of critical acclaim. While Sitko was pleased with the popular response to his work, he was confused as to why it had become so well received and further puzzled by Eric's increasingly withdrawn demeanor. But just as he was attaining professional success, Sitko's world began to crumble around him. Eric became sullen and nonproductive. A conservative element in society launched a virulent attack on Sitko's sexually oriented paintings, which they condemned as perverse, and the fear that arose from these threats forced the owner of the studio where his paintings were displayed to abort his exhibit.

Fear also became the overriding emotion in Sitko's personal life as well. First, the growing critical speculation that Sitko was an Indian impostor, really a Jewish painter formerly named Seymour Miller, began to cause him to question his own cultural identity. The thought that Sitko might actually be a fraud subsequently caused all of his former supporters to shun him in disgust. This sense of growing alienation was even further compounded by a new source of fear: a virulent wasting disease (unidentified in the text, but most certainly AIDS) that had begun to take the lives of his former colleagues, his friends, and most devastatingly, his lover, Eric.

Both literally and figuratively, it is at this moment that his primitive self and his "civilized" self collide. Sitko is forced to evaluate his life even as he stands at the abyss of death. In his night of confusion, he stumbles across an imperceivable barrier designed to protect the children of an Indian village during a ritual known as the Night of the Washing of the Hair. Sitko is arrested and taken prisoner. Further, because he is believed to be an evil spirit whose presence will certainly contaminate the village children, he is hated and treated poorly.

Although he is cruelly interrogated, publicly ridiculed, and thrown into a cell, he soon meets the person who will restore him both physically and spiritually. The name of this person is Patu; although she identifies herself as a "strong woman" of the tribe, Sitko learns that she has miniature male genitalia. The androgynous imagery shared by both Patu and Sitko, as well as the ironic juxtaposition of their position in society, serves as the central bond through which the two become emotionally linked. On one level, he is a criminal, but he is also suffering, and as a "strong woman" of her tribe it is her job to care for him, at least until he is well enough to be sentenced to death. On another level, however, Patu possesses the instinctive knowledge and intrinsic strength of a person whose life has been fortified by a strong cultural identity.

During the time they spend together, they learn much from one another. Through Sitko's paintings and tales of love and loss, Patu learns to overcome her primitive superstitions and to appreciate the universal impact of art. Patu, in turn, teaches Sitko that in order to live fully, in whatever time is allotted on this earth, an individual must first understand and appreciate his or her own ancestral heritage. Then, the individual must choose to use those cultural strengths to help the whole of humanity to live more fully by releasing the spirit from the crippling bondage that is most often caused by irrational fear.

See also Apocalypse: Traditional Primitive; Apocalypticism; Delito; Highwater, Jamake; Patu.

GILES GOAT-BOY; OR, THE REVISED NEW SYLLABUS

Giles Goat-Boy (1966) is the allegorical satire written by John Barth in which he uses the setting of a university as a symbol for the modern world. Within this world, Barth creates a protagonist who is an amalgam of the mythological Fisher King, the sacrificial Christ-figure, and the disillusioned would-be savior of T. S. Eliot's "wasteland" of the modern world.

In spite of the protagonist's initial enthusiastic quest for truth about his mysterious origins, Billy Bockfuss, a.k.a. George Giles, the goat-boy, learns, through his ritual passage from adolescence to maturity, that "departure," "initiation," and "return" are necessary if a hero wishes to emerge from an individual quest with the truth about his life and its purpose on this earth (Olderman 76). Nevertheless, while such a simplistic thematic overview can suffice for a general understanding of the work, readers must grapple with the voluminous and frequently unwieldy text that describes Giles's mysterious birth in the belly of the giant WESCAC (West Campus Automatic Computer), which controls the universe of New Tammany College, if they wish to participate in and learn from both the comic and tragic entanglements that Giles encounters along the way.

While some readers and literary critics eagerly awaited the revelation of this long-promised treatise on independent action, and as such, were up to the challenge of wading through the miasma of words, others were unconvinced by the hype preceding its publication and were, therefore, less than pleased with its cumbersome construct (Morrell 1976, 68–69). In fact, one critic of the novel, Raymond Olderman, sums up the latter position by saying that "reading it is like being imprisoned." However, he encourages readers to enter Giles's world and to accept the central metaphor of University as Waste Land, because they, through Giles's experiences, will learn that

> man's educated consciousness in conspiracy with his instinctual death wish has left him inert, unable to act, unable to accept mythology and its cycles, unable to achieve peace through the single moment's experience of unity, and unable to do even what George does—seek his own redemption instead of merely learning about it (Olderman, 1972, 85).

And while readers have been given this ominous warning before, particularly in the works of such modernist writers as T. S. Eliot in the form of his poem *The*

Waste Land, Barth's work is worthy of the time it takes to explore its truths because its "superb command of literary and linguistic tradition" combined with its "originality of structure" has deemed it worthy of its well-deserved reputation for literary greatness (Morrell 69).

See also Allegory; Apocalypse: Secular; Archetype; Barth, John; Eliot, T. S.; The Fisher King; Symbol; *The Waste Land.*

GLORIANA

Also known as Tanaquill, Gloriana is the embodiment of the reigning queen of Faeryland in Sir Edmund Spenser's long romantic epic *The Faerie Queene* (c. 1590–1609). Her character, whose name means "glorious one," is clearly based upon the personage of Queen Elizabeth I, and the work is dedicated to the monarch. As such, Spenser portrayed the queen as the most wise, virtuous, and regal of all the characters presented in the six extant books included in the work. Moreover, throughout the poem, Gloriana is the object of worship and service for each of the virtuous knights, including a young knight and future king named Arthur, who willingly face incalculable odds in order to do honor to the throne.

See also Allegory; Apocalypse: Traditional Judeo-Christian; Arthur, King; *The Faerie Queene;* Revelation, Book of; Spenser, Edmund; Una.

GLOUCESTER (EARL OF)

Gloucester is the faithful old friend of King Lear in Shakespeare's apocalyptic drama. In the play, Gloucester and his two sons, Edgar (the good son) and Edmund (the evil son), provide a parallel plot that mirrors, in many ways, the events that happen to the restless Lear, a noble king of pre-Christian Britain, and his three daughters, Goneril, Regan, and Cordelia. Gloucester, like Lear, possesses personality traits that make him vulnerable to his evil son. He is affable and approachable. He also has a tendency to make impulsive decisions, and to a greater extent than Lear, he is known for pursuing personal pleasure. Like Lear, Gloucester is superstitious; however, the earl places even more significance than does the king on disturbing cosmic signs that seem to portend the unpredictable behavior of the people around him.

Gloucester, however, is only a shadow of Lear in that he is much weaker in will than the monarch. For example, when his evil daughters force the king to wander into a raging storm, the king also rages over the injustices done to him. Gloucester, conversely, whimpers rather than rages, tends toward depression rather than aggression, and when he is blinded by Lear's son-in-law Cornwall and his evil wife, Regan, Gloucester prefers suicide to living a life with limitations. In fact, he wanders blindly toward what he believes are the cliffs of Dover with full intention of ending his life in a desperate plunge. However, his loving son, Edgar, who is in disguise and otherwise undetectable to his father, convinces him that he has survived his jump and thereby encourages the pitiable old man to go on with his life.

Through the example of Lear's devastating loss of his beloved daughter, Cordelia, and through the generous and loving devotion of his son, Edgar, Gloucester learns valuable life lessons. These lessons come late in life to Gloucester. Nevertheless, it is only through his blindness that he, like Lear, is able to see past his own folly and the deception of appearances in order to appreciate his lot in life.

See also Apocalypse: Traditional Primitive; Cordelia; Great Chain of Being; *King Lear;* Lear, King; Regan.

GO TELL IT ON THE MOUNTAIN

Go Tell It on the Mountain (1953) is a powerful novel by James Baldwin about the African-American experience in 1930s Harlem. In many ways, the novel reflects the childhood experiences of the author himself, and particularly those surrounding his three-year ministry as a storefront preacher. The novel, which contains Christian apocalyptic symbolism throughout, draws heavily on biblical references to tell the story of John Grimes, an adolescent who must make a decision between his attachment to the pleasures of the world and the eternal promises offered to the saints in heaven. According to John R. May, these facts are made clear at the outset of the novel, which

> begins on "the seventh day," the last day of the week and suggestive as well of the last age of the world, and ends on the morning of the eighth—the first day of the new creation, the day of ultimate salvation. It is the fourteenth birthday of John Grimes and the day of his first (and possibly last) experience with salvation (May 1972, 156).

John's "legal" father, Gabriel Grimes, is the full-time caretaker, part-time hellfire and brimstone preacher of the Temple of Fire Baptized in Harlem. A host of other friends and family members are deeply involved in the church. Even with all this support, John still struggles with the decision to become "saved" upon reaching the age of accountability. In the first part of the novel, a series of graphic flashbacks explain why John is in a state of perpetual spiritual and emotional conflict. He is the illegitimate son of Elizabeth, Gabriel's second wife, who had had her son by her lover, Richard, long since dead. Unknown to Elizabeth, her self-righteous husband has also had a sordid past, filled with sins of the flesh, that includes the cruel abandonment of a lover who became pregnant and bore him an illegitimate son. Although Gabriel never had anything to do with the raising of this son, he was devastated when the boy, who apparently had inherited his father's wild ways, eventually died. The preacher's first wife, Deborah, who was a long-suffering victim of childhood rape and marital infidelity, worshiped her husband until the day she died. It was following the deaths of his illegitimate son and Deborah, however, that Gabriel was introduced to Elizabeth, his new wife, by his outspoken and hedonistic sister, Florence. In some ways, Gabriel believed that by marrying a sinner like Elizabeth and raising her bastard son, he would be able to atone for the devastation caused by the sins of his youth.

During their marriage, however, Elizabeth bears Gabriel another son, whom he names Royal, the same name that had been given to his dead illegitimate son. In Royal lies all of his hope. Ironically, however, Royal, too, seems to have inherited his father's temperment and deliberately turns from both his father and the church. The remainder of the novel revolves around the past details of the principal players. The story chronicles the depths of depravity to which Gabriel sinks throughout his life. It reveals the self-righteous cruelty with which he rules his household, and it further explains the fervor with which he searches for assurance of spiritual restoration before his death. Although he hopes that Royal will inherit the spirit of God, it is the ignored and abused John who actually "becomes saved" from his sins and emerges from the hell of his young life with the ingenuous hopes for a redeemed adulthood.

It can only be assumed, however, based on Baldwin's experiences and the subtleties of the narrative, that John Grimes's euphoric condition will be short-lived. In the final scenes of the novel, in which John views the Harlem streets blinded by the light of his dramatic conversion experience, the young man becomes disillusioned with the limitations of a culturally imposed faith. As May summarizes Baldwin's message,

> . . . the real judgment of the novel is not of John's adolescent sins but of white Christianity that has used faith in the crucified Jesus as a way of keeping the black man content with his lot. The image of the heavenly city, already come to earth in the morning streets of Harlem, is the ultimate of ironies. The belief in the new life of eternity—for the black man in America, at least—is self-defeating. There is no life in continued oppression (161).

See also Apocalypse: Anti-Christian; Baldwin, James; Harlem Renaissance; Naturalism.

GOD

God is usually referred to as the supreme, perfect, infallible, all-knowing, omnipotent creator and ruler of the universe. Whether this being is the sole object of worship within a belief system (monotheism), the sole object of worship in spite of an awareness of other gods (henotheism), or one of many supernatural and powerful beings within a system of belief, who influence the forces of the universe (polytheism), references to God (or gods) embody the infinite mind, spirit, and soul, as well as the principles of life, truth, justice, and love (*American Heritage Dictionary* 565).

While the various alternative belief systems involve limitless and sometimes impenetrable complexities, most religions revolve around a belief in one or more gods in which three primary characteristics of the deity usually emerge: power, mercy, and incomprehensibility. This is particularly true in regard to the ancient mythological concepts of God and those originating from the more primitive animistic cultures or societies. In most cases, however, a unity of belief exists in regard to the worship of at least one supreme supernatural power, or a "high God," to whom all must ultimately answer in the execution of their duties.

Ancient Concepts of God

These concepts have their roots in humanity's need to make order out of an otherwise chaotic universe. While early Greek and Roman deities were identified

English nineteenth-century artist William Blake created a vision of the throned Christian God judging Adam.

with the properties of natural elements or with powerful universal forces, such mythologies, like those of Hesiod and Homer, later evolved into the more rationalized concept of God that was presented in the works of Plato and Aristotle.

Eastern Concepts of God

Because of the diversity of the various Eastern cultures, as well as the myriad forms of ritual and worship handed down through history, most Eastern religions are populated with many gods, some of which are benevolent while others are hostile. In the ancient Indian religions, however, the gods or deities are mystical constructs usually revolving around such forces of nature as rain, fire, wind, sky, and storms. In the Hindu belief system, Brahma, or the creator god, is usually recognized along with its other triadic counterparts: Vishnu, the preserver god, and Shiva, the destroyer.

In Buddhism there is an emphasis on self-abnegation or asceticism. The goal is enlightenment; the path of life is made easier by Dharma, or the way of the righteous, and it is only through discipline and the guidance of bodhisattvas, or enlightened ones, that a human can hope to achieve Nirvana, or the state of ultimate peace.

In Chinese concepts of god, beliefs revolve around behaviors rather than specific deities. For instance, Confucius presented a course of action based upon ethical behavior, humanistic wisdom, and political allegiance. Taoism, China's second major religious influence based on the teachings of Lao Tzu, is less of a formal religion and more of a revival consisting of a primitive amalgam of magic, animism, and polytheism.

Western Concepts of God

Much of what is known about the development of Western religions has come about as a result of the Persian practice of Zoroastrianism and its combination with the strongly demonstrated faith of ancient Israel. While the sixth century B.C. marks the actual beginning of the recognition of a monotheistic God who was the supreme creator of the universe, the practices and doctrines related to this omnipotent deity were split between three primary sects: Judaism, Christianity, and Islam.

According to Judaism, God or Jehovah made a covenant with his chosen people through which he led them out of captivity in Egypt into the Promised Land. The Old Testament is filled with historical and prophetic accounts pertaining to the election of this group and promising their return to their rightful homeland after they first suffer for their disobedience against God's laws. The religion of Islam, on the other hand, borrowed liberally from both the Judaic and the Christian systems of belief. In Islam, God or Allah related his teachings to Muhammad, known as the greatest prophet. It is through adherence to these teachings that the Muslims hope to attain their opulent otherworldly rewards.

Christianity became firmly established among the Western religions following the birth of Jesus of Nazareth, otherwise known as Jesus Christ, the Messiah, or the second person in the divine trinity; i.e., God the Father (Abba), God the Son (Christ), and God the Holy Spirit. The power of Christianity was reinforced by the persecution and crucifixion of Christ who died, according to prophecy, for the atonement of humanity's sins. As such, both the witnesses of the event, and, more importantly, the disciples of his ministry, recounted the miraculous events and the profound teachings of Jesus in the New Testament. As a result of such scriptures, as well as the historical reinforcement of clerical teachings, Christianity was later redefined by Martin Luther, and later by John Calvin, who posited that because God the Father was ultimately unknowable, only through repentance, and the belief in Jesus Christ, designated as Lord and Savior, can humanity hope to enter the kingdom of heaven for all eternity.

While detailed coverage of the various contemporary discussions regarding both the existence and nature of God is beyond the scope of this reference work, more specific information regarding the end times or the Last Judgment for believers of the aforementioned religions can be found in the cross-references that follow.

See also Allegory; Apocalypse: Buddhist; Apocalypse: Hindu; Apocalypse: Persian; Apocalypse: Secular; Apocalypse: Traditional Judeo-Christian; Apocalypse: Traditional Primitive; Daniel, Book of; Revelation, Book of.

GOETHE, JOHANN WOLFGANG VON

Goethe (1749–1832) is considered by many to be one of the greatest contributors to world literature as well as Germany's most significant poet. Because of his keen intellect and wide diversity of activities, particularly in the areas of science and politics, Goethe's body of work, consisting of novels, plays, and poetry, reflects his belief that humanity is both related to and responsible for its actions as part of an organic, natural, and holistic universe.

His universal perspective was the result of his rigorous and multifaceted education. Under the strict supervision of his barrister father, Johann Caspar Goethe, and his artist mother, Catharina Elisabeth Textor Goethe, his studies were an amalgam of drawing, music, philosophy, science, theater, and literature.

At age sixteen, Goethe was sent to the University of Leipzig to study law. In spite of his best intentions, the garrulous and attractive young man became easily distracted from his legal studies in the urban collegiate environment, and as such, he began to lean toward other interests, including medicine, music, literature, and socializing. His revelry was interrupted by an unexpected illness that caused him to return to his home for appropriate care.

Upon his return, he became absorbed in the Pietist movement, a German Lutheran reform sect that introduced him to mystical alchemy. Although he continued to nurture this interest, one that would play a prominent role in his most famous work, he eventually recovered from his illness, returned to school, and completed his law degree at Strasbourg in 1771. From 1771 through 1775, Goethe divided his time between the duty of practicing law and his two loves: women and writing. While he seemed to have remarkable success in each of these areas, he soon yearned to break from his past, and so he moved from Frankfurt to the city of Weimar. This move was a propitious one in that it was there where he met the older wife of a member of Germany's ducal court, Charlotte von Stein, who served as his literary inspiration over the next years.

During those years, however, his emotional and avocational interests caused a significant lag in the progress of his works. But by the mid-1780s, his waning adoration for the increasingly possessive Stein aligned with drastic political changes that affected his employment; therefore, in 1786, he decided to move to Italy where, for a period of two years, he renewed his commitment to classical art and completed several previously neglected projects, including the two-volume work *Italian Journey,* published in 1816, *Iphigenia in Tauris,* published in 1795, and the play entitled, *Torquato Tasso,* which he finished in 1789.

Following this prolific period, Goethe returned to Weimar where he soon became involved with an amiable and uncomplicated woman, Christiane Vulpius. Their relationship became scandalous, however, upon the birth of a son in August of 1789, which occurred outside the bonds of marriage. This event caused the couple to suffer a six-year period of social separation until their eventual marriage in 1806. In spite of this sense of isolation, it was also during this time, 1794, that Goethe initiated a close association with the respected dramatist, writer, and historian Friedrich Schiller, thereby forging a collaborative philo-

German romantic poet Johann Wolfgang von Goethe, as portrayed by Johann Heinrich Wilhelm Tischbein in *Goethe in the Country*

sophical and artistic form known as Weimar Classicism. As a result of Schiller's encouragement, Goethe was able to complete what is still considered the world's greatest *bildungsroman,* or novel of education, entitled *Wilhelm Meister's Apprenticeship,* as well as his literary masterpiece, *Faust: Part I.*

The death of Schiller in 1805 had a profound personal effect on Goethe; nevertheless, Schiller's generous legacy to Goethe, a legion of accomplished artists and intellectuals, secured the author's literary success that continued for the following two decades. Although the loss of his inspirational friend and mentor would never be assuaged, Goethe continued to pursue his craft in later works, including revisions of *William Meister's Travels* as well as the final version of *Faust: Part II,* which he completed in August of 1831, but requested that it not be published until after his death. On March 22 of the following year, 1832, death brought a close to Goethe's rich and productive life. Out of respect for his heritage, his artistic accomplishments, and his faithful service to his country, Goethe was ultimately honored with a state funeral after which he was entombed, next to his beloved colleague, Friedrich Schiller, in the mausoleum of the ducal family.

See also Apocalypse: Traditional Judeo-Christian; *Dr. Faustus; Faust; Love in the Ruins: The Adventures of a Bad Catholic at a Time Near the End of the World;* Mephistophiles; More, Dr. Tom; Satan; Science Fiction; *The Thanatos Syndrome.*

GOG AND MAGOG

Gog and Magog, according to several biblical prophesies of the last days of the world, describe the powerful armies that will descend upon the people of Israel and will ultimately be confronted and annihilated by the mighty apocalyptic force of God. Referred to in chapters 38 and 39 of Ezekiel, Gog, in general, refers to the land of Magog (38:2), represented by the descendents of Noah's son, Japheth (Genesis 10:2), and specifically referred to in the text as the "chief prince of Meshech and Tubal" (38:3), which implies the center of the region where Japheth's descendents lived. While the aforementioned information is provided as the only explanation within the scriptural text, some scholars have identified Gog as the historical monarch Gyges, who ruled as the king of Lydia from 685 to 652 B.C. Scholars also agree that while biblical references to Magog are relatively vague, they essentially point to the fact that both the land and its people correspond closely to a specific area located in Asia Minor.

Regardless of the specific geographic location, however, the greatest apocalyptic significance of Gog and Magog becomes apparent in the reading of the New Testament. In the book of Revelation, Satan inspires the heathen armies of these cities to wage war upon Israel. This event, in turn, inspires God to demonstrate His wrath in a dramatic shower of hailstones, fire, and brimstone. Ultimately, this victory heralds the imminent coming of the Messiah (20:8).

The battle of Gog and Magog, however, is not limited to Hebrew texts. In fact, several multicultural explanations exist for the significance of this battle. For example, according to Arabic literature, Gog and Magog represent two mythical northern peoples who had been imprisoned by Alexander the Great behind a large wall. These people, referred to in Arabic literature respectively as Yajuj and Majuj, will reemerge from their imprisonment at sometime close to the Day of Judgment, and at that time, God will destroy these people forever. Perhaps the most unusual reference to Gog and Magog, however, relates to a British legend in which two giants (of the same names) had been conquered and bound to the palace gates at London's Guildhall. To commemorate the binding of these two giants, Henry V directed the construction of two huge statues of the giants to be displayed in Guildhall. Although these statues were first destroyed by the city's Great Fire in 1666, and were replaced in 1708 but were again destroyed during a 1940 air raid, new effigies of the conquered giants were erected in 1953 and remain there to date.

See also Apocalypse: Traditional Judeo-Christian; Apocalyptic Literature; Armageddon; Daniel, Book of; Ezekiel, Book of; Revelation, Book of.

THE GOLDEN BOUGH: A STUDY IN MAGIC AND RELIGION

The Golden Bough (1914) is the popular multivolume collection of worldwide folklore, religion, myth, and magic written by the renowned anthropologist Sir James George Frazer. Considered a seminal work, *The Golden Bough* clearly demonstrates the relationships between ancient rituals and contemporary practices in an effort to trace the evolution of humanity's view of nature, society, and the supernatural.

While the intention of the work was to collect ethnographic information and present illustrations of similarities between cultures, most modern anthropologists question the data as well as the methods of collection. Nevertheless, while his processes may not satisfy contemporary standards of the scientific method, the findings are invaluable in the study of mythology as the basis for the development of all subsequent forms of literature. As such, readers can learn much about the development of human understanding and the reflection of the human condition through various forms of art. Frazer explains that in ancient cultures, people believed that they could control the forces of nature through the use of rituals or magic. Eventually, this belief gave way to the use of religion as a panacea for resolving the conflicts inherent to a chaotic universe. In more recent times, however, Frazer posits that religion has been replaced by an equally iconoclastic belief in science and technology as the solution for the problems of humanity on the earth. This work is valuable for the many things it has to say about humanity's attempt to control the uncontrollable; unfortunately, as is demonstrated in the body of apocalyptic literature, this realization often comes too late.

See also Allegory; *Anatomy of Criticism: Four Essays;* Frazer, Sir James George; Jung, Carl Gustav; Myth; Symbol.

GOLDING, SIR WILLIAM GERALD

William Golding (1911–1993) was the Nobel Prize–winning English novelist whose experience as a teacher in an all boys' school, and whose service in the British Royal Navy during World War II, inspired him to pen his prize-winning apocalyptic parable entitled *Lord of the Flies* (1954). This popular antiwar novel, which was well received as a major feature film in 1963 and was later remade in a 1990 film version, clearly reflects critic John R. May's classic description of primitive apocalyptic fiction (May 1972, 229).

Based upon Golding's observations of flawed democracy, deliberate cruelty, and intrinsic atavism that was demonstrated daily on the playgrounds of the Bishop Wordsworth School in Salisbury, England, *Lord of the Flies* is the first of his novels to reveal the human tendency toward evil that simmers beneath the placid surface of a seemingly civilized society. Perhaps the reason that readers find *Lord of the Flies* both compelling and disturbing is that it shows how a group of supposedly innocent young boys, who have been abandoned on an island paradise in an attempt to keep them safe from the ravages of war, quickly (and ironically) transform their heavenly sanctuary into a hellish Darwinian existence once they have been removed from the restraining influences of society, morality, and adult supervision.

Although Golding's frank observations of humanity's essential depravity were introduced in *Lord of the Flies,* the author continued exploring this aspect of the human condition in his subsequent novels, *The Inheritors* (1955), *Pincher Martin* (1956), *Free Fall* (1959), and *The Spire* (1964). And while his less popular works dealt with similar themes, the following works retain the original flavor of Golding's artistic creative genius: *Darkness Visible* (1979); *Rites of Passage* (1980); a book of essays entitled *A Moving Target* (1982); *The Paper Men* (1983), and the sequel to *Rites of Passage* entitled *Close Quarters* (1987). Golding was one of the few British subjects to have received the royal honor of knighthood just five years before his death on June 19, 1993.

See also Apocalypse: Traditional Judeo-Christian; Apocalypse: Traditional Primitive; Apocalyptic Literature; Apocalypticism; *Lord of the Flies;* Merridew, Jack; Naturalism; Piggy; Ralph; Satan; Simon.

GONERIL

Goneril is the oldest and the most depraved of the three daughters of King Lear in William Shakespeare's apocalyptic drama of the same name. In every way, she is evil personified. Devious, manipulative, and completely amoral, Goneril is the archetypal villainess whose motives are apparent at the opening of the play. She is intelligent but uses this gift as a weapon with which she attempts to exert her will. In Act I Scene I, Lear is weary of the daily duties required of an active monarch and decides to divide his kingdom among his three daughters. In order to determine which daughter receives the greatest amount of land, they must enter in a verbal contest in which they effusively express their love for their father.

Although the premise is certainly false, so too are the responses of both Goneril and Regan. Goneril's hypocrisy is more blatant, her effusion more eloquent, and her spoils of war more substantial than that of her younger sibling. Her victory in this contest is secured to an even greater degree because of her keen awareness of her father's volatility, upon which she eagerly plays.

After the verbal contest, Goneril is charged with housing the aging king. Although he is both her father and still the reigning monarch, Goneril soon lets him know that things have changed now that he is living under her roof. She speaks openly of her doubts about his mental stability. Moreover, she insults and humiliates him directly by informing him that he must reduce the size of his military force of knights and squires because their behavior is too disruptive to her lifestyle. Rather than accept her ultimatum, however, the king resolves to live with Regan, his middle daughter, but again, Goneril's will is served when she surprisingly arrives at Regan's home and urges the younger sister to reject the king unless he is willing to apologize to Goneril. Goneril is committed to enslaving her father, so much so that she is willing to turn him into a beggar unless he agrees to submit to her will.

Goneril's public emasculation of her father demonstrates her cruelty, but such actions are even more pronounced when she directs them toward her husband, Albany. In fact, she takes great pleasure in routinely insulting her mate, not only because she believes that her intelligence is superior to his, but she also interprets his respectful nature as little more than the possession of a weak will.

For this reason, she behaves fearlessly as she blatantly pursues an adulterous relationship with the equally evil bastard son of the Earl of Gloucester,

Edmund. In Edmund, Goneril clearly sees a reflection of herself. He is ruthless, ambitious, and heartless. As such, she is drawn to him to the point that she is ultimately willing to poison her sister, Regan, rather than allow her sibling to win the object of her desire.

See also Apocalypse: Traditional Primitive; Cordelia; Great Chain of Being; *King Lear;* Lear, King; Regan.

GOTHIC FICTION

Gothic fiction is a nineteenth-century literary reaction against the rational influences of the eighteenth-century Augustan Age as represented in the works of Pope, Swift, and Johnson. According to scholars of the movement, gothic fiction combines the

> supernatural element of the ballad[,] the primitive, primeval quality of the epic[,] the extravagance and violence of Elizabethan drama[,] the wildness of pagan Europe. . . . the exoticism of Oriental and Near Eastern tales. . . . the excesses of the chivalric romances[,] the death-gloom of graveyard poetry . . . . [and the] stress on the sublime . . . sensuous, anti- and non-intellectual [thereby] playing on awe, ecstasy, and disorder . . . (Karl 237).

Gothic fiction is also identified easily by the stylistic elements that appear in such works. Frequently, in gothic novels the settings are dark, fearsome, and often feature characteristics of classic horror films such as cobwebbed ceilings, gabled roofs, creaking stairs, and haunting apparitions, either real or imagined. Such fiction also features protagonists, such as Shelley's Frankenstein, who are removed, either by intelligence, immorality, or insanity, from the mainstream of society. Such outsiders, "like Cain, move along the edges of society, in caves, on lonely seacoasts, or in monasteries and convents" (239). Further, as illustrated in the tormented protagonists within the works of Poe, Hawthorne, Dickens, and the Brontes, these outsiders are "driven by strange longings and destructive needs"; they experience "estrangement. . . . and terrible surges of power and devastation." Ultimately, as "tortured iconoclasts," "pure criminals," "saintly psychopaths," or "uncontrollable schizophrenics," they serve an important function in literature because they reinforce the power of myth and thereby endure suffering for their egoism as they "bear the burdens and sins of society" (239).

See also Apocalypse: Traditional Judeo-Christian; Apocalypse: Traditional Primitive; Apocalypticism; *The Blithedale Romance; Faust; Frankenstein, or the Modern Prometheus;* Hollingsworth; Moodie, Zenobia; Myth; Romanticism; Science Fiction; Shelley, Mary Wollstonecraft.

THE GRAIL (OR HOLY GRAIL)

The grail is the legendary symbol, usually taking the form of a dish, a cup, or a chalice, that embodies the complex relationships between medieval romance, ancient myth, and religious allegory. As such, the grail is frequently a central reference within works related to some form of literal or figurative quest. Originating in the ancient Western legend of the Fisher King, it relates the rise, fall, and sometimes the regeneration of a monarch whose kingdom's decay and restoration correspond directly with the actions and fate of the king himself.

Although there are numerous accounts of the grail as well as the quest motif throughout literature, the following examples reflect some of the more accepted views of the grail's symbolic significance. One account describes the cup or grail as the "source of illumination" that originated in the East and must ultimately return to its source. As a part of this account, ". . . the legend tells how it was fashioned by angels from an emerald that dropped from Lucifer's forehead when he was hurled into the abyss. Thus, just as the Virgin Mary redeems the sin of Eve, so the blood of the Redeemer redeems through the Grail the sin of Lucifer" (Cirlot 1971, 121).

Another account, which is perhaps the most widely accepted within traditional literary circles, records the grail as the chalice or cup from which Jesus Christ drank during the Last Supper. Following the supper, one of Christ's followers, Joseph of Arimathea, kept the chalice and used it to catch some drops of blood that had fallen from the wounds of Christ. The legend further posits that Joseph kept this chalice with him throughout the duration of his life, and as long as he had it in his possession, the grail had provided him with all necessary forms of sustenance. After his death, the chalice was apparently handed down throughout various generations of descendents, the last of whom was Sir Galahad, a character who was immortalized in Malory's Arthurian legend, *Le Morte d'Arthur.*

In addition to the predominant view of the grail as a Christian symbol, other critics contend that the vessel is really a female sexual symbol that is associated with another male symbol of a bleeding lance. This view is addressed in extensive detail within Jessie Weston's study of the subject in her 1920 work entitled *From Ritual to Romance.* As such, the grail has been frequently employed by writers throughout most literary periods. It had a significant impact on medieval literature as reflected in Malory's work. Further, it reemerged as a predominant symbol in the works of Victorian authors such as Alfred Lord Tennyson in his poem based on the Arthurian cycle, *Idylls of the King.* Nevertheless, in spite of its roots in antiquity, the grail continues to emerge throughout modern literature and, in fact, became an even more complex focal point around which such authors as T. S. Eliot expressed the spiritual desolation of modern humanity in his epic poem entitled *The Waste Land* (1922).

See also Allegory; Apocalypse: Secular; Apocalypse: Traditional Judeo-Christian; Apocalyptic Literature; Apocalypticism; Archetype; Arthur, King; The Fisher King; Jung, Carl Gustav; *Le Morte d'Arthur;* Myth; Symbol; *The Waste Land.*

GRAVITY'S RAINBOW

Gravity's Rainbow (1973) is Thomas Pynchon's magnum opus that weaves together the threads of a historical epic, the personification of chaos theory, an antiwar diatribe, an irreverent treatment of human sexuality, and a reverent study "about the nature and consequence of origins" (Mendelson 16). In many ways, the scope of the novel, which addresses political, religious, psychological, technological, and philosophical issues as they pertain to the modern world, is embodied within the quest of one man, Lieutenant Tyrone Slothrop, an American working in London for the Army's Allied Intelligence at a time near the end of World War II.

In addition to Slothrop, however, is a cast of over three hundred characters who attempt to escape the boundaries of threatening bureaucracies in order to create their own definitions of what it means to be human in a world poised on the brink of destruction. In this way, they too are like Slothrop. A primary focus of Pynchon's novel is about the "connectedness and coherence of the minute particulars of the world" (15). This central theme of connectedness is evident early in the novel when Lt. Slothrop is being investigated by "the Firm," a secret military organization. The reason for their interest in Slothrop is that he achieves a prodigious erection on the exact sites that Nazi V-2 rockets target for bombing on an average of four and a half days following each of his priapic prophesies.

Realizing that he is the object of the Firm's intricate conspiracy, Slothrop leaves the Army and begins his personal odyssey to find the truth about his origins. He learns that as a child he had been the experimental subject of a Harvard professor, Laszlo Jamf, whose research led him to work for the Nazis in the development and deployment of rockets. During Slothrop's quest for truth, he goes underground, manages to escape into Germany, and eventually finds himself in the maelstrom of madness and mystery known only as "the Zone." Although outside of the Zone, Slothrop found himself beset by paranoia stemming from the pursuit of intricate political and industrial networks, while inside the Zone, he is equally concerned with its "analogous network of black marketeers and dope peddlers with 'connections' . . . of their own" (18).

As he proceeds throughout his own Homeric epic, he becomes increasingly paranoid. In this way he is also connected with the other characters in the novel in that he finds himself psychologically tossed between the figurative Scylla and Charybdis—i.e., the forces of decadence and destruction—that progressively threaten the future of the modern world. The tragic irony of his quest, however, is clearly portrayed in the symbolic meaning of the novel's title as a scientific metaphor for entropy. Specifically, the words in the title represent "[t]he essential pattern of life, from dust to order to dust" (Friedman and Puetz 24), a pattern that, at the end of the novel, is clearly revealed. In this prophetic final scene, set in a European War Theater where the audience is staring at a blank screen screaming, "Come-*on! Start the show!*," a powerful V-2 rocket, like "a bright angel of death" (Pynchon 760), is heading toward the earth as the force of gravity causes a reversal in its rainbowlike parabolic path. All that is left as the rocket comes "screaming" across the sky (3) is the silence of a stunned crowd as it mutely waits its inevitable fate, unable to utter a historical hymn that their world had never been taught to sing (760).

Pynchon's confusing and often unfathomable tome has been regarded by some as an overlong book unworthy of literary merit. Nevertheless, most critics agree with the following assessment of the winner of the 1973 National Book Award:

> Few books in this century have achieved the range and depth of this one, and even fewer have held so large a vision of the world in a structure so skillfully and elaborately conceived. This is certainly the most important novel to be published in English in the past thirty years, and it bears all the lineaments of greatness (Mendelson 1986, 21).

See also Allegory; Apocalypse: Secular; Apocalyptic Literature; Archetype; Entropy; Myth; Pynchon, Thomas; Science Fiction; Symbol.

GREAT CHAIN OF BEING

The great chain of being is a term related to the Platonic concept that the universe is controlled by specific rules of order. This concept has been resurrected, at least in some recognizable form, throughout the body of Western literature, but its appearance is most evident in the works of the Greek Neoplatonists, the seventeenth- and eighteenth-century classicists, and the American Transcendentalists.

According to the Platonic concept, the first quality of universal order is plenitude. This principle relates to the fullness and diversity extant within the universe. The second principle relates to continuity, or the basic elemental interrelationship of all organic forms within the universe. The principle known as gradation refers to a linear hierarchy, or a great chain, in which all universal entities play a part. Essentially, from the basest organism throughout the myriad vegetable, mineral, animal, human, and celestial forms, each entity represents a link in life's chain and plays a specifically designated role in the harmony of the universe that begins and ends with perfection, or God.

Because the concept of the great chain of being is rich with symbolism, writers have applied it within some of the world's most significant works. Perhaps one of the greatest representations of the concept can be found in William Shakespeare's *King Lear* (c. 1605). In this play, when a capable king of pre-Christian Britain decides to divide his land among his daughters (i.e., he stops acting like a king), the great chain is obviously disrupted. As a result of this decision, chaos breaks loose in Lear's universe. First, his "unnatural daughters," Goneril and Regan, begin to treat him like a doddering fool rather than respecting him both as their king and their father. With the kingdom's leadership in doubt, other insurrections and betrayals ensue until the beleaguered king is driven mad by the unexpected chaos that threatens to devastate his world.

Order is restored only when the relationships between the links in life's chain have been returned to their rightful positions. In Shakespeare's tragedy, as in other representative works, such a restoration of order usually comes at a great price. While loss and sorrow are part of this price, the eventual return of universal order, as a result of cataclysmic events, finally provides hope for those who have successfully learned this valuable lesson about life.

Arthur O. Lovejoy's seminal work entitled *The Great Chain of Being: A Study of the History of an Idea* (1936) is a valuable resource for those who wish to understand this ancient concept that provided the framework for the development of some of the world's great literature.

See also Apocalypse: Traditional Primitive; Cordelia; Edgar; Edmund; Emerson, Ralph Waldo; Gloucester (Earl of); Goneril; *King Lear;* Lear, King; Regan; *The Tempest;* Transcendentalism.

THE GREAT GATSBY

The Great Gatsby (1925) is the classic social criticism of American materialism during the "Roaring Twenties" as both personally experienced and fictionally represented by novelist F. Scott Fitzgerald. Essentially, this is the story of a romantic idealist, Jay Gatsby, who will stop at nothing to attain his version of the American Dream. The narrator of the novel is Nick Carraway, a wealthy Midwesterner who works as a Manhattan bond broker. In an effort to be close to his work, but to live outside of the city, Nick rents a house in the Long Island community known as West Egg. His temporary home is well situated between his wealthy cousin's home in the more fashionable East Egg community and the pretentious palatial estate of the mysterious millionaire Jay Gatsby.

As soon as he moves to his new home, Nick finds himself immersed in the reckless lives of his wealthy distant relation, Daisy Buchanan, her boorish husband, Tom, and their friend, and eventually Nick's irresponsible consort, Jordan Baker. Through Jordan, Nick learns that Daisy is unhappily married because of her husband's callousness and flagrant infidelities. This truth becomes evident when Tom introduces Nick to his mistress, Myrtle Wilson, the shabby but licentious wife of an impoverished auto repairman. More importantly, however, Jordan also informs Nick that his wealthy neighbor, Jay Gatsby, was once romantically involved with Daisy during their youth. What Nick does not realize, however, is that he will soon become a pawn in a dangerous game that Gatsby hopes to win by convincing Daisy to become his wife.

Nick is easily manipulated into serving as a go-between for Daisy and Jay. First, he is seduced by the flirtatious enthusiasm of his distant cousin, and soon after, he is further drawn into their societal circle, which revolves around excesses of food, bootleg liquor, and the lavish lifestyle of the dashing, determined Gatsby. Fitzgerald's descriptions of these countless parties, many of which are held at Gatsby's mansion, reveal the boredom, decadence, and futility of America's upper class. Moreover, such parties also serve as a means by which Gatsby nurtures his friendship with Nick in an attempt to grow closer to Daisy.

It is not long after their friendship progresses that Gatsby confides some sketchy details about his past. He reveals that he too had come from the Midwest, but his origins were humble compared with Nick's. These shameful memories of the young James Gatz's poverty, and its devastating result, Daisy's rejection of his proposal, causes him to use his charisma, ingenuity, and self-discipline to amass a fortune with which he hopes to win her heart. Although Gatsby is secretive by nature, he feels that in confiding these details to Nick, he will be able to move ever closer to the attainment of his golden goddess, Daisy Buchanan.

His plan comes to fruition when Nick arranges for the former lovers to meet over tea at his home. To show his appreciation for the gesture, and to create an

F. Scott Fitzgerald criticized American society of the 1920s in his novel *The Great Gatsby.* Here, Daisy Bucahanan (Mia Farrow) listens to Jay Gatsby (Robert Redford) in the 1974 movie based on the novel.

idyllic environment for their reunion, Gatsby arranges for someone to mow Nick's grass and to fill his home with the flowers that Daisy has always loved. Having set himself as the dashing leading man within the perfect romantic scene, Gatsby is clearly overcome by Daisy's allure, and she, in turn, finds him all the more attractive because of his considerable wealth and social influence. As such, unable to contain their excitement within Nick's home, Gatsby invites Daisy to his mansion where he reveals an unrivaled opulence—one he has designed especially to please her. Warmed by the familiarity of his lavish surroundings, Daisy accepts Gatsby's invitation to attend one of his famous parties.

On the night of one particular party, Daisy arrives in her dazzling array and seems to be in her element. Surrounded by Gatsby's extravagant displays of food and finery, she feels irrepressibly drawn to him and overcome by her desire to recapture the innocence of their youth as well as the passion of the present. She is, however, openly disturbed by the vulgarity of Gatsby's riotous guests, and so the two steal away from the festivities and consummate their reunion in an adulterous affair. The reality of their liaison is only part of a dream for Daisy; conversely, for Gatsby, the event is more significant in that it marks the end of his arduous quest. Thinking that he has begun to win her away from her husband, Gatsby decides to forego any further revelry. By making his house off-limits to strangers, he hopes that his mansion will finally become the sanctuary where he alone will enjoy his life's most priceless treasure.

With their sexual reunion as the pivotal point of the novel, what follows reflects the various wages of their sins. Gatsby's impatience to possess Daisy is only equaled by her growing confusion over his persistence. Slowly, Gatsby unveils the less attractive aspects of his past as he boldly reveals a ruthlessness to which Tom Buchanan instinctively responds. The dramatic tension within the tempestuous love triangle builds but finally culminates in a horrendous event that will change each of their lives forever. After a dangerous day of drinking and desperate denial, Daisy drives away from the confrontational scene in Gatsby's car, and in the process accidentally kills Tom's mistress, Myrtle. Myrtle's senseless death occurs outside of her ramshackle apartment above her husband's garage that is located among the ash heaps along the outskirts of town. The folly of their individual lives culminates appropriately amidst the chaotic refuse of the modern world.

What remains is only further confusion. Although Daisy drove Gatsby's car on the night of Myrtle's murder, he gallantly agrees to accept the blame should the accident be traced to his vehicle. In the meantime, his relationship with Daisy is stalled by a sensible distance through which she hopes she will appear uninvolved. Even though much time passes without Daisy's contacting Gatsby, he remains faithful to her while still deluded by his dream deferred. It is in this state of romantic delusion that Gatsby's life is taken. In the ultimate revenge, apparently Tom has told George Wilson, his mistress's husband, that it was Gatsby with whom Myrtle had been having an affair. Therefore, despondent over the death of his wife and the deception of Tom's tale, Wilson shoots Gatsby, and in his last act of desperation, kills himself as well.

In the end, Nick unravels all of the entangled details of his friends' sordid affairs. Furious at Tom for having implicated Gatsby, and disgusted by Daisy's calculating indifference to her lover's murder, Nick presides over the death of his friend, as well as that of the American Dream. This tragedy becomes even more pronounced as Nick finds himself the sole attendee at Gatsby's funeral, with the exception of Gatsby's father, whom Nick consoles with assurances that his son had been a great man. As a result, Nick resolves to remove himself from the trappings of a corrupt society and makes plans to return to the simplicity of life in the Midwest. Before leaving, however, Nick terminates his relationship with his former friends, Daisy and Tom, and provides a fitting epitaph for the moral death of the world that they had come to represent: "They were careless people, Tom and Daisy—they smashed up things and creatures and then retreated back into their money or their vast carelessness, or whatever it was that kept them together, and let other people clean up the mess they had made" (180–181).

See also Apocalypse: Secular; Apocalyptic Literature; Buchanan, Daisy; Carraway, Nick; Gatsby, Jay.

GREENER, FAYE

Faye Greener is the ordinary young actress who comes to Hollywood with dreams of stardom in Nathanael West's apocalyptic novel *The Day of the Locust* (1939). Although Greener, and her ne'er-do-well father, arrive in Los Angeles with the expectation of her becoming the next blonde bombshell, her actual acting experience is limited to a small part in an unimportant film entitled *Waterloo*. Still, in spite of this reality, Faye carries herself with the same illusive airs of the stereotypical American bitch goddess.

Throughout most of the story, Faye's acting is focused less in the professional arena than it is in her personal life. Her gift, it seems, is in beguiling and abusing young men whom she can use for her particular ends. Early in the novel, Faye coldly dismisses the attentions of the protagonist, aspiring artist Tod Hackett, because he has no means with which to further her career. However, while she continually makes it clear to everyone involved that she is saving herself for that special person who can catapult her to stardom, she is, in reality, a cheap imitation, a tawdry tramp, and a fading starlet who is equally used by the succession of hapless men who fade in and out of her meaningless life.

While most of these men have the emotional means with which to protect themselves from her wiles, one ingenuous man, a shy bookish neighbor, Homer Simpson, becomes obsessed with having her in any way he can. The opportunity affords itself when Faye is forced to find a place to stay. Under the guise of their creating a "business arrangement," Faye moves in with Homer and promptly proceeds to dash his dreams of love with the harsh realities of her lascivious behavior.

Ultimately, in yet another act of her selfish cruelty, Faye finally deserts Homer. This event devastates this already psychologically vulnerable man and drives him into a demented frenzy. The novel's climax, which involves the grisly murder of Homer Simpson, is the direct result of Faye's egocentrism and shallowness. It is for her sins, as well as those of others like her, that Homer is sacrificed for the satiation of the mob.

See also Apocalypse: Anti-Christian; Babylon; *The Day of the Locust*; Hackett, Tod; Satan; Simpson, Homer; West, Nathanael.

GROTESQUE

Grotesque is a term that dates back to sixteenth-century Rome when the word *grottesea* defined the grottos or caves existing underneath the city that contained ancient paintings reflecting gross exaggerations of various life-forms. In literature, it was first used in the eighteenth century when it was applied to situations and characters found frequently in satire and comedy, genres that depend upon absurd and incongruous representations of human vice and folly.

Since that time, both the literary term and the writing style have been used by many authors, the most notable of which are Edgar Allan Poe, Flannery O'Connor, William Faulkner, and Joseph Heller. In their works, character development is marked by representations of gross physical, emotional, and/or spiritual exaggerations. Such characters are imbued with physical traits or peculiar behaviors that go beyond recognized societal norms. In some cases, a character might be depicted as having supernatural qualities, a situation within a plot might border on the incredible, or the resolution of a story might seem incongruous with the events preceding it.

Such is specifically the case within the collective body of work of Flannery O'Connor. Known for her Southern gothic portrayals, O'Connor's works portray characters who greatly exceed literary expectations. While such characters are rooted in stereotype, O'Connor takes them beyond the norm in order to convey a greater emotional impact on the reader. For instance, in her novel *The Violent Bear It Away,* the protagonist, Francis Tarwater, encounters several characters or forces that permanently affect him as well as the outcome of the story. Although each of these supporting characters influences the protagonist in a different way, their exaggerated forms, which respectively represent religious fanaticism, psychological obsession, mental defectiveness, or pure evil, lead the main character through a series of escalating events that ultimately lead to a spiritual transformation brought about by nothing less than a violent personal cataclysm.

See also *Absalom, Absalom!;* Apocalypse: Traditional Judeo-Christian; Apocalyptic Literature; *As I Lay Dying; The Narrative of Arthur Gordon Pym; The Violent Bear It Away.*

HACKETT, TOD

Tod Hackett is the protagonist and talented young artist in Nathanael West's novel of apocalyptic despair entitled *The Day of the Locust* (1939). At the outset of the novel, the character is one of many who have migrated to America's West Coast during the 1920s and 1930s in search of promise, profit, or posterity. Although he dreams of becoming a great painter someday, in the meantime Tod supports himself as a costume and set designer for a Hollywood studio. In this capacity, he soon learns that the city is filled with disillusioned dreamers who have left the comfort of their established families in order to endure endless days of drudgery with only the distant hope of making it big in America's shining yet shallow promised land.

As he becomes accustomed to his new life in the city, Tod meets several stereotypical characters, each of whom symbolizes some form of flawed humanity. Because he is particularly lonely and craves female companionship, he is soon smitten by a selfish aspiring starlet, Faye Greener, whose charisma and obvious physical charms consume his thoughts. He is disabused of this notion, however, when Faye, upon realizing his intent, informs him that she could never become seriously involved with a young man of Tod's stature because of his inability to further her acting career.

While he accepts this reality, he continues to observe, and in some instances, participate in Faye's increasingly sordid lifestyle. In an effort to escape his preoccupation with Faye and to keep his dreams alive, Tod becomes obsessed with the details of what he hopes will be the artistic culmination of his life's work, a painting entitled "The Burning of Los Angeles." In this painting, Tod hopes to capture the angst and despair of the enraged émigrés who continue to overpopulate the city. As he contemplates his masterpiece, Tod is gradually introduced to various characters, most of whom revolve around Faye Greener, and each of whom is a grotesque exaggeration of some vile human quality. Although he remains something of an outsider, Tod witnesses numerous scenes of immorality, greed, and violence. These events, both overtly and subliminally, fuel the fires of Tod's artistic imagination.

At its climax, Tod has become sickened by the depravity of the people who surround him. He has also been moved by the pitiable futility of the actions of a shy and innocent Midwesterner, Homer Simpson. Because Simpson, too, has fallen in love with Faye Greener, he has made himself completely vulnerable to her cruelty, thereby leaving himself open to relentless humiliation from Greener, her friends, and her lovers. In the novel's climactic scene, Homer wanders the streets in utter despair after he has been deserted by Faye. Tod witnesses the dazed confusion of the destroyed young man, but is unable to reach him because of a crowd in the streets that has gathered in anticipation of a major Hollywood movie premiere.

The physical separation of Tod and Homer reflects the emotional isolation suffered by all the characters in the novel. However, Tod becomes increasingly concerned for Homer, whose disorientation becomes more obvious. From a distance, Tod can see that Homer has taken a seat on a bench, perhaps to sort out his thoughts about returning to his Midwestern home. But to Tod's horror, Homer disintegrates into madness and engenders the seething wrath of the crowd. The unspeakable event occurs when, in response to the continued taunting of a malicious neighbor boy, Homer rises to chase the youth. The youth, however, trips and falls in his attempt to escape the scene of his crime. In a mindless fury, Homer stomps the boy to death.

Tod witnesses this horror, but he is powerless to assist Homer; instead, he is forced to watch as Homer becomes the city's sacrifice. Homer is quickly lifted by the angry throng and carried through the streets until they descend upon him in a collective mission of utter destruction. In this moment, life and art merge for Tod. And although he has been physically spared by the rescue of a police cruiser, Tod's fragile mind has been permanently seared by his original apocalyptic vision that has ultimately become a ghastly reality.

See also Apocalypse: Anti-Christian; Babylon; *The Day of the Locust*; Satan; Simpson, Homer.

HARLEM RENAISSANCE

The Harlem Renaissance, also known at the time as the New Negro Movement, was an impressive period of literary creativity for the United States. It originated in Harlem, New York, in the 1920s. Since the movement was initiated amidst the inner-city ghettos, the earliest contributions to the genre featured stories containing traditional black dialect, quaint characterizations, and stereotypical situations. Nevertheless, the growing popularity of the Harlem Renaissance eschewed the earlier writings of Charles Chesnutt and Paul Lawrence Dunbar, whose works were more reflective of white culture, and consequently became known more for highlighting the most compelling issues of modern black culture, specifically spirituality, family, and racism. Ultimately, the literary proliferation of such universal themes inevitably resulted in a collective resurgence of black America's artistic confidence and rightful sense of racial pride.

Among the pioneers of the Harlem Renaissance movement were such respected philosophers, writers, and educators as Alain Locke (1886–1954), who, in 1925, published the landmark anthology entitled *The New Negro: An Interpretation*. Soon, his work was followed by that of others, including James Weldon Johnson, who became famous for his two controversial novels, *Autobiography of an Ex-Coloured Man* (1912) and *God's Trombone* (1927). These inspirational works placed Johnson in the position of mentor to new writers within the Harlem group such as the Jamaican immigrant Claude McKay, who wrote *Harlem Shadows,* a collection of verse published in 1922, and a novel, *Home to Harlem,* published in 1927.

Other formidable additions to this emerging literary group included the poet Countee Cullen, whose edition of *Caroling Dusk: An Anthology of Verse by Negro Poets* (1927) brought the vigorous efforts of several talented black authors to the forefront of the literary scene. By this time, the movement was firmly established, and its audience was eager to accept the powerful candor of Langston Hughes's first collection of verse, *The Weary Blues,* as well as his subsequent novel, *Not without Laughter,* published in 1930. In the following year, Hughes introduced yet another significant force in the movement, author and playwright Zora Neale Hurston, who collaborated with him on a play entitled *Mule Bone,* completed in 1931.

As a result of their success, as well as societal conditions, the movement later became represented by such leading writers as Jean Toomer, Richard Wright, William Jourden Rapp, Wallace Thurman, and Arna Bontemps, whose novel entitled *God Sends Sunday* (1931) is accepted as the final work of the Harlem Renaissance.

Fortunately, however, the legacy of this significant body of literature continued as a result of the financial support of such white writers as Carl Van Vechten and others who offered scholarships and other philanthropic opportunities for those who were dedicated to perpetuating black America's cultural and literary tradition. As such, while the movement eventually declined, it did succeed in creating a new breed of black intellectuals whose later, more revolutionary, works reflected the increasing sense of alienation and oppression perpetuated by America's white mainstream society. Their hardships, however, have been permanently recorded in an equally inspirational body of literature created by such imposing figures of the 1960s as James Baldwin, Ralph Ellison, and Imamu Amiri Baraka, and fortunately, the strength of the movement still reverberates through the contemporary works of Alice Walker, Maya Angelou, Chinua Achebe, and Toni Morrison.

See also Achebe, Chinua; Apocalypse: Anti-Christian; Apocalypse: Traditional Judeo-Christian; Baldwin, James; Ellison, Ralph; *Go Tell It on the Mountain; The Invisible Man; Native Son; Things Fall Apart;* Wright, Richard.

HAWTHORNE, NATHANIEL

Nathaniel Hawthorne (1804–1864) was born on the fourth of July in Salem, Massachusetts, the descendent of Puritan ancestors. He is one of America's most widely read authors. This intensely reflective son of a sea captain received his education at Bowdoin College where he met two lifelong friends, Franklin Pierce (a future U.S. president) and Henry Wadsworth Longfellow (a fellow writer), who, among other literary figures, would later greatly influence his life and career.

In the years following his graduation from college, he lived, somewhat reclusively, at home with his mother and sister. Although he socialized minimally in Salem during these years, the primary focus of his life was research into

Nathaniel Hawthorne

America's colonial past. Having had an ancestor who had participated in the Salem witchcraft trials, Hawthorne was fascinated by this period in history. His work reflects his obsession with the past, particularly the psychological consequences of guilt and sin. To some degree, each of his works reveal his fascination with humanity's blatant demonstration of pride, lust, and greed, as well as its suffering through obsession, frustration, and denial. As a result of his personal experiences, Hawthorne's work also reflects his cynicism with humanity's ceaseless albeit futile pursuit of utopian societies.

His perspectives on these and other issues first surfaced in the historical novel *Fanshawe* (1828), which he published anonymously. Doubting its literary merit, he later withdrew it from republication. During the years that followed, Hawthorne continued his work on short stories that could be enjoyed either singularly or as part of literary collections. His first legitimate popular success came with the publication of his stories collected in *Twice Told Tales* (1837).

At the same time that Hawthorne's literary career began to flourish, so too did his personal life; in 1837, the author met Elizabeth Peabody, a famous educational reformer from Salem, who was fascinated by Hawthorne's work. This meeting soon led to his introduction to Peabody's sister, Sophia, who later became the author's wife. Sophia was twenty-nine when they first met; she was also an invalid, so Hawthorne became obsessed with gaining the financial security that would enable him to care for her after their marriage. As such, he went to work as a surveyor in a Boston Customs House. During this time, he also became reacquainted with his old friend Longfellow and other members of the literary community. This renewed camaraderie led Hawthorne, reluctantly, to participate briefly in the utopian society conceived by the Transcendentalist movement known as Brook Farm. Although Hawthorne, unlike contemporaries such as Henry David Thoreau and Ralph Waldo Emerson, had doubts about the viability of a bucolic communal life, he agreed, in 1841, to invest financially in the social experiment with the hope of earning enough money to marry his fiancée.

Many historical accounts exist to document Hawthorne's cynicism for the concept of an ideal society. Still others reveal, with no uncertainty, Hawthorne's personal distaste for the daily labors and general responsibilities that drained the psychological and creative juices from the author during his stay on the farm. For Hawthorne, who worked best in solitude, Brook Farm was a failed experiment that not only distracted him from his writing but also drained him financially without ever providing a monetary return on his investment.

In spite of his lost investment, Hawthorne married Sophia in 1842, a year after their meeting. Their marriage buoyed his spirits, particularly after the couple moved into the Old Manse in Concord, Massachusetts. Formerly the residence of a prolific writer, Ralph Waldo Emerson, the Old Manse similarly served Hawthorne well. It was in the Old Manse that Hawthorne lived both a happy and productive life with Sophia and their first daughter, Una. In this residence he produced his finest collection of short stories, *Mosses from an Old Manse* (1846). The success of this work was, in part, the result of a favorable review by fellow writer Herman Melville. Melville's critical acclaim of Hawthorne's work did much to seal a valuable friendship between the two artists.

After this blissful time, the Hawthornes moved, once again, to Salem where the author returned to work in the Customs House. This mind-numbing work continued until 1849 when, as a result of a political fracas, Hawthorne was relieved from his position. The details of this experience remained fresh in his mind, however, as he began writing his literary masterpiece that combined elements of his personal experiences with psychological musings in a work entitled *The Scarlet Letter* (1850).

With this work, and upon the advice of his publisher, Hawthorne ceased writing short stories and dedicated himself to the development of novels. The result of these subsequent efforts include *The House of the Seven Gables* (1851); a children's book, *The Wonder-Book* (1852); and the apocalyptic novel based on Hawthorne's Brook Farm experience, *The Blithedale Romance* (1852).

In the meantime, Hawthorne's friend Franklin Pierce was elected president of the United States. He appointed Hawthorne as consul for Manchester and Liverpool, England, from 1853 to 1857. After his return from England, Hawthorne published his final novel in 1860, *The Marble Faun*. During this time, his physical health began to fail, and although he published a collection of sketches dedicated to Pierce entitled *Our Old Home* (1863), he continued to work on a variety of projects until he died in May of 1864. He was laid to rest in the Sleepy Hollow Cemetery in Concord, Massachusetts. He was carried to his grave by luminary pallbearers, including James Lowell, Henry Wadsworth Longfellow, and Ralph Waldo Emerson.

See also Apocalypse: Traditional Primitive; *The Blithedale Romance*; Brook Farm; Coverdale, Miles; Moodie, Priscilla; Moodie, Zenobia; Romanticism; Transcendentalism; Westervelt.

HEART OF DARKNESS

Heart of Darkness (1902) is the name of Joseph Conrad's gripping novella, replete with apocalyptic images, that was originally included in a collection entitled *Youth* but was later published as a singular work. Based primarily upon Conrad's real-life experiences as a captain of a steamship that had been stationed briefly in the Belgian Congo, *Heart of Darkness* reflects those experiences and recounts the greed, injustice, and general immorality that emerges when humanity justifies its intrinsic corruption in the absence of a viable theology and in the name of civilization.

The story begins when an unnamed narrator introduces several characters who plan to travel to a remote jungle location on a cruising yawl named the *Nellie*. This opening scene reflects a general characteristic of primitive apocalypse: a peaceful, still setting (May 1972, 229). Such scenes, however, usually serve as the proverbial calm before the storm, which is certainly the case in Conrad's work. While departing from the motionless shores of England's Thames River, the five people aboard the cruiser—the Director of Companies, a lawyer, an accountant, the unnamed narrator, and an experienced seaman, Marlow—engage in conversation while waiting for the river's tide to turn in order to propel them on their voyage. At this point, Marlow spins a seaman's yarn recounting the ruthless exploitation caused, in the name of civilized society, by the Roman colonists. The details provided in this account of violence and greed not only expresses Conrad's view of the injustice of colonizing foreign lands in the name of civilization, but they also foreshadow many of the same senseless activities that they will observe as they travel toward their destination deep inside the jungle.

Following these introductory comments, with which Marlow has mesmerized his audience, he begins yet another tale; this one deals with the circumstances that led up to his present assignment. And although his precise mission is not detailed, nor is the actual destination of their voyage, as events ensue, readers are provided with information suggesting that the passengers are headed to a remote station in Africa that has become legendary for its success in the ivory trade.

As their journey progresses, it is punctuated by a series of fits and starts. With each delay, Marlow observes a progressive state of decay and neglect; broken and rusted machinery and ruined abandoned vessels litter the riverbanks. People, too, are dehumanized, as is presented by his description of emaciated natives whose faces bear the "deathlike indifference of unhappy savages" (80). These observations are most puzzling, particularly in light of the reported success of the center of the operation. Marlow is most disturbed by the horrible scenes of dying natives who appear to be little more than "bundles of acute angles" (82). Their wasted and diseased forms, however, draw a sharp contrast to the man whom he meets when he reaches the operational center of the station. Against the hellish backdrop of countless black near-corpses, Marlow finds an animated "white man, in such an unexpected elegance of get-up that in the first moment [Marlow takes him] for a vision" (83). This man, who resembles "a hairdresser's dummy," is the ivory company's chief accountant and, more importantly, the primary source of information about the mysterious Mr. Kurtz. According to the accountant, Mr. Kurtz, the general manager of the ivory operation, is "a first-class agent," "a respectable person," and an "important" figure renowned within the ivory trade (84).

This glowing account of Mr. Kurtz, in spite of the obvious chaos of the operation, causes Marlow to become obsessed with meeting the man who resides at the center of the mysterious dichotomy. Consequently, as Marlow gets closer to Kurtz's station, he progressively learns more about the man who has become both physically and mentally destroyed by his presence in "the heart of darkness." As he enters Kurtz's world, Marlow soon learns the truth of the matter. The station thrives, not because it is run efficiently, but because Kurtz has turned himself into a godlike character whom the natives both fear and worship because of his terrorist tactics that have resulted in his success in the ivory trade. Clearly, this self-deification, in part caused by their elevation of him as something of a tribal king, reveals that the manager has become unbalanced mentally by his exposure to and participation in the "unspeakable rites" of the natives. Although the specifics of these rites are never mentioned, critics agree that they probably involve human sacrifice. Kurtz's consumption of human organs is a primitive attempt to retain his physical vitality in exchange for the loss of his own humanity, his former position within "civilization," and ultimately the damnation of his soul.

Marlow's discovery of the aforementioned events enables him to complete his personal quest. In addition, by determining the violent truth of the manager's corrupt ivory operation, he also completes his assigned company mission: he relieves Kurtz from his official post. However, soon after Kurtz has been carried to the steamer for his return to England, the diseased madman convulses in feverish death throes. Kurtz's final words, "The horror! The horror!" (147), reflect an acute awareness that is said to occur at the last moment of one's life. In this case, because this astonished exclamation also heralds a corrupt man's entrance into the gates of eternal hell, Marlow is forever changed by the words, as well as what they represent—literally, the unfathomable darkness that is possible within the depth of the human heart.

See also Apocalypse: Traditional Primitive; Apocalypticism; Conrad, Joseph; *The Hollow Men; The Invisible Man;* Kurtz, Mr.; Marlow, Charles; *The Waste Land.*

HEAVEN

According to most world religions, heaven is a term related to the final resting place for the souls of those who have lived according to the laws of their respective God. Heaven is often identified as a garden paradise, an abode in the sky, or a supernatural counterpart of the earth whose streets are "paved with gold" and are lined with "many mansions" as an eternal reward for the religious elect.

The most constant element of all religious depictions of heaven is that of the residence of the supreme deity. While Judaism relates to a Garden of Eden concept, Islam regards their seven heavens as cites of opulence and sensual pleasures. Buddhist and Zoroastrian doctrines describe a wide range of heavenly levels, each equipped with appropriate rewards for varying levels of behavior. Christianity has what is perhaps the most well defined concept of what the righteous can expect as their eternal reward.

For example, according to John 6:38, heaven is the point of origin and return for Jesus Christ. According to Romans 8:34, it is also the place where he will pass final judgment upon the living and the dead. And although the influence of Roman Catholicism initially introduced heaven as the residence of harp-playing winged cherubim, most modern views accept the belief that heaven is the ultimate destination for humankind. And as a reward for human righteousness, God will share his perpetual glory with the blessed, who will forever live in a state of eternal bliss.

See also Allegory; Apocalypse: Traditional Judeo-Christian; *The Divine Comedy; Paradise Lost.*

HELL

Hell is a region below the surface of the earth wherein, according to a variety of religious doctrines, the souls of the wicked will be tormented for eternity amidst the sulfurous flames of infernal damnation. According to Babylonian myth, hell was known as "the place of No-Return." Hebrews referred to it as "Sheol," an abode of unending corruption. The Greeks similarly conceived of the concept of an "unseen land" or Hades, while the word *hell* literally means "the place of concealment."

Some of the more graphic literary depictions of hell, however, appear in the apocalyptic epic *The Divine Comedy,* by Dante Alighieri. According to Dante's book within the *Comedy* called the *Inferno,* there are nine levels of hell, and each

The Inferno, an aspect of hell, a detail from a Byzantine mosaic in the Baptistry, Florence, Italy

level consists of a punishment that is commensurate with the sins committed while individuals lived upon the earth. At the bottom of hell, however, is an icy lake in which Satan is imprisoned as he feeds upon the heads of three of history's greatest traitors: Judas Iscariot, Brutus, and Cassius.

In addition to this literary depiction of hell, the Bible itself, both in the Old and the New Testaments, relays vivid depictions of the various forms of torment that will be endured by the wicked for eternity following the Last Judgment as presented in the apocalyptic Book of Revelation. Nevertheless, whether hell is an actual place wherein sinners will be eternally tormented in a physical sense, or it is a condition of mind, in which the wicked must contemplate their separation from heaven for eternity, hell, or fear of its torment, is ultimately the destination that has served as the central metaphor for the body of apocalyptic thought and literature that has proliferated from the beginning of humanity until the present.

See also Allegory; Apocalypse: Secular; Apocalypse: Traditional Judeo-Christian; Apocalypse: Traditional Primitive; *Paradise Lost*.

HERSEY, JOHN

John Richard Hersey (1914–1993) is the American journalist turned novelist who is best known for his graphic accounts of the destruction that occurred during World War II, specifically his account of an atomic bombing in his novel *Hiroshima* (1946). He was born in China and lived in that country until he was ten years old. He returned to the United States and completed his schooling, graduating from Yale in 1936, after which he became a foreign correspondent for *Time* and *Life* magazines. From 1937 to 1946, Hersey spent time in Italy, Russia, and the Far East.

These travels enabled him to gather material for *A Bell for Adano* (1944), a novel that takes place in Sicily, which won him the Pulitzer Prize in 1945. His travels to Japan and Russia were important to the development of his novels *Hiroshima* (1946) and *The Wall* (1950), wherein he combined his personal observations of the effects of war with various elements of imaginative fiction. These novels are among the most widely read and critically acclaimed of all his works. Hersey is also the author of *A Single Pebble* (1956), *The Child Buyer* (1960), *The Conspiracy* (1972), *The Walnut Door* (1977), and *The Call* (1985).

See also Apocalypse: Secular; Apocalyptic Literature; *Hiroshima*.

HESSE, HERMANN

Hermann Hesse (1877–1962) is the German-born novelist and poet whose literary works deal primarily with a combination Jungian psychology and Eastern mysticism as a pathway for finding self-realization and spiritual fulfillment. His works, on the whole, convey the predominant theme of isolation and individual reconciliation with the polar opposites of life. Nature's intrinsic dualities—light and darkness, good and evil, ignorance and enlightenment, death and regeneration—are pervasive themes in most of his works. Such is expressly the case in one of his more famous novels, *Siddhartha,* wherein the young

John Hersey

Hermann Hesse

protagonist abandons the security of his father's faith and his home in an effort to resolve life's conflicts, through the teachings of Buddha, and thereby attain inner peace.

Although some of his other works, such as *Steppenwolf,* similarly deal with the issue of duality, they do so, respectively, on more of a bestial or cerebral level rather than concentrating solely on the spiritual plane. Consequently, all of Hesse's novels, poems, and even his autobiographical writings reflect his concern with the duality of nature; moreover, they also focus strongly on the difficulty with which the artistic personality contends with such matters and resolves their dilemmas through individual modes of expression. In honor of his contributions to world literature, Hesse received the Nobel Prize in 1946.

See also Apocalypse: Buddhist; God; Jung, Carl Gustav; Myth; *Siddhartha;* Symbol.

HIGHWATER, JAMAKE

Jamake Highwater (1942–), who also writes under the pseudonym J. Marks, is the remarkable playwright, novelist, biographer, journalist, and lecturer who specializes in issues related to Native American culture. While he is most frequently associated with works written for the young adult fiction genre, he has become recognized for his ability to blend primitive myths, Native American legends, and contemporary psychological and artistic concerns in a growing body of apocalyptic fiction that is typified by his powerfully written novel entitled *Kill Hole* (1992).

In many ways, *Kill Hole* is autobiographical fiction that features many of the characters and events that shaped Highwater's early life. Many of the cultural conflicts and chaotic rituals within the novel have their origins in Highwater's own mixed ancestry. Born on February 14, 1942, Highwater is the son of both a Blackfoot and a Cherokee Indian. Like the protagonist in his apocalyptic novel, Highwater's early life was shaped by the fact that his father, an Indian Rodeo stuntman, had died young and had abandoned him and his brother. As such, he, like his main character within the novel, was forced to live for some time in an orphanage, at least until his mother remarried. Upon her remarriage, and his reintegration into her life, Highwater was exposed to the dominant white culture. In spite of his mother's efforts to reign him within the confines of the dominant culture, Highwater initiated his own personal quest for his Native American identity as well as for his identity as an artist.

He had no trouble finding outlets for his creative expression. He graduated from college with dual degrees in music and anthropology. These combined experiences, which leaned heavily on his relevant autobiographical information, provided the foundation for his most popular novel, *Anapo: An American Indian Odyssey,* which was patterned on Homer's *Odyssey* and which blends the lyricism of the oral tradition with the formal structure of a classical literary quest.

His next novel, entitled *Song from the Earth,* examines the close relationship between great art as "good spirits" that positively influence the universe as opposed to art for the more temporal purpose of mere beauty, which is subjective, elusive, and ultimately corruptible. Within his apocalyptic novel *Kill Hole,*

American military personnel view the charred landscape of the Japanese city of Hiroshima in September 1945. American John Hersey reported the apocalyptic effects of the August 6, 1945, atomic blast on six survivors in a 1946 *New Yorker* article, and blast survivor Masuji Ibuse won Japan's highest literary award, the Noma Prize, for his 1969 novel *Black Rain,* based upon survivor accounts.

however, Highwater blends his concerns about blood loyalty and the various bonds of love that unite human hearts with his beliefs regarding the "good spirits" of pure art that can help the human spirit to transcend the cruel and chaotic boundaries that cause senseless suffering throughout an individual's earthly existence.

Although Jamake Highwater has begun to receive well-deserved critical acclaim for his more recent works, he continues to practice his craft while also contributing to the proliferation of the cultural community. Since 1975, Highwater has continued to preach what he practices in his role as a lecturer and consultant to the New York Council on the Arts.

See also Apocalypse: Traditional Primitive; Apocalypticism; Delito; Ghost Horse, Sitko; *Kill Hole;* Patu; Symbol.

HIROSHIMA

Hiroshima (1946) is John Hersey's objective account of the atomic bomb attack on the Japanese city of the same name by the United States government to bring an end to World War II. When the bomb exploded within the center of Hiroshima on August 6, 1945, at 8:15 A.M., everything within a radius of approximately 8,000 feet was completely decimated, and considerable damage occurred far beyond these limits. As a result of this bombing, more than 71,000 people died, and countless others suffered a myriad of physical and emotional effects as a result of both radiation as well as the psychological impact of such a traumatic experience.

While he was on a journalistic assignment in the Far East, John Hersey began to record the devastating details of the bomb's aftermath, which presented the story from the victims' point of view. This report, first published in *The New Yorker* magazine in the August 31, 1946, issue, gave the American people an opportunity to quantify the personal and material loss experienced by six individuals who witnessed the horrors and survived the aftermath of the atomic blast. The impact of this article, which had introduced the universal human factor into what had previously been viewed as merely a military victory, resulted in Hersey's publication of the account, in book form, in November 1946.

See also Apocalypse: Secular; Apocalyptic Literature; *Black Rain;* Ibuse, Masuji.

HOENIKKER, FELIX

Felix Hoenikker is the stereotypical "mad scientist" in Kurt Vonnegut's apocalyptic fantasy entitled *Cat's Cradle* (1963). A Nobel Prize–winning physicist by profession, and an undisciplined tinkerer by choice, Dr. Felix Hoenikker is best known within the scientific community for his developmental work on the atomic bomb dropped on Hiroshima, Japan. This fact, portentous in itself, causes him to become the subject of a book about important people and their recollections of the day the bomb was dropped. The intended book, whose proposed title was to be *The Day the World Ended,* is the inciting action that compels Jonah, the narrator of the Hoenikker saga, to learn more about the man whose mind contained both the curiosity and the technology with which to destroy the entire world.

In Vonnegut's novel, Hoenikker celebrates his own childlike curiosity. And this eccentric characteristic becomes publicly apparent in a speech he delivers upon being awarded the Nobel Prize,

> "Ladies and Gentlemen. I stand before you now because I never stopped dawdling like an eight-year-old on a spring morning on his way to school. Anything can make me stop and look and wonder, and sometimes learn. I am a very happy man. Thank you" (17).

In addition, Hoenikker's penchant for approaching his work as play is also recalled by his youngest son, Newt, who remembers his father's inquiring, "Why should I bother with made-up games when there are so many real ones going on?" (17). The pathetic irony of his philosophy, however, is that his approach to science as child's play, with all of its devastating potential, demonstrates the countless holocausts generated by humankind whose folly, pride, and moral recklessness inevitably thwarts his futile attempts to play God.

Clearly, such is the case when a general representing the Marines approaches the physicist with a peculiar problem—mud. Apparently, both his weaponry and his soldiers' effectiveness have frequently been compromised by the muddy terrain of foreign lands. He urges Dr. Hoenikker to develop some chemical, a small machine, or even a pill that could immediately transform marshy swamps into a state of solid stability. Presented with such an interesting challenge, the physicist begins to research and experiment with materials that could fulfill the general's request. During the process of his investigation, Hoenikker becomes fascinated by a story:

> [It involved] a factory that had been growing big crystals of ethylene diamine tartrate. The crystals were useful in certain manufacturing operations. . . [however,] one day the factory discovered that the crystals it was growing no longer had the properties desired. The atoms had begun to stack and lock—to freeze [after coming in contact with liquid] (38).

The culmination of his inquiry into the subject was the development of a substance, called ice-nine, that could instantly freeze liquids into solid forms that would become impenetrable by any temperature lower than 144.4 degrees Fahrenheit. Thrilled by his discovery, but cautious about its potential, Dr. Hoenikker kept his secret and his prized crystal chip with him at all times. He also carried it with him during his family vacation on Cape Cod during which he eventually disclosed the information to his children. To their astonishment, they were also able to witness its effects firsthand when some of the crystal had become mingled with their dog's water. Instantly, the dog froze. They were convinced, at that moment, of the devastating potential of their father's last gift to mankind (41).

Ultimately, the potential of this "gift" comes to fruition at the end of the novel in an apocalyptic realization of all that they had feared. As often happens in regard to powerful technology, ice-nine eventually made its way into the hands of the corrupt and megalomaniacal leader of the South American republic of San Lorenzo. The republic's leader, "Papa" Monzano, had worshiped Hoenikker, as well science itself, and as such, had given Hoenikker's son, Franklin, a powerful position in his government in exchange for a chip of ice-nine. Moments before "Papa's" death, the leader decides literally to try to "take it with him"; as such, he swallows the chip of ice-nine, and his body predictably becomes frozen solid. Although attempts are made to prevent further contamination, every characteristic of apocalyptic literature eventually comes to pass. Earthquakes, raging seas, relentless storms, panic, and rock slides ensue. One such slide results in the demolition of the tower in which "Papa's" body is held; consequently, a bizarre sequence of events ultimately results in "Papa's" frozen corpse sliding into the sea, whereupon ice-nine begins to reign over the earth.

Only a few people who had been separated by a shifting land mass survive the cataclysm. Among the survivors is the narrator of the story, Jonah, whose new purpose is to detail Hoenikker's folly to any future generations that might exist, and to serve as a living legacy to man's destructive impulses that will always threaten the beauty and the security of the earth.

See also Apocalypse: Secular; Apocalyptic Literature; *Cat's Cradle;* Ice-Nine; Jonah-John.

HOLLINGSWORTH

Hollingsworth is the self-deluded megalomaniac who is a key character in Nathaniel Hawthorne's novel *The Blithedale Romance* (1852). Before he is even presented on the scene, he is first described by another character who has seen him before and was captivated by his persona. When asked if she knows Hollingsworth personally, the character Zenobia exclaims, "No; only as an auditor—auditress, I mean—of some of his lectures . . . ," but she clearly shows her admiration for him by stating, "What a voice he has! and what a man he is! Yet not so much an intellectual man. . . . as a great heart" (48).

Zenobia, however, goes on to lament that such a powerful figure wastes his time in the pursuit of misguided philanthropy. Hollingsworth is deeply committed to gathering money and land with which to build a community for criminal reform. He feels that his own intrinsic superiority and obvious personal gifts require him to share his knowledge and experience with those less fortunate individuals whose myriad personal flaws drive them to criminal misbehavior.

While Hollingsworth is enthusiastic and charming at the outset of the novel, he becomes exceedingly narcissistic and ruthless in the pursuit of his messianic endeavor. His believes that the ends justify the means of his actions. As such, he tests his influence with each of the characters in the novel, and as a result, he exploits each one for whatever gift, be it financial, intellectual, or emotional, that he can use to make his dream come true.

In the process, his divisive influence in the Blithedale community causes one character, Zenobia, to give him her money and, naively, her love, in the hopes of uniting with this powerful man. His use of her money and the rejection of her affections, however, leads her to become despondent and, ultimately, to commit suicide. Similarly, Hollingsworth disappoints the ever-loyal Priscilla. Although Priscilla is Hollingsworth's chosen mate, Priscilla's dreams of being loved and protected by such a powerful man are also dashed by the end of the novel. Ironically, she, the once weak and wan waif, becomes his strength, his support, and his savior. This reversal of fortune occurs immediately following Zenobia's suicide. Hollingsworth, once a giant of a man, ends up as a wasted dreamer who has been haunted and destroyed by his feelings of guilt over Zenobia's suicide. Clearly, Hawthorne uses Hollingsworth to conclude that all philanthropic idealists can lose their souls if they should become blind to humanity in the pursuit of their prideful goals. Through Coverdale, the author moralizes that Hollingsworth "exempli[fies]. . . . the most awful truth. . . . [that] from the very gate of heaven there is a by-way to the pit!" (247).

See also Apocalypse: Traditional Primitive; *The Blithedale Romance*; Brook Farm; Coverdale, Miles; Moodie, Priscilla; Moodie, Zenobia; Romanticism; Transcendentalism; Westervelt.

THE HOLLOW MEN

The Hollow Men (1925) is a significant poem written by a pioneer of the modernist period in literature, T. S. Eliot. Within this work, the writer creates an amalgam that integrates various references of mythological, religious, historical, and cultural significance. In doing so, he also incorporates the stylistic elements of nursery rhymes and liturgical repetition to convey the meaningless existence of those living in the postwar twentieth century.

Essentially, this poem focuses primarily on the "hollow men" reminiscent of the stuffed effigies related to ancient fertility myths. Like Kurtz, the soulless monomaniacal inspiration originating from Joseph Conrad's *Heart of Darkness*, Eliot's "hollow men" wait impotently amidst the ruins of modern society in the hopes of moral and social regeneration. In spite of attempts to make meaning out of fragments of history, myth, and memory, their existence is little more than a mockery of the spiritual decay that embodies a society that has brought about its own inevitable decline.

See also Apocalypse: Secular; Apocalyptic Literature; Apocalypticism; Archetype; Eliot, T. S.; Freud, Sigmund; *Heart of Darkness;* Jung, Carl Gustav; Myth; Symbol; *The Waste Land.*

HUXLEY, ALDOUS LEONARD

Aldous Leonard Huxley (1894–1963) was the English novelist, essayist, and satirist who is best known for his futuristic social satire entitled *Brave New World* (1932). In many ways, the details pertaining to his life greatly influenced both the nature and the quality of his work. Huxley was the grandson of the distinguished biologist T. H. Huxley, and he was also the half-brother of the Nobel Prize–winning physicist, Andrew Huxley. In addition to his scientific influences, Aldous inherited some of his skill in the area of letters as the son of the famous biographer Leonard Huxley and the great-nephew of the notable Victorian poet Matthew Arnold.

Although Huxley's career as a scholar and writer was seriously compromised by keratitis, which resulted in his partial blindness, he managed to graduate from Balliol College, Oxford, England, in 1916, and publish his first two novels shortly thereafter, *Crome Yellow* (1921) and *Antic Hay* (1923). Huxley established himself as a social satirist in these two works and further sharpened his cynical observation of the philosophical and political pretensions of his day in his subsequently published collections of short stories, *Mortal Coils* (1922) and *Those Barren Leaves* (1925).

As he pursued his life and his art in the late 1920s and early 1930s, Huxley became increasingly suspicious of the pervasive and potentially threatening influences of politics and technology, two forces that he believed would ultimately have a dehumanizing influence on the development of future societies. As such, *Brave New World* reflects these concerns and expresses them vividly in an apocalyptic science fiction novel in which the individuality of humanity's body and spirit are replaced by the more efficient reproduction or cloning of various castes of the human species. By showing how science can be more productive through the elimination of independent thought, feeling, and motivation, Huxley ingeniously predicted many of the genetic miracles that currently serve as the hallmark of the modern civilized world. His question of whether or not the human spirit can survive amidst such sterile control is answered by the

Aldous Huxley

suicide of the only "savage" character to be developed within the novel. Even though it is read as a classic example of dystopic science fiction, *Brave New World* continues to serve as a warning to those who value science over the more intrinsic values of human nature.

See also Apocalypse: Secular; Apocalypticism; *Brave New World;* Science Fiction.

IBUSE, MASUJI

Hiroshima-born novelist Masuji Ibuse (1898–1993) is a leading figure in the Japanese literary world. As a student Ibuse majored in French at Waseda University and later attended the School of Fine Arts to pursue his avid interest in painting. He eventually combined his expertise in dialect as well as his gift for vivid imagery to portray the lives of ordinary people within the form of the novel.

Although Ibuse wrote his first story in 1923 while he was still a student, this satirical work, as well as other stories, were later published in a collection entitled *Salamander and Other Stories* in 1929. Ibuse became a formidable literary force who was immediately recognized throughout the 1930s. The work that followed, *John Manjiro, the Cast-Away: His Life and Adventures* (1937), was well received, in addition to his subsequent series of animal allegories, but his greatest success did not come until after the conclusion of World War II. Consequently, while he continued to gain recognition within his own country throughout the 1940s and 1950s, it was not until publication of *Black Rain* (1969), his novel based on primary sources that describes the effects of the atomic bombing on the lives of everyday people, that he received the worldwide attention that had already led him to win the Noma Prize, Japan's highest literary award.

See also Allegory; Apocalypse: Secular; Apocalyptic Literature; *Black Rain; Hiroshima.*

ICARUS

According to the ancient Greek legend, Icarus was the son of the revered Athenian architect and inventor Daedalus, who was famous for designing the inescapable labyrinth for King Minos. He was also famous for designing the legendary wings made of feathers and wax, with which he and his headstrong son, Icarus, escaped imprisonment. Despite Daedalus's stringent moral and practical warnings, Icarus's pride and self-assurance led him to disobey his father. Foolishly, Icarus uses his fabricated wings to fly too close to the sun. As a result of his hubris, the wax on his wings eventually melted, sending the ingenuous youth plunging to his death in the depths of the sea. The mythical story concludes with Icarus pitifully washed ashore on an island whose name, Icaria, was given in commemoration of a young man who was promising but too proud.

See also Apocalypse: Traditional Primitive; Apocalyptic Literature; *Love in the Ruins: The Adventures of a Bad Catholic at a Time Near the End of the World;* Mephistophiles; More, Dr. Tom; Percy, Walker.

ICE-NINE

Ice-nine is the name of a substance that causes liquids to crystallize or freeze as a result of a precise and rigid stacking of atoms. This invention is the fictional creation of an eccentric Nobel Prize–winning physicist, Dr. Felix Hoenikker, who serves as the unwitting agent of death in Kurt Vonnegut's apocalyptic sci-fi fantasy, *Cat's Cradle* (1963). In the novel, Dr. Hoenikker has earned considerable fame for having been instrumental in the development of the atomic bomb that was dropped on Hiroshima. Given Hoenikker's formidable reputation, a Marine general, who had become frustrated by the problems of his troops' having to fight in the mud, asked the physicist to develop something that "could make infinite expanses of muck, marsh, swamp, creeks, pools, quicksand, and mire as solid as [his] desk" (37). Hoenikker's response to this request was the development of ice-nine.

Both the advantage as well as the problem with this substance is that any liquid to become frozen as a result of contact with ice-nine would remain in a solid form unless it could be heated to a melting temperature of 114.4 degrees Fahrenheit. For Hoenikker, this discovery was as exciting as the atomic bomb, but his optimism was seasoned with caution given his knowledge that its misuse could inevitably lead to similarly cataclysmic results. As such, fully aware of ice-nine's dire consequences, the physicist kept a careful account of the entire quantity of this substance and also maintained a high level of secrecy regarding its development. However, on one fateful Christmas Eve, while on vacation in Cape Cod with his three children, Hoenikker decided to divulge his secret to the only three people whom he felt he could trust: his sons, Newt and Franklin, and his daughter, Angela. After having shown them the apocalyptic chip, which he kept in a bottle in his pocket, Hoenikker died later that same evening. Upon his death, his children divided the chip equally. As such, "*ice-nine* was the last gift Felix Hoenikker [had] created for mankind before going to his just reward" (41).

The details of the Hoenikkers, as well as those of ice-nine, are related through a narrator, identified only as Jonah, who learns about the physicist in the process of writing a book about famous people who had been involved with the dropping of the atomic bomb. Although he never actually writes the intended book, *Cat's Cradle* becomes the narrator's chronicle of a good idea turned bad, so bad, in fact, that it results in a global apocalypse of biblical proportions.

As in most literary apocalypses, particularly those related to the Promethean myth, technology serves as a powerful yet dangerous means of seduction for those who are either intellectually or ethically incapable of governing its use. Such is the case with ice-nine. Each of his children eventually trades his or her knowledge and possession of ice-nine in exchange for the attainment of a personal goal. In the case of Hoenikker's middle son, Franklin, however, the wage of his personal sin is the virtual death of most of the planet.

Franklin is motivated to make such a compromise, however, because in his youth, he had felt awkward, unpopular, and socially isolated. His greatest dream was to become someone of importance who could use his meticulous architectural talents to attain respect and status within a society. He is afforded such an opportunity when he travels to a fictional South American location known as the Republic of San Lorenzo. There he becomes employed by its megalomaniacal leader, "Papa" Monzano, who is both iconoclastic in regard to science and eager to harness the talent of the renowned physicist's son. Simply stated, what results from this partnership is Monzano's acquisition of ice-nine in exchange for his nefarious appointment of Franklin as "the architect of the 'San Lorenzo Master Plan'" (61).

Nonetheless, the master plan, fueled by hubris and ambition, never materializes. In the end, "Papa" Monzano dies, but not before he freezes himself solid by swallowing the crystal of ice-nine that he had worn in a vial attached to a neck chain. What follows is a series of apocalyptic events, including rock slides, tornadoes, raging seas, and earthquakes, which result in "Papa's" petrified body accidentally falling into the sea. Considering the effect of ice-nine upon liquid, only moments pass before San Lorenzo and most of its inhabitants experience the end of their utopian world. Although an earthquake causes a piece of land to separate from the mainland, and only a few people survive the arctic apocalypse, the narrator ultimately issues a warning to potential scientific iconoclasts in an effort to save the world from future destruction at the hands of humanity.

See also Apocalypse: Secular; Apocalyptic Literature; *Cat's Cradle;* Hoenikker, Felix; Jonah-John; Prometheus.

IMMELMANN, ART

Art Immelmann is the demonic trickster who undermines the work and the life of Dr. Tom More in Walker Percy's apocalyptic novel *Love in the Ruins: The Adventures of a Bad Catholic at a Time Near the End of the World* (1971). According to John R. May's critical framework for the "humorous secular apocalypse," a necessary ingredient in such plots includes the appearance of an evil archetype whose purpose it is to instigate the prophesied last loosing of Satan in an increasingly corrupt world. Moreover, Immelmann's duplicitous relationship with the novel's ambitious protagonist is also reminiscent of the battle between good and evil that was waged between Christopher Marlowe's prideful necromancer, Dr. Faustus, and his deceitful tempter, Lucifer's eternally damned minion, Mephistopheles.

As quoted in Gary Ciuba's definitive study of Percy's apocalyptic fiction, R. W. B. Lewis finds that such "con artists [as Immelmann] in American apocalypses. . . . have [often] played the false prophet in Revelation 13 and [have routinely] duped their victims into darkly comic days of doom" (Ciuba 1991, 140–141). Certainly, such is the case in Percy's unconventional novel.

Specific parallels between these two unlikely morality plays show Percy's deliberate and sustained attempt to revisit Marlowe's apocalyptic vision as a satirical modern-day parable. First, Dr. More, like Dr. Faustus, is a frustrated scientist steeped in theological tradition with the physician's determination to cure the ills of the world. Similarly, both Mephistopheles and his counterpart, Art Immelmann, serve as cunning foils to their respective protagonists. In each case, these quick-thinking deceivers are acutely aware of their victims' hubris, folly, and delusions of grandeur. Armed with such knowledge, each deceiver tempts his own wary but willing narcissist with promises of fame, fortune, and future fulfillment.

As Dr. Faustus is lured into making a pact with the devil, so too is Dr. More. Faustus signs a contract, in blood, with Mephistopheles in which he sells his soul to the devil in exchange for unlimited knowledge and access to the demon's supernatural power for the period of twenty-four years. In contrast, while Dr. More's impetuous arrangement with Art Immelmann lacks the grave consequence of eternal damnation, it does, however, threaten the modern world with widespread destruction on an apocalyptic scale.

Details from *Love in the Ruins* support such comparisons between the two diabolical con-men. For example, Immelmann "tries to get this Faust to stumble into the pit by offering financing for [More's controversial invention, the Qualitative-Quantative Ontological Lapsometer], a 75 percent return of profits, and the glory of possibly saving the world" (141). Although the complacent doctor initially refuses the offer because he believes that he will obtain funding from a more reliable source, he later falls prey to Immelmann's promise to improve the lapsometer from merely a diagnostic to a curative instrument, thereby guaranteeing the success of their joint venture. After all other sources of hope are gone, More (like Dr. Faustus) signs a contract with the fast-talking fiend and thereby unleashes the destructive forces that he had always feared would consume humanity in a cataclysmic event.

Fortunately for the beleaguered More, the world, however, does not end. Nevertheless, for a time, he previews the pains of hell while watching as chaos reigns over the lecture auditorium known as the Pit. He is spiritually tormented by the sodium brimstone clouds that rise menacingly from the Paradise Estates Golf Course. And he is frightened yet resigned regarding the Bantu rebellion that overthrows the community's social system. Nevertheless, because Percy's protagonist's sins are forgivable, on the whole, and because Dr. More ultimately sacrifices a part of himself—specifically, his irresponsible libertine lifestyle—for the sacramental security of married monogamy, More survives without forfeiting possession of his eternal soul.

In contrast to Marlowe's prideful Faustus who refuses repeated opportunities to repent for his sins, Percy's Faust clearly realizes his mistake of selling out to Immelmann, repents for his decision to collude with the con-man, and recruits the help of his nurse and faithful guardian angel, Ellen Oglethorp. It is only through these efforts that he is ultimately able to break his pact with Immelmann's Mephistopheles and thereby permanently free himself from the ceaseless bondage of a damnable contract.

See also Apocalypse: Secular; Apocalyptic Literature; *The Confidence-Man: His Masquerade; Dr. Faustus; Faust;* Icarus; *Love in the Ruins: The Adventures of a*

Bad Catholic at a Time Near the End of the World; Mephistophiles; More, Sir Thomas; Satan; Smith, Father Rinaldo; Thanatos; *The Thanatos Syndrome.*

THE INVISIBLE MAN

The Invisible Man (1952) is one of two novels written by African-American novelist Ralph Ellison. This book deals primarily with an unnamed black man's attempt to find his own identity within a dominant white culture during the 1930s. Based in part on the author's own experiences, the novel reflects the conflicts of mind, body, and spirit that the narrator endures in an effort to make meaning in a chaotic world, to fight frustration, and to reconcile his role in a racist society while attempting to react to injustice with a sense of personal responsibility.

The Invisible Man is triadic in form, a structure not unlike Dante's apocalyptic treatise on the nature of man entitled *The Divine Comedy* (1321). In Ellison's novel, however, the narrator is guided through a series of natural rather than supernatural cataclysms. Further, he is assisted on his journey toward enlightenment not by wise and loving guides, like Virgil and Beatrice, but by corrupt individuals who are either egocentric or as blind to reality as he. Whereas Dante's narrator is rewarded at the end of his quest by a clear vision of justice, beauty, and truth, Ellison's apocalyptic vision reveals a world of violence and derision where the only hope for survival lies in delusion and the denial.

Given this clear distinction between the two works, it is easy to see the sharp contrast between Dante's work of traditional Judeo-Christian apocalypse as opposed to Ellison's secular apocalypse. In Dante's work, Satan is immobilized in his icy circle of hell; conversely, Ellison's world is a riotous inferno of hypocrisy and hatred that narratively fulfills the biblical prophecy of the last loosing of Satan.

Viewing Ellison's modern apocalypse through this tripartite structure, therefore, enables readers to recognize the prophetic significance of the "Battle Royal," a scene that marks the first phase of the narrator's search for identity. In this scene, which incites the action of the novel, the narrator participates in a degrading spectacle wherein blindfolded blacks battle one another for the entertainment of a white audience. Ironically, the reward for his victorious participation in this humiliating display is a scholarship to attend one of the state's designated Negro colleges. As such, his guides through this journey are Mr. Norton, a white business magnate who financially supports the institution for personal rather than altruistic purposes, and Dr. Bledsoe, the two-faced college president who, under the guise of assisting the narrator, unjustly undermines the young man's future academic success.

In the second portion of the novel, the narrator learns of his deception, but he accepts his fate, leaves his academic dreams behind, and moves into the world of work, located three stories below the ground, at the Liberty Paint Company whose claim to fame, symbolically, is the precise application of black pigmentation to create a perfect shade of white paint. In this next phase of the journey, the narrator, once again, is assisted in his descent into reality by two diabolical guides, Lucius (Lucifer?) Brockway, the traitorous autocrat in charge of quality control at the factory, and Brother Jack, the charismatic albeit duplicitous union organizer for a militant group known as the Brotherhood of Man. Each of these two characters, like the two guides before them, shamelessly exploit the narrator for the furtherance of their own individual causes. In an attempt to establish some kind of identity for himself, the narrator accepts an offer to become a spokesman for the Brotherhood's cause. Consequently, this decision leads him to encounter two individuals who represent the most demonic characters within the novel.

These two characters are known as Ras the Exhorter and the unseen antagonistic force who is unwittingly responsible for the narrator's ultimate decision, known only as Rinehart. Ras the Exhorter, who later becomes Ras the Destroyer, is a caricature of the stereotypical black militant. While the narrator initially accepts Ras's recommendations in the hope that he will find a forum for his own individual expression, he soon learns that Ras has no interest in individuality, which he believes must be sacrificed for the greater good of the Brotherhood. Ras, who incites a riot and literally oversees his created chaos high atop a horse on the streets of Harlem, is Ellison's undeniable representation of one of the "four horses of the apocalypse" who heralds worldwide destruction in the book of Revelation. Ras's violence and single-minded purpose is also responsible for the narrator's climactic decision to escape from the ranks of the Brotherhood and to try, one last time, to find an identity for himself.

Ironically, in his attempt to disguise himself so as not to be accosted by Ras and his followers, the narrator wears dark glasses and a white hat to make himself "invisible" on the streets of Harlem. This disguise, however, not only provides him an avenue of escape from imminent danger, but paradoxically, it is this very abdication of his own identity that leads to his unorthodox path to personal freedom. All of this comes about as a result of his resemblance to another man named Rinehart, who is known for his gambling, womanizing, and spiritual and monetary extortion. The very fact that he is frequently mistaken for Rinehart while wearing his disguise helps the narrator to discover, in the final chapter of the novel, that true freedom lies in a state of figurative (as well as literal) invisibility. Therefore, as the visage of Rinehart, who is "the living symbol" of the world of chaos (May 152), the narrator is finally able to view his surroundings as they are, not as they are interpreted by intellectuals, businessmen, disillusioned societal outcasts, or enraged militants. Further, as he makes a conscious decision to live in a hole, or a cellar, beneath the streets of the city, he is finally free to develop an individual philosophy of life, which he shares within the epilogue of the novel. The narrator's personal revelation, which comes as a result of his hellish journey, is presented at the conclusion of the novel:

> Step outside the narrow borders of what men call reality and you step into chaos—ask Rinehart, he's a master of it—or imagination. That . . . I've learned in the cellar, and not by deadening my sense of perception; I'm invisible, not blind. No indeed, the world is just as concrete, ornery, vile and sublimely wonderful as before, only now I better understand my relation to it and it to me. I've come a long way from those days when, full of illusion, I lived a public life and attempted to function under the assumption that the world was solid and all the relationships therein. Now I know men are different and that all life is divided and that only in division is their true health (576).

See also Apocalypse: Secular; Apocalypticism; Archetype; Bledsoe, Dr.; Brother Jack; Conrad, Joseph; *The Divine Comedy;* Ellison, Ralph; *Heart of Darkness;* Hell; Revelation, Book of; Rinehart; Satan; Symbol.

ISAIAH, BOOK OF

The book of Isaiah is considered one of the great written works of Old Testament prophecy. It was written by a man whose Hebrew name, Yeshayahu or Yeshayaha, loosely translated, means "salvation of Yahweh." It is likely that the time of Isaiah's prophetic ministry to Israel, from approximately 742–687 B.C., occurred during a time of great conflict with Assyria. The early chapters of the book describe how the prophet received his calling, and how his people dealt with the series of invasions by hostile armies; the most significant chapters, 24 through 27, are often referred to by biblical scholars as "the little apocalypse." The reason for this reference clearly results from the depiction of the final battles between the forces of good and evil that are reiterated, in greater detail, throughout the book of Revelation.

Among the specific prophecies mentioned in Isaiah are the desolation of inhabitants of the earth because they have broken the everlasting covenant. Also, according to the prophecy, "the earth shall reel to and fro like a drunkard, and shall be removed like a cottage; and the transgression thereof shall be heavy upon it; and it shall fall, and not rise again" (Isaiah 24:20, KJV). But after a period of suffering, the Lord promises, through the prophet Isaiah, that he will eventually "swallow up death in victory; and the Lord God will wipe away tears from off all faces" (25:8). In response to this, the book of Isaiah also includes an extensive hymn of praise thanking God for his mercy on his disobedient people.

The final part of the prophecy foreshadows much of the detail provided in Revelation in that at the end of the world, God will slay the "leviathan [or] piercing serpent," also known as "the dragon that is in the sea" (27:1). Moreover, he further promises that after the dragon has been slain, "Israel shall blossom and bud, and fill the face of the world with fruit" (27:6). And although the restoration of the city of Jerusalem will be compromised by attempted attacks by hostile nations, God promises that in that time, "the great trumpet shall be blown" indicating that all people will be called to worship in Jerusalem.

See also Apocalypse: Traditional Judeo-Christian; Apocalyptic Literature; Armageddon; Daniel, Book of; Ezekiel, Book of; Gog and Magog; Leviathan; Revelation, Book of.

ISHMAEL

Ishmael is the name of the narrator of Herman Melville's American apocalyptic masterpiece *Moby-Dick* (1851). According to the Latin translation, Ishmael means "God may hear," and in the Hebrew translation, means "he will hear." Also based on the Old Testament origin of the name, Ishmael, in general, has come to refer to characters who are, either by choice or by chance, outcasts from society. Clearly, Melville was aware of these etymological origins in naming the character who would serve as the observer of the apocalyptic events that would eventually destroy everyone on the whaling vessel, the *Pequod.* Melville's Ishmael is the sole survivor of the cataclysmic ordeal that compels him to become a reluctant prophet warning against human pride in *Moby-Dick.*

Ishmael's essential nature is evident in the opening scenes of the novel wherein he confesses to an insatiable and nearly self-destructive curiosity about everything in the world. He is one of literature's many intellectual wanderers who roam the earth in search of meaning in the midst of life's myriad mysteries. For this reason, he is particularly drawn to the mystery of the sea, which for him, "is the image of the ungraspable phantom of life . . . [wherein he believes lies] the key to it all" (3).

In as much as he admits to a preference for maintaining a low profile in whatever interest he pursues, he serves as the perfect foil for the novel's misguided and monomaniacal hero, Captain Ahab. Ahab, in contrast to Ishmael, feels compelled to control his universe, an intrinsic personal characteristic that became pathological after losing a leg to the fierce white whale, an object of his revenge, the malevolent sea mammal Moby-Dick. In spite of their obvious differences, however, the two men share a keen intellect. Whereas Ahab's intelligence is obvious in his dedication to action, Ishmael's intelligence is more internalized and contemplative, a quality that serves him well as both the narrator and an emotionally detached participant in a world controlled by Ahab's descent into madness.

Although Ishmael is very much involved in the activities that occur on the *Pequod,* and is, in fact, eager to bond with his fellow seafarers, it is precisely his ability to maintain a safe intellectual distance from Ahab's virulent vengeance that ultimately saves him from the apocalyptic outcome of the captain's diabolical quest. This characteristic of Melville's narrator has also become something of a literary archetype in that this pattern of the detached yet nearly seduced narrator is repeated throughout literature in general, and apocalyptic literature in particular. One example occurs in a twentieth-century science fiction fantasy by Kurt Vonnegut entitled *Cat's Cradle.* Within this novel, which has similar monomaniacs with similar iconoclastic pursuits, Ishmael's character is re-created in the form of a narrator named Jonah-John. Clearly, both the allusion to the biblical Jonah, and his relationship to a great whale, as well as the first line of Vonnegut's novel, "Call me Jonah" (Vonnegut *CC* 1), as compared with Melville's opening line, "Call me Ishmael," illustrate how Melville's prophet of doom reflects a literary theme of humankind's ignorance of God's omnipotence.

See also Ahab; Ahab, Captain; Apocalypse: Secular; Apocalypse: Traditional Judeo-Christian; Apocalyptic Literature; *Cat's Cradle;* Hoenikker, Felix; Ice-Nine; Jonah-John; Leviathan; *Moby-Dick.*

JOEL, BOOK OF

The book of Joel is one of the prophetic books of the Old Testament that deals with the events leading up to the final apocalypse. The author, whose Hebrew name, Yoel, means "Jehovah is God," was probably a resident of Jerusalem, but considerable debate exists as to the dates during which the work was written. Those who favor a preexilic composition date the work circa 830 B.C. However, considerable evidence also exists that the book might have been composed during the postexilic period dating somewhere around 400 B.C. While such matters are best left as the subject of debate for more learned biblical scholars, lay readers need only know the message of the work, which is primarily an announcement that "the day of the Lord cometh, for *it is* nigh at hand" (Joel 2:1, KJV).

Chapters 2 and 3 of Joel, in particular, take great pains to attract the attention of those who have been living their lives heedless of the pending Day of Judgment. Joel urges his people to "sound an alarm in [his] holy mountain" (2:1), and to prepare for the earthquakes, the desolation, and the darkening of the sun, moon, and stars that will pronounce the coming of the Lord. In order to allay the fears of his people, however, Joel encourages them to keep the faith in God's promise that he will eventually restore their land as well as "the years the locust hath eaten" (2:25) because of their earlier disobedience of his laws.

Another important prophecy within the book of Joel is what is known as the "outpouring of God's spirit," which will cause Israel's sons and daughters to prophesy, its old men to "dream dreams," and its young men to "see visions" (2:28). And as a result of this outpouring, "it shall come to pass that whosoever shall call on the name of the Lord shall be delivered" (2:32). While chapter 3 deals primarily with a recounting of the final apocalyptic battles, as is similarly provided, albeit in greater detail, within other prophetic books of the Bible, Joel's work also mentions the opportunity for Gentiles to fight for the cause of righteousness and to join "the multitudes" of his chosen people on the Day of Judgment "in the valley of decision" (3:14).

See also Apocalypse: Traditional Judeo-Christian; Apocalyptic Literature; Daniel, Book of; *The Day of the Locust;* Ezekiel, Book of; Isaiah, Book of; Revelation, Book of.

JONAH, BOOK OF

The book of Jonah (c. 500–200 B.C.) details the events pertaining to the life of one of the minor prophets in the Old Testament. The setting of the story presented in this parable is a community consisting of postexilic Jews. The purpose of the parable, more than likely, was to cause a resurgence of obedience among a people whose persecution had caused them to doubt God's ways and to seek vengeance on their oppressors rather than justice. As such, Jonah represents his people who, at the time, were less than inclined to follow God's command to spread his word among all people of the earth—including their enemies.

Essentially, God asks Jonah to become a missionary to the neighboring hostile land of Nineveh, a great Assyrian city, which had become known for its excessive decadence. Jonah was reluctant to help his tyrannical neighbors in any way, particularly if such actions would lead to the salvation of their city. So when God directed him to travel to Nineveh, he instead disobeyed the command and fled toward Tarshish (i.e., in the opposite direction of Nineveh and as far away from God as possible).

In his attempt to escape God, Jonah becomes a passenger on a ship; God's will once again becomes readily apparent when the ship is tossed by raging storms. Soon, the others on the ship begin to wonder why God has allowed them suddenly to suffer in this way, and so they decide to draw lots to reveal the cause of their calamity. Not surprisingly, Jonah's lot identifies him as the source of God's wrath, and he is, therefore, tossed overboard in order to save the ship.

This misfortune led him to become swallowed by a great fish, or whale, in which he lives for three days. While imprisoned within the sea creature, he cries out to God for mercy, and this call results in the whale's spitting him out onto dry land. Grateful to be alive and on land, he is still reluctant to serve as a prophet to Nineveh; nevertheless, remembering God's mercy toward him, he obeys the original command, travels to Nineveh, and much to his surprise, the wicked city repents of its evil ways.

Although he should feel pleased to have finally obeyed God's will, his human pride, and the pride of his people, causes him to feel resentful that such an evil city as Nineveh has been saved. Once again, through a series of smaller lessons, God teaches Jonah the importance of both justice and mercy. The biblical account of Jonah's folly serves as the prophet's lasting warning to others, like himself, who attempt to place their own will above that of God's.

See also Apocalypse: Secular; Apocalypse: Traditional Judeo-Christian; Apocalypse: Traditional Primitive; Apocalyptic Literature; *Cat's Cradle;* Jonah-John; Leviathan; *Moby-Dick.*

JONAH-JOHN

Jonah-John is the narrator and protagonist of Kurt Vonnegut's science fiction fantasy entitled *Cat's Cradle* (1963). At the outset of this novel portraying a classic secular apocalypse, Jonah-John, or simply Jonah, is a writer who as a young man feels compelled to chronicle the activities of famous Americans and their recollections of the day that America used the atomic bomb in its attack on Hiroshima. The proposed title of the book, which he never actually writes, is *The Day the World Ended*. Little does he know, however, at the time he begins his project, that his literary research will result in his personal experience with a similar disaster of worldwide significance.

In order to understand the relevance of Jonah's character in Vonnegut's novel, readers must first understand the archetypes upon which the protagonist is based. First, it is no mere coincidence that his name is Jonah. Much like the original Jonah in the Old Testament, Jonah-John understands the considerable challenges he faces as he undertakes his task, and he also encounters both physical and psychological obstacles in the completion of his mission. Furthermore, just as the biblical Jonah finally learns about humility and survives to warn the world of the high cost of human pride, so too does Jonah-John survive an apocalyptic adventure, thereby becoming yet another reluctant prophet whose own warning is delivered in the form of the narrative of *Cat's Cradle*.

Another perhaps even more direct pattern upon which Jonah-John is based is Ishmael, the narrator of Herman Melville's apocalyptic masterpiece, *Moby-Dick*. This relationship is clearly evident in the opening lines of each novel. In Melville's work, the first words are "Call me Ishmael," and in Vonnegut's novel, they are "Call me Jonah." These abrupt introductions by the two narrators convey the prophetic tone of the factual details that comprise their respective tales. Moreover, just as the impartial Ishmael ultimately becomes the sole survivor of the *Pequod's* apocalyptic encounter with the great white whale, Jonah-John's detachment from the iconoclastic society of San Lorenzo enables him to survive a more devastating man-made cataclysm of epic proportions.

Given this background, it is understandable how Vonnegut's Jonah, much like his aforementioned archetypes, begins his journey as a worldly, cynical, and self-absorbed individual who inevitably becomes transformed by the profound revelation of his experiences. Jonah's first significant revelation in the novel regards his making contact with the youngest son of a famous physicist, the eccentric genius Dr. Felix Hoenikker. Although Jonah only intends for Dr. Hoenikker to be one of many subjects for his book, he becomes obsessed with the evolving story of the Nobel Prize winner whom he learns had been directly involved with the creation of the atom bomb. Through the initial cooperation of the scientist's midget son, Newt, Jonah learns two things that would forever change his view of humanity and its role in the universe. First, he learns that before his death, Dr. Hoenikker had discovered a chemical compound that would permanently render temperate liquids into frozen crystalline solids. The product of this discovery, known as "ice-nine," had been produced to assist the government in fighting wars on soggy foreign soil; however, its eventual possession by unscrupulous individuals would inevitably turn Hoenikker's best intentions into disastrous results.

A second lesson that Jonah learns in the novel regards the area of religion and its role in the lives of human beings. As such, although he begins his adventure as a lukewarm Christian, his continued quest for more information about the rabid scientist ultimately leads him toward conversion to the absurd and somewhat nihilistic "religion of lies" called Bokononism. He acquires his knowledge of Bokononism during his visit to the South American republic of San Lorenzo. In short, this religion is based upon the attainment of superior physical and mental health as well as the relentless pursuit of happiness; in short, it's an ever-changing dogma filled with contradictions, bizarre rituals, and humanity's inevitable rebellion. Nonetheless, the "easy-believism" of the religion of lies has caused it to become a threat to the growth of the republic and is, therefore, forbidden by the government. Ironically, however, although no one openly professes the belief for fear of punishment by a gruesome method of public execution, it is widely acknowledged and accepted that most San Lorenzians are secretly involved in its practice, including the leader of the republic himself.

As Jonah's quest leads to a successive series of coincidental epiphanies, his perseverance ultimately leads him to the object of his visit to San Lorenzo. The main reason he travels to this destination is to interview Dr. Hoenikker's middle child, Franklin. What he learns about Franklin from personal experience, however, runs contrary to everything he had heard previously about the reclusive and rebellious ne'er-do-well. Jonah is surprised that rather than meeting an irresponsible drifter, he encounters the illustrious Major General Franklin Hoenikker, the principal architect of San Lorenzo's political and technological future who is prized both for his knowledge and even more for his relationship to Dr. Felix Hoenikker. Assuming that Franklin would be a chip off his famous father's block, "Papa" Monzano, the ambitious and science-obsessed leader of the republic, hopes to harness some of the genius and potential power made possible by the physicist's experiments, not the least of which is ice-nine.

Eventually, as Jonah builds his relationship with Franklin, as well as Monzano's radiantly serene adoptive daughter, Mona, he begins to join the inner circle of San Lorenzo and becomes a trusted figure in the republic. When Franklin, who is destined to be Monzano's successor and the husband of Mona, confides that he loves another and is temperamentally ill suited for rulership, he recommends, successfully, that Jonah become the next leader of the republic. Almost immediately, this opportunity seduces Jonah who begins to plan his political strategies even before the death of "Papa" Monzano. His eagerness to assume his role is further fortified by the understanding that as the leader of San Lorenzo, he will also become the husband of his beloved Mona.

In addition to his political future, Jonah also pursues the study of Bokononism under Mona's tutelage. Although he almost loses her because of her refusal to remain monogamous, preferring the Bokononist practice of literally loving everyone, he capitulates to the religion's liberal moral stance in order to possess—officially, at least—the object of his desire. Nevertheless, while Jonah is involved in both the subtle and obvious machinations of San Lorenzo society, he retains his journalistic objectivity as this man-made utopia is destroyed, as is usually the case, by the prideful and self-serving actions of the novel's principal characters.

In the final chapters of the novel, each of Dr. Felix Hoenikker's children admit to succumbing to temptation. These children also, in essence, sell their souls and thereby compromise humanity in its entirety for the temporary fulfillment of their individual desires. Specifically, Newt, the midget, is enamored with a miniature Russian dancer, with whom he spends one sexually fulfilling week on Cape Cod, only to find their brief but torrid affair concluded with her theft of some of his portion of ice-nine. Angela, the oldest and most responsible albeit admittedly homely child, uses ice-nine as a bribe to win a handsome and successful husband. And finally, Franklin, who had once felt isolated and insignificant in the world, willingly trades his portion of ice-nine for the prestige and power of a high-ranking position under the leadership of Monzano, who is an avid worshiper of science in general, and of Dr. Felix Hoenikker in particular.

Their collective sins inevitably result in one of the most complete apocalypses in American literature. First, Monzano, who takes his last breath on his deathbed, decides to leave this world in a blaze of scientific glory; he removes the vial of ice-nine that he has worn around his neck, swallows the crystals, and becomes immediately petrified in a position of icy triumph. At this point, Jonah reflects on the inevitable impact that the dissemination of ice-nine will have on the world. He recalls a portentous passage in *The Fourteenth Book* of Bokonon, which is entitled, "What Can a Thoughtful Man Hope for Mankind on Earth, Given the Experience of the Past Million Years?" The answer offered in the book "consists of one word and a period. . . . 'Nothing' " (164). As such, the narrator learns the terrible truth that the forces of religion, government, and science, while impressive and reliable for the most part, are ultimately impotent in a world where chaos, human pride, unwavering ambition, and a collective absence of moral responsibility keep humanity from making the right decisions when presented with the dilemma of choice. Consequently, following his realization of the inevitable, Jonah objectively observes the chaotic events that are the wages of their sin. And it is in these scenes that Vonnegut conveys his version of the end of the world. First, a disabled plane drops suddenly from the sky. The ensuing explosion of the plane results in the destruction of Monzano's castle. Rock slides abound, and eventually the earth rends, creating a threatening abyss separating Jonah and a few others from the remainder of the people who are swallowed up by the raging sea. The final cataclysmic event occurs when the unstable rocks of Monzano's tower cause his frigid corpse to be hurled into the sea. Recalling the ultimate horror, much like St. John in the book of Revelation, Jonah closes his eyes and witnesses a scene worthy of the plagues of the Four Horsemen of the Apocalypse,

> There was a sound like that of the gentle closing of a portal as big as the sky, the great door of heaven being closed softly. It was [he recalls] a grand AH-WHOOM. I [Jonah] opened my eyes—and all the sea was ice-nine. The moist green earth was a blue-white pearl. The sky darkened. . . . [T]he sun became a sickly yellow ball, tiny and cruel. The sky was filled with worms. The worms were tornadoes (174).

The descriptively detailed death of their morally bankrupt world is ultimately confirmed in a note that the survivors find under a rock, which apparently had been composed by the religious icon, Bokonon himself.

> To whom it may concern: These people around you are almost all of the survivors on San Lorenzo of the winds that followed the freezing of the sea.

> These people made a captive of the spurious holy man named Bokonon. They brought him here, placed him at their center, and commanded him to tell them exactly what God Almighty was up to and what they should now do. The mountebank told them that God was surely trying to kill them, possibly because he was through with them, and that they should have the good manners to die. This, as you can see, they did (182).

Although there were a number of survivors on that fateful day, only one had been chosen, seemingly from the very beginning of his quest, to deliver a revelation to those living in the last days of a corrupt world. Ironically, the message Vonnegut satirically presents in his apocalyptic tale is as old as humanity itself. Free will, intended as a divinely inspired gift, will ultimately become an eternal curse, as long as humans continue to create institutions, governments, and technology in an attempt to deify themselves.

See also Apocalypse: Secular; Apocalyptic Literature; *Cat's Cradle;* Hoenikker, Felix; Ice-Nine.

JUNG, CARL GUSTAV

Carl Jung (1875–1961) was the Swiss psychologist who is best known for his discovery of archetypes, or universal patterns within humanity's "collective unconscious," that are based on myth, symbols, and religion. This discovery, which clearly had relevance in Jung's analysis of personality types and human relationships, has also had a significant impact on both the development and interpretation of some of the world's finest examples of modern literature.

As a child, Jung was sensitive, pensive, and extremely attracted to the mystical qualities found in Eastern religions. This fascination continued to fuel his imagination even after he was accepted to medical school at the University of Basel where he studied psychiatry and composed a dissertation on the subject of spiritualism and the occult. In the years that followed, Jung's psychiatric studies led him to develop a system for revealing unconscious mental blocks known as the word-association technique, which is still in use to date.

While he was making significant strides in his own area of study, perhaps the greatest influence on the future of his work came as a result of his professional association with the father of psychoanalysis, Dr. Sigmund Freud. At first, their relationship was one of mutual admiration. However, as Jung's views began to stray from Freud's orthodox insistence on sexuality and its narrow range of dream interpretation, Jung branched out by publishing his own theories in a 1912 publication entitled *Psychology of the Unconscious.* In this work, Jung extrapolated on a theory that he had been developing throughout his entire life; essentially, he examined the universal application of mythological symbols as they correlated directly with a cadre of standard psychotic fantasies.

Jung officially split from the psychoanalytical approach of Freud and developed his own theory of analytic psychology. This work, in turn, led him to focus on the spiritual, mythical, and symbolic influences on the development of human personality. These studies eventually led him to create a major work revealing these theories entitled *Psychological Types,* published in 1921, a work that is still relevant in the study of human psychology. The primary premise of the

Carl Gustav Jung

work dealt with the differences between introverted and extroverted personalities as well as his views of the androgynous nature of humans, which concerned the reconciliation of the *anima*, or man's feminine archetype, with the *animus*, or the female's masculine archetype, for the purpose of self-realization. And although these were groundbreaking concepts for the time, both theories are currently accepted as standard means of exploring human personality.

Jung's extrapolation on his theory of archetypes, or original types upon which others are based, has made a significant contribution to the area of literary interpretation. Specifically, Jung posited that within the "collective unconscious" of humanity, major archetypes related to birth, death, power, demons, and God maintain consistent characteristics regardless of the culture in which they have been conceptualized. As such, this technique of using archetypes in literature has added depth to the study of ancient allegories, classical myths, and world religions as well as figuring prominently in the works of such modern writers as James Joyce, William Faulkner, Franz Kafka, Flannery O'Connor, and D. H. Lawrence. And although some have questioned the validity of Jung's abstract and sometimes mystical explanations, his efforts to help writers express the complexity of the human experience is as valuable to the fictional form as are the individual stories themselves.

See also *Absalom, Absalom!* Allegory; Apocalypse: Traditional Judeo-Christian; Archetype; *Faust;* Freud, Sigmund; *The Great Gatsby; The Hollow Men;* Myth; Symbol; *The Violent Bear It Away; The Waste Land.*

KARAMAZOV, ALYOSHA FYODOROVICH

The youngest and most innocent son of Fyodor Pavlovich, the self-indulgent patriarch in Dostoyevsky's *The Brothers Karamazov,* Alyosha, as he is affectionately known, is studying as a novice under the tutelage of an elder named Zosima. Nevertheless, while Alyosha dreams of pursuing a life of monastic service, Zosima recognizes characteristics of worldliness that link him to his father and his brothers, and, therefore, Zosima recommends that Alyosha serve God in the secular world rather than in the clerical one. In regard to his function within the novel, however, Alyosha is the even-tempered, kind-hearted, and compassionate observer and occasional mediator between his volatile father and his anguished brothers.

See also Apocalypse: Traditional Judeo-Christian; Apocalypticism; *The Brothers Karamazov;* Karamazov, Dmitri Fyodorovich; Karamazov, Fyodor Pavlovich; Karamazov, Ivan Fyodorovich.

KARAMAZOV, DMITRI FYODOROVICH 

Also known in the novel as Mitya, Dmitri is the oldest son of Fyodor Pavlovich Karamazov in Dostoyevsky's *The Brothers Karamazov.* Although he displays similar characteristics of his father, such as lustfulness and general self-indulgence, he has an essential nobility that appears briefly in the novel but does not completely emerge until he fails to defend himself during a trial for his father's murder, which he did not commit; he is accused of the murder because of an ongoing feud with his father. Apparently, when his mother died and left an inheritance for her young son, the wastrel father, Fyodor, promised to give his son his due, but selfishly squandered the funds for his own entertainment throughout Dmitri's adult life.

This issue of inheritance was often a matter of public debate, so too was the rivalry between father and son in regard to their relationship with a local siren named Grushenka. Grushenka is powerfully drawn to Dmitri, but she refuses to get involved with a man who has less money than she. As such, the general animosity between father and son suggested the possibility that Dmitri could have

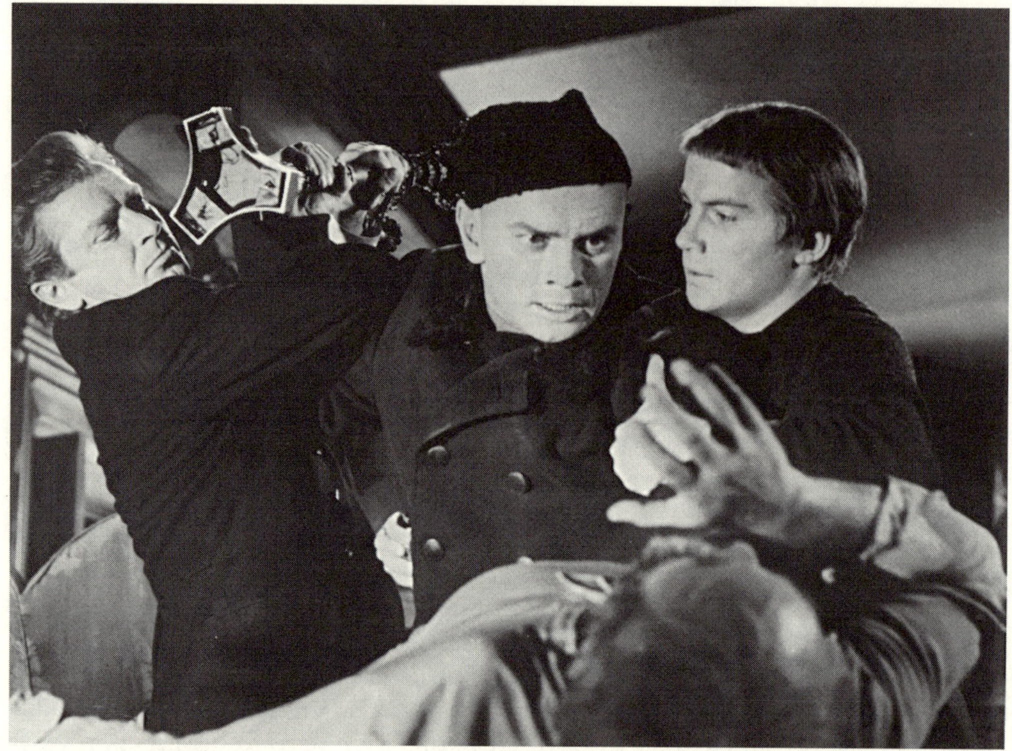

Russian novelist Fyodor Dostoyevsky published *The Brothers Karamazov* in the late 1880s; a movie based on the work was released in 1958. An enraged Dmitri Karamazov (Yul Brynner), restrained by brothers Ivan (Richard Basehart), left, and Alyosha (William Shatner), right, threatens their father, Fyodor Pavlovich (Lee J. Cobb), with a candlestick.

murdered his father, but the truth is that it is Smerdyakov, Fyodor's illegitimate son, who is actually guilty of the crime.

While Dmitri's general temperament suggests that he would react strongly against such an unjust accusation, readers eventually understand his solemn acceptance of his fate—exile to Siberia—because it is motivated by a sense of duty, justice, and respect for the reputation of his former fiancée who had once loved and helped him in the past, in spite of his infidelity to her.

See also Apocalypse: Traditional Judeo-Christian; Apocalypticism; *The Brothers Karamazov;* Karamazov, Alyosha Fyodorovich; Karamazov, Fyodor Pavlovich; Karamazov, Ivan Fyodorovich.

KARAMAZOV, FYODOR PAVLOVICH

Fyodor Karamazov is the lustful, irreverent exhibitionist who is the patriarch of a family of sons in Dostoyevsky's epic novel entitled *The Brothers Karamazov.* Although he is aware that his behavior is often embarrassing and degrading, his buffoonery is encouraged by any demonstration of contempt that comes from observers, and most importantly, from any of his sons.

As a character, he is the embodiment of the seven deadly sins. He is easily angered at Dmitri's rightful requests for his legal inheritance. He is covetous of his money and Grushenka, a local seductress who can match him both in wits and money. Further, he is envious when he learns that Dmitri has managed to work his way into Grushenka's heart. In almost every scene in which he appears, Fyodor displays behavior that is gluttonous, lustful, slothful, and swollen with pride. As such, although each of his children has inherited some small quality of their father's amiable albeit objectionable character, he alone in the novel is the total representation of irrational thought and pure animalistic action.

See also Apocalypse: Traditional Judeo-Christian; Apocalypticism; *The Brothers Karamazov;* Karamazov, Alyosha Fyodorovich; Karamazov, Dmitri Fyodorovich; Karamazov, Ivan Fyodorovich.

KARAMAZOV, IVAN FYODOROVICH

Also known as Vanya, Ivan Karamazov is the embodiment of rationality and intellect in Dostoyevsky's apocalyptic novel *The Brothers Karamazov.* Ivan has had the experience of traveling abroad, and as a result, he has witnessed many injustices in the world that have caused him to question the existence of God. Ivan has made the conscious decision to reject the gift of eternal salvation from a God who would allow suffering to exist within the world.

In his heart, Ivan feels both pity and revulsion for human beings as a result of their intrinsic weakness. He is particularly aware of such weakness as he observes the licentious behavior of his father, the willful aggression of Dmitri, the religious subjection of Alyosha, and the dim-witted logic of his epileptic half-brother, Smerdyakov.

Nevertheless, having clearly given much thought to the essential weakness of human nature, he expounds his views by reciting an enigmatic parable called "The Grand Inquisitor" to his youngest brother, Alyosha. And while he feels secure in his cynicism and rejection of spiritual matters, it is precisely this lack of conviction that causes his soulful torment and gradual mental deterioration when he learns that his own careless rhetoric was responsible for Smerdyakov's murder of their father.

See also Apocalypse: Traditional Judeo-Christian; Apocalypticism; *The Brothers Karamazov;* Karamazov, Alyosha Fyodorovich; Karamazov, Dmitri Fyodorovich; Karamazov, Fyodor Pavlovich.

KILL HOLE

Kill Hole (1992) is the Native American novel written by Jamake Highwater, also pseudonymously known as J. Marks. It typifies John R. May's definition of the traditional primitive apocalypse (May 1972, 229). Within this novel, Highwater combines classical symbolism, Native American myth, and the cataclysmic intensity of the modern world in which to tell his visionary tale about the powerful forces of life, love, ancestry, and art.

In doing so, Highwater introduces an autobiographical protagonist known as Sitko Ghost Horse. The novel begins *in media res*, or in the middle of the crisis that faces him throughout the novel. This crisis involves his accidental wandering across a boundary of an Indian tribe on the night of a special ritual in which the formerly sequestered children of the camp would be blessed and cleansed by good spirits who would help them live in their new terrestrial world. His unintentional disruption of their ritual, however, results in his immediate imprisonment, humiliation, torture, and impending death. Through a series of flashbacks, nightmares, and visions that occur or are recalled throughout his imprisonment, the reader learns of the former happiness Sitko had known before his world fell apart and sent him wandering insanely into a situation that promises to bring his life to a violent end.

Through these flashbacks, the narrative reveals that Sitko's early life was somewhat chaotic and nontraditional. The basic source of his identity is related in the oral recitation of his lineage. Specifically, in those moments throughout the novel when he is either called upon to prove himself or trying to preserve both his identity and his sanity, he delivers the following litany:

> "My name is Sitko Ghost Horse! But I don't know where I come from. My grandmother was called Amana! Her husband was Far Away Son! But he died. She had a child. With a stranger. That child was my mother, Jemina Bonneville! And my father was called Jamie Ghost Horse! And my foster father was named Alexander Milas-Miller. And when I was adopted I was called Seymour Miller. They called me Sy Miller, but I am Sitko Ghost Horse. That is who I am!" (144).

The frequent appearance of this refrain establishes a central theme within the novel: Sitko's quest for his true identity. But while his assertion that he is proud of his Native American identity is admirable, it often masks the confusion of his having been raised by a stern foster father from the dominant white culture who had once been a coworker of Jamie Ghost Horse, both of whom were aerialists in a circus. While the details are never actually presented, it seems clear that Sitko's unreliable natural father disappeared from the family, leaving all the responsibility for Sitko and his older, and understandably embittered brother, Reno, with his hapless mother, Jemina, who promptly placed them in an orphanage due to her inability to care for them properly by herself. After she and Alexander Milas-Miller marry, however, they attempt to retrain the boys into their middle-class American ways. While the older of the two, Reno, openly rebels against such a loss of his heritage, Sitko secretly grapples with the complex issues of his own personal, sexual, and artistic identity.

It is this lack of surety in his identity that specifically causes him trouble when he wanders into the strange tribal camp on the night of their special ritual. Because he is unable to place himself within the world, they too are unable to determine whether he is a good or an evil spirit; thus, he is imprisoned, and because of their primitive superstitions, he is likely to be killed for his lack of conviction. In addition to killing him, the leaders of the tribe also threaten to kill all of the children whose purification and initiation ritual was interrupted by his unfortunate appearance. In essence, the tribe believes that if an evil spirit has invaded the camp before the children have been blessed, then the children must be killed rather than be allowed to grow up under the influence of an evil spirit.

None of this information, however, is presented clearly either to the reader or to Sitko himself early in the novel. It is only after the introduction of a complex character named Patu that Sitko learns the significance of his crime and the brutality he will certainly face at the hands of their primitive leaders. While Patu appears to be a large, slightly deformed woman, and presents herself as an "Earth-Mother" figure, in reality, she is a hermaphrodite—i.e., she looks and acts like a woman, but she also has very small male genitalia hidden beneath her robes. Within their tribe, however, this obvious androgyny is celebrated rather than scorned. As such, she is considered a "strong woman" whose duty it is to care for those who must suffer and wait, whether they be condemned criminals or innocent children. Consequently, as Patu's trust in Sitko grows, so too does the bond that they share that gradually frees him to learn, through Patu's tutelage as well as through dreams and visions, his true identity in the world.

This truth, however, does not come without a cost. The first thing that he learns from Patu is that he has a powerful enemy within the tribe whose intent it is to destroy him. The enemy is the nefarious tribal leader known as Delito, which is translated in Spanish as "crime." Clearly based upon a demonic archetype, Delito has sadistic qualities that are revealed as he conducts an interrogation of his prisoner, Sitko. While in Delito's presence, Sitko experiences excruciating pain, endures verbal humiliation, and fades in and out of a chaotic delirium. Although Patu, as usual, intervenes on Sitko's behalf, readers get the sense of Delito's diabolical qualities as he leaves Sitko's prison cell, "whisper[ing] with a vicious smile. . . . laugh[ing] and hop[ping] on his little legs. . . . [with] the sweet odor of decay [flying] in the wind and [following] after him. An obedient shadow [seems to] trai[l] doggedly in his footsteps. And as he [vanishes] though the door, he le[aves] a fragile trail of cinders and blood" (101).

Another, and perhaps even more powerful lesson that Sitko learns from Patu, however, is one that helps him to heal the wounds of his personal past. Through Patu, an eager audience for both his daytime stories and his nightmarish ravings, Sitko is able to resolve his relationship with a former male lover and fellow artist, named Eric, with whom he had worked and shared his life until Eric's cruel death from a wasting sickness that can be nothing other that AIDS. Most significantly, however, he learns from Patu that his art is the means by which he will regain what has been missing in his life: his ancestral heritage and his joy for living.

Through a series of harrowing near-death experiences, the apocalyptic theme of the novel provides Sitko with a cyclic return to reality. And this return to reality comes as a gift from Patu. Just prior to his scheduled execution, she gives him a piece of clay pottery that she has created with her own hands. She reinforces what he already knows: that with art there is life. But as he also knows, life cannot truly be lived if one lives in fear, as he had done after the death of so many of his friends that left him both unable to create and unable to love. In order to illustrate her point and thereby unify the work with an explanation of its central metaphor, Patu tells him to take the clay bowl with him "wherever [he] go[es.]" But before she surrenders custody of it, she drives a small hole into the bottom of the bowl and explains to the puzzled Sitko that it is a "kill hole" (193). She rationalizes her actions to Sitko as follows: "This bit of clay is a living creature from the earth. And now I have killed it. Now the spirit of the bowl is free to go with you. Now both the bowl and you, my friend, are free at last" (194).

Realizing the wisdom of this explanation, Sitko himself is set free. And as he notices that the door of his cell is open, he leaves his confinement behind him, along with his fear of death, his fear of professional persecution, and his fear of losing someone he loves. By doing so, he proves that in spite of the inevitable cruelty and chaos in the earthly world, he can follow the path of the totemic fox who leads him out of the woods, and begin again to celebrate his life, his art, his sexual orientation, and his ancestral heritage because he is finally free from the bondage of fear.

See also Apocalypse: Traditional Primitive; Apocalypticism; Delito; Ghost Horse, Sitko; Highwater, Jamake; Patu.

KING LEAR

King Lear (c. 1605) is considered by some to be the greatest tragedy written by William Shakespeare. Although the work emphasizes historical rather than religious apocalyptic doctrine, it can rightfully be classified within John R. May's category of traditional primitive apocalypse. According to May, such works contain specific elements: paradisiacal conditions that are disrupted by pervasive evil influences and the acceleration of evil deeds causing widespread chaos until the evil cycle is eventually broken by a clear awareness of reality that usually results from considerable suffering and/or loss (May 1972, 229). Such is certainly the case for the protagonist of *King Lear.*

This is a saga of Lear, an aging king of pre-Christian Britain. Although he is in good health, he decides that he is tired of the relentless rigors of rulership and, therefore, intends to divide his formidable kingdom among his three daughters, Goneril, Regan, and his favorite child, Cordelia. This division of property, however, comes at a price. The daughters must perform for their pampered father by offering elaborate public declarations of their love for him. Naturally, he expects that all of his daughters will be lavish with their praise, but he believes that his youngest, Cordelia, will be the most effusive, which, in turn, will justify his giving her the largest portion of his kingdom. The result, however, runs counter to his plan. As expected, the two older daughters, Goneril and Regan, have no problem bartering meaningless words for valuable land. Their fawning efforts are clearly exaggerated and false, yet Lear complacently accepts their accolades as truth and plans to award them accordingly. He is shocked and greatly disappointed, however, when Cordelia, his favorite child, defies the dubious pattern set by her sisters and plainly states that she loves him as a dutiful daughter should, "nor more, nor less." While Lear should be honored by her candor, respect, and reluctance to offer him insincere flattery, instead he is quickly angered by his wounded pride. Consequently, as an act of thoughtless retri-

King Lear, central figure of William Shakespeare's circa 1605 tragedy, was portrayed by Yuri Yarvet in a 1970 Russian movie. The play fits John R. May's category of a traditional primitive apocalypse: an earthly paradise temporarily overcome by evil that causes temporary chaos before a return to a more somber reality.

bution, he immediately disinherits his beloved Cordelia and spitefully divides his land equally between her two diabolical siblings.

This action leaves Cordelia the singular option of being given in marriage to the king of France. Cordelia is devastated by her father's actions, but she is soon calmed by the integrity of her actions and the devotion of her new husband. Lear quickly regrets his impetuous decision after spending one month in the hostile atmosphere of Goneril's home. During that time, not only does she force him to reduce the number of knights within his military entourage, but she also maliciously places his faithful friend, the Earl of Kent, in the stockade. Finding these actions abominable, Lear sends Kent to the home of his second daughter, Regan, to prepare her for his arrival. Although he believes that playing one sister against the other will ensure a comforting welcome, he soon learns of their conspiracy to humiliate and destroy him when, upon his arrival at Regan's, she demands that he apologize to her sister before she will accept him in her home.

With the growing awareness of the unfeeling avarice of his two manipulative "unnatural" offspring, Lear madly wanders into a hovel on the heath in the midst of a raging storm. Clearly, the upheaval of the storm is paralleled in the agonized musings of the forlorn king. The rapid decline of Lear's physical and mental health causes Kent to enlist Cordelia's help in saving her father. Without question, she dutifully and lovingly sends attendants to retrieve her ailing father, while, at the same time, she enlists the French army to set up camp on Britain's shores where she plans to reunite with the disenfranchised monarch. Concurrently, however, Goneril and Regan are joining forces against them.

While this drama of love and betrayal occurs within Lear's family, a parallel struggle simultaneously occurs within the house of the Earl of Gloucester. This is significant in that Gloucester, like Lear, is also prideful, impetuous, and ignorant of the intricacies of human nature. Moreover, he also has two children who are polar opposites. Edgar is his loyal, loving, and legitimate son; Edmund, on the other hand, is Gloucester's bastard son who has been raised without love and without the legacy of legitimacy. These factors embitter Edmund and cause him to seize pleasure and power by any means possible.

Inevitably, both the paths and the purposes of these two families become intertwined within the play. Because Goneril and Regan, who are described as "tigers not daughters," are eager to destroy both Lear and Cordelia in order to retain their land, and because Edmund is motivated to destroy his unloving father and claim his due, the evil forces unite, for a time, causing widespread destruction. When Goneril and Regan learn that Lear and Cordelia, assisted by the French army, will be returning to reclaim his land, they fortify their efforts, defeat the French army, and take their relatives as prisoners. While this should satisfy the two evil sisters, it is only a small victory because they have yet another score to settle. This second, perhaps more insidious, rivalry involves Edmund, Gloucester's bastard son, as the object of both women's desire. Finding this situation intolerable, Goneril, the older and stronger of the two, murders her younger sister, Regan, in jealousy over Edmund, and then, in desperation, she stabs herself.

Even though they are dead, their evil plot lives on in the edict that when Cordelia comes to shore, she must be hanged to punish Lear. And although events occur to soften the heart of Edmund to the point that he tries to rescind the order to kill Cordelia, his efforts come too late. As such, the play ends with Lear's fleeting happiness resulting from his reunion with Cordelia, his inevitable mental decline and broken-hearted death that immediately follows Cordelia's, and the restoration of order in the kingdom under the capable leadership of Gloucester's devoted son, Edgar.

According to noted critic Joseph Wittreich, all of these actions, in spite of their complexity, conform to the model of literary apocalypse. He refers to key elements of the play and concludes,

> In *King Lear,* majesty may fall to folly; but the foolish king, persisting in his folly, by the end of the play becomes wise. There is a resurrection; and even if there is death, death is a deliverance from the horrors of this life. All of the evil perish, along with some of the good; but some of the good also survive and, under this aegis, history continues (Wittreich 1984, 185).

See also Apocalypse: Traditional Primitive; Cordelia; Edgar; Edmund; Gloucester (Earl of); Goneril; Great Chain of Being; Lear, King; Regan.

KURTZ, MR.

Mr. Kurtz is the enigmatic chief of the inner station of a European-owned ivory company operating deep in the Belgian Congo in Joseph Conrad's psychological drama *Heart of Darkness* (1902). Before coming to his position with the ivory trading company, Mr. Kurtz had been a highly educated European gentleman whose personal gifts included public speaking, music, art, poetry, and political savvy. Many of these talents, in fact, prepared him well for his subsequent success as an ivory merchant in Africa, in spite of the deplorable conditions under which he was forced to operate.

Nevertheless, as is revealed through the narrator's journey into the jungle, where he hopes to investigate some mysterious circumstances surrounding the operation as well as to meet the renowned Mr. Kurtz, readers come to understand how quickly a civilized person can deteriorate, both physically and mentally as well as spiritually, after having been removed from the social and moral restrictions that serve as the hallmark of a "civilized" society. In this novella, Kurtz exemplifies such a rapid personal decline and thereby reveals the frail human barrier that barely separates civility from savagery.

Although his initial intentions had been honorable—i.e., to use his expertise to develop a profitable ivory trading station—several factors contributed to his inevitable fall. The first and most significant factor was his sense of personal pride. Much like Goethe's *Faust* and Christopher Marlowe's *Dr. Faustus,* Kurtz had already surpassed most humans in his personal accomplishments and had yearned for even greater knowledge, skill, and power. Just like the deluded protagonists of other apocalyptic works, this overwhelming pride blinds Kurtz to the ultimate knowledge that the pursuit of wealth, power, and honor are never worthy enough goals for which to trade one's humanity, civility, or, more importantly, one's immortal soul.

As such, Kurtz, like his Faustian archetype, falls prey to the seductive influence of his Mephistophelean manager who diabolically raises the stakes of their deadly game each time a new goal has been achieved. Further, the manager, like Mephistopheles, delights in the growing frustrations of a foolish man, like Kurtz, who is relatively unaware of the damnable futility of his superhuman ambitions. Therefore, it is this overriding ambition that causes Kurtz to lose his humanity in the pursuit of his fleeting goals. Although he is initially considered to be one of the most prominent performers in the operation (and as such, he has been promised the proper machinery, tools, and shipping vessels with which to perform his ivory trading operation), he soon learns that the law of the jungle precludes the law of modern society. Consequently, the delays, interruptions, and a growing sense of desperation lead him to behave with a cruelty and ruthlessness that he deems necessary to build a thriving ivory trade. In short, since he cannot rely on science and machinery to attain his goal, he learns to use the rules of the jungle to become successful in the African ivory trade.

As a consequence of his personal magnetism and natural authority, he is revered by the natives who come to worship him as a god, but he is also feared by them because of his endless exploitation. They come to trust him because he becomes an active participant in their primitive rituals—"unspeakable rites" that most likely involve human sacrifice and cannibalism in order to sustain the physical strength of a tribal leader. Because he accepts his role as their god and has willingly become one of their own, they tolerate his growing despotism, which often involves their being shackled, starved, and forced to work, at gunpoint, until they are discarded amidst the relentless jungle overgrowth after having been literally worked to death.

Although the natives resign themselves to their fate because they are happy to be in the presence of their "god," Kurtz, their willing icon, conversely, becomes slowly crazed by the reality of his personal moral decline. Just as remnants of his old books and paintings can be found abandoned along the path leading to him, Kurtz has gradually discarded all behaviors and sensibilities that had once defined him as a paragon of civilized humanity.

Marlow, the primary narrator of the tale, as well as the sea captain who had been commissioned to recover a steamship and to investigate Kurtz's station, finds little more than the remains of the great and respectable man whom he had once hoped to meet. And although he had been given many clues about Kurtz's progressive depravity along his journey, Marlow is ill prepared to find the cadaverous visage of a "hollow man" who had been decimated by his materialistic ambition, and who later became immortalized in a poem of the same name by the modernist poet T. S. Eliot.

Heart of Darkness ends soon after the close of Kurtz's pitiable life. But before he dies, Kurtz, much like his other Faustian counterparts, becomes pathetically aware of the darkness that he will face for eternity as a result of his pact with his personal demons. This moment is poignantly captured in Marlow's following observations of the dying monomaniac,

> Anything approaching the change that came over his features I [Marlow] have never seen before, and hope never to see again. . . . It was as though a veil had been rent. I saw on that ivory face the expression of sombre pride, of ruthless power, of craven terror—of an intense and hopeless despair. . . . [And in his final moments, during which his life seemed to pass before his eyes,] he cried out twice, a cry that was no more than a breath: "The horror! The horror!" (147).

See also Apocalypse: Traditional Primitive; Apocalypticism; *Dr. Faustus; Faust; The Hollow Men;* Mephistophiles; *The Waste Land.*

LEAR, KING

King Lear is the fictional sixteenth-century ruler of pre-Christian Britain in William Shakespeare's tragedy of the same name. At the outset of the play, Lear is an aging monarch of "fourscore and upward," or over eighty years old. In spite of his chronological age he remains physically and mentally strong, and he is considered both a capable and respected leader. His real problem early in the play is not senile dementia, as it may be later in the play. His problem relates to foolishness, irresponsibility, and willful pride. These traits are demonstrated almost immediately in a twofold manner: first, he shirks his solemn duty by making the hasty and selfish decision to abdicate his throne prematurely; second, he impulsively chooses to divide his kingdom (although not his title as king) among his three daughters, Cordelia, Goneril, and Regan—not according to loyalty or merit, but according to solicited public displays of elaborate and insincere flattery. In other words, the daughter who verbally expresses her love most dramatically will inherit the greatest share of Lear's kingdom.

It is clear in the opening scenes of the play that Lear favors his daughter Cordelia over the others, and in fact, plans to live with her during his retirement years. But in conducting this foolhardy contest, he greatly underestimates each of his daughters, and this will inevitably lead to the downfall of his comfortable world. First, believing that Cordelia loves him the most, he expects her to lavish him with the greatest public exhibition of love and praise. He does her a disservice in this expectation, however, in that she is too sincere with her affection and too respectful of her father to try to manipulate him with such a tawdry display. Instead, he is taken in by the idle flattery of Goneril and Regan, the two competitive siblings who are eager to usurp their father's power. As a result of his impetuous and egocentric request, he feels compelled to keep his word by dividing his kingdom among the two evil daughters, while willfully disinheriting his beloved Cordelia.

With this arrogant decision, Lear initiates the systematic destruction of his formerly fulfilling life by violating the ancient philosophical concept known as "the great chain of being." According to this philosophy, the universe contains an established order under which every living being is placed; each creature has a designated position or is a specific link in life's chain. This hierarchy of life posits that if someone has been given the responsibilities of a king, he must fulfill that role to the best of his ability until it is no longer possible to rule responsibly, due either to infirmity or death. Moreover, if anyone of lesser station (or a subordinate link) attempts to seize sovereign control, or even if a child attempts to overthrow parental authority, then the hierarchical order linking all living beings will be greatly upset. The "great chain" will be broken, unleashing the forces of chaos upon the universe. This philosophy incites the action in Shakespeare's play and shapes his characters' lives.

Chaos comes first during Lear's stay with his oldest and most powerful daughter, Goneril. He is stunned by her unwillingness to treat him with respect and the sudden reversal in her formerly obsequious displays of affection. Instead, she progressively undermines his authority, questions his mental capacities, and denies him each of his regal whims. She insists that he dismiss his knights and squires for their disruptive behavior. Lear's pride, however, makes it impossible for him to accept this degradation, and he sends his faithful servant Kent to announce his arrival at the home of his second daughter, Regan.

Instead of being welcomed by Regan, however, he is astonished and angered when he learns that Kent has been inhospitably received. Further, he is dismayed when Goneril arrives on the scene and Regan demands that Lear first apologize to his eldest daughter before she will agree to accept him in her own home. At this point, the sisters' unnatural conspiracy to usurp their father's sovereign authority becomes evident to Lear. The maddening realization that his world has suddenly turned upside down sends him fleeing into a fierce storm, accompanied by his servant Kent and a wise companion known only as the Fool.

As a result of the cumulative conspiracies and injustices against him, Lear's heart becomes heavy and his mind becomes weak. He slowly descends into madness. It is while he is in this deranged state that he ironically comes to see the cruel realities of the world for the first time, not as a self-pitying and pampered monarch, but simply as a man. Eventually his suffering is ameliorated by the loving intercession of Cordelia, who demonstrates in deeds, not words, her love for her father. Under her guileless care and that of her physician, Lear begins to find peace. But, after a temporary restoration of both his authority and his sanity, he learns to his horror that Cordelia has been murdered. In the closing scenes, Lear carries Cordelia's dead body, acknowledging that she has been sacrificed for his hubris. Somewhat restored by both this awareness and his profound suffering, he dies, leaving a disturbing legacy for all those whose willful actions threaten to topple the predestined order of the universe.

See also Apocalypse: Traditional Primitive; Cordelia; Edgar; Edmund; Gloucester (Earl of); Goneril; Great Chain of Being; *King Lear;* Regan; Shakespeare, William.

LEVERKUHN, ADRIAN

Adrian Leverkuhn is the protagonist of Thomas Mann's retelling of the Faustian legend in his apocalyptic novel, *Doktor Faustus.* In his portrayal of the deluded idealist, scholars agree that Adrian is not only a reflection of Mann's personal history as it relates to Germany, but he is also symbolic in that his individual development correlates directly with the decline and fall of his native country itself. His physical characteristics also reflect the naturalistic and deterministic philosophies that were popular during the time in which the saga takes place. For example, in her discussion of Adrian's physical appearance and personality traits, Gunilla Bergsten notes the following correlation between the character and his national heritage:

> Heredity and milieu determine Adrian's life as much as the lives of the French naturalists' heroes. His bluish-greyish-greenish eyes are explained as a mixture of his parents' blue and black eyes; Mann obviously intended an allusion to the mixture of blond Nordic stock and dark Alpine stock that forms the German national physiognomy. Adrian's migraine headaches and his penchant for speculation are inherited from his father; since the romantics, melancholy pondering has been designated a Nordic trait. Adrian's musical talent comes from his mother; Mann thus portrays musicality as the South's contribution to the German soul ("Historical View" 72).

In addition to the elements of nationalism reflected in the work are issues related to the psychoanalytical theories of Sigmund Freud. These are represented in Adrian's various neuroses and their traumatic causes, which tend to produce characters like himself and the other damaged Germanic individuals represented throughout the novel. The most important aspect of the novel, however, is Adrian's commitment to repeat the Faustian pact with the demonic forces of the universe in exchange for the promise of achieving the highest level of the musical art form. It is this deluded commitment without regard to personal cost that reveals much about Mann's observation of the German consciousness and its inevitable susceptibility to corruption. Mann's views on this subject appear in Bergsten's essay:

> Music is calculated order and chaos-breeding irrationality at once, rich in conjuring, incantatory gestures, in magic of numbers, the most unrealistic and yet the most impassioned of arts, mystical and abstract. If Faust is to be the representative of the German soul, he would have to be musical, for the relation of the German to the world is abstract and mystical, that is, musical—the relation of a professor with a touch of demonism, awkward and at the same time filled with arrogant knowledge that he surpasses the world in "depth" (84).

Ultimately, as a consequence of this quest for "arrogant knowledge," Mann's Faust joins the ranks of his deluded fictional predecessors. And just as their stories remain as apocalyptic legacies to others who might be tempted to raise themselves above the level of their creative source, Leverkuhn's music remains as yet another haunting reminder of a human quest for perfection that is unwittingly obliterated by the eternal sacrifice of one's singular—or, in this case, national—soul (Bergsten 1986).

See also Apocalypse: Secular; Apocalypse: Traditional Judeo-Christian; Apocalyptic Literature; Archetype; *Doktor Faustus; Dr. Faustus; Faust;* Freud, Sigmund; Goethe, Johann Wolfgang von; Mephistophiles; Satan; Zeitblom, Serenus.

LEVIATHAN

Leviathan is a Hebrew word meaning "the coiled one" or "that which gathers itself together in folds." References to this primordial monster clearly originated in early Canaanite literature. Later references to a whale or "the great dragon of the sea" reflect the Israelites' familiarity with the term as presented throughout the Bible, in the books of Job, Psalms, Isaiah, and Jonah.

In general, references to the leviathan, particularly within the body of apocalyptic literature, serve a symbolic function related to the devastating power of one of God's creations. According to most accounts, God plans to keep the monster in check until the end of a particular era, or until he has had enough of humanity's recklessness. Then the leviathan will briefly unleash its wrath upon mankind, only to be vanquished by God's power at the end of the world.

The presence of a leviathan, used in both a literal and figurative sense throughout the body of Western literature, foreshadows the condition of a pending cataclysm. For example, in the book of Jonah the protagonist is subsumed into the "belly of the beast" until he is willing to submit to God's will. A parallel of this occurs for the protagonist of Kurt Vonnegut's science fiction fantasy *Cat's Cradle,* in which another Jonah witnesses destruction on a grand scale and is tasked with warning future generations of a similar fate.

While there are many examples to support the apocalyptic literary associations with the leviathan, there is perhaps no more devastating account than that presented in Herman Melville's American apocalyptic masterpiece, *Moby-Dick.* So central to the understanding of the work is the legend of the leviathan that Melville uses several pages at the beginning of the novel to provide an extensive multilingual etymology of the word. This section, entitled "Extracts," details the use of the word in various biblical references as well as in classical literature. For a complete discussion of the specific role of the leviathan in Melville's opus, readers should refer to the entries in this volume entitled "Ahab, Captain," "Melville, Herman," and "*Moby-Dick.*"

See also Apocalypse: Secular; Apocalypse: Traditional Judeo-Christian; Apocalypse: Traditional Primitive; Apocalyptic Literature; *Cat's Cradle;* Ice-Nine; Jonah, Book of; Jonah-John.

LEWIS, C. S.

C. S. Lewis was the beloved British teacher, scholar, and author whose intelligence and fanciful imagination successfully blended faith, fiction, and fantasy into an impressive and memorable collective body of work. He was born Clive Staples in 1898 in Belfast, Ireland, to a devoted mother and a father who was a successful attorney, though mostly absent. Lewis's rich interior life began during his childhood, soon after the death of his mother. In order to escape from the realities of loss and loneliness, Lewis and his older brother spent countless hours creating intricate tales drawn from the literary classics that had been made available to them in their father's expansive library.

This early exposure to great literature prepared him for his study in an English boarding school, as well as for his rigorous curriculum at University

C. S. Lewis in 1974

College, Oxford. Although his studies were interrupted by his military service during World War I, he returned to school and graduated with honors from Oxford in 1923. From 1925 to 1954, he was a tutor there and earned the esteemed position of fellow at Magdalene College. A personal account of the psychological, philosophical, and theological experimentation he explored during those years is thoughtfully presented in his 1956 autobiography, *Surprised by Joy.* While the autobiography and some of his early wartime poems provide readers with valuable insights into the author's personal quest for truth, they are, of course, not the works for which he has become most widely known.

It was the publication of *The Allegory of Love: A Study in Medieval Tradition* (1936) that brought Lewis his greatest critical acclaim. In this work, the author conducts a critical exploration of myth and its essential contribution to the English literary tradition. During his years at Oxford, Lewis became involved with a group of scholars who reawakened his interest in spiritual matters. Particularly through his close relationship with Charles Williams, Lewis was inspired to write a series of books containing religious themes: *The Problem of Pain* (1940), *The Screwtape Letters* (1942), *Christian Behaviour* (1943), *The Great Divorce* (1945), *Miracles: A Preliminary Study* (1947), *Mere Christianity* (1952), and *Reflections on the Psalms* (1958).

In addition to these formidable works of literary and theological scholarship, Lewis decided to resurrect his early fascination with fantasy and magic and melded it with mythological and Christian themes in a science fiction space trilogy comprised of the following novels: *Out of the Silent Planet* (1938), *Perelandra* (1944), and *That Hideous Strength* (1946). In the first of these novels, Lewis's protagonist travels to Mars (Malacandra) in order to explore the philosophical consequences of earth's (Thulcandra's) original fall from grace, the temptation of fear, and the triumph of faith. In *Perelandra,* Lewis's protagonist once again travels through space, this time to Venus (Perelandra), where he is charged with influencing the planet's first "mother" to avoid temptation and to choose obedience in order to avoid the same spiritual fate as that of earth, the "silent planet," which can no longer communicate with God. In the last book of the trilogy, Lewis departs from the extraterrestrial experience and focuses rather on the spiritual battles being waged in contemporary England. In this work, which is markedly different from the previous two, Lewis was greatly influenced by his friend Charles Williams, who had extensive knowledge of the Arthurian legend. Thus, *That Hideous Strength* blends Christian themes with Celtic myths. Lewis's obvious disdain for the demonic philosophy of logical positivism culminates in an ultimate battle of truly biblical proportions.

While this science fiction trilogy reveals much about the author and his intellectual and spiritual views, the novels failed to receive the widespread recognition that they actually deserved. In his next foray into the world of fantasy, Lewis resurrected the stories of his own lonely childhood and made an indelible mark as a writer of a series of children's fiction. Thus, the *Narnia Chronicles,* featuring a mythical animal kingdom as a thinly veiled allegory, eventually brought him to the public's attention. The seven books in this series, which has become a juvenile literary classic, include *The Lion, the Witch, and the*

Wardrobe (1950), *The Horse and His Boy* (1954), *The Magician's Nephew* (1955), and the final apocalyptic novel, appropriately entitled *The Last Battle* (1956).

Although in his later years he maintained a reputation as one of Oxford's most popular teachers, in the last decade of his life Lewis accepted the honorable appointment at Cambridge—his former rival institution—of Chair of Medieval and Renaissance Literature. In addition to achieving popular acclaim later in life, it was also during his later years that he aroused something of a scandal when he met and married a former Jew and Christian convert, fellow writer Joy Davidman. Although she died not long after their marriage, he helped to raise her son and maintained his faith by continuing to write, and most importantly, to teach at Cambridge, until his death in Oxford on November 22, 1963.

See also Apocalypse: Traditional Judeo-Christian; Archetype; Arthur, King; Merlin; Myth; *Out of the Silent Planet; Perelandra;* Ransom, Dr. Elwin; Science Fiction; Symbol; *That Hideous Strength;* Weston, Edward Rolles.

LORD OF THE FLIES

Written by William Golding in 1954, this novel won the Nobel Prize as an apocalyptic parable of a paradise lost. Clearly, Golding's personal experience as a schoolmaster of an all-boys' institution, as well as his distinguished service in the British Royal Navy during World War II, provided him with sufficient proof that the human condition is intrinsically evil, a theme that he explores most poignantly in *Lord of the Flies,* as well as in each of his subsequent novels.

The inciting action of the novel involves the air evacuation of a group of young boys from a British academy in order to save them from an atomic attack at the center of war-torn England. The novel begins with the emergence of the boys from their crashed plane on a deserted tropical island. When they realize that there are no adults in their midst, the natural leaders of the group try to restore the type of order with which they were familiar at their all-boys' school. The symbolic means by which they call their members to order is a conch shell that one of them has found on the beach. Not unlike a heralding bell or resounding trumpet, this conch serves as an indicator of authority and a token of decorum that temporarily keeps them from fearing their unknown fates.

First among those boys to establish the early rules on the island is Ralph, the pragmatic British schoolboy and protagonist of the novel, who stresses the importance of civility and order amidst their chaotic situation. The other natural leader to emerge from the group is Jack Merridew, Ralph's foil and the undisputed antagonist of the novel, who is recognized as the former leader of the school's choirboys. But Jack soon revels in the unregulated environment and establishes himself as the chief hunter of the group.

It is clear from the outset of the novel that the forces of order vs. chaos, good vs. evil, and restraint vs. rebellion are to be reenacted on this island paradise, much like in the Genesis account. Similarly, the eternal struggle between these dichotomous universal forces quickly transforms their earthly paradise into a terrifying inferno, which both stuns its survivors and sears them forever with the awareness of their destructive natural instincts.

At the beginning of the novel, Ralph's common sense approach to their circumstances causes him to cling desperately to the familiar democratic practices of their former school days. Jack, on the other hand, eagerly discards all vestiges of order as quickly as he discards his choirboy's uniform. From the moment that his naked body is warmed by heat of the sun, Jack's natural atavistic instincts rise to the surface, bringing forth his repressed bloodlust. He becomes a natural enemy to everything that Ralph and his orderly cohorts represent. Consequently, it is not long before the younger boys are forced by their disparate leaders to choose sides. While initially most of children choose the security that Ralph offers them, their fears of the island soon subside. Because of this lack of fear, as well as their reluctance to maintain a false sense of order in their unrestricted paradise, many of the boys soon choose play over work. By succumbing to this temptation, their choice heralds the ascent of an evil influence that overtakes the island, which is represented by the "hunters" who choose to join Jack in his bloodthirsty pursuits.

While most of the boys are soon divided between the two camps representing the forces of good and evil, there are two additional characters who are distinctly different from either Ralph or Jack, as well as from the other boys on the island. Each in his own way is distinctive because of his apparent weakness, yet the inner strength that emerges within the two throughout the drama eventually causes them to become the unwitting objects of human sacrifice at the point when chaos overtakes the island. The first of these two sacrificial characters is Piggy. As an overweight, bespectacled asthmatic, Piggy is an unlikely candidate for survival within a Darwinian universe. However, he soon overcomes his fears and rises above the former school yard ridicule by exerting his exceptional intellect, a valuable quality that initially keeps the others from harm and provides them with both the means and the hope of an eventual rescue. Simon is also different from the other boys in the group. Although he is strangely withdrawn, prone to ascetic "spells," and spiritually inspired by the natural beauty of his surroundings, Simon also distinguishes himself through his kindness to the "littluns," his selfless assistance to those in need, and his faithful pursuit of truth in spite of the diabolical fear that threatens to destroy the island and its desperate inhabitants.

The sacrifice of these two characters functions in the same way as that of primitive cyclical myths. The spilling of their innocent blood symbolically appeases the force of evil that had reigned over the island. Thus, the novel concludes, true to the pattern of traditional apocalyptic literature, with the emergence of the boys from the chaotic flames that they had created to consume Ralph, the remaining voice of reason on the island. Ironically, this fire, intended for destruction, figuratively marks the return of reality and literally serves as a signal fire that attracts a passing British naval vessel. Finally, although the young savages are stunned and confused by the arrival of a naval officer, who serves as an emissary from the "grown-up" world, Ralph alone stands ready to face reality amidst the ravages of the scorched former paradise, as he weeps "for the end of innocence [and] the darkness of man's heart" (Golding 1954).

See also Apocalypse: Traditional Judeo-Christian; Apocalypse: Traditional Primitive; Apocalyptic Literature; Golding, Sir William Gerald; *Heart of Darkness;* Merridew, Jack; Piggy; Ralph; Satan; Simon.

LOVE IN THE RUINS: THE ADVENTURES OF A BAD CATHOLIC AT A TIME NEAR THE END OF THE WORLD

This satirical novel by Walker Percy (1971) addresses the author's concern for the portentous decline of humanity's spirituality. Using the landscape of dystopian science fiction, Percy's novel takes place at an undesignated time in the near future of America. It is a time when political, religious, and social schisms threaten to destroy an increasingly immoral world. Percy's protagonist, Dr. Tom More, narrates events that occur over a four-day period, culminating ironically on Independence Day—July 4th—as he sits and waits for the imminent cataclysm with the belief that only he has the means to save humanity from its spiritual ills.

Central to the story is Tom More's reliance on Yeats's apocalyptic vision voiced in the poem "The Second Coming": "Things fall apart; the centre cannot hold; /Mere anarchy is loosed upon the world." In More's world, the signs of such anarchy are abundant. First, traditional political parties have evolved into absurd factions. For example, the party formerly known as Republicans is now known as the Knothead party "whose members suffer from apoplexy and bowel disorders, while the Democrats have been driven to form the fiercely liberal Left party and are prone to abstraction, morning terror, and impotence" (Ciuba 1991, 133). Next, the Roman Catholic Church has split into two distinct groups. The American Catholic Church now represents the conservative view, while a more radical adherence to the dictates of the Holy Roman Empire is espoused by the Dutch Reform denomination. As a result of political and moral decline, social unrest is also evident in More's world. A group of black extremists known as Bantu guerrillas threatens insurrection against the white leisure class. Meanwhile, the white leisure class is concerned less with security and salvation than with the pursuit of self-serving hedonism.

Tom More recognizes such societal ills because he is sorely afflicted by them. He has already dissociated himself with the political factions. Moreover, he has abandoned religious faith following his wife's abandonment and his daughter's untimely death from a cruel cancer. He has become reliant upon alcohol and unbridled sex with virtual strangers in an effort to numb himself from the reality of his meaningless existence.

Throughout the novel, More reflects on the oft-repeated quote, "Physician, heal thyself." But at the beginning of the novel, he can neither heal himself nor anyone else; he can only diagnose societal ennui by using his questionable invention, More's Qualitative-Quantitative Ontological Lapsometer. Using this instrument, he performs readings on the various operational centers of people's brains and "diagnoses the maladies of the soul through the signs of the body"

(138). While More is convinced of his instrument's diagnostic effectiveness—to the point that he writes what he believes to be an incontrovertible article for publication—his colleagues are less impressed with the culmination of his efforts. Their doubt, however, is based less on the modified encephalograph itself than on the fact that More has been hospitalized intermittently in a mental institution as a result of the general "sense of abstraction" and recurrent "morning terrors" that drive him to alcoholism and keep him in a state of perpetual anticipation of impending doom.

Perhaps his colleagues fail to see the dangers that More sees because they are similarly oblivious to the outward signs of their world's demise. In describing the community in which he lives, More makes frequent references to the intrusion of vines that creep menacingly into the edifices of their residential area, Paradise Estates. Although he perceives that this suburban subdivision is gradually becoming subsumed by the pervasive vegetation of the surrounding swamp (a symbolic reference to the decadent society of ancient Babylon, which was famous for its pretentious Hanging Gardens), no one other than More seems to recognize that the vines (much like society's spiritual malaise) threaten to overrun their world. Nor do they find anything unusual about other evidence of the decline of everyday life, such as the broken appliances and abandoned automobiles that litter homes and roadways because "things [have simply] stopped working and nobody want[s] to be a repairman" (54). Metaphorically, this is also the case with the decay of the human spirit; therefore, More egocentrically wields his invention as he embarks on his quest to become the savior, or "repairman," of the soul.

The only distraction that takes him from his primary mission in life appears in the form of various women. Each one, however, is somehow as fragmented as he. Doris, his former wife, loves More but becomes disenchanted with him as his spirituality wanes following the unmerciful death of their devout daughter, Samantha. She becomes absorbed in Eastern philosophy and runs away with an Englishman-mystic who uses her money to develop his own religious center in Cozumel, Mexico, where Doris accidentally dies. Next, Moira, the ingenuous clinician with a fascination for ruins, a disjointed understanding of history, and an insatiable bad taste in literature, art, and music, is little more than a willing nubile body. For More she serves as sex object, but also as a replacement for his dead daughter. Thus, he spends time musing about ways to bring her happiness and enjoys the simple pleasures she brings into his life. Lola, on the other hand, is a large, maternal, sexual, self-possessed woman who thrives in the faux grandeur of her manufactured plantation, Tara, and cares for him with her defiant will, a carbine rifle, and protective affection. The final and most constant woman in his life is his nurse, Ellen Oglethorpe. She is a stalwart, no-nonsense Presbyterian who pragmatically anticipates his every need. Much like the stereotypical "Girl Friday," Ellen accepts her boss—and later her husband—for the man that he is. She recognizes and occasionally admonishes him for his faults, but she believes in the validity of his work and is ultimately a devoted helpmate for her indulgent but well-intentioned sinner/saint.

Ellen demonstrates her dedication to More when together they confront the most menacing force in the novel, the diabolical Art Immelmann. "Immelman's appearance seems like the last loosing of Satan in the novel's already devil-ridden world" (Ciuba 140). His literary comparison to Faust's Mephistopheles is blatantly portrayed when the insistent confidence-man gains the weakened More's trust through collusion, flattery, and deception. Under the guise of helping More to modify his machine in order to provide sufferers not only with a diagnosis but a supposed cure, Immelmann convinces More to sign a contract with him in order to promote the machine: he convinces More to sell his soul to the devil, thereby unleashing the terrible power of the device. The devastating results of this contract quickly become apparent as a simple medical demonstration of the Lapsometer turns into a chaos of repressed lust and rage. Unconcerned with the instrument's potential, Immelmann recklessly distributes More's invention at random, an act that Immelmann hopes will produce immediate profits but one that ultimately leads More to prepare for the inevitable end of the world.

The remainder of the novel chronicles More's recognition of his gross error in judgment. He quickly comprehends his contribution to the pending cataclysm as societal chaos escalates in the form of the Bantu revolt. More prepares for the end of the world by storing his various women, his collection of Great Books, and provisions of canned foods and cases of Early Times bourbon in adjoining rooms of a dilapidated Holiday Inn. While in his ruined fortress, he vows to cancel his contract with Immelmann and to recover all the misappropriated prototypes of his invention in order to save the world from destruction. And although she initially is tempted by Immelmann's offer to work for him, it is Ellen who actually helps More to save himself.

Ironically, in spite of his angst and his scrupulous preparations, the end as More imagines it never really comes. It is this simple fact that leads to More's personal salvation. "Having failed to create a utopia, [his] salvation comes at last from discovering that love has been corrupted almost everywhere he looks and can only be found in the most unlikely place amid his own self-ruin" (147). In the epilogue of the novel, five years have passed since the cataclysmic July 4th, and the reader finds a new Tom More. Although he is still concerned about humanity's decline, he is no longer obsessed with thoughts of preventing it. Instead, he settles down with Ellen in an uncluttered existence where he is restored by her steadfast devotion and the love of their children. The novel concludes appropriately on December 25, when Tom realizes "It is Christmas Day and the Lord is here, a holy night and surely that is all one needs" (343). He is clearly transformed. No longer does he need the relentless spiritual pursuit of his former life with Doris. Neither does he rely on the mind-numbing effects of alcohol abuse, nor does he need the desperate physical couplings with other lost souls. Finally, within the ruins of his former self, he finds his own salvation. Amidst the chaos of the universe he submits to the uncertainties of love, and he twines himself, like ivy tendrils, about his wife in their new bed, where he now believes that "all good folk belong" (343).

See also Apocalypse: Secular; Apocalyptic Literature; Babylon; Immelmann, Art; More, Dr. Tom; Percy, Walker; *The Thanatos Syndrome*.

MCCLELLAN, CLARISSE

Clarisse McClellan is the idealistic and impassioned seventeen-year-old neighbor of fireman Guy Montag in Ray Bradbury's apocalyptic novel, *Fahrenheit 451*. The two meet during a serendipitous evening walk at a time and in a neighborhood where people rarely communicate with one another. Although most of the community is insular and paranoid about the presence of a "fireman" whose job it is to burn the books prohibited in their society, Clarisse is unafraid as Montag approaches her. She explains her lack of fear by recounting her uncle's assessment of her: "I'm seventeen and I'm crazy. My uncle says the two always go together" (Bradbury 7).

In contrast to the world-weary Montag, everything about Clarisse reflects the innocence and promise of one who has not yet succumbed to societal cynicism. For example, she delights as she walks in the rain and tastes the raindrops. She is enchanted by the color that remains on her chin after she rubs a dandelion on it. Montag also observes that "[h]er face [is] slender and milk-white, and in it [is] a kind of gentle hunger that touche[s] over everything with tireless curiosity" (5). This curiosity is contagious, and Montag becomes drawn to her ingenuous optimism. He is confounded by the lack of fear she shows in his presence. She merely asks him why he burns books, whether or not he has read any of them, how he feels about his work, and, most importantly, whether or not he is happy. This question haunts him, both on that night and in the nights to come, because although he replies that he is indeed happy in his work, he knows that she intuitively perceives his dissatisfaction with his life and seriously questions the validity of his work.

Throughout the novel, the specter of Clarisse looms largely in Montag's memory, even when he learns that she has moved from her home and is presumed dead. Her disappearance, obviously linked to her secret association with the fugitive band of "Book People," leads Montag to do the unthinkable. He goes against his government, his society, and his former self by reading a previously confiscated book. This event changes his life forever. It is thus through his brief relationship with Clarisse that Montag is inspired to transform himself. His life-affirming action paves the way for a new society.

See also Apocalypse: Traditional Judeo-Christian; Bradbury, Ray; *Fahrenheit 451;* Montag, Guy; Phoenix.

MALORY, THOMAS

Thomas Malory (c. 1408–1471) was the English writer (although some believe that he was Welsh) who is famous for his imaginative prose portrayal of the rise and fall of King Arthur and the knights of the Round Table in *Le Morte d'Arthur.* Little biographical information exists on Malory, nor is much known about his particular interest in the Arthurian cycle. Apparently Malory had served as a member of the British Parliament about 1445, but he must have demonstrated behavior or attitudes that ran contrary to the dictates of the monarchy. According to the author's own notes preceding the text, the work was written while he was imprisoned. Based on historical documents, this particular incarceration occurred during the ninth year of King Edward IV's reign, which would date the completion of the work to 1469 or 1470. Malory's subsequent infractions, which remain obscure, sent him to prison so frequently that he died there, never having seen his work in print. It was not published until 1485, fourteen years after his death.

See also Apocalypse: Traditional Judeo-Christian; Apocalypse: Traditional Primitive; Arthur, King; *A Connecticut Yankee in King Arthur's Court; The Faerie Queene;* Fisher King; *The Golden Bough: A Study in Magic and Religion;* Merlin; *Le Morte d'Arthur;* Myth; Symbol.

MANN, THOMAS

Thomas Mann (1871–1950) was the Nobel Prize–winning German novelist and essayist who is best known for his penetrating psychological novels dealing with the apocalyptic elements that express the duality within the artistic temperament. This temperament is one with which the author was extremely familiar in light of his own personal heritage. His father, a wealthy grain merchant and a renowned member of the senate in Lübeck, a city located near the Baltic Sea, was typical of the conventional middle class, which he willingly represented. In contrast, Mann's mother came from a German-Latin American heritage. She was less conventional and more passionate, encouraging Mann's own intrinsic artistic drives. Most of Mann's fiction reflects this autobiographical duality in that it collectively examines the role of the artist who is continually forced to confront the powerful influences of societal convention.

In the year of his father's death, 1891, the author remained in Lübeck in order to finish his schooling, while his family made the move to the more welcoming environment of Munich, the capital of Bavaria. After the completion of his education, he joined his family and went to work, at the same time auditing classes at the local technical university. His writing career began in 1894 with the appearance of *Gerfallen,* a story about a "fallen woman." While he followed this work with another novel just four years later, his reputation as a serious writer was established firmly upon the publication of a series of novels dealing with the naturalistic, multigenerational saga of a Lübeck family entitled *Buddenbrooks.*

As his work progressed, so too did his political leanings, an evolution that is reflected in his two well-received novellas, *Tonio Kroger* and *Tristan.* But this prevailing theme of an insensitive ruler in opposition to a sensitive artist is per-

Thomas Mann

haps best portrayed in *Death in Venice,* his successful novella that appeared in 1912. In the years that followed, Mann's growing alienation from German nationalism in favor of the democratic ideal distanced him from his family members, particularly his brother. This sentiment is chronicled in his representation of a corrupt prewar society in his second major novel, *The Magic Mountain* (1924). As a result of this novel and similar subsequent works, Mann was invited to participate in an extended lecture tour. However, his antigovernment views had begun to have negative consequences for the author. In 1933, he was urged by his children to move to Switzerland to avoid political persecution.

During the years in Switzerland, Mann was at work on a biblical tetralogy that included the following works: *Joseph and His Brothers, The Tales of Jacob, Young Joseph,* and *Joseph in Egypt.* (While living abroad in 1943, he published another work in the series entitled *Joseph the Provider.*) While he was writing these works, he was also becoming known for his growing public statements against the tyranny of Nazism, which resulted in his loss of German citizenship in 1936.

Mann then settled in the United States, where he was a noted lecturer at Princeton University in New Jersey until 1941. He became an American citizen in 1944, which provided him more freedom in his political writings. While in the United States, Mann continued to denounce the Nazi regime in both his lectures and his writings, the most memorable of which is his interpretation of Goethe's Faustian legend entitled *Doktor Faustus* (1947). In this work, Mann exposes the corrosive influence of Nazism on the creative temperament specifically and on humanity in general. He continued writing on variations of this theme even after he returned to Europe in 1952, where he settled permanently. Mann continued to be productive in both his life and his art, but before completing his final work, a comic novel entitled *Confessions of Felix Krull, Confidence Man,* the author died on August 12, 1950.

See also Apocalypse: Secular; Apocalypse: Traditional Judeo-Christian; Archetype; *Doktor Faustus; Dr. Faustus; Faust;* Freud, Sigmund; Leverkuhn, Adrian; Mephistophiles; Myth; Zeitblom, Serenus.

MARLOW, CHARLES

Charles Marlow is the primary narrator of Joseph Conrad's apocalyptic vision, *Heart of Darkness* (1902). This skilled sailor of the open seas and experienced captain of ocean vessels is traveling on fresh water on an assignment that will take him to the center of the Belgian Congo to investigate the mysterious events regarding the operation of his company's ivory trade. He is presented from the outset of the novella as something of a sage. His "sunken cheeks," "yellow complexion," "ascetic aspect," and "meditative" mood (Conrad 66) reveal Marlow's "Buddha-like" countenance, which reflects the realm of experience from which he speaks. And like most sailors who are renowned for their romantic yarns, he is a natural participative narrator in the story that reflects his life's most compelling physical and psychological journey.

Readers follow Marlow as he moves farther from the civilized world into the heart of the savage African jungle, where the rules of the modern world gradually cease to exist. During one disturbing stop in his voyage, Marlow arrives at the company's lower station where he is stunned by an overwhelming sense of waste. Rusted tools, machinery, and abandoned vessels litter the shores and raise questions in his mind about their disuse and disrepair. What is even more disturbing to Marlow, however, is the horrible revelation of human decay. Everywhere he looks he sees gangs of chained African workers with hollowed eyes, emaciated bodies, and broken spirits. This collective human refuse, he learns, is the means by which the ivory operation proliferates. These sick savages are clearly being worked to death, then thoughtlessly discarded, all for the profit of the ivory trade.

Amidst this hellish reality, in a company building, Marlow soon finds a character who presents a sharp contrast to his ruinous surroundings. This man, the company's chief accountant, is the epitome of British colonial correctness. While his fastidiousness in itself heralds a serious contradiction within the workings of the company, this fussy, starched, "fashion model" of a man is important because he is the first to provide Marlow with information about the great and respected general manager of the operation, Mr. Kurtz. The accountant, convinced of Kurtz's prominence within the organization, provides nothing but superlatives in his descriptions of this icon of the ivory trade. Sensing that this Mr. Kurtz is at the center of the mysterious events he has been sent to investigate, Marlow is committed to meeting the manager as the culmination of his personal quest.

His pursuit is thwarted by delays until he decides to join a caravan of black workers on a 200-mile trek that will ultimately take him to the company's central station. Upon his arrival at the station, fatigued and shamed by his inability to keep up with the others, Marlow is disappointed to learn that the steamship he had been commissioned to captain has been sunk and is lying on the bottom of the river. The man who delivers this disturbing news, along with the fact that it will probably take months to fix the vessel, is the overwrought and chaotic manager of the central station. Marlow takes an immediate dislike to this disagreeable man, whom he considers a "chattering idiot."

Later, Marlow meets and speaks with one of the manager's minions, who, in hope of obtaining privileged information about the company, invites the weary traveler into his own quarters. Once inside the opulent room of this "papier mache Mephistopheles," as Marlow refers to him, he learns more about Mr. Kurtz, reinforcing the Faustian theme surrounding Kurtz's diabolical ambition and increasing Marlow's curiosity about the operation's enigmatic general manager. Much of this information is corroborated by another minor character, a leader of an expedition. He reveals that the many delays in repairing the disabled steamer revolve around Mr. Kurtz's reported "illness," which has kept him out of touch with his subordinates for nearly nine months.

When the necessary parts arrive to make the steamship seaworthy, Marlow is focused more than ever on meeting the mysterious Mr. Kurtz. But this leg of the journey is fraught with peril. When savages attack, his helmsman is killed by an arrow. In the midst of confusion and about to turn back, Marlow spots the long-awaited inner station where Kurtz reportedly is to be found. At the station, he is greeted by a Russian, one of Kurtz's workers. Clearly devoted to his leader, the Russian tells of Kurtz's method of operation and reveals the reason for the station's success in the ivory trade. Kurtz, having established himself as something of a god in the midst of the natives, has figuratively sold his soul to the devil by enslaving native workers, threatening them at gunpoint, and working them literally to death for the acquisition of a profitable and massive ivory supply.

The most disturbing revelation about Kurtz, however, is the Russian's account of his leader's personal decline during the past few months. Clearly debilitated by some strange and prolonged disease (a soul sickness?), Kurtz is reportedly near death. The Russian sends natives to deliver the general manager to Marlow, who will escort the fallen leader back to England. Although Marlow is shocked by Kurtz's deathly appearance, he is also astonished by his frightening impact on the local natives, who strongly protest the removal of the man whom they have come to worship as their god. The sad irony, however, is that instead of having control over the natives, Kurtz has himself been subsumed by their savage ways. He has participated in their "unspeakable rites," and, in doing so, has become little more than a savage and diabolical madman.

Upon secretly witnessing Kurtz's participation in the savage ritual on their last night at the inner station, Marlow begins to understand the depth to which a human being can descend once he has been removed from the threads of theology, morality, and conscience that weave the fabric of a so-called civilized society. While witnessing these events, Marlow more poignantly realizes how fragile this fabric is and that he, like Kurtz, could be equally susceptible to the degeneration of his spirit and humanity after prolonged exposure to similar circumstances.

Although Kurtz finally dies, speaking the profound truth of the depravity of the human heart with a Faustian lament, "The horror! The horror!," Marlow soon learns that he, too, has been infected to some degree with this degenerative moral disease. This becomes evident upon his return to Europe, where he meets with Kurtz's former fiancée who begs Marlow to tell her love's last words. Throughout the story Marlow is presented as a man who prides himself in never having spoken a lie, but now he realizes that he is no more immune to corruption than any other human. For the benefit of the grieving "intended," he lies about Kurtz's last words, telling her that her name was the last sound that had passed the dead man's lips. The novella ends, therefore, with Marlow's understanding that he and Kurtz, the object of his obsessive quest, are really two parts of a human whole. Thus, he emerges from the experience with the mature insight that humanity is an inseparable amalgam of darkness and light, and it is up to each individual to decide the ultimate path to take on the seductive and chaotic journey from life to death.

See also Apocalypse: Traditional Primitive; Apocalypticism; Conrad, Joseph; *Dr. Faustus; Faust; Heart of Darkness;* Kurtz, Mr.; Mephistophiles.

MARLOWE, CHRISTOPHER

The free-thinking English poet and dramatist Christopher Marlowe (1564–1593) wrote tragedies such as *Tamberlaine, Dr. Faustus, The Jew of Malta,* and *Edward II,* which were considered some of England's greatest dramatic works until the appearance of those by his famous contemporary, William Shakespeare, who was born just two months after Marlowe in February 1564. As the first son of a successful middle-class shoemaker who later earned the status of church warden, Marlowe's early life was a comfortable, unremarkable one. At the age of fifteen, Christopher received his first scholarship to the Corpus Christi Cathedral School, after which he earned the more prestigious award, the Archbishop Matthew Parker Scholarship to Cambridge. Having accepted the award, it was expected that he would major in theology and take his holy orders, leading to a career in the clergy. Although Marlowe made use of his stipend and graduated with a Bachelor of Arts degree in 1584, he did not join the clergy.

While some speculate that this decision resulted from his disillusionment with the church, the more probable cause for his decision to not enter the clergy was his secret involvement with the political intrigues that proliferated between Protestants and Catholics at the time. In 1587, after Marlowe had already earned the necessary credits for a Master of Arts degree, the university refused to confer it because it questioned his covert activities. Some argue that the church's decision was based on the fact that Marlowe had used its money but had failed to join the clergy. Others believe that Marlowe, like the rebellious protagonists in his novels, was secretly an atheist—a fallacious assumption that historians continue to discredit. Whatever the case, the university's decision to deny his degree was quickly reversed after the institution received a letter from the Queen's Privy Council, which assured the college that Marlowe was, in fact, performing valuable services for the state (i.e., spying on Roman Catholic activities). Moreover, the college was chastised for unfairly judging Marlowe's participation in activities that academicians could not completely comprehend.

Marlowe's major dramatic works all resonate with a familiar Renaissance theme: the meteoric rise of ambitious egotists whose actions result in the devastating consequence of divine judgment . This is certainly the case in *Tamberlaine* (1590), *The Jew of Malta* (c. 1589–1593), *Edward II* (1592), and his apocalyptic interpretation of the Faust legend, *The Tragical History of Dr. Faustus* (c. 1592–1593). In addition to writing in the dramatic form, Marlowe is also known for his significant works of both narrative and erotic lyric poetry, two popular forms of literary entertainment in Elizabethan England.

Although his literary endeavors brought Marlowe considerable success, his continued political activities and their resultant legal entanglements began to threaten the future of the promising young artist. An event that marks his first brush with the law occurred in September of 1589, when Marlowe and a friend, Thomas Watson, were involved in a sword fight that led to the death of a local innkeeper's son, William Bradley. The investigation of the incident resulted in Marlowe's brief incarceration in the Newgate Prison for a period of only one week; Watson was acquitted after five months on the grounds of self-defense. But the imbroglio brought Marlowe to the attention of the local authorities, a situation that may have led to his untimely death.

Marlowe's involvement with fellow author Thomas Kyd instigated a fatal scenario. On May 12, 1593, Kyd, who was also being investigated for his political involvements, was arrested on the charge of atheism. After his home was searched, and after he had been subjected to torture, Kyd claimed that the condemning heretical materials found in his room had actually belonged to Christopher Marlowe, with whom he had lived in 1591. Kyd's charge of Marlowe's atheism was subsequently supported by the questionable claims of a man named Richard Baines, who decried Marlowe as a vociferous religious skeptic. When his charge was brought before the Queen's Privy Council, a warrant was issued for Marlowe's arrest. Although Marlowe was released, the Council had placed severe limitations on his activities. Nevertheless, the dramatist was allowed to accept a dinner invitation at a tavern just outside of London that was owned by a wealthy widow, two local con-men, and a spy who served as a double agent. While this suspect company was not unfamiliar to the rebellious Marlowe, the drinking and revelry of the day resulted in a boisterous tavern brawl over a bar tab. Official accounts of the event indicate that Marlowe, who was actively involved in the fight, was accidentally stabbed in the skull directly over the right eye, an injury resulting in his immediate death. Historians agree that Marlowe's "accident" was most likely part of an intricate plot to kill the author for his subversive political activities. Although there is no conclusive position on the matter, the facts remain that twenty-nine-year-old Marlowe's mysterious death occurred on May 30, 1593, and that none of the accused was ever convicted of the crime.

See also Apocalypse: Traditional Judeo-Christian; Apocalyptic Literature; *Dr. Faustus; Faust; Love in the Ruins: The Adventures of a Bad Catholic at a Time Near the End of the World;* Mephistophiles; More, Dr. Tom; Shakespeare, William.

MELVILLE, HERMAN

A renowned nineteenth-century novelist, short-story writer, and poet, Herman Melville (1819–1891) penned two of the most profound apocalypses in American literature. The lesser-known of these two works is *The Confidence-Man* (1857). The other is one of the world's most widely read apocalyptic novels, the highly symbolic and allegorical masterpiece, *Moby-Dick* (1851).

Born in New York City on August 1, 1819, to Allan Melvill (the "e" was added later) and Maria Gansevoort Melvill, the future author was raised in an environment of security and material comfort. This was partly a product of his father's success as an importer of French luxury apparel, and partly of his mother's aristocratic heritage. Her wealthy ancestors were included among the early Dutch settlers of Albany, New York. In addition to these favorable circumstances, Melville was fortunate to have within his ancestral lineage a number of illustrious relatives known for their bravery in battle and adventurous world travels.

Melville's idyllic childhood soon came to an abrupt end. After having suffered a devastating bankruptcy and a subsequent physical and mental breakdown, his father died of pneumonia in January of 1832. His mother moved with the children to a small town in upstate New York for the support of her wealthy relatives. But young Melville, at age eleven, was clearly traumatized by the loss of his beloved father and by the circumstantial poverty that made him feel insecure and isolated from his wealthier cousins.

During the years spent near his maternal relatives, Melville attended the prestigious academy known as the Albany Classical School. He was unable to complete his studies there for financial reasons, leading to a less formal completion of his education while he worked as a clerk in his uncle's bank. Although it appeared that Melville might succeed in pursuing a business career, subsequent family tragedies necessitated additional moves. He accepted a job as a schoolmaster in Massachusetts so that he could still be assisted by his uncle's family. Disillusioned by the instability and meager income of that profession, Melville decided in 1839 to follow the example of several of his ancestors by setting out to sea to find his fortune. Signing up as "the boy" on the *St. Lawrence,* a British ship, Melville spent nearly five years traveling around the world and amassing material for several of his early novels. This experience resulted in his signing up for work in 1841 on the whaling vessel *Acushnet.* This provided much background material for *Moby-Dick,* such as the whale hunting process and the monetary value of whale oil.

After little over a year on this vessel, however, Melville decided to jump ship during one of its stops in the Marquesas Islands. Bored with whaling by this time, and curious about the Edenic existence of the inhabitants of a valley known as Typee, Melville, along with sailing companion Tobias Greene, happily lived among the natives for a few months. By all reports, the two were treated hospitably by the natives, but Melville's growing suspicion that rumors about the natives' practice of cannibalism might be true caused him to escape from the island by boarding another docked whaling vessel that had stopped on the island.

For the next several years, Melville wandered from job to job and island to island until he decided, in late 1843, to join the U.S. Navy. This decision led to his return to Boston, Massachusetts, where he was eventually discharged from service. It was at this point in his life that he was persuaded by family and friends to begin his literary career by recording the exciting details of his South Sea adventures in fictional form. Thus, his novels *Typee* (1846) and *Omoo* (1847) established Melville's literary reputation as a successful travel writer.

Bolstered by this newfound respectability, Melville decided to take a wife. In 1847, he married Elizabeth Shaw, the daughter of a formidable Supreme Court justice. Soon the growth of his family, which included two sons and two daughters, necessitated the vigorous pursuit of his writing career. It was during these years that Melville proved to be most prolific. His efforts quickly resulted in a prodigious body of work: *Mardi* (1849), *Redburn* (1849), *White Jacket* (1850), and most importantly, Melville's favorite work, *The Whale,* which was published in 1851 as *Moby-Dick.*

It was also during these years that the Melvilles purchased a farm in Pittsfield, Massachusetts. In one respect this move proved to be fortuitous: it resulted in his meeting and developing a friendship with Nathaniel Hawthorne, a fellow writer who was similarly drawn to humanity's dark side. But Melville's finances began to falter from the expense of running a farm. Once again, Melville drew upon the monetary support of his wealthy uncle while continuing to earn money as a writer of short stories for such periodicals as *Harper's* and *Putnam's.* Ironically, while these short stories were well received, *Moby-Dick,* the effort that Melville considered to be the artistic culmination of his life's work, as well as the subsequent novel *Pierre* (1852), received unfavorable reviews from critics and popular audiences alike. This response stunned the author and initiated a period of deep mental depression. Even an extensive voyage to Palestine and the Mediterranean, financed by his father-in-law with the hope of returning the writer to his former health, did not help. Upon his return, Melville attempted to revive his enthusiasm for writing by publishing two works: *Israel Potter* (1855) and a cynical apocalyptic allegory, *The Confidence-Man* (1857). The overwhelmingly negative reaction to these works, as well as his continued disappointment over public reaction to *Moby-Dick,* eventually led Melville to the decision to terminate his career as a writer of fiction.

Although this decision resulted in an immeasurable loss to the literary world, Melville did continue to compose poetry, mostly for himself. His mental depression eventually subsided after taking a brief junket on a clipper ship. He decided to sell his burdensome farm, move his family to New York City, and resign himself to a more practical existence—as well as to relative obscurity—by taking a job as a customs inspector, a position he held from 1866 to 1885.

At this time, as a result of the death of several of his wealthy relatives, Melville received a sufficient inheritance to retire as a day laborer in 1886. While this legacy afforded him the opportunity to revive his writing career, he was still so embittered by the reception of his earlier works that he chose never to publish another word of fiction, a vow that he kept until his death on September 28, 1891. At the time of his death he was remembered only as a minor writer of adventure stories. Fortunately, his works were rediscovered in the early 1920s. It was not until then that he finally received—posthumously—the critical respect that was long overdue for the brilliant writer of *Moby-Dick,* one of the greatest apocalyptic novels ever written and one of the most significant masterpieces in the collective body of American literature. (Melville 1961, 1964)

See also Ahab, Captain; Apocalypse: Traditional Judeo-Christian; Apocalyptic Literature; *The Confidence-Man;* Ishmael; *Moby-Dick.*

MEPHISTOPHELES

Mephistopheles is the personification of the devil in the legend of Faust. The legend originated in the anonymous *Faustbuch* (or Faust-book), (1587), was skillfully developed in Christopher Marlowe's *The Tragical History of Dr. Faustus* (1604), and was later redefined in Goethe's *Faust* (Part I, 1808; Part II, 1832).

According to the various representations of the legend, Mephistopheles, a minion of Lucifer, is damned to an eternity of suffering in hell because he is a fallen angel. In the original anonymous treatment of the character, Mephistopheles—in search of other potentially damnable souls—offers Faustus, the scholar, theologian, physician, and magician, a seemingly irresistible deal. With Lucifer's permission, he proposes a pact that will endow Faustus with unlimited knowledge, physical freedom, and Mephistopheles's boundless diabolical service for a period of twenty-four years in a contractual exchange for Faustus's immortal soul.

While each subsequent portrayal of the character contains similar details, Marlowe's Mephistopheles is sympathetic in that having once known eternal bliss, he recklessly casts it aside, plunging him into an infinite abyss devoid of the presence of God. In contrast to this portrayal, Goethe's depiction of the character renders Mephistopheles as a more heartless, cynical, malevolent demon than Marlowe's. The circumstances involving worldly temptation and its eternal consequences, however, remain consistent throughout each of the works.

To illustrate humanity's intrinsic curiosity and desire for both omniscience and omnipotence, many novelists have created characters—like Mephistopheles's prideful victim, the megalomaniacal Faust—who are willing to gamble everything for a glimpse of Godlike power. This archetypal trend has become particularly evident in the works of twentieth-century writers such as Walker Percy, whose Faustian scientists, physicians, and seekers willingly face apocalyptic outcomes offered by Mephistophelean characters in exchange for the promise of societal and/or self-deification. One prominent example of such a deluded character is Dr. Tom More, the protagonist of Percy's two apocalyptic novels, *Love in the Ruins* (1971) and *The Thanatos Syndrome* (1987).

In the earlier of the two novels, Tom More is a lapsed Roman Catholic, a complacent alcoholic, and a fanatical believer in cataclysm who is convinced that the end of the world is near and that he is responsible for preventing the imminent apocalypse. He comes to this conclusion after having been driven away from his faith and his fellow man as a result of disappointment and devastating loss. Believing that he alone understands the societal ills of modern man—a spiritual and psychological disconnection from God—More embarks on a personal journey in which he hopes to save America from its progressive state of ruin.

His hope for the future lies in his encephalographic invention known as More's Qualitative-Quantitative Ontological Lapsometer. With this instrument, More believes that he can scan the human brain, or Carl Jung's concept of the psyche, and locate specific cerebral centers that have been damaged by exposure to sodium ions, the suspected cause of the spiritual malaise and societal apathy he sees around him.

Such an invention might have serious implications in the psychiatric community, but his efforts and his device are viewed with significant skepticism by his former colleagues because of his recent personal and professional decline. Although Tom tries to comply with his colleague's recommendations and prevailing philosophies, he soon becomes desperate to convince them of the impending doom that will certainly result from their ignorance. Thus More, as Dr. Faustus, heedlessly contracts with an obsequious con-man, the Mephistophelean Art Immelmann. By promising to improve Dr. More's invention so that it will become a popular and profitable venture, Immelmann seduces Dr. More into signing away his intellectual freedom. More thus unwittingly accelerates apocalyptic events by placing the device's immeasurable power in Immelmann's diabolical hands.

The sequel to *Love in the Ruins, The Thanatos Syndrome,* reintroduces a new and somewhat improved Dr. Tom More. This time, Dr. More is more subdued. Having learned that the world did not end without his intervention, and having been involuntarily incarcerated for a period of two years, More seems less likely to question the universe and more content to live amidst the ubiquitous ruin of middle-class America. During the years he spent in jail, he had both the time and the solitude to sort things out and to define his priorities. Eventually, he becomes content with pursuing the small pleasures of daily life, most of which focus on his research and his wife and former nurse, the practical Presbyterian, Ellen Oglethorpe.

This idyllic state of affairs changes when Dr. More once again makes a random connection between the peculiarities he observes in his personal and professional lives. Although he is reluctant to resurrect his previous paranoia, he can't help but notice significant changes within his patients and his wife. Clearly, based on his observations, he senses a collective separation of self involving the suppression of the super-ego and the subsequent escalation of the id. In other words, the bestialism that resulted from overexposure to sodium has somehow become reintroduced into society.

Ultimately, More learns that it is via a diabolical plot named Project Blue Boy that the local water supply is being contaminated by heavy doses of sodium. In addition, More discovers that this contamination has led to a proliferation of sexual abuse and exploitation among children within the affected areas. Thus, More, as Faust, must once again confront the forces of evil. This time, however, he resists the temptation to sign a contract that would unwittingly place him in collusion with Van Dorn, the Mephistophelean perpetrator of this heinous crime. As a result of this refusal to symbolically sell his soul to the devil, More restores order to his chaotic world. His actions impact on previously immoral legislative dictates and release the children from continued abuse. His efforts also lead to the punishment of the various perpetrators in appropriate degrees. On the personal level, they heal his once faltering marriage. And in regard to his influence on humanity, his experience—like that of Faustus—remains on record as a warning to those who might otherwise succumb to the devil's tempting invitation to pursue hubris and folly at the cost of eternal damnation.

See also Apocalypse: Secular; Apocalyptic Literature; *Dr. Faustus; Faust;* Freud, Sigmund; Immelmann, Art; *Love in the Ruins: The Adventures of a Bad Catholic at a Time Near the End of the World;* Marlowe, Christopher; More, Sir Thomas; Satan; Smith, Father Rinaldo; Thanatos; *The Thanatos Syndrome.*

MERLIN

Merlin is the ancient sorcerer, sage, and soothsayer who appears prominently throughout various versions of the romantic Arthurian legend. Although his personage is fictionally altered, depending upon its Christian or non-Christian origins, the following characteristics remain static: he is a wise man with supernatural abilities, whose existence is inextricably linked with the fates and fortunes of at least two famous British kings.

Although his character is an amalgam of both British and Welsh traditions, Merlin's first fictional appearance occurred in a ninth-century work by Nennius entitled the *Historia Britonum.* However, it was not until Geoffrey of Monmouth penned the *Historia Regnum Britanniae* in 1137 that the legend of the magician began to take shape. Later in the twelfth century, the character reappeared in Robert de Boron's French trilogy, which owes much to Geoffrey's detailed portrayal. But it was Sir Thomas Malory's *Le Morte d'Arthur* (1490), based upon de

Merlin, wearing his sorcerer's hat, was a prominent figure in Arthurian legends. Dan Beard drew this Merlin for Mark Twain's *Connecticut Yankee in King Arthur's Court*.

Boron's poems, that brought the magician to a literary prominence that later resurfaced in Edmund Spenser's *Faerie Queene* (1589–1596).

One of the more accepted views of Merlin's origin, and the one that is presented initially in the Vulgate cycle, is that he was the son of an Incubus father (a demon spirit who has sex with sleeping women) and a mother who was a Welsh princess. While growing up in the court of Vortigern, the king of the Britons, Merlin was able to use his powers to predict the inevitable victory of the Britons over the rival Saxons. Later, as a sorcerer and adviser to King Uther Pendragon, Merlin cast a spell causing the monarch to sleep with Queen Igraine, who by some accounts was another king's wife. This union produced an heir to the throne—King Arthur—whom Merlin would serve in his legendary kingdom.

Some of the specific feats that have been attributed to Merlin, particularly those detailed in the Christian accounts of the legend, include his prophesies regarding the Holy Grail and his recommendation that King Arthur build a round table to ensure the equitable treatment of each of his knights. Furthermore, it is believed that Arthur sought Merlin's advice in selecting each of the knights who would sit around the king's table. Related accounts also hint that Merlin was responsible for the supernatural transport of the mysterious monoliths of Stonehenge from Ireland to England. But the most poignant and ironic element of Merlin's nature is his complete vulnerability to the enchantments of females, such as the Lady of the Lake or Nimue, who use their power to subdue him in order to suit their purposes. Merlin's sentimental portrayal as a wise man who is undermined by his ill-fated passions is explored in detail in *Idylls of the King* (1859) by Alfred Lord Tennyson.

Although his legend is centuries old, the beloved magician has endured as the subject of twentieth-century literature. He is featured in the narrative poem *Merlin* (1917) by Edward Arlington Robinson, as well as in the ten-hour dramatic epic by experimental German author Tankred Dorst, *Merlin: Or, The Wasteland* (1981). But the most memorable contemporary portrayal of Merlin's duality is captured in the farcical social satire written by the American writer and humorist, Mark Twain: *A Connecticut Yankee in King Arthur's Court* (1889).

See also Apocalypse: Secular; Apocalypse: Traditional Judeo-Christian; Arthur, King; *A Connecticut Yankee in King Arthur's Court; The Faerie Queene;* Malory, Thomas; Morgan, Hank; *Le Morte d'Arthur.*

MERRIDEW, JACK

Jack Merridew is the innocuous name given to the diabolical antagonist of William Golding's prize-winning apocalyptic novel of lost innocence, *Lord of the Flies.* In this novel, a planeload of schoolboys crash-lands on a deserted coral island during an escape from a bombing raid on their English school yard during the Second World War. Although the pilot dies in the plane crash, survivors immediately emerge from the wreckage. The first to be identified in the text is the novel's protagonist, an attractive adolescent and natural-born leader named Ralph. Soon after, however, the antagonist—the opposing dark force who will eventually destroy their island paradise—is introduced as Golding's narrative unfolds.

As Ralph surveys the tropical landscape and assesses the situation, amidst the haze rising from the terrestrial heat, his "eye [is] first attracted to a black, bat-like creature" whom he sees "danc[ing] on the sand." This "creature" appears "bullet-headed" from a distance, due to the black cap that covers his bright red hair. In spite of his perilous circumstances, Ralph notices, the distant figure is frolicking wildly, with "his black cloak circling." Upon closer inspection, Ralph observes that this apparition poses no immediate threat because it is only Jack—a bright-eyed boy who appears "crumpled and freckled, and ugly without silliness" (16–17).

Such a paradoxical introduction presages Golding's major premise that the potential for evil intrinsically exists within all human beings, even within seemingly innocent choirboys like the novel's antagonist, Jack Merridew. Devilish potential such as his is usually kept in check by responsible adults, rigid school rules, or the moral guidelines of a civilized society. But humanity's predisposition for aggression, as represented in Jack's rebellious character, will inevitably emerge once these restrictions have been removed. Such becomes the case the moment that the plane deposits the schoolboys on the island. Most of the children are frightened and concerned about their fates. Jack, in contrast, feels immediately freed from the confines of the civilized world, an emotion that is manifested in his dance of liberation on the coral sands of the deserted beach.

This contrary aspect of Jack's character is poignantly portrayed early in the novel, and it stands out in sharp relief against his surroundings and the behavior of his other schoolmates. First, the island is serene and lush, much like a newly created Garden of Eden. Second, the only inhabitants of the island paradise are its indigenous creatures and, after the crash, the innocent children, all boys, whose ages range approximately from six through twelve. The third and perhaps most significant contrast reveals that the boys are, for the most part, eager to accept Ralph's authority and willing to obey his orders in the hope that they will be saved and returned to the order of their former world. But Jack, seemingly unafraid of his new surroundings, neither accepts Ralph's position of authority nor participates in activities that will lead to the group's possible rescue. Thus, within the setting of this newfound Eden, Golding places Ralph and Jack in distinct adversarial positions. He observes— from a safe literary distance—as they battle over the bodies and souls of the other boys on the island in an effort to determine which force will inevitably reign supreme over this microcosm of the modern world.

Jack's initial behavior foreshadows the gradual escalation of his primitive instincts, as well as his demonstrative rejection of former civility. Whereas others are concerned with maintaining a signal fire that will lead to their rescue, Jack relies on his cunning and agility as he makes a game of their circumstance. In an attempt to usurp Ralph's power, he appoints himself "chief" of a group of "hunters" who become fixated on killing wild animals. The acquisition of meat becomes an issue on the island despite the fact that there is still a great bounty of seafood and fruit to be shared by all. The real purpose of the hunt becomes evident when Jack succumbs to his primitive urges as he paints his face, using charcoal and clay. This act marks Jack's transformation from civility to savagery:

> Beside the pool [of water], his sinewy body held up a mask that drew [the others'] eyes and appalled them. He began to dance and his laughter became a bloodthirsty snarling. . . .[T]he mask was a thing on its own, behind which Jack hid, liberated from shame and self-consciousness (Golding 58).

From this moment, Jack succumbs to his bloodlust, and soon he forgoes any remorse for the act of killing. In fact, he celebrates it, as well as his own success in the endeavor. Thus, his confidence, further fueled by his apparent victories in the wild, eventually seduces the others to join in his bestial revelry, with the exception of Ralph, Piggy, and Simon. In recompense for their resistance to comply with Jack's new order, Piggy's valuable glasses are stolen, and he eventually falls to his death, dashing his brains upon the coral rocks. In an even more blatant act of savagery, the saintlike character Simon is mistaken for a jungle beast during a feverish nighttime hunting ritual. Ironically, Simon has come bearing information that will allay the fears of the group. But he is mercilessly silenced as Jack's army of hunters converge on his darkened form and butcher him, while ritually chanting, *"Kill the beast! Cut his throat! Spill his blood! Do him in!"* (Golding 141).

The final act of terror initiated by Jack and his savages, however, represents the obliteration of order by the forces of chaos. Jack no longer hides his murderous intentions; rather, he determinedly imperils everyone on the island by setting a blazing fire that he hopes will coax Ralph from his hiding spot so that he can finally kill his rival and reign supreme over his infernal paradise. This act, however, ironically leads to their being spotted by a British naval vessel and their subsequent rescue. Thus, Ralph escapes Jack's savage attack and reasserts himself as the leader of the boys. Jack's future after the rescue is no doubt uncertain. The temporary triumph of good over evil is sadly overcast by the attitude of the naval officer who rescues them. He sees their life-and-death struggle as little more than child's play, and in these few utterances, reflects the future fate of a world in which boys like Jack eventually grow up only to attempt to destroy the world with larger and more devastating weapons of war.

See also Apocalypse: Traditional Judeo-Christian; Apocalypse: Traditional Primitive; *Lord of the Flies;* Piggy; Ralph; Satan; Simon.

MILLENNIALISM

Also sometimes *millenarianism, millennialism* is a term originating from the Latin for the number 1,000 that represents a philosophy consistent with many Christian denominations. According to chapter 20 of the New Testament account of the book of Revelation, the prophetic writer is given a vision portraying the seizing and binding of Satan in a bottomless pit. Concurrently, all Christian martyrs who have been long dead will be resurrected and will reign on earth with Christ for a period of one thousand years, or "the millennium."

While specific Protestant sects, such as the Adventists and the Jehovah's Witnesses, maintain unique views of this thousand-year reign, in the majority of Protestant denominations the millennial period simply reflects a time of great peace, the welcomed absence of evil, and the fulfillment of God's promise that the righteous will enjoy a thousand-year dominion over the earth.

An aspect of eschatology, or the study of "last things," millennialism as a belief attempts to provide tangible answers for humanity's persistent questions about what will happen to people on earth after Armageddon—but before the time of God's final judgment. Finally, while millennialism is predominantly a Christian concept, sociologists point to evidence such as predominant characters and symbols that reflect similar beliefs in non-Western cultures.

See also Apocalypse: Traditional Judeo-Christian; Apocalypse: Traditional Primitive; Eschatology; *The Origin of the Brunists;* Revelation, Book of.

MILLER, JUSTIN ("TIGER")

"Tiger" Miller is the photojournalist whose efforts transform a devastating mining accident in a small Pennsylvania town into a bizarre media circus in Robert Coover's apocalyptic novel, *The Origin of the Brunists* (1966). In the novel, Miller is both figuratively and literally an outsider in the town that experiences a mining disaster in which ninety-seven men are killed and only one, Giovanni Bruno, survives the blast.

The reader is introduced to Miller shortly after the explosion, opportunistically taking photographs of the dead miners as their bodies are recovered, interviewing and photographing grieving widows and deranged observers, and planning his cataclysmic coverage of the event for the front page of his newspaper, *The West Condon Chronicle.* His efforts result in the dramatic headline, "MIRACLE IN WEST CONDON" (92). This headline ignites a smoldering undercurrent of religious fervor already extant in the town. Miller recognizes that it is the media's function both to inform and to entertain, and he begins to research his project by infiltrating the developing millenarian cult. Revolving around the survivor of the blast, Giovanni Bruno, the cult eventually becomes known as "the Brunists."

While the accident devastates the already dying mining town, it invigorates "Tiger" Miller and drives him to perpetuate the apocalyptic fervor that increasingly engulfs the citizens of the community. Although he attempts to ingratiate himself to the grieving community, and specifically focuses attention on the survivor's vulnerable sister, Marcella, he is held under suspicion by the more zealous members of the cult. Marcella is physically attracted to him, and for a time he is allowed easy access to the machinations of the cult.

Tiger begins to confuse his self-created journalistic fiction with the reality of their situation when he encourages Marcella's affection. Although he is attracted to her, it is less for her real self than for the role in which he has cast her. Thus, in his journalistic representations of her, he describes a virginal icon, "a wonderfully erotic/religious figure: a blend of *'forest greenness, and church masonry and northern stars'* " (Dewey 1990, 104). In reality, however, she is a devoted sister to the mining victim whose simple faith in the cult is in direct conflict with her powerful sexual desire for Miller. Because he wants to worship her, and especially to rescue her from the fanatical cult that he has helped to create, he seriously miscalculates her reaction to his behavior during an encounter in the print shop.

Miller plans to save Marcella from the group by asking her to marry him. Just as he has orchestrated the events in the town, he similarly orchestrates their encounter in a back room of the *Chronicle.* Although during their meeting Marcella expresses her clear sexual desire for him, she becomes unnerved by his reluctance to consummate their relationship as well as by his scripted revelation that he does not believe in the Brunists and that he further wishes to take her away from the cult through marriage.

Humiliated, dismayed, and devastated by Miller's lack of faith, Marcella runs from Tiger's fictional world and retreats into the world created by the millenarian cult inspired by her brother. By doing so, however, she unwittingly recedes from reality and ironically becomes the virgin martyr of the cult that Miller has helped to perpetuate.

It is her return to the cult and her subsequent decline in mental and physical health that expose Miller to the group as the "dark one," or the archetypal Antichrist that threatens to undermine the group's faith. Consequently, on the night of the apocalyptic gathering on the Mount of Redemption, the Brunists observe him in their midst and descend upon him in an enraged ritual of destruction. He survives the attack and is hospitalized for his wounds. Marcella, however, is killed in the melee. Miller briefly berates himself for having played Judas to her Christ-figure. Thus, even after her death, he demonstrates his choice to deify her rather than to grieve for the real woman who had invited him to participate in life through genuine passion and love.

Miller eventually recovers, at least physically, through the professional and sexual ministrations of his previous lover, a lascivious nurse he calls "Happy Bottom." And although their relationship promises none of the intense honesty that Marcella's love offered, he is content to remain in familiar territory, with Happy Bottom, as an observer and exploiter of his own fictional world, "forever cushioned . . . from the vital connectedness" of real life (105).

See also Apocalypse: Traditional Judeo-Christian; Apocalyptic Literature; Bonali, Vince; Millennialism; Naturalism; *The Origin of the Brunists.*

MILTON, JOHN

The renowned English scholar and poet John Milton (1608–1674) is best known for his magnum opus, *Paradise Lost*, the story of mankind and its subsequent fall from grace, which was published in 1667. Milton was born into a relatively prosperous family. His father John was a London scrivener—a legal writer—as well as a moneylender. His mother, Sarah Jeffery, was a subdued but well-respected woman who was known for her generous nature and her charitable efforts and contributions within the community.

Encouraged by his father, who was also a minor literary composer, Milton's destiny was shaped by his inherited love of literature. This proclivity was nurtured by his studies at Christ's College in Cambridge, where after an initial incompatibility with his first tutor, he maintained a fulfilling and academically satisfying relationship with his subsequent mentor. In 1632, Milton graduated from Christ's College with a Master of Arts degree and some academic distinction. From his academic pursuits he gained a lifelong love for ancient history, classical literature, romance languages, and Bible study. Because his father approved of young Milton's interest in these compelling areas of scholarship, he provided his son with the financial support necessary for the budding writer to pursue his continuing independent study on these subjects while living at home.

One of the first works resulting from his efforts, and one that was indicative of Milton's considerable talents, was the elegy entitled *Lycidas* (1637), inspired by and dedicated to one of his dear friends who had died at a young age. Recognition of this work subsequently drew attention to an earlier masque—a work that is intended for dramatic presentation—entitled *Comus,* that had been written in honor of the inauguration of John Ederton as the new Lord President of Wales (1634).

Following these early successes, Milton decided to expand the scope of his personal scholarship by traveling abroad. Thus, in 1638, after the death of his mother and the marriage of his brother, Milton embarked on a trip to the classic cities of Italy—Rome, Venice, Geneva, and Florence—and returned to England in 1639 with a renewed interest in Italian art, religious literature, and music. Inspired by this experience, and influenced by several of the world's great literary epics, he began contemplating his own work of epic proportions. It would rival the ancient epics such as Homer's *Odyssey* and Virgil's *Aeneid,* Dante's ecclesiastical epic *The Divine Comedy* (c. 1307), and the more contemporary epic romance, Edmund Spenser's *The Faerie Queene* (1595).

Although Milton was consumed by such a literary ideal, the practical side of his nature and the political issues of England led him to two other avenues of expression. First, he established a school in London, along with his two nephews Edward and John Phillips, where he served as a classical tutor. While working in this capacity, he also began producing highly inflammatory pamphlets dealing with corruption in the Anglican church. In 1641 and 1642, he published five pamphlets attacking Episcopalian bishops and supporting the less stringent system offered by the Presbyterian sect. As a result of these efforts, Milton ultimately came to the conclusion that an individual's spiritual life is really one's own personal responsibility, and that individual growth in this area is not to be achieved by adherence to denominational doctrines but rather by one's own individual interaction with biblical texts.

While the author was beginning to come to terms with some of the world's more controversial issues of scholarship and spirituality, he also became interested in pursuing more conventional institutions such as marriage. Thus, in 1642, Milton hastily married seventeen-year-old Mary Powell, who was so different from him in temperament, political and religious views, and educational background that she soon left him to return to her parents. During their time apart, Milton became so obsessed by the general issue of marital incompatibility and the church's rigid stance against divorce that he embarked on another campaign of pamphlet writing. This time he attacked both the political and religious institutions and laws which, in his own experience unfairly prohibited divorce. Ironically, in 1645, while he was in the midst of this activity, his wife returned to him and bore him five children. She died in 1652.

Despite his reputation as a divorce advocate, Milton took a second wife, Katherine Woodcock, in 1656. Unfortunately, she lived only another two years. In 1663, Milton took his third and final wife, Elizabeth Minshull, with whom he lived until his death.

The writer came to appreciate the stability of marriage, which enabled him to pursue his scholarship with such vigor that he began to lose his eyesight. Although he required the assistance of a scribe to record his apocalyptic masterpiece that he hoped would "justify the ways of God to men," he completed his work, *Paradise Lost*, in 1665, and it was published two years later. In this twelve-book opus, Milton not only addressed the fall of man in a more humanistic manner than did Dante, but he also featured personal and spiritual battles over the political battles of Virgil. But, most importantly, he successfully emulated the epic form that he had so long admired in the work of Homer and achieved his formidable scholarly goal that he had been incubating for nearly twenty years of his life.

Although the author could have concluded his literary efforts upon the publication of his ultimate masterpiece, he was eventually persuaded by friends and fellow scholars to continue the spiritual saga of humanity, the ultimate victory of Christ over Satan, and the rewards of eternal salvation in his 1671 work, *Paradise Regained.* Also published in that same year was another masterwork with a biblical foundation, *Samson Agonistes.* In this work, the author used the classical plot pattern of the Greek tragedy to reveal the excruciating details of the vanquished biblical hero of the same name.

These works represent a full life of scholarship, insight, and spiritual devotion that enabled Milton, attentively nursed by his wife, to enjoy his remaining years in a state of personal and professional fulfillment as well as spiritual tranquillity. Fortified with the knowledge that his works were attaining both popular and critical acclaim, Milton died peacefully on November 8, 1674, having earned a well-founded reputation as one of the world's greatest contributors to classical literature.

See also Apocalypse: Traditional Judeo-Christian; Apocalyptic Literature; *The Divine Comedy;* God; Heaven; Hell; Satan.

MIRANDA

Miranda is the daughter of the deposed Duke of Milan in William Shakespeare's apocalyptic tragicomedy, *The Tempest* (c. 1611). Miranda's name literally means "a wonder," and she is the epitome of innocence. Her soft-hearted naiveté is not merely the result of idealism but the result of her separation from the corrupt influences of the civilized world. Miranda and her father Prospero had been exiled from their homeland after a political coup. They were placed in a ramshackle vessel and given only a few provisions, with the expectation that their ship would ultimately crash upon the rocks. Miraculously, the father and his three-year-old daughter washed up on the shores of a deserted island, and there they lived in tranquil isolation for the following twelve years. During that time, Prospero studied magic in order to avenge the serious wrong that had been done to him and his child.

Although Miranda is fifteen years old when readers first encounter her as an individual character, she is remarkably innocent. In fact, placed upon this deserted island paradise, she is Eve-like. Her lack of experience with other more manipulative members of society has kept her tender and trusting, naturally toward her father, but even toward Caliban, the monstrous creature also imprisoned on the island. Her tender nature causes her to be upset on the occasion when another ship crashes onto their deserted island home. Unaware that her father's magic has caused the ship and its particular inhabitants to wash ashore, she is deeply concerned about the safety of all those who may be on board.

The person with whom she is most concerned, of course, is the handsome young Ferdinand, the son of her father's former rival, the King of Naples. She comes upon him as he is getting his bearings on the island, and when their eyes meet, theirs is the classic case of love at first sight. Their meeting is especially beautiful because, in her innocence, she is devoid of the guile that usually accompanies courtship rituals. And although her genuine candor surprises the smitten Ferdinand at first, he is overwhelmed and relieved to have found such a perfect woman in such an unexpected location. The two almost immediately declare their love for one another, and Miranda agrees to Ferdinand's proposal of marriage provided that her father will approve of the union.

Fortunately, Miranda does not know that it has been her father's design all along that Ferdinand would arrive on the island. When Prospero uses magic to render himself invisible to observe their initial meeting, he is extremely pleased by the possibilities of their union. In fact, it is partly his daughter's joy that leads him away from his original plan for vengeance and causes him to pursue a course of reconciliation with his former enemies. Thus, it is the force of love—Prospero's for Miranda and Miranda's for Ferdinand—that enables the deposed Duke to receive his long overdue apology, to become restored to his former nobility, and to enjoy the promise of familial fulfillment that will certainly follow his blessing of their most perfect union.

See also Apocalypse: Traditional Judeo-Christian; Apocalypticism; Caliban; Ferdinand; Prospero; *The Tempest.*

MISS LONELYHEARTS

Miss Lonelyhearts is the concise novel written by Nathanael West (1933). It contains various symbolic elements that cause the work to span the distinct apocalyptic classifications established by John R. May (May 1972, 229). First, as a representation of primitive apocalypse, *Miss Lonelyhearts* represents the "ritual return to chaos . . . in American life. Nature, the works of man and human misery are all symbolic of the chaos of existence. It is this chaos that Miss Lonelyhearts—the priestess of twentieth-century America—must impose order upon" (211).

It is this need to impose order amidst the chaos of humanity that motivates the novel's protagonist "Miss Lonelyhearts," a male journalist who writes responses in the agony column of a newspaper called the New York *Post-Dispatch.*

During the course of his work, Miss Lonelyhearts receives no less than thirty letters per day, each one symbolizing the wretched lives of the countless suffering masses. The letters he receives serve as desperate pleas for help to solve some of life's most impossible problems.

For example, at the opening of the novel, Miss Lonelyhearts describes the letters and the people who write them. One writer, known only as "Sick-of-it-all," agonizes over her lot in life as a good Catholic woman. In spite of her religious beliefs and her deteriorating health, she has been forced to endure the repeated indignities involved in being "man and wife," not the least of which has been the reluctant bearing of seven children within the span of twelve years (2). Thus, her letter details the mental, physical, and spiritual anguish she and countless others like her must endure. Next, he receives a letter from "Desperate," a sixteen-year-old girl who matter-of-factly wonders if she should commit suicide because of her problem—a gross physical deformity that has left her without a nose on her face. The letter is even more pitiful in its plea for encouragement to retain some hope for future happiness because she is "a good dancer . . . [has] a nice shape and [her] father buys [her] pretty clothes" (2). Sadly, the journalist can find no words with which to comfort her. The final letter to which Miss Lonelyhearts must respond on the same day is a heartbreaking request for advice from "Harold S," an older brother of a thirteen-year-old girl who has clearly been taunted because she is a deaf-mute; the greater problem, however, is that she has been sexually abused and impregnated by a neighbor (3). Having nowhere else to turn, the boy writes to Miss Lonelyhearts for advice on how to save his sister from the inevitable shame she will suffer in society and from the physical beatings she will receive from her irate mother.

Partially because Miss Lonelyhearts is the son of a Baptist minister and partly because of his sensitive nature, the journalist is obsessed with the Christian apocalyptic response to chaos in the universe: no matter what the question, Christ is the answer. However, Miss Lonelyhearts feels unable to impose his spiritual solution on his readers because Shrike, the diabolically cynical editor of the paper, uses the journalist's belief in Christ-as-restorer-of-order as "his particular joke" with which to torment the earnest protagonist (3). Thus, from fear of Shrike's intimidation and to some degree from fear of his own creeping doubt, Miss Lonelyhearts suppresses his initial response and relies instead on empty platitudes that he knows will never placate his readers' physical pain or soothe their suffering souls.

Miss Lonelyhearts's problem is that his job as an advice columnist was never intended as a serious position. The agony column was first conceived as a joke—a publicity stunt. On a practical level, Miss Lonelyhearts welcomed the job because he believed that it would eventually turn into something better, like an ongoing gossip column. What he didn't count on, however, was that his readers, with their "inarticulate expressions of genuine suffering," would "take him seriously." Thus, "for the first time in his life, he is forced to examine the values by which he lives. This examination shows him that he is the victim of the joke and not its perpetrator" (32).

In spite of this ironic twist of fate, Miss Lonelyhearts desperately seeks a source for answers. In his own mind, he runs the gamut of humanity's perpetual search for life's meaning, and this quest is reflected in Shrike's malicious recommendations: "Art! Be an artist or a writer" (34). He also discusses the options of drugs and suicide, but Shrike summarily states what Miss Lonelyhearts unfortunately knows to be true: "Neither the soil, nor the South Seas, nor Hedonism, nor art, nor suicide, nor drugs, can mean anything . . ." to the suffering masses (35).

While his letters reflect the growing chaos of the modern world, he notices similar entropic intrusion into his personal life as well. On a day when he tries to take comfort in the order of his own private universe, his logic is defied by buttons rolling under beds, pencil points breaking, and a host of similar indignities that confirm his growing loss of control. These events are similarly reflected in the escalating complexity of his personal relationships. For instance, Shrike's cynicism seems to become more pervasive. His experiences with women—Betty, his sometime fiancée, Mrs. Shrike, the libidinous wife of his boss, and Fay Doyle, the "Broad Shoulder[ed]" wife of a crippled meter-reader—not only fail to give him solace, but, in every case, they serve to complicate his life with greater frustration and despair.

Therefore, in order to steel himself against the vicarious pain of the letters and against the ubiquitous neediness and, in some cases treachery, of the women in his life, Miss Lonelyhearts decides that it's best to become solid and impermeable, like a rock. Clearly, the rock—the solid foundation upon which Christ built his church—serves as a powerful symbol of Christian apocalypse. But unlike other Christian apocalyptic novels in which long suffering ultimately leads to genuine hope, Miss Lonelyhearts as the rock only deludes himself and inadvertently brings about his own destruction.

The first occasion in which he experiments with his new philosophy occurs when Shrike picks a fight with him for insulting his wife: "Miss Lonelyhearts stood quietly in the center of the room. Shrike dashed against him, but fell back, as a wave that dashes against an ancient rock" (51). To his dismay, Shrike backs down and even seems congratulatory in response to the journalist's refusal to fight. However, unaware that by hardening his heart he is committing emotional suicide, Miss Lonelyhearts continues to "remain calm and solid" (52). When Betty confesses that she is pregnant with his child and threatens to get an abortion, he responds by asking her to marry him and live happily according to her rural Connecticut fantasy. But his response to her problem is automatic, not sincere, because since deciding to become a rock, he has also begun to lose his identity. Even though he had only told her what she wanted to hear, "he did not feel guilty. He did not feel. The rock was a solidification of his feeling, his conscience, his sense of reality, his self-knowledge" (56).

Through these trials, Miss Lonelyhearts believes that he has been tested by God and has "been found perfect" (56). He mistakenly feels that he has finally transcended the troubles of this life by his complete identification with God. "His identification with God was complete. His heart was the one heart, the heart of God. And his brain was likewise God's" (57). Ironically, it is when he feels most invulnerable to humanity's ills that he himself becomes most susceptible to danger.

At the conclusion of the novel, West indicates that Miss Lonelyhearts's "religious experience" (56) leads him to misread the murderous intentions of the cuckolded cripple, Peter Doyle, whose wife has had an affair with the journalist. Therefore, in an effort to become God, in all his mercy, he runs toward the cripple with open arms to embrace him. He is unaware that Doyle is carrying a gun that has been wrapped, ironically, in the remnants of Miss Lonelyhearts's old life—a newspaper filled with hollow words. Ultimately, just as the inadequacy of words made it impossible to alleviate the suffering of the masses, so too do they serve as an inadequate shield to protect a deluded martyr from the chaos of the universe.

See also Apocalypse: Anti-Christian; Apocalypse: Traditional Judeo-Christian; Apocalypse: Traditional Primitive; *The Day of the Locust;* Shrike; West, Nathanael.

MOBY-DICK

One of the greatest American apocalyptic novels, *Moby-Dick* was written by Herman Melville in 1851. The story revolves around a mysterious and malevolent great white whale that attacks whaling vessels and has maimed and killed whalers. One of his most significant victims is Captain Ahab, whose previous encounter with the great white caused him to lose his leg and to vow revenge, regardless of the cost, by hunting and killing the great beast of the sea.

At the beginning of the novel, the narrator—a curious wanderer of the world named Ishmael—follows his call to experience the adventures of the sea by serving on a commercial whaling vessel, the *Pequod*. He soon learns, however, that the ship's captain, Ahab, is less interested in killing whales for their valuable oil than he is in using his crew and his vessel to destroy the whale that left him limping pathetically on a false ivory limb fashioned from the jawbone of a whale. The narrator becomes the unwitting observer of a dance of death that escalates as Moby-Dick torments his victim with occasional sightings, and the determined captain pursues the leviathan nearly halfway around the world in order to exact his revenge.

Although the novel defies concise analysis because of its moral and metaphysical depth, it is essentially a microcosm in which the vast human drama is played out on a smaller scale, within the confines of a relatively small ship sailing upon the limitless universal sea. Within this microcosm, there are other characters who represent basic human characteristics that become evident through their interactions with the central character, Captain Ahab, as well as with Moby-Dick himself. For example, Starbuck serves as Ahab's idealistic but superstitious first mate. He is typical of those individuals who have the best intentions—in his case, to deter Ahab from this dangerous pursuit—but whose fears ultimately render them impotent against the more formidable forces of pride and anger that fuel the wills of powerful characters such as Ahab. Next, the microcosm includes Stubb, the second mate. Stubb is an obsequious disciple who willingly accepts Ahab's commands; he represents those individuals whose unquestioning allegiance to a corrupt authority contributes to, rather than resolves, the problems of the world. On the other hand, Flask, the third mate on the *Pequod*, is merely a stupid, selfish, and sometimes cruel follower of Ahab's commands. He follows not for any particular loyalty to his leader, but merely because he personally enjoys the hunting, tormenting, and killing of whales.

Although he is of little import for his own merit, his real significance lies in his representation of the materialistic and mindless masses who willingly support a cause if it furthers their own selfish purposes. Because the world holds so many like him, he is dangerous solely in regard to the power that comes from his compatriot's great numbers.

The final and perhaps most important character in the novel is Moby-Dick himself. Clearly, Melville intends for this leviathan to be larger than life, with a potential for destruction that is of biblical proportions. His physical appearance has unique significance. His coloration as a "white" whale makes him impenetrably mysterious and a one-of-a-kind creature in the universe. His stunning absence of color is only magnified by his enormous size. He possesses an innate, somewhat supernatural intelligence that compels him to demonstrate his power against his greatest and most intelligent enemy—man—represented by Ahab.

In these and other ways Moby-Dick, the great white whale, is intentionally enigmatic as a literary figure. For Ahab, of course, the whale is pure evil. However, for others, including numerous literary critics, Moby-Dick is symbolic of God's power, and in some views the whale is considered an agent of God who delivers his wrath upon a prideful humanity that continues to disregard the laws of God's universe in favor of its own pitiably futile pursuits.

See also: Ahab; Ahab, Captain; Apocalypse: Traditional Judeo-Christian; Apocalyptic Literature; Ishmael; Leviathan; Melville, Herman.

MONTAG, GUY

Guy Montag is the futuristic fireman of Ray Bradbury's controversial novel of extreme government censorship, *Fahrenheit 451* (1953). Montag is a ten-year veteran of a force whose work has changed significantly from that of the firefighters of today. In Montag's world, homes have been constructed out of fireproof materials; hence, the squad's work has long since been redirected toward a new enemy, the fire of knowledge. According to the fire chief, the symbolic representative of government, literature is considered to be the historical source of society's discontent; therefore, the possession of books is strictly forbidden. Those who are caught with a hidden cache risk the burning of their books, and in some cases even the burning of their homes. At the beginning of the novel, Montag also believes that books promote too much independent thought, and that those who read will inevitably question authority. This is a dangerous thing in a world that relies on societal apathy to accept nuclear war as commonplace and human life as devoid of individual value.

In the pursuit of his duties as a professional book burner, however, Montag becomes curious about why people risk their lives in order to save their books. He begins to confiscate texts from each "crime" scene, and in secret, tries to find meaning in a new world of thought. Soon he meets Clarisse, a young neighbor who—unlike his jaded, somnambulant wife—finds joy in living and introduces him to the value of books. Increasingly, as a result of meeting people who explain to him the wonders of reading, Montag becomes disillusioned with his vocation. His wife discovers his hidden books and mocks his interest in them to visitors in their home, creating a dangerous situation for all. Soon Montag learns that his wife has turned him in to the authorities, which results in his having to burn his own home to the ground.

By this time, Montag can no longer accept life in his former world. He flees to the home of Faber, his book mentor, and is sent "underground" to a secret book-loving community to escape society's inverted form of justice, demonstrated by the fierce attack of a vicious mechanical hound. During his escape, in a symbolic gesture indicating the birth of a new self, Montag crosses a cool, cleansing river, and immediately his energy is restored.

As he walks along an abandoned railroad track toward an unknown future, he sees the distant fires of his new society. Finally, in the company of the "book people," he learns the value of truth, independence, and the love of ideas, and he joins them in memorizing books in order to save them from extinction. Montag's journey ends as he turns his back on a world that is destroyed by nuclear attack and begins his long journey home toward a place and time where people are free to become whole.

See also Apocalypse: Traditional Judeo-Christian; *Fahrenheit 451;* McClellan, Clarisse; Science Fiction.

MOODIE, PRISCILLA

The pallid, fawning half-sister of the spirited Zenobia in Nathaniel Hawthorne's *The Blithedale Romance* (1852), Priscilla is introduced early in the novel as a pitiful supplicant whose only wish is to become part of the experimental community of Blithedale in the hope that she can worship at the feet of her majestic sibling, Zenobia. Although her careful ministrations are curiously amusing at first, Zenobia becomes increasingly annoyed at the younger woman's undying devotion. The reason for this annoyance is that for most of the novel, Zenobia does not know that Priscilla is indeed her half-sister.

Readers will note that a compatible relationship between the two women seems most improbable until the narrator, Coverdale, reveals the truth of the two women in a detailed discussion with a peripheral character, "Old Moodie." Old Moodie, it seems, was once a wealthy and influential man who had married well and had gained significant respectability in his community. Through a series of shady dealings and resultant financial reversals, Old Moodie took to wandering the streets in shame and despair. To protect his wife and daughter, he had entrusted their care to his brother, who ultimately provided Moodie's daughter—the headstrong and beautiful Zenobia—with a sizable inheritance and an exaggerated sense of self-esteem. Although Zenobia's life continued in considerable comfort, Old Moodie slowly recovered enough to marry again after the death of his disillusioned first wife. The child of his second more meager union was the shadowy, self-deprecating Priscilla.

Perhaps because of her proximity to Zenobia, or perhaps because of her exposure to a healthy outdoor environment, Priscilla soon thrives emotionally and physically at Blithedale. This transformation does not go unnoticed by the other principal characters. Zenobia finds Priscilla's change disturbing because the younger woman is now presenting her with a sense of competition. Hollingsworth, the charismatic object of Zenobia's attention, is also attracted to

Priscilla, not only for her looks but for her generous spirit and unquestioning worship of his ideas, all of which seem to grow in the world they have begun to create together.

Just as Priscilla becomes strong in her own right, her life is drastically changed by the ignominious interference of Zenobia and her nefarious former husband, the evil magician Westervelt. In an effort to eliminate the competition—and despite the younger woman's love and loyalty—Zenobia plots with Westervelt to take Priscilla from Blithedale (and away from Hollingsworth) and transform her into the mysterious, clairvoyant "Veiled Lady" featured in Westervelt's traveling magic show. Although it is never directly stated, it can be assumed that the only reason Priscilla agrees to participate in this degrading pact is to please her beloved Zenobia. Zenobia now sees her way clear to win Hollingsworth's heart, but she does not count on his discovering Priscilla during one of these performances. Perhaps because he loves her, and certainly because he needs her to boost his ego and his plans, Hollingsworth calls to Priscilla. She responds by casting off her veil and embracing him in confirmation of their love.

As has always been the case for Priscilla, her happiness is short-lived. Certainly she has won Hollingsworth, but it is because of this truth that Zenobia, distraught over the loss of her money and her honor, commits suicide by drowning herself in a river. Before doing so, however, she vows to haunt Hollingsworth for the rest of his life. This is the case at the conclusion of the novel. In the unchronicled years that pass between his rescue of Priscilla and his final reunion with Coverdale, Hollingsworth becomes a mere shadow of his former self. True to her character, however, Priscilla remains loyal to and supportive of the once indomitable man who wanted to reform the world. In this way, Hawthorne shows that sometimes the quiet flame of the meek is more durable than the blazing hubris of the strong.

See also Apocalypse: Traditional Primitive; *The Blithedale Romance;* Brook Farm; Coverdale, Miles; Hollingsworth; Moodie, Zenobia; Romanticism; Transcendentalism; Westervelt.

MOODIE, ZENOBIA

This exotic and egocentric feminist serves as the compelling principal character in Nathaniel Hawthorne's apocalyptic novel, *The Blithedale Romance* (1852). In spite of the author's protestations, the character of Zenobia is based upon one of his contemporaries, social critic and feminist writer Margaret Fuller, with whom he briefly shared the Brook Farm transcendental experience. Zenobia's personality, much like Fuller's, is a complex amalgam of sensuality, cynicism, passionate histrionics, and detached malevolence.

The fact that Zenobia is not her given name, but one that she has chosen to suit herself, says much about her character. The original Zenobia, a sultry and ambitious queen, was known for her manipulative quest for unlimited power and glory. Similarly, Hawthorne's Zenobia, despite her regal bearing, is superficially civil, but she demonstrates a subversive ruthlessness that threatens anyone who stands in the way of her personal plans.

At the beginning of the novel, however, she is presented as a welcoming earth mother, based on the Edenic archetype of Eve (Hawthorne 44–45). As though she has bloomed directly from the earth, like the exotic flower with which she adorns her hair, she nurtures and encourages each new resident of Blithedale with the strength of her character, the skill of her work, and the warmth of her smile. Behind this smile, however, lies a darker side, one that first presents itself during a lascivious verbal exchange between her and Coverdale. She then attempts to use her feminine wiles to capture the real object of her attention: Hollingsworth, the charismatic but megalomaniacal social reformer of the group. She envisions their union as the combination of strengths that will give birth to a perfect new world over which they will share dominion. Hollingsworth, however, has other plans. As the novel progresses, it becomes increasingly evident that neither her love nor her money are enough to win the heart of this calculating character. Clearly, Hollingsworth prefers the companionship of her plain half-sister, Priscilla. This realization sends Zenobia spinning out of control. As a result, she desperately covenants with the evil magician, Westervelt, who arranges to exploit the conciliatory Priscilla in a traveling magic show that will take the woman away from Blithedale and, more importantly, away from Hollingsworth.

These plans, however, are subverted by the overriding will of Hollingsworth, and Zenobia, sensing her loss of control, becomes despondent as a result. Specifically, she feels humiliated when she learns that Hollingsworth has not only taken advantage of her affection but also her fortune in an attempt to transform Blithedale into his own monarchy for societal reform. Unable to go on, given the knowledge that she has been beaten at her own game, Zenobia arranges to have the last word in the only way that she can. She drowns herself in a nearby river. Consequently, the very thing that she could not accomplish in life she accomplishes in death. As a result of Zenobia's suicide, Hollingsworth becomes wracked with guilt and thus forfeits his dream of rehabilitating all the world's criminals except for one wretched sinner: himself. And although in his final days Priscilla remains by his side, there are no dreams left for the broken and penitent Hollingsworth because Zenobia has won; she has succeeded in vanquishing him from the grave.

See also Apocalypse: Traditional Primitive; *The Blithedale Romance;* Brook Farm; Hollingsworth; Moodie, Priscilla; Romanticism; Transcendentalism; Westervelt.

MORE, DR. TOM

The angst-ridden protagonist of Walker Percy's cataclysmic satire, *Love in the Ruins: The Adventures of a Bad Catholic at a Time Near the End of the World* (1971), Tom More appears again in Percy's apocalyptic tale, *The Thanatos Syndrome* (1987). In the beginning of the first novel, *Love in the Ruins*, the reader finds more than a lapsed Catholic in Dr. Tom More. He is a despondent and cataclysmic man who, having abandoned his faith in God following the merciless death of his beloved daughter, struggles to find order and happiness in a chaotic and often cruel universe.

Tom More's personal struggles are revealed in the first few paragraphs of the novel. He ponders his philosophical dilemma: "Either I'm right and a catastrophe will occur, or it won't and I'm crazy. In either case the outlook is not so good" (Percy *LR* 3). And so, in the opening scenes, More ponders humanity's fate, his own role in the universe, and his perceived responsibility for preventing an apocalyptic end to the modern world. According to Dr. More, the problem is simple: man has forgotten about God and has thereby sickened his soul. The solution, he believes, rests solely in correct application of his invention, More's Qualitative-Quantative Ontological Lapsometer, a device he hopes will be able to "probe the very secrets of the soul [and] diagnose the maladies that poison the wellsprings of man's hope" (6). But in spite of his efforts to maintain control over this powerful device, his pride has caused it to get into the wrong hands. More feels that its uncontrolled use will directly result in the destruction of life as he knows it; ergo, as he is the one who created the device, he feels compelled to assume responsibility for saving the world.

While his actions and their consequences seem clear to him, others doubt their validity—and with good reason. It seems that for years, the once respected Dr. More has steadily declined into an alcoholic haze punctuated by a series of meaningless love affairs, intermittent institutionalizations, and delusions of messianic grandeur. He hasn't always been this way, but disturbing events in his life have led him to agree with the Yeatsian perspective that "things fall apart" ("The Second Coming"). And in More's seemingly contented life, they certainly did. The first soul-shaking event occurs when his loving and devout daughter Samantha is stricken with a disfiguring and aggressive form of terminal cancer known as neuroblastoma. As his daughter's precious face grows mercilessly out of proportion, so too, ironically, does her faith in God. This cruel dichotomy, however, only serves to render the first devastating chink in More's fragile armor of Roman Catholic faith.

After their daughter's death, More and Doris, his wife of many years, find their relationship falling apart. Without faith at the core of their marriage, and without the ability either to comprehend or confide their emotional pain, both begin to fill the increasing gap between them with other pursuits. Doris soon finds comfort in the arms of oriental mysticism, to which she is introduced by an opportunistic Englishman, while More absorbs himself in the predictable yet elusive comfort of Early Times bourbon.

After Doris deserts him, partly because he is a reminder of their shared loss, partly because he is disdainful of her spiritual exploration, but mostly because of his increasingly drunken self-absorption, More begins a secular pursuit of happiness that helps, at least temporarily, to dull his pain. In this abstracted state, More becomes the fascinated collector of various women who enter his life. Because of his abstraction, he is unable to love any one woman; he can only love women in general. While each of his women is different from the others, More feels compelled to maintain relationships with all of them because each woman partially fulfills the growing needs of his fractured sense of self. For example, Moira, the nubile but daft clinician, finds great pleasure in visiting the ruins of modern society and entertaining herself with the sentimental poetry of

Rod McKuen, the commercial orchestrations of Mantovanni, and the questionable insights of *Cosmopolitan Magazine's* editor, Helen Gurley Brown. While Moira personifies the cultural dearth of modern humanity, she also possesses the eagerness of a child. In many ways, More loves her primarily because he can take care of her, something he is unable to do for his deceased daughter, Samantha. Lola, on the other hand, differs greatly from the young nymph in that she is a determined, idealistic, and self-contained woman. Her father sees her as an innocent who is alone in the world, and he asks More to take care of his daughter in his absence. Ironically, it is Lola who becomes Tom's eager lover and complacent caretaker whenever he overindulges and recklessly does harm to himself. Finally, among the other women in More's life is the steadfast and pragmatic nurse, Ellen Oglethorpe. While she clearly disapproves of More's foolishness and, for the most part, declines physical intimacy with him, she admires his work and serves him faithfully by anticipating and fulfilling the majority of his personal and professional needs.

None of these distractions, however, can quell More's increasing abstraction and paranoia. His problem centers around an imminent sense of cataclysm. Everywhere he looks, More sees the decline of society. In his world, it is considered lawful and even ethical to murder disabled infants, demented geriatrics, and anyone whose quality of life has been diminished by circumstances. While these are but symptoms of societal disease, "the cause of public catastrophe [More believes] goes back to a spiritual crisis. Tom recognizes that every faction in politics, society, and religion testifies to a more profound, underlying split in the psyche that [he] can gauge with his lapsometer" (Ciuba 138).

While his former colleagues have all but dismissed him as a result of his professional and moral decline, he becomes seduced by the insistent flattery of the diabolical con-man, Art Immelmann, who shows More how he can improve his device to cure, rather than merely diagnose, spiritual malaise. Thus, Faustian pride and desperation win over logic and instinct when More agrees to become a partner with the Mephistophelean Immelmann, who has promised that he can help More win both the prestige and the profit his genius deserves.

This heedless decision, however, ironically results in the catastrophe he has hoped to prevent. The dreaded event occurs on the day More gets the opportunity he has been waiting for: he is invited to demonstrate his invention during an irreverent assembly consisting of medical students and colleagues in which doctors are pitted against one another in a semiserious diagnostic duel. During More's dramatic demonstration of his lapsometer, all agree that the device has the potential to alleviate the major ills of modern man. The opportunistic Art Immelmann is fueled by the initial enthusiasm of the audience, and he distributes several prototypes of the instrument among the crowd. Well aware of the disastrous consequences, More is horrified by what he witnesses. Almost immediately, the reckless application of the lapsometer causes the room to explode in a chaotic conflagration ignited by ideological conflict, unbridled lust, and uncontrollable rage.

For the remainder of the novel, More systematically repents his rash partnership with Immelmann and pursues his own spiritual restoration through his attempts to regain control over the device and its potentially devastating uses.

Concurrently, More also attempts to take control over his personal life, but his efforts are humorously futile. He creates a fortress of books, women, and liquor in a dilapidated Holiday Inn that he hopes will sustain him during the ultimate anticipated apocalypse.

When the end of the world does not come, and Ellen Oglethorpe successfully saves him from the spiritual treachery of Art Immelmann, Tom More finds himself redeemed both by love and by his personal cataclysmic experience. Thus, he and Ellen marry and have a family. Most significantly, Tom More becomes restored by the realization that his daughter's example of unquestioning faith and days filled with meaningful work and gratifying relationships are the greatest medicines with which to treat the ills of the modern world.

In the novel's sequel, *The Thanatos Syndrome,* in which he again serves as Percy's protagonist, the reader finds a somewhat reformed Dr. Tom More. His reformation, however, was assisted by his two-year incarceration for the illegal sale of amphetamines and barbiturates to sleep-deprived truckers. Reflecting on his time in jail, Tom realizes that the enforced separation from society has provided him with sufficient time and solitude in which to heal. He is no longer paranoid about the end of the world, and he no longer feels compelled to save humanity through the application of his invention.

Soon after he returns home and resumes his meager practice, he realizes that things have undergone a subtle change in his absence. On the home front, his wife Ellen Oglethorpe has become a renowned winner of countless bridge tournaments. Tom notes her independence, her emotional distance, and her total absorption in her newfound avocation, in which she seems to possess a superhuman ability to memorize her opponents' cards. He also notices that her speech has become terse and that she has become more physically assertive than she had been previously.

More also becomes aware of strangely similar behaviors in several of his patients. Soon after he resumes his practice, he makes several obvious connections among cases. In all of his patients, he notes a marked absence of their previously diagnosed psychoses; in their place, however, he recognizes the following shared mannerisms: monosyllabic speech; photographic recall; random thought processes; a discernible apathy; and, in the cases of his female patients, a recurrence of provocative sexual posturing. Such observations lead More to suspect some sort of collective disorder in which patients no longer possess their former spiritual restlessness, their hopes, or their dreams. Much like he feared in the previous novel, these people demonstrate the devastating effects of rampant bestiality that he believed resulted from acute sodium overdoses. As a result of these findings, More concludes that each of his patients is "devoid of all life . . . [and all that remains is] an emptied self that signifies the death-in-life [experience] of a condition he calls the thanatos syndrome" (Ciuba 255).

In order to confirm his suspicions, More enlists the help of several people, including his libidinous distant cousin and respected epidemiologist, Dr. Lucy Lipscomb; former colleagues Bob Comeaux and Max Gottlieb; and his spiritual sounding board from the earlier novel, Father Rinaldo Smith. After considerable intrigue in which all of the characters play a role, their collective efforts reveal a nefarious plot of apocalyptic consequences.

Once again, power has gotten into the wrong hands. However, this time More learns that the extent of his previous paranoia has been exceeded by the reality of a corrupt society. By identifying the new culprit as the former nemesis—sodium overdose—More, Lipscomb, and particularly Father Smith expose a complex plot intended to rid society of "the scourge and curse of life on this earth, the source of wars, insanities, perversions—in short, those very pathologies which are peculiar to *Homo sapiens*" (Percy *TS* 211). This plot, known by insiders as Project Blue Boy, involves the contamination of local drinking water with a sodium formula that causes the spiritless bestial behavior that More previously feared and had attempted to cure with his lapsometer.

The potential horror of such a plot is underscored in the novel by Father Smith's confession to More. In this confession, Father Smith recalls the myriad atrocities that occurred during the Holocaust. His descriptions of irreverence for the human spirit, the megalomaniacal dictates, and the expendability of less-than-perfect lives bring More to realize that the same apocalyptic conditions exist in the foundation of Project Blue Boy. He learns that everything he fears has become a reality, and he uncovers the ultimate consequences of bestiality run amok. What he discovers is the shocking revelation that several proponents of Project Blue Boy are deliberately contaminating the children in a day care center, reducing the children's inhibitions in order to subject them to continual sexual abuse.

After a series of ingenious machinations, More finally succeeds in facing this unspeakable societal demon. Ultimately, with the help of his faithful cohorts, Project Blue Boy is terminated. The diabolical physicians and scientists who participated in the insidious experiment are appropriately punished, and for the most part, the systemic contamination of affected individuals wears off. Thus, More has achieved what he could not in the earlier novel: he is society's savior—at least for now. While he and Father Smith believe that the thanatos syndrome will still exist as the predominant disorder of the twentieth century, More reconciles himself to making the world a better place on a much smaller scale than he had originally intended. Through his efforts, pediatric and geriatric euthanasia have been discontinued. The perverse child care facility has been permanently closed. The perpetrators of the crimes against children are being appropriately rehabilitated, and their talents are being productively applied. Father Smith's reclaimed Hospice becomes the primary residence for comforting the outcasts of society, and More himself is reunited with his wife and renewed in spirit. It is this affirmation of life over death that concludes the novel and leaves the reader with a belief in the joy of new beginnings that come about only after the conclusion of apocalypse.

See also Apocalypse: Secular; Apocalyptic Literature; *Faust;* Immelmann, Art; *Love in the Ruins: The Adventures of a Bad Catholic at a Time Near the End of the World;* Mephistophiles; More, Sir Thomas; Satan; Smith, Father Rinaldo; Thanatos; *The Thanatos Syndrome.*

MORE, SIR THOMAS

The English martyr Sir Thomas More (1478–1535) was at once religious zealot, intellectual humanist, author, statesman, and scholar. He was executed as a traitor after his refusal to recognize the sovereignty of King Henry VIII over the papal authority of the Roman Catholic Church. His remarkable yet controversial biography was written by his son-in-law, William Roper, in 1557, but his compelling life story was also immortalized in the modern drama by Robert Bolt, *A Man for All Seasons* (1961).

The son of the prominent British barrister, Sir John More, Thomas was born on February 7, 1478. As a young man he served as a page for Cardinal Morton, and later he attended Canterbury Hall in Oxford. More became one of England's most respected scholars, a reputation aided by his close relationships with the Dutch scholar Desiderius Erasmus and the dean of St. Paul's Cathedral, John Colet. Together, More and his colleagues developed a group known as the Oxford Reformers whose collaborative efforts greatly promoted the philosophical and artistic movements that occurred during England's Renaissance.

Although More's initial profession was in the field of law, his profound religious convictions had at one time inclined him toward the priesthood. But while he remained an extremely devout follower of the faith, in 1505, he chose to marry, and had four children by Jane Colet. Following her death in 1511, More married again, this time to the widow Alice Middleton, who brought one daughter into the union.

Given the stability of his faith and his family, More became extremely successful in a number of government positions. As an overseas envoy of the court, a skillful court official, and a respected member of the British Parliament, More received an honor never before bestowed upon a layman. Under the leadership of his friend, Henry VIII, More received the title of Lord Chancellor of England in 1529.

This friendship became the impetus for the most difficult decision of More's life. The problem arose when King Henry VIII decided to divorce Catherine of Aragon in order to marry one of her maids of honor, Anne Boleyn. As divorce was clearly a violation of Roman Catholic Church law, More could neither morally nor professionally condone the king's decision. In order to avoid conflict on this issue, More resigned his chancellorship on the basis of poor health. But when Parliament created a law requiring that all royal subjects sign an oath acknowledging the supremacy of the king's Church of England over that of the Holy Roman Church, More refused. Thus, regardless of their previous friendship, More's defiance of the royal dictate resulted in his trial for the charge of treason, his incarceration in the infamous Tower of London, and his public beheading on July 6, 1535.

Although More was martyred for his faithful fight against secular sovereignty, he is remembered through two significant works. The first, entitled *Utopia,* was written in 1516. This work, which features a free and perfect world devoid of misery and injustice, has served as the basis of countless fictional representations in Western literature. In fact, one author who was fascinated by More's dilemma, Walker Percy, used the renowned scholar's name for his cataclysmic character—Dr. Tom More—in his dystopian novels, *Love in the Ruins* (1971) and *The Thanatos Syndrome* (1987). However, it was More's final work, "A Dialogue of Comfort against Tribulation," written in 1534 during his imprisonment, that ultimately served as proof of his great courage and steadfast faith.

Based upon these recollections, as well as the courage and determination with which he led his life, he was canonized in 1935—nearly four-hundred years later—by Pope Pius XI.

See also Apocalypse: Traditional Judeo-Christian; *Love in the Ruins: The Adventures of a Bad Catholic at a Time Near the End of the World;* More, Dr. Tom; *The Thanatos Syndrome.*

MORGAN, HANK

Hank Morgan appears as the time-traveling protagonist in Mark Twain's popular social satire, *A Connecticut Yankee in King Arthur's Court* (1889). As the novel opens, the narrator of the tale—identified only as M. T. (Mark Twain)—recalls his meeting an animated fellow who told an interesting story during their tour of England's Warwick Castle. This provocative tourist, whose name he later learns is Hank Morgan, visits M. T.'s home later that same evening and begins to relate his incredulous journey through time and space to a very interested listener. Although he is clearly fatigued upon his arrival at M. T.'s home, he nonetheless begins to recount the bizarre details of an incident that began with a blow to the head during a brawl between the workers in his place of employment. Becoming quickly exhausted, he asks for a place to rest but placates his anxious audience by directing him to a book containing a day-to-day chronicle of the events that inspired his fantastic written "treasure" (Twain *CY* 6).

According to Hank's personal account, before his bizarre adventure began he had been a superintendent and master mechanic in an American firearms factory located in Hartford, Connecticut. Hank is knocked unconscious by a coworker wielding a crowbar. When he awakes, he is no longer living in nineteenth-century America. Instead, he finds himself facing the point of a spear held by a knight named Sir Kay from sixth-century England. Puzzled by his surroundings but inquisitive about the possibilities of using his advanced knowledge in a medieval era, he agrees to follow the knight, who leads him to the fabled royal court known as King Arthur's Camelot.

While in Camelot, he quickly becomes acquainted with the two people who will figure most prominently throughout his stay in England. First, he meets a page named Clarence, who helps the confused Connecticut Yankee to get his bearings in the medieval monarchy and who will continue to serve him faithfully in the years to come. But most significantly, Hank meets the court's master magician, Merlin, who immediately becomes suspicious of Hank's appearance and his potentially threatening power. Merlin immediately influences King Arthur's decision in the strange matter, and Hank's welcome to Camelot concludes with his being stripped of his anachronistic clothing, thrown into a dank prison cell, and sentenced to be burned at the stake on a date within the month.

Realizing that Merlin will become his nemesis during his time in England, Hank plots a number of ways in which to diminish the credibility of the great magician. He plans to use his advanced technological knowledge to confound the court with his own brand of magic. The first incident occurs on the day of his scheduled execution. Fortunately, Hank is aware that the chosen day and

Hank Morgan, the Yankee of Mark Twain's 1889 novel *A Connecticut Yankee in King Arthur's Court*, was portrayed by Western humorist Will Rogers in a 1931 film. Sandy, the woman with whom Morgan falls in love, was portrayed by Myrna Loy.

time of the debacle corresponds with a rare eclipse of the sun. Based upon this knowledge, he sends Clarence to the court with the announcement that the sky and the sun will grow dim if anyone attempts to go through with the execution. Although they begin the spectacle, before anyone can set fire to his stake the eclipse occurs as he had predicted, and his apparent prescience frightens the court into setting Hank free from his fiery fate.

Seeing this natural event as a demonstration of powerful magic, Merlin reinforces his resolve to destroy his rival and thereby retain his high position in King Arthur's court. In spite of Merlin's considerable efforts to challenge Hank's abilities, the nineteenth-century Yankee's remarkable ingenuity repeatedly stumps the ancient sorcerer at every turn. Inevitably, following a bombastic display in which Hank combines his knowledge of plumbing, fireworks, and theatrical presentation, Merlin's credibility and his position in the court are usurped by the proudly ambitious newcomer.

Throughout the remainder of the novel, readers are treated to Hank's farcical situations as he attempts to adjust to the demands of his medieval setting. Readers are amused as he stuffs himself into an unwieldy suit of armor, and they are increasingly impressed by the contributions he makes to the kingdom.

Hank is very successful, with the help of his page Clarence, in bringing education to the ignorant commoners. He appoints Clarence as the trainer in a newly established "Man Factory" in which talented individuals, handpicked by Hank himself during his travels throughout the countryside, are taught to build firearms, tools, machinery, and even a primitive telecommunication system by which the various hamlets in the kingdom are linked by a system of telephone wires.

Clearly, the more powerful Hank becomes, the more determined Merlin is to even the score and to restore himself to his rightful place as the king's primary adviser. Eventually, after a series of escalating adventures through which Hank attempts to destroy the entire chivalric system and supplant it with nineteenth-century values, his reign of popularity comes to a close. After killing an opposing knight in a duel by shooting him with a gun, he is attacked by the entire force of the knights of the Round Table. Given no other choice, Hank shoots eleven knights and sends the remainder of the troops running in fear. Obviously, these actions make Hank an enemy of the court. His skill and his page Clarence are all he has to combat the resurgent forces of the Dark Ages. What follows is an apocalyptic conflagration in which he pits his nineteenth-century technology against the divinely inspired forces of the medieval kingdom. Although he successfully defends his fortress, he is undermined by his own human frailty. While walking among the dead and the wounded on the battlefield of the Sand Belt, he is stabbed by one of Arthur's knights who implores the Yankee for his help. Clarence takes his master to a cave where Hank begins to recover. To their surprise, a displaced but kindly old woman offers to nurse Hank back to health. He realizes too late that he has been duped. The vengeful Merlin has assumed the disguise of the old woman and casts a spell on Hank that puts him to sleep for the next thirteen centuries. According to Merlin's plan, the spell is broken, but only after Hank himself revives in the nineteenth century.

Although Hank succeeds in returning to his own time, somewhat confounded by his incredible "dream," it is not long before he begins to age rapidly. Soon, a progressive fragility overtakes him, and he ultimately dies, never having understood the revelation delivered to him during his personal apocalypse. Thus, he failed to learn that modern man must be careful not to deify self as he attempts to harness the wonderful but terrible power of technology. Moreover, humanity must learn to understand the depth of the individual spirit, and it must also learn never to underestimate the world's underlying superstitions. Most importantly, human beings must learn to respect the powerful forces of religious faith, which—in spite of the influences of technology—continue to define a society, regardless of the time in which individuals play out their personal dramas.

See also Apocalypse: Secular; Apocalypse: Traditional Judeo-Christian; Arthur, King; *A Connecticut Yankee in King Arthur's Court; The Faerie Queene;* Malory, Thomas; Merlin; *Le Morte d'Arthur*.

LE MORTE D'ARTHUR

A prose rendition (c. 1469) of the Arthurian cycle, *Le Morte d'Arthur* relates the triumphs and tragedies of King Arthur and his knights of the Round Table. This work, which was written while author Thomas Malory was imprisoned and published after his death, presents a nostalgic view of the social and political forces that produced the chivalric or courtly romantic tradition. The vivid detail portrayed in this prose narrative depicts the gallantry of the knights, the pageantry of medieval tournaments, the mythological quest for the Holy Grail, supernatural enchantment, and the human drama revolving around Arthur, both as a man and as a king.

Published in 1485, the importance of this work to world literature cannot be overstated. *Le Morte d'Arthur* clearly served as an inspiration for Edmund Spenser's *The Faerie Queene* and Alfred Lord Tennyson's *Idylls of the King.* It has even generated twentieth-century interest in the social satire written by Mark Twain, *A Connecticut Yankee in King Arthur's Court.*

See also Apocalypse: Traditional Primitive; Arthur, King; *A Connecticut Yankee in King Arthur's Court; The Faerie Queene;* The Fisher King; *The Golden Bough: A Study in Magic and Religion;* Malory, Thomas; Merlin; Myth; Symbol.

THE MYSTERIOUS STRANGER

An apocalyptic novella, *The Mysterious Stranger* was written by Mark Twain in 1898 and published posthumously (1916) by his editors, Albert Paine and Frederick Duneka. The tale, as it appeared in its final form, deals with a young boy from Eseldorf (meaning "jackass village"), Austria, who meets a "mysterious stranger" in 1590 and begins a relationship that will forever change his life and that of his closest friends.

The protagonist and secondary characters in the novel, respectively, include Theodor Fischer and his constant companions, Nicholaus Bauman and Seppi Wohlmeyer. It doesn't take long for the reader to recognize the author's familiar boyhood persona in Theodor and the autobiographical recollections as revealed in his friends. But unlike his American counterparts Tom Sawyer and Huck Finn, the Austrian version of Twain's main character eventually learns more than he ever wanted to know about life, death, and the nature of humanity through his association with the strange yet compelling antagonist, Philip Traum (meaning "dream").

The story begins in a town described by Theodor as a boy's "paradise." More precisely, Eseldorf is described as a kind of backward community that places little value on formal schooling and is concerned primarily with children's observance of church rituals and traditional Christian beliefs. Theodor notes the town's prevailing opinion that "knowledge was not good for the common people, and could make them discontented with the lot which God had appointed for them" (Twain *MS* 2). Thus, their minds, hearts, and souls are entrusted to the two diametrically opposed village priests, the fearsome and diabolical Father Adolf and the beloved and beleaguered Father Peter.

It is Father Peter who initiates the action in this tale by his innocent remark, "God was all goodness and would find a way to save all his poor human children" (3). Father Peter's well-intended comments are overheard by the town's vindictive astrologer, who exposes the priest for such heretical views. The result of the astrologer's accusation is the bishop's suspension of Father Peter, which, in turn, leads to the sinister Father Adolf's acquisition of his flock and to great financial hardships for Father Peter and his niece. Thus, it is Father Peter's future that becomes the topic of great concern for Theodor, Seppi, and Nicholaus, whose fathers respectively are the church organist, an innkeeper, and a local judge. It is during one of their many conversations about life, and specifically about Father Peter, that the boys take out a pipe and prepare to enjoy a secret smoke. They soon realize that they have forgotten the flint necessary to light it. However, even before they can lament the situation, the solution to their problem appears in the form of the "stranger," Philip Traum, who is immediately welcomed into the group with his comment, "Fire? Oh, that is easy; I will furnish it" (6). It is with this dubious symbolic gesture that the novel's antagonist is introduced at a time when the "way [seems to have been] prepared for the appearance of a savior" (May 1972, 77).

Theodor and his friends are mesmerized by the charismatic personality of the boy, who confides that he is actually called Satan, although he is really Satan's nephew, and only uses the name Philip to conceal his identity from less understanding people. While he reveals his essential nature to the boys, they are relatively unafraid because he dazzles them with his supernatural powers and compellingly expresses his challenging worldview. This view, when first stated, reveals Satan's conviction that the whole problem with the human race is the existence of its *"Moral Sense"* (Twain *MS* 13), or the condition that causes it to choose right from wrong; more often than not, however, it chooses wrong.

Father Peter calls upon this moral sense when he approaches the boys and tells of his latest troubles: he has lost his wallet, which contains only a paltry sum, and enlists their help in finding it. Moments later, in the exact spot where Satan has just stood (he has now dematerialized), Father Peter notices his wallet. While he is both surprised and happy that he has found it, he admits that the large amount of money it holds is not his. The boys, however, are not surprised; they are gleefully certain that Satan has caused this miracle to save the bereft priest from financial ruin. Although they suggest that the priest keep the money, Father Peter foreshadows coming events by saying, "[the money] isn't mine. I can't account for it. I think some enemy [must have left it;] . . . it must be a trap" (15). Nevertheless, upon their insistence, and their promise to sign a paper acknowledging that they have witnessed its serendipitous acquisition, the priest concedes by accepting the money.

This decision to succumb to temptation leads to Father Peter's arrest and trial following the virulent accusations of the town's astrologer. Once again, the priest and his niece are subjected to poverty and humiliation, and the convicted priest is thrown in jail. Curious about the conditions of imprisonment, Theodor prompts Satan to use his supernatural powers to show him a jail, but when he sees the horror of a man's torture on a rack and the subsequent vision of the cruel exploitation of women and children in a French factory, Theodor decries such actions by calling their perpetrators brutes. This comment causes Satan to launch into his lecture on the fallibility of the moral sense once again, and he asks Theodor not to malign poor animals, or brutes, as though they possessed this despicable quality that often destroys humanity.

Throughout the remainder of the novel, the boys seek Satan's occasional intervention in unsatisfactory circumstances, but they become increasingly horrified by the callousness and cruelty that often results from his dubious actions. Through his intervention in the lives of the townspeople, many innocent victims eventually suffer and die, and Theodor is helpless to stop it. But Satan finally tires of Theodor's idealism and delivers his ultimate revelation: there is no reason to be concerned either with the events of this life or the consequences of an afterlife. He confirms this position during his final farewell to Theodor, in which he asserts: *"Life itself is only a vision, a dream. . . . Nothing exists save empty space—and you!"* (author's italics) (72). While it is surprising that the author fails to refute such a nihilistic stance, it is even more disquieting when the novel concludes with Theodor's disillusioned final recollection: "He [Satan] vanished, and left me appalled; for I knew, and realized, that all he had said was true" (74).

The novel's controversial conclusion of the meaninglessness of life has long been a subject of considerable critical debate. Some critics proffer that the work's disturbing finale reflects the editors' calamitous attempt to piece together the fragments of Twain's work after his death. The majority, however, agree with the predominant position that the novel's conclusion is merely a reflection of the pathological pessimism that plagued the once great author during the final years of his life. Certainly, sufficient evidence exists to support either side of the debate; however, Twain's biographical information seems to provide the most convincing resolution. In defense of his disagreeable apocalyptic vision, readers should be reminded that at the time he was drafting this work, Twain had suffered the loss of his wife, two daughters, and a considerable fortune, and was himself in declining physical health. Consequently, *The Mysterious Stranger,* while an unsettling tale, should be recognized for its rich symbolism and the general treatment of its apocalyptic theme, and the disillusioned author should not be judged harshly for his final statement to the world. Instead, Mark Twain—one of the world's most beloved humorists and lecturers—should be remembered for his earlier, socially redeeming contributions to the American novel as a literary genre.

See also Apocalypse: Secular; Apocalypticism; *A Connecticut Yankee in King Arthur's Court;* Nihilism; Satan; Twain, Mark.

MYTH

Myth has historically been the result of humanity's attempts to find life's deepest meanings. Rooted in antiquity, revealed in religious rituals, and liberated in the literature of both primitive and advanced cultures, myth is not only "an eternal mirror" in which humanity views itself (Bierlein 1994, xiii), but it is also "the basis of morality, governments, and national identity"(5).

While most readers think of the classical texts of Thomas Bulfinch and Edith Hamilton when considering the topic of mythology, other explorers of the human mind and spirit, including such notable scholars as Carl Gustav Jung, Sir James G. Frazer, Mircea Eliade, and Joseph Campbell, have dedicated their professional lives to helping people understand "what is constant and universal in

[the] human experience" (xiv). While various myths have their origins in primitive belief systems, they include similar characteristics that relate to the natural, supernatural, and cosmic order of things as they pertain to the concerns of man. Regardless of their cultural origins, most myths deal with humanity's principal concerns, not the least of which are creation, life, death, and divinity. Each of these concerns has resulted in various types of myths.

First, the type of mythological reference with which readers are most familiar revolves around cosmology, or the origins of the universe. For instance, according to the ancient Babylonian, Hebrew, and Native American myths, water is the primordial substance from which life, as represented by certain gods, originally emerged. In other cultures, such as Chinese and Hindu, the world was born within the center of a great egg. Following closely behind cosmological myths are those related to the creation of humanity's primal parents, such as the Babylonian Apsu and Tiamat, or the Hebrew Adam and Eve.

Next, as a natural progression of the origin of man, come myths related to the transitional human phases such as birth, initiation, marriage, and death. Countless myths exist to personify these transitions through life. For example, the death and resurrection motif is presented in the myth of Osiris and Persephone, while the significance of marriage is represented by the divine union of the Greek Zeus and Hera, as well as that of the Hindu deities, Lakshmi and Vishnu.

While concern for such remote deities is relevant to understanding the basic human rituals, the necessity for other myths that explain the extraordinary individuals or events in society is evident in the wide array of archetypes such as the tricksters, the god-kings, and the saviors within a culture. As a result, re-creations of such mythological characters as the Greek god of fire (Prometheus); the Egyptian Pharoah; Horus the sun god; and, most notably, Zoroaster, Buddha, and Jesus as saviors pervade the collective body of world literature and thereby reveal the universal truths of existence according to man.

See also Allegory; Archetype; God; Jung, Carl Gustav; Symbol.

MYTH OF MAITREYA

See Apocalypse: Buddhist.

THE NARRATIVE OF ARTHUR GORDON PYM

This short nineteenth-century novel of fantasy and adventure (1838) was written by one of America's foremost masters of the macabre mystery, Edgar Allan Poe. One of the more fascinating features of the work is that while it is presented as a factual narrative of a savage sea adventure, it was really intended as a literary hoax. The intent was so successful that, in some cases, even the most avid of seamen were hard to convince that the work was one of fiction rather than fact.

Part of the reason for the novel's realism in regard to seafaring details is that it draws on Poe's own personal experiences on various sailing vessels during his youth and early adulthood. His enthusiasm for sea travel—combined with his taste for horror and supernatural occurrences—made this apocalyptic work one that served as an inspiration for other writers, such as Melville, who pursued similar topics in their cataclysmic tales.

Many details of the story reflect verifiable parallels between the life of the author and that of his fictional protagonist. For example, in the novel, Arthur Gordon Pym is the son of a successful sea merchant whose trading port is Nantucket. During his stay at a boarding academy, Pym befriends one Augustus Barnard, whose ancestry is also traced back to the sea. Together they decide to run away from school and pursue their personal adventures by setting sail on a small vessel of their own.

They are returned to dock by the crew of a whaling ship that accidentally runs into their tiny vessel. Undaunted by this temporary setback, the young men manage successfully to stow away aboard an old sailing ship, and they embark on an apocalyptic adventure filled with the overwhelming forces of both the natural and supernatural worlds. Throughout their voyage, they encounter such things as cannibalistic savages, wild pursuits, mutiny at sea, and the full cataclysmic array of nature's ravaging forces including wind, rain, and earthquakes. Even though the ending of the novel is ambiguous, with its reference to a supernatural hulking figure that emerges from the mist, the novel on the whole is a classic representation of the Gothic horror tale, and it reflects the apocalyptic temperament that permeates the collective body of Poe's literary work.

See also Apocalypse: Traditional Primitive; Apocalyptic Literature; Apocalypticism; Gothic Fiction; Poe, Edgar Allan.

NATIVE SON

This is a naturalistic novel written by a leader of the twentieth-century black American literature movement, Richard Wright (1940). The favorable critical reaction to this bold novel, which is a virulent attack against racial oppression, helped make the work an immediate literary success. Through its progressive development, the novel challenges society to examine its profoundly negative impact on the life of a young black man, Bigger Thomas, who is trying to tough it out in a Chicago slum. The three sections of the novel entitled "Fear," "Flight," and "Fate" reflect the stages of the main character's personal decline as a black youth who becomes increasingly crushed between his violent impulses and the unfamiliar landscape of the white world.

The first section, "Fear," introduces twenty-year-old Bigger Thomas, his impoverished yet close-knit family, and their squalid living conditions in a crowded one-room Chicago tenement. Their unavoidable lack of privacy serves as a daily reminder to Bigger of the degradation that permeates the city's Black Belt. The only escape from his bleak existence comes when Bigger goes to the movies; the films he enjoys most are those that reflect the opulence and freedom of the white world. Here, in the darkened theater, Bigger freely fantasizes about living as a white person and dreams of what he might become if he were ever given a chance to prove himself. In this section of the novel, the reader experiences the sharp contrast between Bigger's fantasy life and his reality, which is filled with the inane musings of ineffectual friends, punctuated by his angry outbursts, and characterized by an escalating series of neighborhood crimes.

But Bigger's luck soon changes with the chance of a lifetime: he gets a job at the luxurious home of a wealthy white family, the Daltons. Although he initially feels isolated and displaced, his performance as the family's chauffeur soon delivers him from the trappings of his recent past. In his new position, Bigger receives good pay, a room of his own, and an easy work schedule. In addition, it leads to a friendship with the family's liberal daughter Mary and her friend, Jan Erlone, who is a Communist Party organizer. While this friendship and forced familiarity seem initially liberating, Bigger soon feels more awkward and resentful than ever, particularly during a night when he has been urged to eat and drink with his two new cohorts. Because Mary becomes too drunk to get to her bedroom herself, Bigger must help her and at the same time keep from being discovered by her parents. Unfortunately, in the confines of Mary's bedroom, Bigger's underlying fear and his sexual arousal toward the young white woman combine in a disastrous result: while trying to keep her quiet by covering her face with a pillow, Bigger accidentally smothers Mary. The climax of the "Fear" section occurs as Bigger, in a confused frenzy, disposes of Mary's body by dragging her to the basement, severing her head with a hatchet, and stuffing her in the flaming furnace, which the Daltons have instructed him to tend.

The second section of the novel, entitled "Flight," begins the morning after Mary's murder when he realizes that he has betrayed his new friends and is now a pariah in the Dalton home. He soon feels the weight of alienation from all of humanity, and in a series of desperate actions, attempts to cover his tracks. In his terror he involves his girlfriend Bessie. She creates even more complications for him, and Bigger has to kill her and dispose of her body in the air chute of an abandoned building. At the end of this section of the novel, Bigger is once again alone as he flees to a solitary rooftop where he must face the hard reality of his deeds. Eventually, he must also face the entrapment of police gunfire, the wrath of vigilantes, and his ultimate humiliating capture when he is subdued, like an animal, by the icy blasts of a fire hose.

The final section of the novel, "Fate," begins with the coroner's inquest and a rapid trial that takes only a week. During his incarceration, Bigger is forced to examine his life through his interactions with other characters in the novel. The character Max, his attorney from the Communist Party, attempts to convince the jury that society must share the burden of Bigger's guilt. A visit from Reverend Hammond allows Bigger to become lost in the mysticism of Christ's sacrifice on his behalf, but soon, the real vision of a burning cross near the courthouse results in Bigger's eventual rejection of religious faith. Finally, Bigger confronts all the forces of society in a compelling courtroom scene. Not surprisingly, although society itself is also on trial, Bigger is convicted of his crimes. Ultimately, he accepts his fate with a clear understanding of the circumstances that have shaped his life, the consequences of his own choices, and the willingness to die with a sense of dignity and peace that has eluded him throughout his unfortunate young life.

See also Apocalypse: Traditional Judeo-Christian; *The Divine Comedy;* Harlem Renaissance; Naturalism; Thomas, Bigger; Wright, Richard.

NATURALISM

Naturalism is the term used for the nineteenth-century literary movement that reflects the biological theories of Charles Darwin, the determinism of Hippolyte Taine, the positivism of Auguste Comte, and the socialism of Karl Marx. The essence of this movement is a direct rejection of the emotional subjectivity and escapism that characterized Romanticism in that it requires the writer's objective examination of the human experience. Just as Darwin's work documents the "struggle for existence" among different biological species, characters in naturalistic novels are portrayed according their mental, emotional, and spiritual strengths and weaknesses as they struggle to adapt to a changing world comprised of uncontrollable social forces that threaten their survival.

Early authors who espoused the movement in their blatant rejection of the Romantic genre include Flaubert, Balzac, Stendahl, Daudet, and Maupassant. French author Emile Zola is perhaps best known for translating the scientific method into fictional form by codifying the principles of literary naturalism. In an effort to apply the scientific method to the creative process, naturalistic authors such as Zola and his devotees developed and observed their characters' circumstances with a detached curiosity. Thus, a great attention to historical detail and the careful recording of onerous social conditions served as the foundation of this fictional genre. Because oppressive social and economic factors loomed so largely within these works, the characters themselves were little more than social experiments. Consequently, their doomed fates, usually the result of weak bodies, minds, or spirits, were pitied but were mourned less deeply than those of their Romantic predecessors.

While literary naturalism gained popularity in France, England, and later in Germany, American authors soon became best known for definitive works that demonstrated their own rejection of both Romanticism and realism. One of the first American writers to experiment with the new fictional mode was Stephen Crane, who initially published his novel, *Maggie: A Girl of the Streets,* under an assumed name. While his subsequent literary efforts continued to reflect naturalistic elements, other American writers such as Frank Norris, Jack London, and Theodore Dreiser best typify the philosophy and its developmental techniques in their novels. For example, Norris's *McTeague* (1899), London's semi-autobiographical *Martin Eden* (1909), and Dreiser's *An American Tragedy* (1925) illustrate how individuals, in all of their flawed humanity, are no contest for the crushing forces of biology, a depressed economy, and the ubiquitous limitations of a proletarian society. Also, several writers of the Harlem Renaissance continued this tradition by illustrating how these same principles work against African Americans in a predominantly white culture.

See also Apocalypse: Anti-Christian; Apocalypse: Traditional Judeo-Christian; *Go Tell It on the Mountain; Native Son;* Thomas, Bigger.

NIHILISM

Nihilism is the term that describes the historical Russian intellectual movement that flourished during the 1860s. With a focus upon individualism and rational thought, as opposed to societal reliance upon traditional authority, nihilism (originating from the Latin *nihil,* meaning "nothing") pertains to man's belief in only those things that are utilitarian in use or empirical in proof.

As one of the originators of the nihilistic literary movement, Russian author Ivan Turgenev is responsible for the nihilistic portrayal of his protagonist, Bazarov, who serves as the free-thinking pragmatist of his novel, *Fathers and Sons* (1862). Other contributors to the philosophical movement were authors Nikolai A. Dobrolyubov and Nikolai G. Chernyshevsky. The latter's book, *What Is To Be Done?* (1863), supported the views of the movement's most prominent spokesman, Dmitri Pisarev. According to Pisarev, society should reject the dated notions of aestheticism, sentimentality, and intellectual idealism in favor of materialism, substantive proof, and the verity of the natural sciences. Thus, for a time, those whose interests mirrored the authoritarian notions of religion, politics, and artistic expression were spurned by the "new men" of society whose efforts reflected the revolutionary spirit of the age.

Although the nihilistic movement began to wane in regard to literary expression, for a time it took root within the Russian agrarian communities that had practical goals to achieve and relatively little to lose. As a result of its association

Novelist Ivan Turgenev contributed to the nihilistic literary movement in Russia in the 1860s.

with rebellious uprisings, in the late 1870s, the nihilistic philosophy began to disintegrate. What had once been a noble experiment in social reform had gradually become little more than a justification for wanton terrorism and violence against the established social order.

See also Apocalypse: Secular; Apocalypticism; *The Confidence-Man: His Masquerade; The Mysterious Stranger*.

O'CONNOR, FLANNERY

Mary Flannery O'Connor (1925–1964) was the only child of Regina Cline and Edward Francis O'Connor, Jr. Born on March 25, 1925, in Savannah, Georgia, O'Connor's early life was ordinary until 1938, when the family moved to Atlanta because of her father's job in real estate and construction. Later that year, Flannery and her mother decided to move to the more rural Milledgeville, Georgia. When Flannery's father became gravely ill, he moved back with the family for a short time and died on February 1, 1941.

It is rare that the death of a writer's parent has so significant an impact on the work of the artist as in Flannery O'Connor's case. But while still a young writer, she was diagnosed with the same disease that had killed her father. This incurable blood disease, known as disseminated lupus erythematosus, progressively jeopardizes the function of all of the major organs in the body. Thus, the awareness of the gravity of her illness clearly had an impact on both personal and professional decisions that inevitably shaped the artist's work.

At the outset of her professional life, Flannery O'Connor decided to enter Georgia State College for Women, which was later renamed Georgia College, in her home town of Milledgeville. Her studies included dual majors in sociology and English. During her years at this institution, from which she graduated with an A.B. degree in June 1945, O'Connor gained a notable level of local recognition for her early attempts at storytelling. Because of her gifts in writing and drawing, O'Connor received a journalism scholarship for study at the State University of Iowa. While enrolled there, *Accent* magazine published her first story, "The Geranium" (1946). O'Connor graduated with a Masters of Fine Arts degree in 1947 and subsequently enrolled for postgraduate study in the highly regarded Writers' Workshop. This resulted in her being honored in 1948 with a designated place at a prestigious artists' colony in Saratoga Springs, New York.

At the conclusion of her formal education, O'Connor decided that she would not return to the South but would try living in New York City. But she soon realized that she was temperamentally ill suited for city life and decided to move in with two friends, both classical scholars, Robert and Sally Fitzgerald, in Ridgefield, Connecticut. While still living in Ridgefield, O'Connor visited her mother in Georgia during a Christmas vacation. It was en route to this visit that she became ill with what she believed was acute rheumatoid arthritis; however, a later investigation at Atlanta's Emory University Hospital confirmed the devastating diagnosis that she had, in fact, developed the fatal blood disease that had taken her father's life.

Because of the problems related to this illness, O'Connor soon moved back to the South to benefit from her mother's constant care. She and her mother moved from their home in Milledgeville to the Cline family dairy farm on the outskirts of Andalusia, Georgia. It was at this residence that the writer observed characters and events that would figure prominently in many of her stories. Although she was frequently too ill to write, the author became acutely aware of the dwindling commodity of time. She made the best of it by writing whenever possible, receiving many visitors, and maintaining a lively correspondence with several of her friends. This correspondence, much of which surrounds the publication of her major works, the complexities of her faith, her love for live, and the power of her friendships, appears in a collected edition that was published posthumously, *The Habit of Being* (1979).

It is in this revealing collection of letters that readers can learn much about the forces that propelled Flannery O'Connor to literary success. The entries also reflect several dominant themes that appear prominently in her work. First, O'Connor uses these letters to express her candid and fervent views about Christian philosophy in general, and in particular, her powerful faith in Roman Catholicism. O'Connor's correspondence also reveal details about people in her life, including her emerging literary characters, who suffer from the deadly sin of pride. Because of her belief that pride is responsible for the fall of humanity, she forces many of her protagonists to come face to face—often violently—with mysterious and sometimes grotesquely portrayed messengers. These messengers deliver the revelation of great sin in order ultimately to help the protagonists become "saved" or restored to a spiritual state of grace, even if this does occur just moments before their death.

This sense of restoration through divine or supernatural intervention not only played a key role in O'Connor's personal life. This same theme—primarily that of salvation through Christ—remains a constant in the small but powerful body of her work. These works include two novels, *Wise Blood* (1952) and *The Violent Bear It Away* (1960), in addition to other efforts including a nonfiction book of essays and discussion, *Mystery and Manners* (1969); *The Complete Stories of Flannery O'Connor* (1971); the collection of personal letters, *The Habit of Being* (1979); and a collection of book reviews written for Catholic newspapers, *The Presence of Grace* (1983).

Although Flannery O'Connor's life and career were cut short because of lupus and a resultant host of physical complications, for the most part, her last days were spent in the way in which she had always chosen to live. When she could, she enjoyed visits with friends; between hospital stays she worked diligently on her second collection of short fiction, *Everything That Rises Must Converge,* which was published posthumously. And finally, in August of 1964, with affection, wit, and faith intact, she died of kidney failure at the young age of thirty-nine, leaving a legacy of literature that would cause her to be remembered as one of the most important writers of American short fiction.

See also Apocalypse: Traditional Judeo-Christian; Grotesque; *The Violent Bear It Away*.

ONE HUNDRED YEARS OF SOLITUDE

This 1967 apocalyptic masterpiece written by the leader of the Latin American magical realism literary style, Gabriel García Márquez, was clearly influenced by the author's admiration of the multigenerational works of Southern author, William Faulkner. In many ways its protagonist, Jose Arcadio Buendia, is patterned on the monomaniacal Thomas Sutpen of Faulkner's *Absalom, Absalom!* in that he envisions and ultimately creates his own city of Macondo in the middle of a Latin American swamp.

Parallels can be drawn consistently between the two works. Their themes are essentially the same: the inexorable rise and fall of several generations within a basically corrupt family, and their apocalyptic destruction by the forces of nature. The events of García Márquez's novel reflect elements of biblical myth as well as the historical details relating to the century between the postcolonial 1820s and the 1920s. In addition, much like other biblically based myths, the work conforms to a triadic structure in which Part One describes the founding of the paradisiacal community; Part Two develops the theme of evil intrusion in the form of gypsies, merchants, and modern society; and Part Three involves the descent of a plague of insomnia, the creation of a "memory machine," and the miraculous intervention of Melquiades, an indomitable gypsy scribe who restores Macondo's historical memories in the apocalyptic manuscripts that actually form the narrative content of the novel.

See also *Absalom, Absalom!*; Allegory; Apocalypse: Traditional Primitive; Apocalyptic Literature; Archetype; *As I Lay Dying;* García Márquez, Gabriel; Myth; Revelation, Book of; Sutpen, Thomas; Symbol; *Terra Nostra*.

ONTOLOGY

Christian von Wolff introduced the term ontology in the eighteenth century to identify a new area of metaphysical speculation. Literally defined as the study of the individual self or its essential "being," this abstract concept may be categorized somewhere between the study of psychology (individual mental processes) and the study of natural philosophy (the individual mentality in relationship to the stimuli of the natural world). Thus, ontology deals with reality itself as something both unique and separate from the individual who subjectively interprets or perceives this reality.

In twentieth-century literature, the ontological perspective is reflected in the works of specific authors, such as Walker Percy, who have been recognized for their studies in psychology as well as for their close observation of human life and its myriad responses to societal stimuli. In two of Percy's apocalyptic novels, *Love in the Ruins* (1971) and *The Thanatos Syndrome* (1987), the author focuses on the collective loss of humanity's ego or its essential self in response to the ubiquitous threats resulting from advances in technology. To personify this problem of loss of self, or damaged ego, Percy introduces a protagonist, Dr. Tom More, who deals with the issue in the two works. As a psychiatric physician with an abiding interest in Roman Catholic theology and an obsession with the pervasive forces contributing to societal decline, Dr. More himself is one of the proverbial walking wounded of the modern world.

Although he tries to suppress his own "morning terrors" and recurrent "abstractions" by overindulging in alcohol and sex, he also attempts to find the solution to the declining mental stability of modern man by inventing an instrument with which to diagnose the origin of individual mental disorders. He calls his dubious invention More's Quantitative-Qualitative Ontological Lapsometer. It is a modified encephalograph through which he can scan the brains of afflicted individuals and locate the precise hemisphere and center of lapsed brain function. Armed with this diagnostic data, More hopes to make his contribution to science, and ultimately to save the world from certain doom, by treating his patients with greater accuracy and thereby restoring their damaged essential selves.

In these novels, Dr. More and most of Percy's secondary characters individually relate to the troubling, confusing, and often comedic circumstances of their lives. Each one also demonstrates the ontological process itself by showing the ways in which their individual "realities" or perceptions often differ significantly from the realities of others who share the promising yet precarious experience of life in the modern world.

See also Apocalypse: Secular; Apocalypse: Traditional Judeo-Christian; Apocalypticism; Freud, Sigmund; *Love in the Ruins: The Adventures of a Bad Catholic at a Time Near the End of the World;* More, Dr. Tom; *The Thanatos Syndrome.*

THE ORIGIN OF THE BRUNISTS

The Origin of the Brunists, a 1966 apocalyptic and naturalistic novel by Robert Coover, is an attempt to reveal the many ways in which humanity copes with the chaos of the universe. Coover's first metafictional effort, the novel depicts the impact of a devastating mining disaster on the citizens of a small Pennsylvania town. The town, West Condon, is representative of working-class America in the mid-twentieth century. Prior to the inciting action of the story, the town has already begun to die. Economically, its decline is marked by the closing of coal mines, once a thriving industry, and the subsequent increase in unemployment for countless immigrant workers. Culturally, the town is also fading because the young people have started to move away, disillusioned with the impoverished reality and the small-town dreams of their ancestral Catholic and Protestant families. But it is the riveting impact of the mine explosion, killing ninety-seven men and leaving only one survivor, that causes the townspeople to seek answers amidst the random destruction that has permanently ravaged their lives.

The individual pursuit of such answers creates Coover's fictional three-ringed circus. In one ring is the ringmaster, a photojournalist named Justin "Tiger" Miller, who decides to exploit the disaster in a series of increasingly cataclysmic stories in his newspaper, the *West Condon Chronicle.* In another ring is a group of disillusioned miners, led by the perpetual realist Vince Bonali, who call themselves the "Common Sense Committee." This group, with the collective mentality of the religious right, the Ku Klux Klan, and drunken vigilantes, makes its peripheral presence known in the latter part of the work. However, it is justifiably the center ring of the novel, the tightly knit circle of the millenarian cult known as "the Brunists," that commands the reader's attention in its attempt to impose a strident spiritual order on its tenuous temporal world.

The Brunists adopt their group's name from the sole survivor of the mining disaster, local resident Giovanni Bruno. Even though the town was already filled with an assortment of religious fanatics, mystics, and prognosticators prior to the accident, the shattering event propels these people into an accelerated effort to discover signs, symbols, or something that will make sense of their situation. The first sign comes in the form of a cryptic note written by miner and former preacher Ely Collins, who was a beloved member of the community before being killed in the blast. His wife believes that his note, which reveals Ely's call to return to preaching, is also a warning to those who have fallen away from their faith. Another sign soon becomes evident when Giovanni Bruno awakens from his coma insisting that, while trapped in the mine, he witnessed a vision of the Blessed Virgin in the form of a white dove. This symbolic message, which may be little more than the ramblings of a brain-damaged miner, is confirmed by one of the town's more delusional characters, Eleanor Norton, who claims that the vision portends the imminent end of the world.

Such thoughts, planted in the fertile soil of the town's desperation, cause the Brunist cult to grow rapidly. Also noticeable are the ritual music, sacred meetings, and celestial white robes that increasingly separate the elite from the rest of the community. Empowered by its millenarian message, the evangelical elitists spread the news of the pending apocalypse that will occur on the hilltop of the mine, a previous make-out spot that has recently been renamed the "Mount of Redemption." Although their initial efforts are somewhat suspect, the group is soon validated by Justin Miller's sensational headlines that begin with the revelation of Giovanni Bruno's survival, thereafter known as the "MIRACLE IN WEST CONDON."

Given the response to the first article, Miller revs his media machine with the help of his Speedographic camera and "Hilda," the beleaguered printing press of the *West Condon Chronicle*. At first, Miller is an outside observer in the close-knit community, but he soon discovers that by pretending to believe in the Brunist doctrine, he can tap the flow of daily information that proliferates within the group and thereby chronicle the fiction he feels compelled to create. Meanwhile, as the religious fervor accelerates, so too do the efforts of some local miners—led by the pragmatic Vince Bonali—who become known collectively as the "Common Sense Committee." Although their actual behavior becomes a mockery of the purpose indicated by their name, they nevertheless serve as a realistic foil to the Brunist ideology and Miller's fabricated sensationalism.

In spite of the committee's feeble attempts to thwart the millenarian movement, Miller's exploitation of the cult continues with the unwitting assistance of Bruno's devoted sister, Marcella, who is powerfully attracted to the charismatic journalist. Miller, however, only perceives her in the role of the virginal icon whose good works and gentle spirit inspire the group. Clearly, he does not love her, and—because of his personal lack of depth—he *cannot* love her. But when he realizes the potential danger of the cult, he proposes marriage to Marcella—not out of love, but only with the intention of casting himself in the role of her savior.

This effort fails miserably. Instead of leaving the group as he requests, Marcella becomes disillusioned with Miller's exploitation both of her beliefs and her love. She runs from him, retreating to the security of the Brunists, and visibly begins to wither from her lost dreams and his failure to understand her needs. Her personal retreat from reality is first marked by her stunned and disheveled appearance on the night of their cataclysmic near-consummation in the press room of the *Chronicle.* It is later increasingly reflected in her apparent mental and physical decline following the encounter. Finally, on the night of the predicted end, when Marcella is accidentally hit by a car as she wanders vacantly in the middle of the road, the group identifies Miller as the cause of her martyrdom: an Antichrist whom they will later attempt to immolate on the Mount of Redemption amidst the ill-fated apocalyptic frenzy.

However, in spite of their predictions and rituals, and in spite of the thunderous storm and the subsequent mud slide, the world does not end on the designated date. Nor does it end on the days indicated in a series of future predictions. Nevertheless, the Brunist cult persists by perpetuating its own collective fiction, which continually evolves, developing finally into a worldwide gospel of the coming apocalypse.

Miller's personal fiction continues as well—through his superficial and primarily physical relationship with a licentious nurse he calls "Happy Bottom." The novel ends as she ministers to him during his recovery from the assault on the Mount, and their future together promises to become one in which they will both feel safe. Together, they form a covenant in which sex and the daily pursuit of personal pleasure will insulate them from the chaos that reigns in the world outside themselves. It seems, therefore, that the only true survivor of the community's cataclysm is Vince Bonali. Although he loses his job, his reputation, and nearly ruins his marriage as a result of his "committee's" exploits, he alone survives with a renewed belief in God, and paradoxically, a resolute acceptance of the randomness of life in the universe.

See also Apocalypse: Traditional Judeo-Christian; Apocalyptic Literature; Bonali, Vince; Coover, Robert; Millennialism; Miller, Justin ("Tiger"); Naturalism.

OUT OF THE SILENT PLANET

The first book in a trilogy created by religious and early science fiction writer C. S. Lewis (1938), *Out of the Silent Planet* was followed by sequels *Perelandra* (1943) and *That Hideous Strength* (1945), works that create fictional characters and familiar yet equally fictional worlds through which the author examines the eternal battle between the formidable forces of good and evil.

One of the characters who appears in each of the novels within the series is Dr. Elwin Ransom, a philologist from Cambridge, England. Ransom is kidnapped during a walking tour of England's pastoral countryside and is taken via a spaceship to the mythical planet of Malacandra, which the author intends to represent Mars. Ransom's kidnappers on this otherworldly voyage include

Devine, a nefarious former childhood schoolmate, and his accomplice Weston, who is a physicist eager to learn the ways and to exploit the potential means discovered on the lush planet of Malacandra. The only obstacles preventing them from making progress in their previous attempts to explore the planet have been the creatures known as *seroni.* Based on their limited perspective of the strange extraterrestrial life-forms, they attempt to resolve their problem by offering Ransom as a human sacrifice. In this way they hope to placate what they believe to be primitive creatures prone to such simple distraction.

Although their mission is a malevolent one, Ransom is unaware of his fellow voyagers' intended purpose for including him on the trip. Given this innocence of purpose and his general interest in the luminous landscape of their heavenly destination, he eagerly explores Malacandra. He feels instinctively attracted to the land and its creatures, which conjure mental references both to the spiritual works of John Milton and to the compelling ancestral images depicted in Greek mythology.

But Ransom's initial euphoria is soon disrupted by his realization that Devine and Weston plan to offer him to the strange cadre, consisting of six *seroni.* Although Ransom is less afraid of these creatures than are his earthly companions, the intended transaction is thwarted when another beastlike creature—identified by the others as a *hrossa*—emerges from the water. Amidst the chaos of the attack, Ransom manages to escape, and thus begins his personal exploration of Malacandra. In his quest for knowledge and experience in this strange and beautiful new world, he also learns of the negative lore related to Thulcandra—his home planet earth—as well as its relevant position within the universe's solar system, which is referred to on Malacandra as the Field of Arbol.

Much of his newly acquired knowledge comes from the simple observation of his surroundings as he wanders the strange planet, on his own, for nearly two full days. His isolation, as well as his escalating fear, is eventually interrupted by his encounter with a *hrossa,* one of the Malacandran sea creatures, whose name he learns is Hyoi. Because Ransom's career in philology involves the study of historical linguistics, he manages to develop a crude system of communication. Hyoi takes him back to his village, where Ransom lives among the other *hrossa* for a few weeks and learns their views about their own planet as well as the one from which he has come. He learns that they are primarily a community of singers, dancers, and poets, essentially mild-mannered, peace-loving creatures. They relate that Malacandra is governed by a higher being known as an Oyarsa. Further, they tell Ransom that the entire universe was created by Maledil the Young, who lives and rules simultaneously with a highly evolved spirit known as the Old One. Of greatest interest to him, however, is their limited knowledge of his own earth, which they state has been relegated to the unfavorable position of a "silent planet." When questioned further on this topic, they can only confess their limitations and refer him instead to the *seroni,* or the celebrated thinkers of the planet, who would certainly have the answers for his more probing questions. Content for the time being in his new surroundings, Ransom lives happily among the *hrossa,* who share the basic moral standards of the other inhabitants of the planet, the *pfifltriggi* (toadlike artists and tradespeople) and the *seroni* (human-shaped cerebral beings), who together comprise the collective order known as a *hnau*. Clearly, what C. S. Lewis intends to convey to readers with his introduction of the peaceful coexistence of the diverse creatures on Malacandra is the sense of paradisiacal harmony that the inhabitants of earth might have experienced had it not been for the disobedience and immorality that led to mankind's fall.

As Ransom continues on his journey, he gradually gets to know the other inhabitants of the planet. The *seroni*, in particular, provide him with insights that imply that his planet's violent history and willful independence have been the cause of its broken communication with its creative force, as well as with the other planets whose people remain content to follow the ethical and moral guidelines set forth by their more respectable and law-abiding rulers. Although he is disturbed by the *seroni* view of his world, he is reminded of the corruption of his two fellow travelers, Devine and Weston, who are eventually held accountable to the great Oyarsa for killing Ransom's friend Hyoi and two other *hrossa*. The two are obviously ignorant of the severity of the situation, as well as the language of Malacandra, so Ransom must serve as an interpreter for the evil earthmen and must attempt to justify their actions to a higher authority.

In speaking for Devine, his former schoolmate, Ransom is used by his fellow human's base materialism, which serves as the primary motivation for all of his selfish actions. Speaking for Weston, however, is another matter. Ransom recognizes that the scientist is even more dangerous than his cohort in that he is willing to sacrifice anyone or anything to his idolatrous worship of science and technology. Further, Weston reveals his spiritual ignorance in his assertion that earth is, in his opinion, a superior planet that has within its power the potential to devastate inferior beings such as those who inhabit Malacandra. Upon hearing such unenlightened views, the Oyarsa rules that both Weston and Devine are "bent" creatures; the peaceful Malacandrans have no other word that comes close to describing the force of evil they embody.

As a merciful punishment for their crimes, the earthmen are sentenced to return to earth and allowed just enough fuel to reach their destination before their craft is destroyed. However, before leaving for earth, the Oyarsa tells Ransom that although Thulcandra has been controlled for a time by a "bent" Oyarsa, the Creator—Maledil—has not completely given up on the planet. Thus, Ransom is heartened by the knowledge that there will be an effort to reclaim earth from the "bent" rule that has caused it to be separated from its creator's voice. There will at some point in the future be a final struggle between good and evil that will ultimately determine the fate of the silent planet. Thus, although the problems that exist on earth—represented by the corrupt Devine and Weston—are not resolved in this novel, they serve as an appropriate springboard for similar explorations that continue in *Perelandra* and culminate in *That Hideous Strength.*

See also Apocalypse: Traditional Judeo-Christian; Apocalypticism; Lewis, C. S.; *Perelandra;* Science Fiction; *That Hideous Strength.*

PARADISE LOST

A 1667 apocalyptic work by John Milton, *Paradise Lost* has been viewed by many to be the greatest literary epic of all time. In essence, it contains all the classic elements of apocalyptic fiction: visions, supernatural occurrences, the battle between good and evil, divine intervention, and justice and retribution. In short, it is the story of humanity and its initial fall from grace—a fictional account of the Old Testament Genesis story.

The epic begins with a rumor spread by Satan regarding the creation of a new world and its noble creature called man. The legion of fallen angels holds a council and decides that Satan should fly from hell to earth in order to investigate the situation. Although he experiences great difficulty in reaching his goal, Satan finally views the objects of his curiosity and is initially astounded by their beauty and their innocence. It is while he overhears their conversation about God's prohibitions to them that he conceives his insidious plan for their inevitable downfall. After a series of otherworldly events, he disguises himself as a serpent, speaks to Eve when she is alone in the garden, and convinces her to disobey God's commands and to eat the fruit from the Tree of Knowledge. When she does so and is not immediately punished, she becomes exhilarated by the possibility of gaining new knowledge. She eventually confides in Adam, who out of love for his mate shares the fruit, initiating the devastating consequences of their foolish decision. Almost immediately, their peace is disrupted by a quarrel, and for the first time they are ashamed of their nakedness when they are together.

Because of their sin, God in heaven is grieved and sends Michael the Archangel to escort the first couple out of paradise. The angel reveals a vision to Adam that disturbs him because it portends the suffering that they and their descendents will soon endure. But, at the same time, the angel encourages Adam to hold fast to God's plan as his offspring—Jesus Christ—will eventually come to earth to atone for their sins. At this point, fully aware of the magnitude of their loss, Adam and Eve are escorted out of paradise by sword-wielding angels and prepare to live out their lives under the sentence of God's judgment, which will prohibit them from ever returning to paradise.

See also Allegory; Apocalypse: Traditional Judeo-Christian; Apocalyptic Literature; *The Divine Comedy;* God; Heaven; Hell; Milton, John; Revelation, Book of; Satan.

PATU

Patu is the "strong woman" who serves as something of a guardian angel for the embattled protagonist of Jamake Highwater's apocalyptic novel *Kill Hole* (1992). At the outset of the novel, Patu is the highly superstitious caretaker of her tribe's prisoner, Sitko Ghost Horse, who has accidentally violated a sacred tribal ritual and has thereby endangered the lives of all the small children in the village. Because of the severity of the alleged crime, Patu is understandably wary of the stranger who has become her charge. She secretly wonders whether the rumors that she has heard about him are true and is concerned that he might be an evil spirit who has come to destroy their tribe.

Because of her personal and spiritual strength and her instinctive nurturing tendencies, she gives Sitko the opportunity to prove himself in her presence. What he does in an effort to impress her, however, reveals the level of superstition that controls the society in which she lives. Thus, because he is a portrait painter by trade, Sitko tries to flatter his caretaker by rendering her portrait out of charcoal on the walls of the adobe hut where he has been imprisoned. In a reaction common to many primitive cultures, Patu is immediately terrified and begins to rub her image from the wall for fear that the artist has captured her spirit. It is this initial encounter that leads the way for the first dialogue between Sitko and his captors. It is also through Patu that Sitko learns much about his alleged violation and the devastating consequences of his "crime." He also learns about the androgynous identity of Patu, a half-man/half-woman, who is not reviled by her people but revered because of her uniqueness and her strength.

Because Patu demonstrates the protective and nurturing characteristics of a woman and also possesses the hermaphroditic characteristic of miniature male genitalia, her function in the story has both literal and figurative significance. For example, as they get to know more about one another, Patu learns that Sitko suffers greatly from a sense of alienation he feels within the modern world. First, he is a half-breed. Although he comes from a predominantly Native American culture, his heritage has been diluted by his mother's mixed parentage and by her subsequent marriage to a wealthy Jewish man. This man served as Sitko's foster father and called the child by the name Seymour Miller, rather than his given name of Sitko Ghost Horse. Patu also learns that as an artist, Sitko's form of expression has caused him to achieve both critical recognition and societal revulsion because of its graphic sexual content. She understands this duality because even as she gets to know him, she finds it difficult to determine whether or not his work is good or evil. Finally, Patu identifies deeply with Sitko because of his homosexuality. Much like Patu herself, Sitko has the artistic and nurturing qualities of a woman, but he is also an ardent lover as a man who makes love to another man. Thus, she pities him for the many dilemmas he faces in his life, and, in time, his genuine concern and gratitude toward her become clear enough for her to defend him, even if it means going against the superstitious regulations of her tribe.

One of the areas in which Patu's power as a "strong woman" comes into play is her ability to disempower the diabolical official, Delito, who is intent on killing Sitko. Ever vigilant, Patu monitors Delito's whereabouts, and on the occasions when he uses deceit to frighten and torment the unsuspecting Sitko, Patu's virtuous presence leaves Delito no recourse but to flee from her power and goodness.

Throughout the novel, therefore, Patu is a significant force in the healing of Sitko's life. And through their daily interactions, their communal meals, and their shared confidences, Patu teaches Sitko the importance of holding onto the power of love. Further, she teaches him to be proud both of his ancestry and his artistic gifts, and, most importantly, she teaches him that the only life worth living is one that can be lived freely and without the crippling influences of hopelessness and fear.

See also Apocalypse: Traditional Primitive; Apocalypticism; Delito; Ghost Horse, Sitko; *Kill Hole.*

PERCY, WALKER

A writer who considered himself primarily a novelist, Walker Percy (1916–1990) has seven major fictional works to his credit, although his writing career included a number of contemplative and acerbic essays and more than fifty literary reviews. Born in Birmingham, Alabama, on May 28, 1916, Walker is still hailed as one of America's great Southern writers, in spite of his unwillingness to be so categorized. His ideas, a curious amalgam of existential, philosophical, religious, scientific, linguistic, and cultural influences, resulted from a series of events in his early life that clearly shaped both his world and his art.

In his posthumously published collection of essays, *Signposts in a Strange Land* (1991), Percy submits that his parents' death while he was still a young man greatly influenced his future. After his father committed suicide in 1929, he moved to his bachelor uncle's house in Greenville, Mississippi, along with his mother and his brothers. A few years later, Percy's mother died in a car accident, which left the boys in the care of his uncle, William Alexander Percy, who officially adopted them in 1931.

During the years spent in Greenville, Percy became immersed in both literary and popular culture. His uncle, who was also an author, customarily entertained such literary luminaries as Carl Sandburg, Langston Hughes, and William Faulkner. That their influence was felt by Percy is evident from his first literary foray as a gossip columnist while attending Greenville High School. Percy was deeply interested in the scientific method, and upon graduation decided to pursue the field of chemistry. He enrolled at the University of North Carolina, from which he received a B.S. degree in 1937. Following this educational experience, Percy decided to pursue a medical career by enrolling in Columbia University's College of Physicians and Surgeons, where he ultimately earned an M.D. degree in 1941. Oddly enough, however, at the end of his studies he decided that he was less well suited for medicine than some of his other classmates. Instead, he began a voyage of self-discovery that included participation in a regimen of psychotherapy and a dedicated involvement with popular culture explored through his continual movie-going.

These experiences clearly ignited his intrinsic curiosity, and, ironically, just as he became interested in the true nature and purpose of man, fate intervened.

Walker Percy at home in Covington, Louisiana, in 1987

He contracted a mild case of tuberculosis stemming from his work as a resident at New York's Bellevue Hospital. This illness, both a blessing and a curse, required a convalescence of two years, during which he found the time and the freedom to embark on his philosophical quest in earnest. He read a series of great books, which included the work of Camus, Dostoyevsky, Tolstoy, and Kafka, among others.

In 1944, after his recovery from a relapse of the disease and after having absorbed an impressive body of philosophy and literature, Percy was convinced that he was more interested in the exploration of humanity's collective mind and soul than merely the exploration of its physical body. Although this was a lonely, contemplative time for Percy, he eventually took two important steps that would form a foundation for the remainder of both his life and his work: (1) he met and married Mary Bernice Townsend, and (2) within the year following their marriage, both he and his wife converted to Roman Catholicism.

These experiences, along with the financial security he gained from the estate of his deceased uncle, enabled Percy to build his family—he had two daughters—and to move to the small, comfortable town of Covington, Louisiana. There, in 1950, he began his official literary career by publishing essays in respectable national journals. In the years that followed, Percy began to work within the genre of the novel, and although he had discarded several early drafts, he eventually published his much-revised book, *The Moviegoer*, in 1961. This effort was followed by others, several of which present apocalyptic themes: *The Last Gentleman* (1966), *Love in the Ruins: The Adventures of a Bad Catholic at a Time Near the End of the World* (1971), *Lancelot* (1977), *The Second Coming* (1980), and *The Thanatos Syndrome* (1987).

Although he continued his reflective and insular life until his death on May 10, 1990, the prodigious body of his work lives on. Through these works, readers will continue to enjoy his satirical yet compassionate character portrayals, and they will share the private fictional journeys of the alienated modern "Everyman" who struggles to find a sense of belonging, a soul-inspiring faith, and a thread of hope for a world that becomes increasingly absurd and devoid of meaning.

See also Apocalypse: Traditional Judeo-Christian; *Love in the Ruins: The Adventures of a Bad Catholic at a Time Near the End of the World; The Thanatos Syndrome.*

PERELANDRA

Perelandra (1944) is the second work in the trilogy of science fiction novels dealing with apocalyptic themes written by one of England's most beloved authors, theologians, scholars, and lecturers, C. S. Lewis. Taken as a whole, the space trilogy deals collectively with the temptation of human hubris and its relationship to the spiritual fall of humankind. In an effort to highlight the key aspects of human nature that make it susceptible to such a fall, Lewis first introduced readers to *Out of the Silent Planet* to illustrate how intellectual pride, ruthless ambition, and rapacious materialism have caused the earth, referred to in the trilogy as Thulcandra, to become severed from communication with the other planets who still hear and obey the word of Maledil, the God of the universe.

The observer, participant, and translator of this tripartite extraterrestrial allegory is Dr. Elwin Ransom, a philologist—professor of ancient languages—whose linguistic abilities make it possible for him to communicate with the inhabitants of other planets. In *Out of the Silent Planet,* Dr. Ransom is kidnapped by two corrupt space travelers from earth: Devine, a grasping materialist, and Weston, a megalomaniacal physicist who plans to exploit the planet Mars—Malacandra—by stripping it of its resources and making it inhabitable for a human colony under his own rulership. Given the circumstances of his arrival on Malacandra—a human sacrifice for the placation of the threatening Martian life-forms—it is understandable that throughout most of the first novel in the trilogy, Dr. Ransom is tentative, fearful, and overly cautious as he learns the truth about both Malacandra and his own planet, Thulcandra. His facility with languages, however, helps him learn much about the Malacandran life-forms, the eldila or powerful angels that protect it, and the great leader or Oyarsa, Maledil, who governs the entire universe. Clearly, Ransom's purpose in the first novel is to illustrate that the only way that humanity can ever hope to hear the word of God and begin to defeat the forces of evil is to overcome the fear that is the opposing force of humanity's greater gift, faith.

Having learned this lesson, and after having shared it with a few fellow scholars and close friends, Ransom begins his second and most significant journey in *Perelandra*. The novel opens when the narrator, supposedly C. S. Lewis himself, travels upon the bidding of his longtime friend, Ransom, to discuss some "business." In spite of the fearsome mental forces that threaten Lewis to turn away from his appointed duty, he persists and eventually meets with Ransom. Ransom reveals that he has been beckoned by Maledil and will be accompanied by the eldila during his voyage to a new and unspoiled planet, Perelandra (Venus), for a purpose that is as yet fully unknown to him. Although his friend has doubts about Ransom's tale, particularly when he views the coffinlike vessel in which Ransom will travel through space, Ransom's lack of fear and overriding faith convince him to assist the traveler by executing the details related to his appointed mission.

The mission of his voyage to Perelandra, Ransom eventually learns, is similar to the dilemma that was presented to Adam and Eve at the time of the earth's birth: faithful obedience versus free will. Although he doesn't fully understand why he has been selected, Ransom is the perfect choice for such a mission. First, as a human and member of a fallen species, he understands the pain that results from living on a planet overrun with ruthlessness and depravity. Second, his experience on Malacandra has taught him the importance of overcoming the temptation of fear with the power of faith. It is this experience and knowledge that will enable him to keep Perelandra free from the fallen fate of earth—the "silent planet"—and thereby give the universe a fresh start.

As part of his mission, Ransom soon meets a Green Woman whom he realizes is the Venusian equivalent of earth's first planetary "mother," Eve. Like Eve, the Green Woman is curious and vulnerable, and because she is still in search of her designated mate, alone to make her own decisions. Upon meeting her, Ransom realizes what he must do. He must protect her not only from her own folly, but he must also keep her out of the clutches of the seductive Satan, who has possessed the physical body of his former kidnapper and nemesis, the physicist Weston. Weston has made a pact with Satan in exchange for the promise of colonizing the planet with others of his own kind. But in his ignorance of spiritual matters, he fails to realize that Satan is only using his body as an instrument through which he will seize control over the new inhabitants of Perelandra and destroy it in the same way that he destroyed the former paradise on earth.

Clearly, Ransom's responsibility is a formidable one. But before he is required to confront the enemy once again, he is given the opportunity to appreciate the limitless beauty and undeniable value of living in an unspoiled world. Ransom's travels throughout the lush fecundity of the Perelandrean landscape fill him with more physical pleasure than he could ever have imagined. The air is more fragrant, the fruits are more delectable, and the flowers are more glorious than he had ever known on earth. His senses are overwhelmed by the wonder of the unspoiled planet. While traveling from island to island in the Perelandrean paradise, Ransom also becomes attuned to the beauty and power of the land and sea creatures that are equally awesome in their uniquely magnificent displays. He comes to love this land and its inhabitants, and it is this appreciation of the pristine planet that empowers his emotional commitment to the preserving of its perfection.

This inner conviction comes just in time for a sequence of conflicts with evil forces that threaten Perelandra. First, he learns that Satan, through Weston, has begun to prey on the vulnerability of the Green Woman. As he did with Eve in the earthly garden, Weston empathizes with the Perelandrean Eve, whom he consoles as a woman usurped of the power to live where she chooses, a queen who has been forced to wait too long for her king, and a natural mother who yearns for fulfillment that can only come by bearing the offspring she so greatly desires. Fortunately, she shares her thoughts and feelings with Ransom, and in return she unwittingly convinces him that the pleasure they experience in the present will be available in the future only if someone—namely himself—is willing to physically fight for the right to preserve paradise.

At this point, the protagonist's name and purpose become clear. Just as Christ returned to the earth in order to offer Himself as the physical "ransom" for the potential salvation of its fallen inhabitants, Ransom himself must now fight with Weston/Satan, at the possible cost of losing his own life, in order to thwart the diabolical plan to similarly corrupt the Perelandrean planet (Venus, embodied in the Greek goddess of love).

Thus, in the climax of the novel, specifically in chapters 12–14, Ransom suffers many of the same temptations, tauntings, and trials faced by Christ at Gethsemene and Golgatha. After a vicious, prolonged, and ultimately deadly battle, Satan/Weston is vanquished, and although Ransom bears a wound in his heel not unlike that of the Achilles myth, he emerges victorious, finds shelter in a cave, and is eventually restored to glorious health.

Although C. S. Lewis masterfully blends a number of different myths and legends within this beautifully written novel, little can prepare the reader for its final chapters in which Ransom reaps the reward of his personal sacrifice. In the end, he is awed to be called into the presence of Perelandra's newly united queen, the Green Woman, and her long-awaited king. He also learns that his sacrifice has spared the couple from a firsthand battle with the forces of evil; Maledil has informed them of the danger they had faced and the terrible fate from which they have been saved. As a reward for his selfless act of courage, Ransom is provided with a prophetic apocalyptic promise, not unlike that of the biblical Book of Revelation. In this promise Ransom learns that his actions have caused Maledil to reconsider the distance he has kept from Thulcandra, the silent planet. Although at an appointed time in the future great plagues and suffering will befall its inhabitants, another final battle between good and evil will be waged, and the next time the forces of goodness will reign for eternity. Thus, the novel ends with a vision of Thulcandra (Earth), Malacandra (Mars), and Perelandra (Venus) celebrating a joyful reunion in a universal "Great Dance" in which all creatures of the universe will experience the "splendor, the love, and the strength" (222) that has been destined for all of God's creatures since the beginning of time.

See also Apocalypse: Traditional Judeo-Christian; Apocalypticism; Archetype; Lewis, C. S.; Myth; *Out of the Silent Planet;* Ransom, Dr. Elwin; Science Fiction; *That Hideous Strength;* Weston, Edward Rolles.

PHOENIX

A one-of-a-kind mythical creature, the phoenix is a legendary bird that shares the characteristics of a pheasant and an eagle. According to Arabian legend, this creature, sensing the end of its natural life in the present cycle, prepares for its death by creating a nest of aromatic resins and wood. While building this nest, the phoenix sings funereal melodies and flaps its wings to fan the flames of an incendiary transformation ritual in which both the nest and the creature are consumed in flames that ignite from the nest's exposure to the penetrating rays of the sun. The conclusion of the myth, however, is said to occur approximately five hundred years later when a new phoenix rises majestically from the same ashes and bone marrow that were the remains of the original rite.

The myth of the phoenix is traditionally used in literature to symbolize the concept of "periodic destruction and recreation" (Cirlot 1971, 253). Moreover, in apocalyptic literature, based on traditional Judeo-Christian values, the phoenix "signifies the triumph of eternal life over death" (254). In general, however, the symbol of the phoenix is one that relates to inevitable regeneration and ultimately to the "successful completion of a process" (254).

This universal affirmation of life appears frequently in literature of the end times, particularly in works within the science fiction genre. The image is featured prominently in two such works: Ray Bradbury's *Fahrenheit 451* (1953) and Pat Frank's *Alas, Babylon* (1959). In both of these stories, the regeneration of a dying society is the central theme. In *Alas, Babylon,* an accidental detonation of a nuclear weapon results in the utter destruction of the United States, with the singular exception of a small band of people who live in an area of Florida where the winds have failed to carry the full force of deadly radiation. This stunned band of survivors, led by a reluctant but natural-born leader, learns how to adapt to their devastated environment by using survivalist techniques and learning the value of cooperative work, thereby ensuring the regeneration of the human race. In this work, references to the phoenixlike characteristics of the survivors and their techniques are woven throughout the text.

Bradbury's *Fahrenheit 451* is even more blatant in its use of the phoenix to symbolize universal regeneration. In his novel, society has been numbed by the proliferation of incessant world war. In order to retain control of the masses and to maintain unquestioned allegiance to governmental initiatives, special emphasis has been placed on exaltation of the physical senses. In this society, people seek pleasure through constant recreational drug use, they are continually entertained by wall-to-wall interactive television, and their collective sport of choice is viewing the pursuit and capture of so-called criminals who are terminated routinely on the nightly news.

One of the greatest crimes of this period is the possession and/or reading of books. Books have been banned in this society because they are known to incite independent thinking, which more often than not leads to the questioning of governmental decisions and individual action. This text, then, deals literally with the incineration of thought: the essence of humanity. The burning of hidden caches of literature is the official function of "firemen" who arrive on a discovered crime scene, douse the contraband with kerosene, and set fire to the books, ideas, homes, and even individuals who defy the government's authority.

In spite of such efforts to control people's minds, once again, an itinerant community of "Book People" rises amidst the ashes of a dying society. This wandering band of fugitives—consisting of academics, literati, and intelligent people with questioning minds—subsists in camps along the fringes of society. Their sole purpose is to preserve the dying beauty and power of literature by having each person memorize a favorite book in an effort to preserve the great works for a time when civilization is once again ready to emerge from the ashes and bring the glory of the written word to light.

See also *Alas, Babylon;* Apocalypse: Traditional Judeo-Christian; *Fahrenheit 451;* Science Fiction.

PIGGY

Piggy is the overweight, asthmatic, bespectacled victim in William Golding's apocalyptic parable, *Lord of the Flies.* As one of the survivors of a plane crash resulting from an attempted escape from an imperiled boys' school in war-torn England, Piggy is immediately represented as ill suited for survival on the coral island where their plane makes its crash landing.

It is assumed that prior to the beginning of the novel, he has been a pampered child whose "auntie" has attempted to keep him well fed (i.e., nurtured) and overdressed (i.e., overprotected) to prevent the chills that might instigate his respiratory problems. Although she loves him, and he understandably loves her for her efforts, she is neither able to help him overcome his countless fears nor protect him from the interminable ridicule he experiences on the school yard of an all-boys' academy. Thus, he is presented in the novel as the stereotypical childhood weakling upon whom the infinite ranks of burgeoning bullies descend whenever parental or academic authorities abandon their watch.

Golding portrays Piggy with a realism few writers could match, perhaps because of his own experience as a schoolmaster in an all-boys' British academy. There he witnessed on a daily basis the Darwinian struggle for existence: the stronger boys perpetually preyed upon the weak. The discerning reader accustomed to witnessing such senseless acts of cruelty within human nature immediately fears for Piggy and instinctively shudders at his inevitable fate. Although Piggy has few physical qualities that can assist him in an atmosphere where only the "fittest" will survive, he does possess one superior quality: the mental agility to make him a valuable resource as the boys begin their doomed adventure on a deserted island.

Throughout the novel, Piggy's eyeglasses reflect—both literally and figuratively—the power of his intellect. Thus, he "sees" the need to provide some kind of order following the chaos resulting from the plane crash. Further, he is the first to "see" the conch shell on the beach and to understand its mythical significance: to calm the raging seas and to establish the societal order of the ages. Moreover, it is Piggy's glasses that become instrumental in providing hope for their rescue when the lenses are used to generate a signal fire to mark their location on the island. Given such insights and services, he is a valuable assistant to the group's natural leader, Ralph, who is presented as a virtual "golden boy." Ralph's strength, experience, maturity, and confidence identify him as the pragmatic representative of civility amidst the savagery that develops and threatens to ensnare them, like the nefarious undergrowth of the island.

In spite of Piggy's considerable contributions, he remains the object of ridicule on the island. He is particularly targeted by the novel's antagonist, Jack Merridew, and his ruthless henchmen. While Jack comprehends the value of

Piggy's mental strength, he derides him at every opportunity, negating both his prescient warnings and his practical recommendations that may help get the boys rescued from their perilous plight.

One of the reasons that Jack is opposed to Piggy's suggestions is that Jack is in his element on the island. In fact, within a short time—without the restrictions of an adult authority figure—Jack has been transformed from a traditional school yard bully into a savage killer. He is jealous of Ralph's initial authority over the boys, and his innate brutality begins to surface. Piggy's safety becomes progressively threatened throughout the novel. Jack's delight in killing the wild pigs that roam the island reflects his joy in tormenting the weak and obese child. It also foreshadows the antagonist's determination to hunt and kill Piggy when he realizes that he must destroy Piggy in order to possess his glasses. With the glasses, he can start the fire needed to cook the meat of the animals he has killed.

Although allusions to Piggy as the force of intellect, the unadaptable weakling, and the predators' prey appear throughout the novel, it is Piggy's savage murder that reveals Golding's belief that the forces of brutality will often overcome the powers of reason when left ungoverned by a higher authority. Other characters disappear, die, or are murdered in the novel. But it is the senseless death of reason—represented by Piggy's death—that causes Ralph, in the final words of the novel, to lament the ultimate fate of humanity. Sadly, the meaningless end to Piggy's pitiable life has caused Ralph to lose his innocence. In its place is the undeniable reality that savagery will always seethe silently in the hearts of men. The illusory veil of civility cannot alter the course of humanity toward self-destruction. (Golding 1954)

See also Apocalypse: Traditional Judeo-Christian; Apocalypse: Traditional Primitive; *Lord of the Flies;* Merridew, Jack; Prometheus; Ralph; Satan; Simon.

PILGRIM, BILLY

Billy Pilgrim is the fictional protagonist of the apocalyptic science fiction novel *Slaughterhouse-Five,* by Kurt Vonnegut, Jr. Much like the first American colonists to arrive in the New World, Billy literally is a reluctant pilgrim who must form a bridge between the past and the future in an effort to help his fellow citizens cope with the sobering realities of their present lives.

By trade, Billy is an optometrist who has attained a modicum of success. The occupation is as symbolic as his name. Before the novel's end, he accepts his designated mission to "prescribe corrective lenses" for the people who live on earth. In order to gain this perspective, however, Billy must first become "unstuck in time" and travel to the alien planet of Tralfamadore, where he learns the ultimate dreadful fate of the earth. He is not unfamiliar with destruction, having witnessed the 1945 firebombing of Dresden during World War II. Upon his return from the war, Pilgrim is abducted by aliens and taken to Tralfamadore. The omnicient Tralfamadorians assure Pilgrim that the earth's days are numbered. Unlike humans, who generally feel immune to such apocalyptic warnings, the Tralfamadorians have adopted a credo that helps them to keep things in perspective. Pilgrim is given a revelation and commissioned to travel through time and space. He delivers his prophetic message—"So it

Optometrist Billy Pilgrim (Michael Sacks), protagonist of Kurt Vonnegut, Jr.'s, *Slaughterhouse-Five,* talks to his dog after being jolted from earth to a zoo on the planet Tralfamadore, in a 1972 movie based on the book.

goes"—in order to save the "Earthling souls" from the psychological torment of their inevitable fate.

See also Apocalypse: Secular; *Cat's Cradle;* Science Fiction; *Slaughterhouse-Five; Or the Children's Crusade: A Duty Dance with Death.*

THE PILGRIM'S PROGRESS

A classic religious allegory, *The Pilgrim's Progress* was written by John Bunyan (Part I, 1678; Part II, 1684) under the following complete title: *The Pilgrim's Progress from This World to That Which Is To Come: Delivered under the Similitude of a Dream Wherein Is Discovered, the Manner of His Setting Out, His Dangerous Journey; and Safe Arrival at the Desired Countrey.* As has often been noted in regard to this work, at the time of its publication part I of *The Pilgrim's Progress* was second only to the Bible in popularity among readers. This popularity tends to confirm the high regard for the work's thematic significance: the human spiritual journey toward eternal salvation. Although the language of the text is biblical in tone, it is presented with the clarity and simplicity of a folktale. Moreover, its characters are familiar to all levels of readers. Christian, the protagonist in the story, is named both literally and figuratively to represent Christians in general as they journey through life's temptations and trials: from "the City of Destruction" they attempt to reach heaven—"the Celestial City"—at the end of their life's quest. Readers also identify with the qualities of the other characters in the story, whose names reveal their specific functions within the work: Mr. Worldly Wiseman, Faithful, Hopeful, Evangelist, Despair, Ignorance, and the archetypal demon, Apollyon.

Through Christian's journey in part I of the work, readers can appreciate the moral lesson of repenting and seeking forgiveness of sin. But most important is Christian's triumphant arrival at heaven's open gates. There he is greeted with resounding trumpets and the gleeful welcome of the redeemed. There is a sense of spiritual optimism as the story ends with the explanation that the truth of human salvation had actually been revealed to Christian in a dream.

While in many ways part II of *The Pilgrim's Progress* is similar to the first part of the work, it focuses more on the journey traveled by Christian's wife, her four sons, and her companion Mercy. Christian was relatively unassisted in his quest, but his wife and her companions have the assistance of Mr. Greatheart, who provides counsel, encouragement, and physical strength in the face of conflict. Bunyan introduces additional characters such as Mr. Valiant-for-Truth, Mr. Ready-to-Halt, Mr. Feeble-Mind, and a host of others, apparently to encourage readers to be more charitable toward those who possess obvious human frailties.

This simple tale successfully embodies the human experience from birth to death and beyond, to eternal salvation. Its popularity as a classic work of literature remains undisputed. Just as the work can be appreciated for its own considerable merit, so can readers give credit to its author. Bunyan's own life as a humble working man and inspired preacher has made the spiritual journey seem more attainable for all of life's "pilgrims" who wish to "progress" to their heavenly destinations.

See also Allegory; Apocalypse: Traditional Judeo-Christian; Bunyan, John; Myth; Symbol.

POE, EDGAR ALLAN

A mentally unstable and enigmatic American poet, novelist, journalist, and short-story writer, Edgar Allan Poe (1809–1849) is best known for his intense morbidity and for his early development of a literary genre that would become recognized as detective fiction. Born on January 19, 1809, in Boston, Massachusetts, where his actor parents were currently performing, Poe's early life was both itinerant and chaotic. The death of his father in 1811 and his mother in the following year caused him to suffer greatly. The poverty and alienation no doubt contributed to his brother William's early death and to his sister Rosalie's becoming certifiably insane.

Moved by the children's tragedy and prompted by her own childlessness, Mrs. John Allan, the wife of a prosperous tobacco merchant, arranged for the informal adoption of the intelligent but sullen child. Thus, Edgar lived with the Allans, and even spent five years with them in England, before returning to Richmond, Virginia, in 1820. Although the family was relatively prosperous for the times, the psychological aspect of Edgar's upbringing is somewhat questionable. In fact, considerable critical debate exists about the severity with which

Edgar Allan Poe

John Allan treated the boy. Most agree that Allan's high expectations and personal volatility were at least partly responsible for Poe's self-destructive and disturbed personality. The seminal event in the young man's life that terminated his relationship with his foster father involved Allan's arrangement to have his son accepted into the prestigious West Point Academy. After admission, the young man's gambling, general distraction, and myriad profligate exploits led to his expulsion from the school in 1831 and Allan's subsequent disowning of the troubled young writer.

This pattern of promise followed by disappointment continued as Poe pursued his literary profession. Early in his career, he had received minor recognition for poetry collections that included, most notably, *The Raven and Other Poems* (1845). As a result of these small successes, he drew the attention of various respectable magazine editors. However, while Poe's work—particularly in the areas of editing and literary criticism—was generally well regarded, his work habits were continually interrupted by bouts of erratic personal behavior. Despite this unpredictability, he managed to piece together a journalistic career by working at a succession of publishing houses; he did not stay long with any publisher because of the disruptive effects of his chronic alcoholism.

Poe's general instability also led to financial difficulties. He subsisted by living with his paternal aunt, Mrs. Maria Clemm, which led to Poe's marrying her thirteen-year-old daughter (his cousin) Virginia Clemm in 1836. There is no doubt that Poe loved his young, frail wife (she died from tuberculosis in 1847). His poems reflect an obsession with pallid and childlike women who share many of his wife's personal characteristics. His devotion to Virginia and his despair at her death drove him into a deeper and more destructive level of alcoholism, compounded by his experimentation with various mind-altering drugs such as opium. The tormented artist, originator of gothic fiction, thus brought about his own demise just two years after his wife's death. And although details prior to his death are sketchy, it is known that Poe succumbed to an alcohol-related illness while drinking in an alehouse. He was taken to a nearby hospital in Baltimore, Maryland, but all attempts to restore him to health failed, and he died on October 7, 1849.

See also Apocalypse: Traditional Primitive; Apocalypticism; Grotesque; *The Narrative of Arthur Gordon Pym.*

PROMETHEUS

The God of Fire in Greek mythology, the name Prometheus literally means "forethinker," and according to legend he was the son of a Titan and a sea nymph. He is best known for his intelligence, his resistance against tyranny, and his generosity to humankind. The Greek poet Hesiod is responsible for the generation of two legends about the young Titan. The first is the tale of Prometheus's inevitable rebellion against Zeus's despotic rule. Their conflict revolves around the issue of meat from animal sacrifice and a disagreement about its most worthy recipients. According to Hesiod's account, Zeus dictates that the gods should receive the choicest morsels, while Prometheus uses his cunning to arrange for the best parts to go to man. Because Prometheus is sympathetic with the burdens of humanity, he urges Zeus to allow people to have the power of fire in order to cook their food, warm their bodies, and light their way. After realizing that Prometheus has tricked him, Zeus exacts his revenge by hiding fire from mere mortals. Undaunted, Prometheus prevails, steals the hidden fire, and brings it to earth according to his original plan.

As punishment for his rebellion against Zeus, and as a warning to mankind, the god creates a beautiful woman named Pandora, meaning "all gifts." Tempted by her charms and endowments, one of which is a magic jar, Prometheus's brother, Epimetheus ("hindsight"), ignores his more insightful brother's advice. He marries her, opens the jar (better known as Pandora's Box), and unwittingly unleashes all manner of chaos, disease, and evil upon the earth.

Hesiod's second treatment of the legend reflects the same initial conflict between Zeus and Prometheus, but the punishment of the second legend involves the Titan's being chained to a rock on Mt. Caucasus. Each day, a vulture attacks him and tears out his liver, which grows back, allowing for the torment to begin anew each morning. Although this punishment is seemingly unendurable, Prometheus is able to withstand the torment because of his knowledge that someday a mortal woman and a male god will produce a savior who will rescue him. After suffering for nearly thirteen generations, his savior, in the form of both a god and a mortal man, releases him from his bondage. This savior—ironically the son of Zeus and a mortal woman, Alcmene—is the immortal hero Hercules, a legend in his own right.

Both legends of Prometheus are significant to the collective body of Western literature. His name has become synonymous with intelligence, civilized culture, and scientific application. Because of these compelling components, as well as his "redemption" by a "savior" who was both god and man, the Promethean myth has served as the inspiration of ancient writers such as Aeschylus, who based his Greek tragedy *Prometheus Bound* (undated) on the exploits of the hero. In addition, Romantic writer Mary Wollstonecraft Shelley used the legend as an inspiration for her 1818 science fiction novel, *Frankenstein, or the Modern Prometheus.* It is not surprising that her husband, fellow Romanticist Percy Bysshe Shelley, was affected by her work and was therefore compelled to reply formally to Aeschylus's tale in his lyrical drama entitled *Prometheus Unbound,* written in 1820.

Although the legend reemerged strongly in the nineteenth century, it has come to hold even more significance in the literature of the twentieth century as a result of the rapid proliferation of science and technology. One example of a modern adaptation of the Promethean myth can be seen in Ray Bradbury's futuristic apocalypse entitled *Fahrenheit 451.* In this novel, fire is equated with technology as a powerful and destructive force when placed in the wrong hands. Thus, the elemental force is misused in the novel by a corrupt government (Zeus?) whose aim it is to keep its citizens "in the dark" by using fire to burn books (Promethean intelligence). The rationale in the novel is not unlike that of Zeus in Hesiod's myth. Because the government fears that books contain ideas, and ideas cause individuals to question government—such as its involvement in perpetual sieges of war—books are banned and other sensory pleasures are provided in order to keep the people from questioning the status quo. Fortunately, however, in Bradbury's novel, a wayward "fireman" who had formerly burned books learns for himself the value of history, philosophy, and ideas in general. Thus, he saves the world from an eternal intellectual darkness by following a small flame that leads to an itinerant band of "book people." These outcasts memorize full texts in order to prepare civilization for a more favorable moment in time when humanity will literally "see the light of ideas" and use it to guide them toward a better world where they can set themselves free from aggression and its state of tyrannical darkness.

See also Apocalypse: Traditional Primitive; Apocalypticism; Archetype; *Fahrenheit 451; Frankenstein, or the Modern Prometheus;* Myth; Science Fiction.

PROSPERO

Prospero is the protagonist of William Shakespeare's apocalyptic tragicomedy, *The Tempest* (c. 1611). As the story begins, readers learn that he is the exiled Duke of Milan who was ousted from his position by a plot between his ruthless brother Antonio and a rival leader, the King of Naples. The Duke, however, was at least partly responsible for his expulsion from office because his intellectual curiosity and his philosophical pursuits kept him from attending to the more practical duties of his office. In an attempt to devote more time to his studies, Prospero evidently turned over many of his governmental responsibilities to his brother Antonio. Antonio, in turn, plotted the murder of his brother by sending him out to sea, along with his three-year-old daughter Miranda, knowing full well that the weakened vessel on which they sailed was likely to be destroyed in the event of even a mild storm at sea.

Prospero and Miranda thus had set sail, and thanks to the thoughtfulness of his former counselor, Gonzalo, the reluctant seafarers had enough food, clothing, and sufficient books from his library to begin a new life on an abandoned island somewhere in the Mediterranean. During the twelve years during which the two live on the island, Prospero pursues his study of white magic in the hope of avenging his wrongful exile. Also during that time, Prospero is assisted by two "spirits"—one basically good and one basically evil—who help him in both the practical and supernatural matters with which he is concerned. Prospero uses Ariel, a good "spirit of the air," to help him learn the secrets of enchantment (he has released the sprite from his imprisonment in a pine tree, the result of a curse by an evil witch). Prospero also uses the evil creature Caliban, a half-fish, half-man whose mother is the witch who imprisoned Ariel, but whose father is the devil. While Caliban's earthbound, irredeemable nature is a clever foil to the more generous spirit of Ariel, he too serves Prospero as more of a slave by drudging reluctantly through years of manual labor inspired solely by his admiration for Prospero's beautiful daughter, Miranda.

Ariel finally helps Prospero to initiate his revenge by stirring up a tempest, after which Prospero's former enemies and their attendant shipmates are cast upon the shore of his island. Prospero behaves in a godlike manner as he uses magic to arrange for the union of his daughter with a noble and deserving young man, Ferdinand. With Ariel's help Prospero successfully confronts his former foes, much like God on the throne of judgment, and causes them to repent for their ill-conceived actions. After gently punishing the guilty and rewarding the innocent, Prospero forgets about revenge and settles for a spirit of reconciliation brought about by the example of the pure and gentle Miranda and her love, Ferdinand. Prospero then releases both Ariel and Caliban from their servitude. Moreover, Prospero is restored to his rightful position as Duke of Milan. This time, however, he will renounce his use of magic and will rule effectively, inspired by the responsibility and love that he has learned during his reign on the island.

See also Apocalypse: Traditional Judeo-Christian; Apocalypticism; Ariel; Caliban; Ferdinand; Miranda; *The Tempest*.

PYNCHON, THOMAS

The works of twentieth-century American novelist and short-story writer Thomas Pynchon (1937–) revolve around the themes of alienation and the personal quest for identity within the chaos and corruption of modern times. Pynchon was born in Glen Cove, New York, in 1937. In 1957, he received his Bachelor of Arts degree from Cornell University. During his years at Cornell, the author also completed two years of military service with the U.S. Navy. After graduation he worked briefly for the Boeing Aircraft Company in Seattle, Washington, later moving to California, where he began his writing career in earnest.

His first notable work, published in 1963 and greeted by favorable critical reviews, was a quixotic and cynical farce of the modern Western world entitled *V.* Pynchon's next novel, *The Crying of Lot 49* (1966), became something of a critical—and underground—success because of its irreverent observations of corrupt and conspiratorial practices within the Tristero System, an absurd and impenetrable futuristic bureaucracy. Because of the popular theme of this work, its fixation on modern conspiracies, and its subversive exploits of the novel's memorable protagonist, Mrs. Oedipa Maas, *The Crying of Lot 49* helped to establish Pynchon as a favorite among American avant-garde artists of the twentieth century.

Although the popular and critical success of his works helped to confirm his status among the modern American literati, Pynchon firmly established his place within the ranks of great writers with his most enigmatic novel, *Gravity's Rainbow* (1973). In this prescient work, Pynchon returns to his successful conspiratorial theme. Those who have revisited this novel in most recent years, however, are sure to notice the increasing relevance of the protagonist's paranoid fantasies in light of the late twentieth-century's technological revolution. The novel's main character, Tyrone Slothrop, understandably suffers an increasing sense of alienation from the modern world in which he lives and works. His existence, he feels, is gradually reduced to little more than an abstraction, and as a result, identity is ultimately sacrificed to the rapacious man-made god of modern technology.

While Pynchon continues to write novels, such as *Vineland*, published in 1990, he has also created memorable works in the short-story genre. According to literary critics, his most notable efforts in this area are considered to be "Entropy," published in 1960, and the 1964 story, "The Secret Integration," a tale about small-town bigotry that later appeared in a collection of stories with similar themes: *Slow Learner,* published in 1984.

See also Apocalypse: Secular; Apocalyptic Literature; *Gravity's Rainbow;* Slothrop, Lieutenant Tyrone.

RALPH

Ralph is the archetypal "fair-haired boy" who serves as the voice of reason and the practical protagonist of William Golding's apocalyptic parable, *Lord of the Flies* (1954). As the first to emerge from the wreckage of a plane carrying a cargo of young schoolboys that had flown from England in an effort to escape from bombs being dropped during the war, Ralph is also the first to determine the circumstances that initiate the action of the novel. He declares to another survivor nicknamed Piggy that they have crashed on a coral island, that there are no adults to be found, and that they should devise a method to search for other boys who might also have survived the crash.

With these declarations, the level-headed twelve-year-old assumes the role of a natural leader whose instincts compel him to create a modicum of order out of their chaotic situation. As he continues to assess their status, he consoles the shaken Piggy by reminding him that he is a capable swimmer, but more importantly, he announces his ingenuous conviction that his father, a commander in the navy, will eventually come to rescue them. Temporarily calmed by Ralph's assurances, Piggy begins to use his formidable intellect to assist Ralph in finding a solution to their problem. He soon succeeds in doing so by spotting a conch shell in the water and explaining to Ralph the value of such a discovery. Ralph, however, soon intercepts the shell and establishes himself as the voice of authority on the island by blowing into the shell, thereby creating a "strident blare" (Golding 14) in the hope of assembling the other children who might be alive somewhere on the island.

While Ralph is a paragon of democratic virtue, his initial naiveté prevents him from understanding the potential evil that is unleashed on the island in the unrestrained characters of Jack Merridew, a bloodthirsty ex-choirboy, and his sadistic minion, Roger. From the outset of the novel, Ralph (the force of good) and Jack (the force of evil) contend for control of their island paradise. Ralph's approach, which is an extension of the familiar rigidity of the all-boys' school from which the inhabitants of the island originated, initially comforts the survivors. They are eager to view him as the group's natural leader; they observe the rules of order he sets in place regarding the authority of the conch shell and the following of traditional parliamentary procedure. However, when Ralph insists on (1) maintaining the signal fire to facilitate their rescue, (2) building shelters, (3) accounting for and feeding the "littluns" (the younger boys), (4) instructing the boys regarding issues of sanitation, and (5) conducting routine meetings to assess the status of their situation, he soon encounters opposition from Jack and his growing number of supporters.

Ralph's strength is his intrinsic ability to create order out of chaos. However, as happens in many similar novels when humans are removed from the restrictions of civilized society and left to their own natural devices, undesirable qualities like sloth, greed, pride, anger, and the whole range of personal weaknesses come to the fore and result in chaos, confusion, and—ultimately—in destruction. Sensing the apocalyptic escalation caused by the "loosing" of the satanic Jack and his loyal follower, Roger, Ralph laments as the boys begin to wander slowly into the camp. Soon play becomes more valued than work, hunting becomes more important than maintaining a signal fire for rescue, aggression becomes the means of maintaining authority, and death is the cost of rebellion against the dark forces of human nature.

In spite of his earlier noble efforts, Ralph eventually realizes that common sense is no match for the destructive instincts of humanity, particularly in an environment where there is an absence of traditional regulatory systems. He also becomes increasingly aware that he will eventually be killed, just like his two friends, the intelligent Piggy and the spiritual Simon, whose "weaker" natures made them temperamentally unfit to contend in the Darwinian struggle for existence set up by Jack's brutal force that gradually wins control of the island. Still, Ralph uses his cunning to resist the diabolical forces that ultimately—both literally and figuratively—destroy their island paradise. At the end of the novel, Ralph alone is aware of the devastating potential of human nature, and that humanity's childlike innocence (as in the story's Edenic archetype) will always disappear forever once humanity succumbs to the temptations that inevitably unleash the forces of evil into the world.

See also Apocalypse: Traditional Judeo-Christian; Apocalypse: Traditional Primitive; *Lord of the Flies;* Merridew, Jack; Piggy; Simon.

RANSOM, DR. ELWIN

Dr. Elwin Ransom is the unwitting protagonist, observer, and narrative translator of the fanciful apocalyptic science fiction trilogy by the noted scholar, teacher, and writer, C. S. Lewis. The character of Dr. Ransom serves as Lewis's central thread, weaving together the following three allegorical novels of humanity's fall and its promised redemption: *Out of the Silent Planet* (1938), *Perelandra* (1944), and *That Hideous Strength* (1946). In the space trilogy, Ransom is first introduced as a kidnapped prisoner on a spaceship headed to Malacandra (Mars), where his captors, the materialistic Devine and the evil Weston, plan to use him as a human sacrifice in order to distract the alien inhabitants from their plans to colonize the Malacandran planet. Ransom's skill as a college professor and linguist specializing in ancient languages enables him to escape his fate by communicating with the Malacandran life-forms that inhabit the strange and threatening planet. Ransom's function in this first novel, therefore, is to demonstrate how the fearful nature of humanity perpetually keeps it from communing with the more benevolent forces of the universe. In time, he learns to trust as a result of his relationship with some of the planet's generous and thoughtful creatures. This trust leads him to learn the truth of his own planet (earth, called Thulcandra in the story) from a universal perspective. This truth is made painfully evident to him when he learns that Thulcandra was once in direct communication with the other more beneficent planets in the solar system (the Field of Arbol). However, because of the corrupt influences that took root quickly after the creation of the planet, it has been quarantined—kept separate from the other more innocent planets—in an effort to subdue the virulent spread of corruption. Thus, Thulcandra has become known as the "silent planet" because its inhabitants can no longer hear or directly communicate with Maledil, the god who is considered by the Malacandrans to be the divine creative force of the universe.

Although Ransom is saddened by the state of his seemingly doomed planet, he returns to Thulcandra fortified by the knowledge that the potential for goodness still exists in the universe. Further, through his personal experiences on Malacandra he has returned fortified by a newfound faith that has wiped away his former fears and has made him open to communication with the eldila, powerful angelic entities who inhabit and care for the Malacandran planet. This communication leads to his involvement in the subsequent space adventure, detailed in the most beautifully written novel of the trilogy, *Perelandra.* The title of this second novel refers to the fictional name given to the planet Venus. Although he is beckoned to Perelandra for an important mission he doesn't fully understand, this time his fears are replaced by trust in the wisdom of Maledil and the protection provided by his guardian eldila. Thus, when he arrives on Perelandra he freely explores the lush beauty of the unspoiled landscape. Unlike Malacandra, where he was constantly fleeing fearsome creatures, on Perelandra he encounters less-threatening yet magnificent beasts and delights in the sensory pleasures of myriad fruits and flowers reminiscent of the biblical Garden of Eden. After being refreshed by his idyllic surroundings, Ransom soon learns the full purpose of his voyage. Simply stated, his purpose is to protect Perelandra, which is as yet uninhabited by a human-type species, from succumbing to the same fate that spoiled the once pristine paradise on Thulcandra. One of his major tasks, therefore, is to meet with a Green Woman who is the Perelandrean counterpart to Eve. Destined to be the queen "mother" of the new inhabitants of the planet, she must first understand and turn away from the forces of evil before she is allowed to unite with her future king and "father" of Perelandra.

When Ransom meets the Green Woman, he realizes that the forces of evil are already present on the planet. His former captor, the evil physicist Weston, has made his way to Perelandra and has entered into an agreement with Satan in exchange for his exploitation of the rarefied new world. Weston's body is possessed by the demonic spirit, and it is through him that the Green Woman begins to question the rules that require her to move from island to island rather than to remain in a fixed location from day to day. And just as the serpent caused Eve to question the motives behind God's rules, Weston's empathy with the Green Woman's circumstances of waiting for her mate and waiting for her children cause her to consider using her free will rather than continuing to obey the laws set forth by Maledil. Realizing this, Ransom intercedes and explains the consequences of disobedience and the high price of separation from the universal creative force. Thus, he inevitably enacts the literal function of his name by serving as the Christ-like "ransom" for the Perelandrean paradise: he must directly fight Weston/Satan in order for the forces of good to vanquish the forces of evil that threaten the future salvation of the planet. As his reward for his courageous intervention, he is returned to Thulcandra with the promise that his planet will one day have a final apocalyptic battle between good and evil, and that the next time, good will reign supreme.

Although Lewis could have stopped at this point in his allegorical treatise, he continued to use Ransom as the pivotal point around which the actions of the final novel, *That Hideous Strength,* ensue. His place in the final novel, however, is more peripheral. Clearly, he has already fought and won a great battle, but as a result, he has been left with a permanent and mythically relevant wound in his heel that forces him to serve more as a guide to the action than its primary character. In this novel, Ransom possesses all the spiritual and empirical wisdom he has gained from his former travels through space. Those experiences, understandably, have caused him to become more pensive and mystically attuned to the natural wonders of his present surroundings in England, the primary setting of Lewis's final novel in the trilogy.

As a spiritual guide, he is both emboldened and empowered by his former guardians, the eldila, who had protected him on his previous journeys. It is through their continued communication with him that he develops a small following, one of whom is the protagonist and representative of the force of good in the world, the neglected wife of an egocentric scholar, Mrs. Jane Studdock. Conversely, her husband Mark Studdock represents the evil that takes the form of intellectual pride as he works, with others of his same kind, to control the world by the manipulation of language, media, and essential truth in his demonic place of employment, the National Institute for Coordinated Experiments (N.I.C.E.) in Belsbury, England.

Following the introduction of this diametrically opposed couple, Ransom fades into the background of the novel. But his mystical and magical influence, as inspired by the efforts of the recently awakened Celtic magician Merlin, is felt as the ultimate battle between good and evil draws to its climactic close and vividly fulfills the apocalyptic promise revealed to him at the end of his Perelandrean voyage. In conclusion, throughout the entire trilogy Ransom not only demonstrates Christ-like qualities and serves as a biblically inspired message of divine revelation, but he also typifies the classic mythical hero in that he is spirited away to pursue a noble quest. Next, he wanders through a threatening labyrinth of experiences in which he confronts life-threatening beasts. Finally, his wisdom serves as an inspiration for those who join him in his fight for goodness that eventually vanquishes the forces of evil in the ultimate spiritual battle that is fought during his time on Thulcandra.

See also Apocalypse: Traditional Judeo-Christian; Apocalypticism; Archetype; Arthur, King; Merlin; Myth; *Out of the Silent Planet; Perelandra;* Satan; Symbol; *That Hideous Strength;* Weston, Edward Rolles.

REGAN

Regan is the middle daughter of the aging monarch, King Lear, in the tragic 1605 Shakespeare play of the same name. Regan's prime motivation in all that she does is to follow in the footsteps of her older sister, Goneril. While Goneril initiates much of the action that ensues in the apocalyptic drama, Regan's middle-child "me too!" nature makes her seem less powerful than her sister. In many ways, however, she is much more cruel. For example, after Lear has divided his kingdom between his two eldest daughters because they have showered him with the greatest degree of idle flattery, Lear spends one month living with Goneril. But because Goneril will not treat him with the respect and unquestioned adoration he believes is his due, he leaves her home in order to live with Regan instead.

Regan begins to show her malicious nature by encouraging her husband Cornwall to seize Lear's messenger, the Earl of Kent, and throw him in stocks for insulting her servant, Oswald. Not only does she show disrespect for the Earl, whom Lear has sent to announce his pending visit, but when Cornwall orders the Earl to remain bound until noon, Regan shows "one-upsmanship" by increasing his suffering with the words, "Till night, my lord; and all night too."

Her disrespect for authority is further demonstrated upon Lear's arrival. Clearly, the King underestimates the cruelty of his second daughter because, although it's obvious that he has left Goneril's home in anger, Regan surreptitiously contacts Goneril, who greets Lear unexpectedly when he reaches Regan's home. Instead of offering her father comfort, Regan seals her callous covenant with Goneril by forcing the king to apologize to the older sister, in public, before allowing him to stay in her home.

This loyalty to her older sister, however, is short-lived. After Cornwall is murdered, Regan kills the servant who slew her husband. She then immediately reinstates the rivalry between herself and Goneril. She does so by pursuing Edmund, the sinister character with whom Goneril is having an adulterous relationship. In her pursuit, she is more free than Goneril to do as she wishes because her husband is dead and Goneril's is not. Thus, she essentially bribes Edmund with all of her worldly goods in order to win his affection and thereby top her sister. Goneril reacts in an act of jealous rage, poisoning Regan in order to keep her from winning the man who is the object of her diabolical obsession. But Regan's death is not to be bitterly grieved, because like her sister, she was an "unnatural" offspring who was determined to fulfill her own will, regardless of the devastating impact it may have had upon others.

See also Apocalypse: Traditional Primitive; Cordelia; Goneril; Great Chain of Being; *King Lear*.

REVELATION, BOOK OF

This last book of the New Testament scriptures (c. A.D. 90–96), is both an inestimable prophetic archetype and perhaps the most significant contribution to the apocalyptic literary genre. While easily identifiable by its customary title, the book

Apocalypsis Sancti Johannis, or Revelation of St. John, is one of the greatest examples of block-book printing.

of Revelation is also identified by different names based upon various printed and denominational versions of the text, some of which are: the Revelation of Jesus Christ to St. John the Divine (King James version); the Revelation to John (Revised Standard version); the Apocalypse of the Blessed Apostle John (Ronald Knox version); and the Apocalypse of St. John the Apostle (Douay edition).

In spite of its various translations, this complex yet instinctively intelligible book serves two important purposes for its legions of readers. First, it summarizes the historical conditions, political implications, and individual crises of faith for early believers who banded together following the death of Jesus Christ. Second, and most importantly, the work, in its entirety, serves as the most cogent expression of the Christian apocalyptic prophecy that has continued to sustain the hopes of faithful followers for nearly two thousand years.

Authorship

Throughout the centuries, considerable debate has centered on the identity of the author of the prophetic work. The writer, of course, identifies himself as John, but exactly which John remains enigmatic for both Old and New Testament scholars. According to the views of Greek and Hebrew scholars in regard to the text itself, the writer of the work indisputably "gives his name as John in four places: Revelation 1:1, 4, 9, 22:8. [However, n]owhere does he claim to be one of the twelve apostles" (*Anchor Bible* 28). In additional support of this view, such scholars also assert that the writer of the text makes no claim to have ever

The book of Revelation includes a description of four horses whose riders will terrorize the world's inhabitants. German artist Albrecht Dürer created a woodcut in 1498 of the horsemen, from left to right, Death, Famine, War, and Conquest.

had a personal acquaintance with Jesus during his lifetime. Moreover, while the text was originally composed in the Greek language, literary scholars suggest that the writer's mastery of the language was marginal at best, casting further doubt upon both the chronological origin and the authorship of the work. Perhaps the greatest source of speculation, however, comes from the recognized fact that many of the apocalyptic scriptural and noncanonical texts were actually written pseudonymously by authors who lived many years after the events they recorded. These authors apparently believed that by assigning the names of recognizable historical or religious authorities to such texts, the prophesies put forth would be more readily accepted.

In contrast, Christian scholars of the text cite a number of reasons suggesting the opposite view: that it was indeed St. John the Apostle who authored the Book of Revelation. Among the primary reasons supporting this assertion are the apocalyptic book's specific diction and close stylistic resemblance to the other written gospels of St. John. Additional evidence can be found in a recorded second-century document prepared by Justin Martyr, *Dialogue with Trypho the Jew.* Chapter 81 clearly identifies the author of the apocalyptic work in the following fragment: "And with us [was] a man named John, one of the Apostles of Christ, who in the revelation made to him. . . ." (*Open Bible* 1181). But perhaps the most convincing support for St. John's authorship of the work relates to the historical events, political atmosphere, and crises of faith that seem to have prevailed during the proposed time in which the work was composed.

Historical Significance

Clearly, as in most of the earlier Jewish apocalypses and related noncanonical prophetic literature, the Book of Revelation was composed during a time of great spiritual confusion and political persecution. The early followers of Christ, including those who had witnessed or had heard of his teachings and miracles as well as his crucifixion, resurrection, and ascension, were convinced that Jesus was indeed the promised Messiah who would deliver them from the suffering of the earthly world. Thus, after Christ's ascension, many early Christians were concerned about the fulfillment of His promises after His death. They became convinced that Christ would one day have to return to the earth in order to demonstrate His ultimate triumph over evil and establish a welcomed reign of peace.

While their faith was strong, several factors contributed to the need for something that would bolster confidence in their convictions. One factor involved the passage of time. Near the end of the first century of Christian activity, some believers had already begun to grow tired of the wait for Christ's Second Coming. Their impatience was compounded by other more pressing factors that had begun to threaten both their collective spiritual beliefs and their physical existence. These factors revolved around the escalation of power within the Roman Empire. At this time, the practice of emperor worship had become something of a social as well as a political obligation. While the meager numbers of early underground Christians had previously posed no threat to the Roman government, their increasing public resistance against the idolatry of emperor worship eventually became problematic for the Roman authorities.

Obviously, this mounting threat caused problems for the Christians as well. Some of the believers were clearly confused in regard to which course of action to take. Many began to waver by capitulating to Roman rule in order to survive. Some even abandoned their faith prematurely out of fear for their lives and those of their families. Still others, however, became the focus of much political scrutiny because of their deliberate refusal to serve Rome in favor of serving their Lord. As a result, many of the more staunch believers endured sustained persecution at the hands of the Roman authorities. It was not unusual for Christians to be convicted of crimes they had not committed, and there were others who were frequently forced to pay unjust penalties for alleged infractions in order to avoid governmental retribution. In spite of such injustice at the hands of the Roman leaders, there still remained those who chose martyrdom or public execution over living with the shame of denying their faith in the Messiah.

These diverse reactions to the changing times and circumstances could have initiated the divine "revelation" to St. John, who at the time was himself a prisoner after being banished by the emperor Domitian to the Isle of Patmos as punishment for his faith. Based upon these historical events, it is reasonable to assume that St. John the Apostle could indeed have been the writer of the apocalyptic book that was intended to deliver a divinely inspired message of warning and hope to the seven churches of Asia, throughout which the practice of Christianity had firmly begun to take root.

Theme of the Work

Like earlier apocalyptic canons, the Book of Revelation is a prophetic work. Also, like previous apocalyptic literature, it reflects the following common characteristics: (1) It was a divinely inspired revelation brought to the writer by an angel. (2) The visions contained within the text reflect a knowledge of otherworldly locations and characters. (3) The work itself focuses on divine judgments of good and evil along with commensurate rewards or punishments in an afterlife. (4) It features the last days of humanity as fraught with fear and frailty, susceptibility to temptation by false prophets, and a growing apostasy. (5) It reflects a series of signs and symbols that portend the great and inevitable temporal and spiritual battles that will be fought both in heaven and on earth. (6) Finally, it promises that the forces of evil will ultimately be vanquished and that the righteous will finally be rewarded by sharing eternity in the presence of God (Reddish 20–23).

Signs and Symbols

Within the twenty-two chapters of the Book of Revelation, countless cryptic references to numerology, mythical creatures, color, animal imagery, and astral formations abound. While such matters serve as grounds for considerable and continued debate, the following details reflect some of the predominant symbols that contribute to the ongoing interpretation of the work.

NUMBERS

Among the numbers featured within Revelation is the frequently used number seven. According to scholars of numerical symbolism, "Seven [is s]ymbolic of perfect order, a complete period or cycle" (Cirlot 1971, 233). This number is used frequently throughout the apocalyptic work. The "seven churches" of Asia represent the various states of faithfulness, corruption, and apostasy that will exist at the time of the end of the world. The great book of the future that God the Father holds in His hand remains closed with "seven seals." When a great angel asks who is worthy to open the book and no one replies, the prophet is saddened. But soon, amidst the supplicants at the throne stands Christ, figuratively "a Lamb as it had been slain, having seven horns and seven eyes, which are the seven Spirits of God sent forth into all the earth" (Revelation 5:1–6). One by one, as the Son of God opens each of the "seven seals," the divine judgments that will prepare the earth for the last days are sequentially revealed. Following the revelations of the seven seals come the "seven angels" who sound the "seven trumpets." The seven trumpets, respectively, represent the following events: (1) the hail and fire that will scorch the grass of the earth; (2) the burning mountain (volcano?) that will fall into the sea, turning part of the sea to blood and causing the death of sea life and the destruction of seafaring vessels; (3) a great burning star—Wormwood—that will fall from the heavens and cause death by contaminating rivers and other sources of drinking water; (4) the partial darkening (eclipsing) of the sun, moon, and stars, which will visibly strike fear into the hearts of men; (5) the falling of a star that will open hell's bottomless pit and release a plague of locusts to torment "only those men which have not the seal of God in their foreheads" (9:4); (6) the sixth trumpet heralds the release of the four horsemen of the apocalypse who, with their beasts and their inscrutable armies, will terrorize the inhabitants of the earth and thereby devastate "the third part of man" (9:15); (7) and finally, the seventh trumpet heralds the appearance of "a mighty angel come down from heaven, clothed with a cloud . . . his face [is] as it were the sun, and his feet as pillars of fire" (10:1). Although the prophet begins to write down all that he has witnessed, this seventh angel commands the prophet to stop writing, and instead commands him to swallow a little book holding the final secrets of the end times. The book is sweet to the taste and bitter to the stomach, but the prophet is urged to digest this information and to preach its contents upon his visionary release to "many peoples, and nations, and tongues, and kings" (10:11).

MYTHICAL CREATURES

The first series of mythical creatures is revealed with the opening of the seals. First, they convey numerological symbolism, and secondly, they reflect other apocalyptic events. Specifically, these creatures are collectively known as the Four Horsemen of the Apocalypse. The number four frequently refers to "the earth . . . terrestrial space . . . the human situation . . . the external, natural limits of the 'minimum' awareness of totality, and, finally . . . rational organization" (Cirlot 232). This use of numerical symbolism seems to reflect the human understanding of the various plagues that will befall the earth with the arrival of each of the deadly four horsemen whose relevance may be interpreted as follows: the first "White" horse represents *conquest* of the earth; the second "Red" horse represents the *slaughter* that will ensue from worldwide war; the third "Black" horse represents the *famine* that will decimate those who are living at the time; and the final "Pale" horse represents the ultimate *death* of both the planet and its inhabitants (Benet 345).

The next mythical creature within the Book of Revelation is the "great red dragon, having seven heads and ten horns, and seven crowns upon his heads" (Revelation 12:3). According to universal mythology of both primitive and classical origin, the dragon is "a kind of amalgam of elements taken from various animals that are particularly aggressive and dangerous, such as serpents, crocodiles, lions as well as prehistoric animals" (Cirlot 85). Such an interpretation is reflected in the words of the apocalyptic prophesy that tell of the dragon's great battle in heaven with Michael the archangel and his armies, who ultimately vanquish the dragon and thereby "cast out, that old serpent, called the Devil, and Satan, which deceiveth the whole world. . . ." (Revelation 12:7–9).

The next appearance of mythological or otherworldy creatures comes in the form of two beasts. The first beast, according to scripture, will "rise up out of the sea, having seven heads and ten horns, and upon his horns ten crowns, and upon his heads the name of blasphemy." Having been given its power by the dragon, its appearance is also an amalgam: it looks like a leopard, has a bear's feet, the mouth of a lion, and one head that bears the scars of a deadly wound. In addition, this beast, who worships the dragon, has been empowered to blaspheme the name of God, to wage war on the saints of the world, and to cause those who are not written in the Lamb's book of life to become his captives, thereby forfeiting their salvation (13:1–10). The second beast, however, reflects a more diabolical duplicity. Although he has two horns like a lamb, he speaks like a dragon. For this reason, he is more deadly than the first beast, whom he causes the remaining people of the earth to worship. It is clear that the people will initially be deceived by his dual nature, particularly in light of the prophesy that he will be able to perform miracles and charm crowds with his obvious power. Such power will bring him allegiance from the unwary inhabitants of the earth, but after a time, his countenance of the lamb will be overshadowed by the influence of the dragon in his nature. Thus, he will cause his devotees to suffer and die unless they submit to wearing a number that will identify them as his own. This number, which will be placed either on their foreheads or their hands, is the symbolic number 666. At this point, John the prophet makes note to all who might fall prey to such deception: "Here is wisdom. Let him that hath understanding count the number of the beast: for it is the number of a man; and his number is Six hundred threescore and six" (13:11–17).

The next and perhaps most significant animal depicted within the Revelation is the lamb. The symbolism of the lamb was first found in the apocalyptic book of Enoch. "It signifies purity, innocence, meekness (as well as unwarranted sacrifice)" (Cirlot 175). This symbolic representation is similarly carried out within John's Apocalypse, in which the Lamb (Jesus Christ or the Messiah) will eventually reign on Mount Zion along with the "one hundred and forty-four thousand" righteous elders, presumably from the twelve tribes of Israel, "who were redeemed from among men, being the first fruits unto God and to the Lamb . . . [who come to their position because] in their mouth[s] was found no guile; for they are without fault before the throne of God" (Revelation 14:1–5).

Although countless other symbols exist throughout the apocalyptic final book of the New Testament, readers should note that the conclusion of the "revelation" to St. John suggests the complete fulfillment of all Old Testament prophesy. Among such matters is the fall of the great and perverse city of Babylon that has been inspired by and reenacted within various forms of apocalyptic literature. Another predominant theme that appears in the final chapters of the work is the binding of Satan for a period of one thousand years. The retention of Satan leads to a thousand-year period of peace, during which the righteous will reign with Christ; this time is often referred to in religious literature as the "Millennial Kingdom." Following this time, however, comes "the last loosing of Satan," another predominant feature of apocalyptic literature. At this point, both heaven and earth will be poised for the great final battle of Gog and Magog. At the conclusion of this battle, the ultimate revenge—as promised within apocalyptic prophesy—comes to pass. The wicked who still remain on the earth at that time will be destroyed by fire, and Satan, their deceiver, will be "cast into the lake of fire and brimstone, where the beast and the false prophet . . . shall be tormented day and night for ever and ever" (20:1–10).

The final prophetic fulfillment, however, occurs with the creation of a "new heaven and a new earth." Within this promise also lies the creation of a New Jerusalem and God's restoration of the city belonging to the twelve tribes of Israel. Upon witnessing this revelation, John hears God's pronouncement to those of the earth who choose to remain faithful:

> Behold, the tabernacle of God is with men, and he will dwell with them, and they shall be his people, and God himself shall be with them, and be their God. And God shall wipe away all tears from their eyes; and there shall be no more death, neither sorrow, nor crying, neither shall there be any more pain: for the former things are passed away. . . . Behold, I make all things new.

At this point, God tells John to "Write: for these words are true and faithful" (21: 3–5). And so he did, as is evidenced in this book, the Revelation of St. John, which is rightfully considered by many to be the greatest literary apocalypse ever written, and one that will surely continue to inspire other writers until the end of time (*Anchor Bible* 1975).

See also Apocalypse: Traditional Judeo-Christian; Apocalypticism; Babylon; Eschatology; Symbol.

RINEHART

Rinehart is the unseen multifaceted character who represents the chaotic forces of a so-called civilized society in Ralph Ellison's apocalyptic novel, *The Invisible*

Man (1952). Although he is never an actual participant in the plot of the novel, the reader learns about his role in society because of his distinctive appearance. Rinehart is characterized as a black man-about-town who is easily identified by his dark glasses and his stark white hat. The narrator of the novel—the Invisible Man—learns about Rinehart when he inadvertently dons the same accessories in order to escape the wrath of a rabid black militant who is a prominent figure in a powerful organization known as "the Brotherhood."

While wearing the glasses and the hat, the narrator is repeatedly mistaken for the enigmatic Rinehart, and this recurrent event makes him eager to learn more about the mysterious man behind the mask. What he finds is that Rinehart is, at the very least, a questionable character. But in his search for Rinehart, the Invisible Man paradoxically stumbles upon the answer to his own search for identity. His description of Rinehart, as well as the narrator's own personal epiphany, is detailed in the novel as follows:

> Can it be, I thought, can it actually be? And I knew that it was. I had heard of it before but I'd never come so close. Still, could he be all of them: Rine the runner and Rine the gambler and Rine the briber and Rine the lover and Rinehart the Reverend? Could he himself be both rind and heart? What is real anyway? But how could I doubt it? He was a broad man, a man of parts who got around. Rinehart the rounder. It was true as I was true. His world was possibility and he knew it. He was years ahead of me and I was a fool. I must have been crazy and blind. The world in which we lived was without boundaries. A vast seething, hot world of fluidity, and Rine the rascal was at home. Perhaps only Rine the rascal was at home in it (Ellison 498).

Given this newfound knowledge, the protagonist ultimately finds his identity, his purpose, and his long-sought means of living amidst the chaos of the modern world. The solution to all of his problems can only be found in a life of invisibility. Moreover, lest the reader doubt that this revelation is the intended central metaphor for the work, Ellison's own words confirm his conception of his fictional creation:

> Rinehart is my name for the personification of chaos. He is also intended to represent America and change. He has lived so long with chaos that he knows how to manipulate it. It is the old theme of *The Confidence-Man*. He is a figure in a country with no solid past or stable class lines; therefore he is able to move about easily from one to another (qtd. in May 1972, 148).

See also Apocalypse: Secular; Archetype; *The Confidence-Man: His Masquerade;* Gatsby, Jay; *The Hollow Men; The Invisible Man; The Mysterious Stranger;* Symbol; *The Waste Land.*

ROMANTICISM

A literary and artistic movement (1798–1832) that developed in the late eighteenth century as a reaction against the logic and reason of the Neoclassical period, Romanticism was initiated by the thought of Swiss-born French philosopher Jean-Jacques Rousseau. Romanticism reflects the priorities of its progenitor: it places great value on individualism, the reverence of nature, an inclination toward passion over reason, a rejection of societal regulation, and an exaltation of the sensual, exotic, mystical, fanciful—and often forbidden—aspects of the imagination.

While the Romantic movement first crystallized in Germany, as is reflected in the works of Goethe, Schiller, and most notably in the philosophical tomes of Immanuel Kant, the movement flourished in the literature of England at the end of the eighteenth century. While authors such as William Blake, William Cowper, and Robert Burns introduced Romantic elements in their work, it is commonly agreed that the official emergence of the Romantic period in literature began in 1798 with the publication of *Lyrical Ballads,* a collection of works by Samuel Taylor Coleridge and William Wordsworth. So surprised was Wordsworth by the reaction to their joint effort that in 1800, they published a revised edition of *Ballads.* It contains a detailed preface that remains to this day a philosophical guideline for the tenets of the Romantic literary movement. Other writers such as Keats, Byron, and Shelley also contributed to the movement. Although France developed its own Romanticists, including Victor Hugo, George Sand, Stendhal, and Dumas, Romantic influences soon made their way into the consciousness of American writers as well.

Although some of the more mystical elements of early Romanticism were replaced by the more humanitarian interests of the American culture, several authors emerged as the Romantic voices of the new continent. And while some authors, particularly the Transcendentalists such as Emerson, Whitman, and Thoreau, were concerned more with the idealism of the period, the following authors were most notable for their Romantic contributions: Nathaniel Hawthorne, Herman Melville, and Edgar Allan Poe. Collectively and individually, their works explored the infinite possibilities of the natural world, the mystical aspects of the supernatural realm, the ecstatic fruition of unbridled sensuality, and the agonizing obsessions that lead to madness.

Ultimately, while this great body of cross-continental work fascinated readers for a time, the movement as an official literary period faded and essentially ended in England in 1832. Nevertheless, the legacy of the Romantic period lives on in its powerful symbolism and fantastic imagery that continue to influence, to some extent, the finest literature of the world.

See also Blake, William; *The Blithedale Romance;* Emerson, Ralph Waldo; Melville, Herman; *Moby-Dick;* Poe, Edgar Allan.

SATAN

Satan, Beelzebub, the devil, the Evil One, and Lucifer, are all common names referring to the supreme evil spirit, the prince of darkness, the serpent of the Garden of Eden, the Red Dragon in the Book of Revelation, and, according to Christian theological tradition, the once illustrious fallen angel who vengefully becomes the tempter and deceiver directly responsible for the spiritual fall of mankind. Specifically, the word *Satan* is derived from the Hebrew word *shatan,* meaning "adversary"; the term *devil* comes from the Greek word, *diabolos,* meaning "slanderer"; Beelzebub, originally a Philistine deity, is known in the Bible's New Testament as "Lord of the Flies," or when referred to as Beelzebul, the translation means "Lord of Dung." Regardless of the terms used, this character is considered the lord of the underworld: the ruler of hell.

Although this force had its origins in the apocalyptic literature of the first and second centuries B.C., and was founded in the Babylonian and Zoroastrian tradition, it also had counterparts within the ancient mythological worlds in the forms of the Greek god, Pluto, and the Egyptian sage, Seth. The archetype of the devil pervades the collective body of world literature, and various authors, particularly from the medieval period, are largely responsible for the pictorial and conceptual renditions of the evil spirit as we know it today.

Perhaps one of the earliest literary poets to depict Lucifer, the fallen angel, in the depths of hell was Dante Alighieri who developed an entire infernal cosmos within his work, *The Divine Comedy.* John Milton's *Paradise Lost* also represents the deceptive force that led to the fall of man. Similarly, the medieval legend of Dr. Faustus pervades Western literature: the devil, as represented by Mephistophiles, takes advantage of humanity's pride and insatiable quest for knowledge by offering men a pact. The price, however, is high: in exchange for omniscience, omnipotence, and the uninterrupted pursuit of pure pleasure, at least for a time, a man must pay the ultimate price—the interminable damnation of his soul and the eternal awareness of his own foolish aspirations. The most famous versions of this legend appear within the works of Goethe, Marlowe, and in the twentieth-century works of Paul Valery and Thomas Mann. Such Mephistophilian characters, however, are not restricted to traditional legendary portrayals.

Characters based on the satanic archetype frequently appear in American literature. For example, within the apocalyptic genre, several characters emerge as

William Blake's *Satan Rousing the Rebel Angels*

demonic representations. Westervelt, the nefarious magician in Nathaniel Hawthorne's novel, *The Blithedale Romance*, clearly depicts the sinister nature of the devil and his destructive influence on susceptible humans. Similarly, the character—actually named Satan—is the perverted antagonist who tortures the innocent throughout Mark Twain's social satire entitled *The Mysterious Stranger.* Herman Melville also reveals the archetypal trickster in his novel, *The Confidence-Man: His Masquerade*, and Beelzebub himself appears to terrorize the abandoned young group of atavistic boys in William Golding's *Lord of the Flies.* In addition to these classics, Southern writers such as Flannery O'Connor, William Faulkner, and Walker Percy frequently feature demonic characters who contribute to the downfall of their unsuspecting prey. Clearly, as long as humanity has a mind to delude, a body to seduce, and a soul to damn, this powerful legendary, symbolic, and very real force will be inextricably linked, through literature, with the human condition.

See also *Absalom, Absalom!*; Allegory; Apocalypse: Traditional Judeo-Christian; Apocalypse: Traditional Primitive; Archetype; Caliban; *The Divine Comedy; Doktor Faustus; Dr. Faustus; Faust; The Golden Bough: A Study in Magic and Religion;* Hell; Immelmann, Art; Jung, Carl Gustav; Mephistophiles; Myth; Percy, Walker; Revelation, Book of; Sutpen, Thomas; Symbol; *The Tempest; The Thanatos Syndrome.*

SCIENCE FICTION

Science fiction is the literary genre that evolved from the revival of a type of literature that was formerly known as "scientific romance." Early examples of such literary works include the strange creatures found in Jonathan Swift's *Gulliver's Travels* (1726); an imaginary trip to the moon recorded in Voltaire's *Micromegas* (1752); and, of course, the unforgettable attempt to use science and technology to create a new life-form, indelibly recorded in what some consider to be the first work of science fiction, *Frankenstein* (1817), written by Mary Wollstonecraft Shelley.

While traces of this genre were only marginally apparent in the following years, the mid-nineteenth century introduced works containing similar elements by authors such as Herman Melville, Edgar Allan Poe, and Nathaniel Hawthorne. It was not until the late nineteenth century, however, that the works of Jules Verne and H. G. Wells ignited a resurgence of interest in the literary portrayal of technological potential.

This renewed interest in the science fiction genre was becoming evident within the broad spectrum of the literary community. Consequently, in the early twentieth century, a pulp-fiction editor named Hugo Gernsback made a commitment to reintroduce the genre's creative elements, such as "charming romance intermingled with scientific fact and prophetic vision," when he reprinted specific technology-based excerpts by Jules Verne, H. G. Wells, and Edgar Allan Poe in the first issue of his new periodical, *Amazing Stories*, which appeared in April 1926 (Hartwell 1993, xiii).

As a result of the popularity of this periodical and the tremendous interest in works of this genre, science fiction was accepted as an official art form. It

Orson Welles, arms raised, directs members of the "Mercury Theatre of the Air" at a 1938 rehearsal. Welles so successfully adapted H. G. Wells's 1898 science fiction classic *War of the Worlds* that on October 30, 1938, listeners believed a war was actually under way.

became the focus of national attention on October 30, 1938, the evening before Halloween, when prominent actor Orson Welles used his radio program "Mercury Theatre of the Air" as a vehicle to produce a compelling dramatization of the H. G. Wells novel, *War of the Worlds* (1898). In this instance, what was clearly intended as an experimental form of entertainment quickly resulted in widespread panic among his radio listeners. And in spite of numerous announcements that the performance was only a dramatization and that the events portrayed in the broadcast were not happening in real life, the nation was riveted by the fictional "news bulletins" announcing a Martian invasion with the appearance of monsters storming a small town in the state of New Jersey. Clearly, from the early reactions of terrified listeners throughout the northeastern part of the United States, audiences were as yet unfamiliar with the new literary genre; thus, the inevitable pandemonium. Although the confusion was eventually quelled, that particular radio performance marks the official initiation to the world of the modern science fiction literary movement.

In the decades that followed, the science fiction genre seemed to bifurcate: some authors placed a greater focus on machinery, while others became more concerned with technology's impact on humanity. This schism is apparent even today between authors such as Isaac Asimov, whose works greatly favor technological advancement, and the technophobic tales of such humanitarian-based writers as Ray Bradbury.

Currently, partly as a result of advancements in nuclear technology, international efforts in space travel, and the pervasive influence of television and film, the science fiction genre now thrives. Its artistic legitimacy is marked annually with conventions and a number of international literary awards for those who have chosen either the vocation or the avocation of "reaching for the stars" (Hartwell 1993).

See also Apocalypse: Secular; *Brave New World; Cat's Cradle; A Connecticut Yankee in King Arthur's Court; Fahrenheit 451; Moby-Dick; The Narrative of Arthur Gordon Pym; Out of the Silent Planet.*

"THE SECOND COMING"

The definitive apocalyptic poem, entitled "The Second Coming," was written by one of the twentieth century's greatest poets and dramatists, the English author and Irish nationalist William Butler Yeats. This powerful yet short work, which was first published in *The Dial* in 1920, reflects the poet's cyclic view of history. Further, as a reflection of the poet's foundational interests in theosophy, metaphysics, and symbolism, this poem incorporates his visionary view of the modern thermodynamic concept of entropy, or matter's gradual tendency toward cataclysmic change, as represented by his central metaphor of a swirling "gyre." The author's use of this complex symbol is expertly detailed in the biographical information provided about Yeats and his work in the *Norton Anthology of English Literature* (5th edition, volume 2), as follows:

> In his [Yeats's] poems of the 1920s and 1930s, winding stairs, spinning tops, "gyres," spirals of all kinds, are important symbols; not only are they connected with Yeats' philosophy of history and of personality, but they also serve as a means of resolving some of those contraries that had arrested him from the beginning. Life is a journey up a spiral staircase; as we grow older, we cover the ground we have covered before, only higher up; as we look down the winding stair below us, we measure our progress by the number of places where we were but no longer are. The journey is both repetitious and progressive; we go both around and upward. Through symbolic images of this kind, Yeats explores the paradoxes of time and change, of growth and identity, of love and age, of life and art, of madness and wisdom (1931).

Although this description of the poetic masterpiece addresses Yeats's theme in general, one specific line in the poem, "Things fall apart; the center cannot hold," has been adopted as an apocalyptic anthem by countless twentieth-century writers, most notably including Britain's T. S. Eliot, Nigeria's Chinua Achebe, and America's psychologically probing Southern satirist, Walker Percy. In essence, most authors who borrow from this seminal apocalyptic work are similarly concerned with the inevitable chaos that relentlessly threatens the stability of the modern world. For example, Yeats's prophetic alarm that "anarchy is loosed upon the world," that "the blood-dimmed tide is loosed, and everywhere/The ceremony of innocence is drowned" reflects the growing apostasy that has threatened to blind modern man to demonic influences in the world since St. John introduced such images in the New Testament prophesy, the Book of Revelation. Such subtle disintegration of humanity's moral fabric is further illustrated by Yeats in other lines of the poem: "The best lack all conviction, while the worst/Are full of passionate intensity."

Such conditions of chaos and depravity are characteristics that clearly define the collective body of apocalyptic fiction and that, in turn, serve to further confirm Yeats's prediction: "Surely some revelation is at hand." The "revelation" that Yeats predicts, one that is mirrored within the body of apocalyptic literature, is that if humanity is to continue experiencing its cyclic path toward self-destruction, then the only possible consequence of its deliberate rebellion and unchecked recklessness will be the world's inevitable consummation by "the rough beast"—Satan—whose "hour [will cyclically] come round at last."

See also Apocalypse: Traditional Judeo-Christian; Apocalyptic Literature; *The Hollow Men; Love in the Ruins: The Adventures of a Bad Catholic at a Time Near the End of the World; The Thanatos Syndrome; Things Fall Apart; The Waste Land;* Yeats, William Butler.

SHAKESPEARE, WILLIAM

William Shakespeare (1564–1616) was the English poet, actor, and dramatist whose works, written during the Elizabethan and early Jacobean periods, have caused him to become regarded as one of the greatest playwrights in literary history. Although early practices of recording birth certificates have caused some speculation regarding the specific birthdate of the author, it is widely believed that the dramatist was born on April 23, 1564, to John and Mary Shakespeare, in Stratford-upon-Avon, Warwickshire, England.

Similarly, little is known about Shakespeare's young life, except that he was the son of a shop owner of moderate financial means who had held several municipal offices in the family's agricultural community. Scholars also agree that the young bard's first formal education probably occurred at the King Edward IV Grammar School in Stratford, and it was here where he first studied the languages of Latin and Greek as well as the works of classical Roman dramatists. Unlike many major dramatists, however, Shakespeare never received a formal university education.

While considerable debate still exists regarding Shakespeare's early years, most scholars have contented themselves with his comparatively well known mature life and works. One such detail is confirmed in the records of a marriage license issued on November 28, 1582. This document confirms Shakespeare's marriage to Anne Hathaway, a woman nearly eight years his senior, when Shakespeare was just eighteen years old. Similarly, baptismal records acknowledge that on the following May 26, Anne gave birth to their first child, Suzanna. Later came the birth of twins Hamnet and Judith; records indicate that Hamnet—Shakespeare's only son—died at eleven years of age on February 2, 1585. This incident was at least one contributing factor leading to Shakespeare's move to London either later in that same year or early in the next.

Although no specific information exists to confirm either the number or the chronological order of Shakespeare's earliest works, most scholars agree that by 1585 he was already considered both a skilled playwright and a budding actor.

William Shakespeare

The plague that devastated London in the 1590s caused a temporary halt to his acting career. The city's theaters were closed between June 1592 and April 1594. During that time, however, it is believed that he supported his family on money provided by his benefactor, Henry Wriothesley, the Earl of Southampton, to whom Shakespeare had dedicated his first two narrative poems, *Venus and Adonis* and *The Rape of Lucrece* (1593).

In 1594, by the time the plague had subsided in London, records indicate that Shakespeare was already a member of the Lord Chamberlain's acting company, the most popular dramatic ensemble in Queen Elizabeth's court, and the theatrical status symbol for England's upper class. Shakespeare's increasing personal popularity and financial success is evidenced by the fact that, in May of 1597, he was able to purchase a home known as New Place, considered by his contemporaries to be the second largest dwelling in Stratford. In addition, several years later the author made another real estate transaction: the purchase of an agriculturally rich property, which subsequently provided him a sizable income that he would enjoy throughout the remainder of his life.

By that time, Shakespeare also enjoyed considerable security within his profession. The bard and his company of fellow actors—called the King's Men—received a patent from Queen Elizabeth's successor, King James I, whose patronage further supported the efforts of his group. In addition to his work for the court, Shakespeare and other leading actors of the community formed an alliance that would enable them to build and operate a new playhouse, the Globe Theatre, one of the most famous theaters of the period. As a result of some ambiguous leasing disputes, however, Shakespeare and his associates later decided to form another dramatic company known as the Blackfriars. This group eventually built a second theater that enabled them to perform entirely within the structure, providing them with more favorable conditions than the former external arrangements of the Globe.

Of greatest significance, of course, is the considerable body of work Shakespeare completed throughout his lifetime. Although there is significant critical debate concerning the dates of composition for many of his works, most agree that they appeared as follows. His comedies include *The Comedy of Errors* (1592–1593), *Two Gentlemen of Verona* (c. 1592), *The Taming of the Shrew* (c. 1593), *Love's Labours Lost* (1594–1595), *A Midsummer Night's Dream* (1595–1596), *The Merchant of Venice* (1596–1597), *The Merry Wives of Windsor* (1597–1600), *Much Ado about Nothing* (1598–1599), *As You Like It* (1599–1600), *Twelfth Night* (1599–1600), as well as two works known as his "dark comedies," *All's Well That Ends Well* (1602) and *Measure for Measure* (1604–1605). In addition to his comedies, Shakespeare composed an impressive body of historical works, based on English nobility and classical Roman figures. These historical plays include *Henry IV*—Parts I, II, and III—(1597–1598), *Henry V* (1598–1599), *Richard III* (1594), *Richard II* (1595), *King John* (1596–1597), and *Julius Caesar* (1599–1600).

While Shakespeare's comedies and historical plays were, for the most part, critically acclaimed in their ability to capture both the nuances of character and the complexities of the English language, the highest point of the dramatist's career occurred at the beginning of the seventeenth century when he produced his famous tragedies, many of which are still considered among the greatest examples of Western literature. These tragic tales include *Hamlet* (1600–1601), the serious satire *Troilus and Cressida* (1600–1602), *Othello* (1604–1605), *King Lear* (1605–1606), *Macbeth* (1605–1606), *Antony and Cleopatra* (1607–1608), *Timon of Athens* (1607–1608), and *Coriolanus* (1608–1609). At the twilight of his career, after having probed the psychological complexity of his characters as well as the depths of the human spirit, Shakespeare's final works reflect a highly symbolic and experimental combination of tragedy and comedy. These efforts include *Pericles* (1608–1609), *Cymbeline* (1609–1610), *The Winter's Tale* (1610–1611), and his final play, *The Tempest* (1611–1612).

William Shakespeare's prolific writing career continued to sustain him creatively throughout his lifetime. As a result of this prodigious body of work, as well as his favorable investments, Shakespeare, who was happy to have witnessed the marriage of both of his daughters, continued to provide for them after their marriages. Shakespeare and his wife also continued to enjoy his retirement years at his comfortable estate, New Place. Ultimately, however, after a full and productive life, William Shakespeare died on April 23, 1616, and was buried beneath a monument at Stratford Church (Wittreich 1984).

See also Apocalypse: Traditional Judeo-Christian; Apocalypse: Traditional Primitive; Apocalyptic Literature; Apocalypticism; *King Lear; The Tempest.*

SHELLEY, MARY WOLLSTONECRAFT

Mary Shelley (1797–1851) was the English novelist whose romantic idealism and intelligent, independent spirit reflected the values of her unconventional parents, William Godwin, a respected scholar, and Mary Wollstonecraft, best known for her pioneering efforts as an ardent feminist. Although Mary's parents had formerly been considered nontraditional regarding such formal institutions as marriage, they adjusted their views when they learned they were expecting a child. Unfortunately, less than two weeks after Mary's birth, her mother died, leaving Godwin to his own devices until he remarried a widow, with two children of her own, to take care of his infant daughter.

As a young girl, the emotional trauma of losing a birth parent, as well as her unhappy relationship with her stepmother, caused young Mary to become obsessed with issues of abandonment. The imaginative stories that emerged during her writing career often centered on creatures who suffered from loneliness or loss. These feelings subsided when, after a series of rebellious demonstrations, she was placed in the care of a more favorable foster family from 1812 through 1814. It was in the home of the Baxters of Dundee where she met the man who would speak to her soul but who would cause yet another scandal in the young woman's life: the poet Percy Bysshe Shelley. There was an immediate, passionate attraction between the two. Although Shelley was already a married man, the couple, nevertheless, eloped within a year of their first meeting. Mary soon gave birth to a daughter, and the couple suffered the unfortunate death of the child. The bigamous entanglements of Shelley's marriage led to his wife Harriet's eventual suicide. Though tragic, it enabled the couple to marry. Following their union, the couple soon had two children, a son named William and a daughter named Clara, and became part of a circle of friends consisting of other prominent members of their local literary community.

The circumstances of their relationship—the legal entanglements, and the expenses resulting from their travel abroad to escape the criticism of their nontraditional lifestyle—led to a series of financial reversals and additional personal tragedies. Not only were they required to ask their friends for money to support their family, but the family itself was stricken, first in 1818 by the death

Mary Wollstonecraft Shelley, author of *Frankenstein,* from an 1841 painting by R. Rothwell

of their infant daughter, and again in the following year with the death of their three-year-old son, William. Although their spirits were briefly lifted only five months after William's death by the birth of another son, Percy Florence, Mary's whirlwind lifestyle drew to a close in 1822, when her beloved husband drowned while sailing with a friend in Italy.

Rocked by the tragedy of her husband's death and overwhelmed by the burden of raising a child on her own, she was again devastated when her father-in-law refused to provide financial support for her son unless she would agree to place the child in the custody of a more conventional guardian. Obviously, her nature prevented her from making such a decision. The problem was eventually resolved when Shelley's son by his first wife died, leaving Mary's son both the title—Lord Shelley—and the estate that had rightfully belonged to his father.

Even though her personal circumstances improved, it is clear from Mary's writing—the majority of which was written and published after her husband's death—that the woman continued to struggle with a profound sense of loss. But while her protagonists, as well as her minor characters, all suffered from varying levels of anguish, her romantic perspective prevailed: her works focused heavily on the healing power of personal restoration and the importance of emotional reconciliation.

In regard to the overall body of her work, Mary Wollstonecraft Shelley is best known for her conventionally Gothic novel, *Frankenstein, or the Modern Prometheus* (1818). This apocalyptic tale, reportedly influenced by such works as Milton's *Paradise Lost* and several of the works of William Shakespeare, deals with psychological themes similar to those that appear in her later romances, *Valperga* (1823), *The Last Man* (1826), and *Lodore* (1835).

Ultimately, despite her rebellious youth, her capricious yet passionate marriage, and the devastating loss of several children, Mary Wollstonecraft Shelley lived the remainder of her life as both a fulfilled artist and a loving mother. She maintained a close relationship with her son Percy, as well as his wife and their children, and, in the end, enjoyed the richness and stability of a family life that she had always longed for, until her tranquil death in 1851.

See also Apocalypse: Traditional Judeo-Christian; Apocalyptic Literature; *Frankenstein, or the Modern Prometheus;* Grotesque; Myth; Prometheus; Romanticism.

SHRIKE

The character of Shrike, the predatory feature editor and antagonist of Nathanael West's apocalyptic novel, *Miss Lonelyhearts,* bears similarity to the following definition of the noun *shrike* provided in *The American Heritage Dictionary* (2nd college edition, 1982): "Any of various carnivorous birds of the family Laniidae, having a hooked bill and often impaling its prey on sharp-pointed thorns or barbs of wire fencing" (1135). Just as the winged scavenger hovers deliberately in search of vulnerable prey, so too does the literary character heartlessly stalk, directly target, and viciously and repeatedly impale his victim, the novel's protagonist, "Miss Lonelyhearts," upon words chosen to trap and destroy him with diabolical and surgical precision.

At the outset of the novel, it is clear that Shrike, the feature editor for the New York *Post-Dispatch*, is charged with increasing his newspaper's circulation by any means possible. Thus, he creates an agony column as a publicity stunt to attract readers. The stunt backfires for the unwitting male journalist, who becomes known as Miss Lonelyhearts. Although the column had originally been viewed as a joke, it soon becomes evident to everyone involved that the world is filled with hopeless people whose letters are "stamped from the dough of suffering with a heart-shaped cookie knife" (West 1). While this situation creates a progressive moral dilemma for the novel's protagonist, it serves merely as an ongoing form of entertainment for the cynical and malicious Shrike.

In every way, Shrike is Miss Lonelyhearts's foil. Miss Lonelyhearts takes his letters seriously; Shrike turns every horrible story into a joke. While Miss Lonelyhearts relies heavily on his fervent belief in Christ as the solution to the world's ills, Shrike makes a relentless mockery of the journalist's religious zeal.

Not surprisingly, Shrike's purpose in this apocalyptic novel is to serve as a "warning sign of impending disaster" (May 1972, 118). Moreover, he can be considered a literary representation of a "loosed Satan who precedes the final catastrophe" (114) of the novel, and, finally, he serves as a mocking observer when the protagonist's spiritual quest is unjustly terminated by the empirical chaos of the universe.

See also Apocalypse: Anti-Christian; Apocalypse: Traditional Judeo-Christian; Apocalypse: Traditional Primitive; *Miss Lonelyhearts*.

SIDDHARTHA

German author Herman Hesse visited India before World War I and wrote the novel *Siddhartha* (1922) based upon his observations of the culture. While the novel is not apocalyptic per se, it does deal with the cyclical concept of enlightenment and regeneration that is common to many of the world's Eastern religions.

The Siddhartha character is based loosely upon the life of the first Buddha: Gotama Buddha (c. 563–483 B.C.). As the protagonist of the novel, his personal growth is chronicled from his early impetuosity to the eventual fulfillment that he finds in his later years. His quest for personal growth begins as he leaves the comfortable environment of his home and the dictates of his father's Brahmin beliefs, and sets out on his own in search of Nirvana: the attainment of eternal peace.

During his life's journey, Siddhartha goes through several phases. With the completion of each phase, the protagonist learns valuable lessons regarding the contradictions inherent to the human condition, particularly those related to finding a balance between joy and sadness, confidence and fear, life and death. He pursues his goal first by attempting to live an ascetic life. He learns, however, that deprivation, silence, and fasting fail to bring him the enlightenment he seeks. Next, he attempts to find fulfillment by indulging in the pleasures of the flesh. Once again he learns that wealth, excess in food and drink, and even the companionship of an enthusiastic courtesan fail to bring him the peace that he seeks.

After he has become determined to abandon his quest, he travels to a quiet river, and in the serenity of that moment he receives the enlightenment he had fervently sought in the past. What he learns is to be still, to be quiet, and to listen. By doing so, he finds that even though humans are often separate from one another, they can still find love, security, and peace within their own hearts. This realization then becomes the focus of his life, and by the end of the novel, Siddhartha finally accepts life's complexities and contradictions as merely parts of the whole, enabling him ultimately to attain wisdom and his long-desired state of spiritual bliss.

See also Apocalypse: Buddhist; God; Hesse, Hermann; Myth.

SILKO, LESLIE MARMON

Leslie Marmon Silko (1948–), the renowned Native American poet and novelist from Albuquerque, New Mexico, grew up in the Laguna Pueblo; her experiences there provided her with the folklore, myths, and rituals necessary to detail the apocalyptic conditions suffered by various dispossessed peoples within the modern world. Silko's formal education began with her attendance at Bureau of Indian Affairs schools, and led to her graduation with honors from the University of New Mexico in 1969, where she received her Bachelor of Arts degree.

Soon after graduation, Silko began to work on her writing in earnest with the publication of several short stories, followed by a collection of poems under the title *Laguna Woman*. With this and subsequent works, Silko has established herself as a reputable voice of the Native American people. In her writings she continually demonstrates her commitment to helping a dispossessed culture find its clear narrative voice within the cacophonous body of Anglo-American literature.

One of her earliest successes in this area came when her book, *Ceremony* (1977), became known as the first novel to be published by a Native American female writer. This story, which combines a nonchronological narrative form with that of Native American mythology, recounts the devastating experiences of Tayo. A half-breed who returns as a disenfranchised World War II veteran, Tayo is eventually restored to spiritual wholeness by the strength and support of his native culture.

Her next collection, entitled *Storyteller* (1981), continues to celebrate her ethnicity. It features a combination of poetry, photography, fiction, and tribal stories that have been perpetuated by the Native American oral tradition. Her subsequent work also reflects her tendency toward stylistic experimentation. Presented in its original epistolary form, *The Delicacy and Strength of Lace: Letters between Leslie Marmon Silko and James A. Wright* (1986) has done much to reveal her personal observations of the complexities of human nature. Yet her most recent and most mature work, a powerful apocalyptic novel entitled *Almanac of the Dead* (1991), postulates the cataclysmic outcome of an environmental and cultural revolution in which Native Americans, who are sensitive to the needs and preservation of nature, tire of the destructive practices of the predominant white culture, and pledge to restore the environment—at any cost—to its pristine and ultimately sacred condition.

See also *Almanac of the Dead;* Apocalypse: Traditional Primitive; Apocalypticism; *Kill Hole.*

SIMON

Simon is the shy and somewhat eccentric young man who reflects the spiritual aspects of human nature in William Golding's apocalyptic novel, *Lord of the Flies.* According to an insightful essay by literary critic Donald R. Spangler (included in the Casebook Edition of Golding's novel), Simon's function within the work is that of a Christ-figure who is ultimately sacrificed at the hands of evil forces for his attempt to provide peace and salvation for a group of schoolboys who have been abandoned on a deserted tropical island (Golding 211).

In this apocalyptic parable, other characters in addition to Simon maintain a symbolic significance through which the author develops his intricate plot and his theme of human depravity. For example, among the major characters within the work are Ralph, the protagonist and pragmatic voice of order and reason, and Piggy, Ralph's intuitive barometer and intellectual guide. Serving as their foils within the novel are the major antagonist, Jack Merridew—the corrupt former choirboy whose instinctive brutality turns the island paradise into an infernal wasteland—and his sadistic minion, Roger, who supports Jack, not only because he believes that it's necessary to kill in order to survive, but mostly because he enjoys watching the suffering and death of both animal and human life. The only thing missing in this assembly, therefore, is the spiritual aspect of human nature, which is obviously expressed through the thoughts and actions of the benign and beloved sacrificial character, Simon.

In support of this view, Spangler and other scholars refer to the text and note Golding's diction as the source of such critical speculation. For example, the reader's introduction to Simon as an unusual character comes early in the novel when the as yet nameless choirboy "flop[s] on his face in the sand," presumably from the heat of the tropical setting. Obviously accustomed to such a scene, however, one of his cynical schoolmates remarks in disgust that the fallen choirboy is "always throwing a faint." Eventually, this boy is identified as Simon (17–18).

In addition to these superficial allusions, Simon is more specifically described by the author as "a skinny, vivid little boy, with a glance coming up from under a hut of straight hair that hung down, black and coarse" (20). This depiction, not unlike the illuminated renditions of Christ as they appear on liturgical materials, illustrates Golding's intention to portray Simon as a Christ-figure. In spite of his powerful literary implication, Simon is little more than a benign simpleton to the others on the island during the early parts of the novel. On occasion, however, the reader is given hints of his uniqueness. For instance, he is not frightened, even at night, by the mysterious foliage that covers the inner portion of the island. He is fascinated by the fragrant and mystical candlelike flowers and reverent toward the serene sanctuary provided by the jungle's dark regions.

However, while the others feel that his peculiar observations and his frequent disappearances are strangely uncommon, they never fail to notice that his simplest actions reveal his essential spirit of generosity. For example, when the other older children are busy building huts, maintaining signal fires, or preparing for the hunt, Simon alone shows his Christlike concern for the little ones on the island by climbing the tall trees and throwing down the ripest fruits to the young children who need his help. Further, he provides moral support for his older peers whenever it is needed, and he is supportive of Ralph when he attempts to resolve the mystery of the "beast" that is posing a threat to their lives. Simon's role is illustrated when Ralph embarks on a journey to the more remote regions of the coral reef and expresses his fears that he will get lost in the process. In response to Ralph's fears, Simon knowingly assures his friend by telling him, "You'll get back all right." Ralph dismisses his friend's optimism by telling him that he is "batty," but Simon reiterates his promise by saying, "No, I'm not. I just *think you'll get back all right*" (103). Not surprisingly, Simon's prediction proves correct, and Ralph returns safely.

While these illustrations are sufficient in themselves to draw the Simon-Christ parallel within the novel, Spangler's critical observation takes things one step further by drawing allusions to Simon's reenactment of Christ's travails at Gethsemane and Golgotha. For example, the critic notes that when Simon ascends the mountain in order to identify the source of the others' fears, his

> kneeling and sweating accord directly with the story of Gethsemane; moreover, Golding's description reinforces those associations by half raising popular pictorial renderings of the person of Jesus and of the Agony in the Garden: Simon kneeling in a[n] "arrow of sun," with "head tilted slightly up," sweat running from his "long coarse hair" (213).

Further, in Spangler's reference to Simon as Christ on Golgotha, the critic notes how "Simon falls, in accord with gospel accounts of Jesus' ascent to the cross, and losing consciousness, regains it only after shedding blood, the nosebleed of the boy analogous to the lance-wounding of Jesus in the details of the crucifixion" (213). In spite of this convincing evidence, the decisive scene in which Simon is portrayed as a Christ-figure in the novel occurs on the night of the ritual hunt.

After his ascent to the mountaintop, where he learns the truth of the "beast" that threatens the children, Simon is eager to return to them with the proverbial "good news" that they can be saved from their fears if only they will listen to what he has to tell them. But just as the teeming crowds of Christ's time ignored his message because they had been so caught up in providing a ritual sacrifice, Simon falls victim to a similar fate. In a weakened condition from his ordeal on the mountain and his subsequent injuries related to his falls, he crawls toward the throng engrossed in its primitive hunting ritual unaware that their bloodlust has blinded them to his identity. Just as the Jews failed to realize, at the time of the crucifixion, that Christ had come to give them a message of salvation, so too do the youthful savages mistake Simon for the "beast" from the darkness. Consequently, they attack him in a blind, moblike rage, unaware, at least for the moment, that they have all participated in the murder of the one person who had risked his own life in order to deliver them a message that would save them from the ignorance and fear that, according to Golding, is intrinsic to the human condition.

See also Apocalypse: Traditional Judeo-Christian; Apocalypse: Traditional Primitive; *Lord of the Flies;* Merridew, Jack; Piggy; Ralph; Satan.

SIMPSON, HOMER

The retired bookkeeper Homer Simpson appears in Nathanael West's apocalyptic novel, *The Day of the Locust* (1939). As a hopeful émigré to Hollywood during its golden era of the 1920s and 1930s, Homer forms an ill-fated relationship with a neighboring starlet, Faye Greener. Although Homer feels that he is in love with this egotistical blonde bombshell, she has no use for him until he can get her out of a financial bind by offering his home as a temporary place for her to stay. Thus begins their "business arrangement" in which she lives with Homer in an unspoken agreement for sexual favors.

The more he does to help Faye, however, the more cruelty and disrespect she shows him. As the novel progresses, so do the humiliating events that inevitably emasculate Simpson and ultimately drive him to the brink of madness. Because he becomes increasingly intolerant of her drunken and lascivious antics with other men, Faye deserts Homer. This ultimate rejection, in spite of his overt generosity, causes him to wander the crowded streets on the evening of an anticipated movie premier.

In his deranged state of mind, Homer's maddened musings are interrupted by the cruel pranks of a spoiled and malicious neighbor boy. After Homer responds to the taunting and the boy attempts to run, the child unexpectedly trips and falls. His fall provides Homer with the opportunity to unleash his repressed desperation and rage by stomping the boy to death.

At this point, Homer himself becomes the *pharmakos*—the animal offering of Greek tragedy—that must be sacrificed for the redemption of a hopeless society. Thus, after killing the boy, Homer is promptly targeted by the enraged mob, raised above the crowd and carried through the streets like a beacon of wrath, and is ultimately trampled to death by the atavistic hoard of disillusioned idealists who, like Homer himself, have been cheated of their Hollywood dreams.

See also Apocalypse: Anti-Christian; Babylon; *The Day of the Locust;* Greener, Faye; Grotesque; Hackett, Tod.

SINNERS IN THE HANDS OF AN ANGRY GOD

This classic "fire and brimstone" sermon was delivered in 1741 by Jonathan Edwards, a zealous eighteenth-century theologian who is considered by some literary scholars to be "the greatest artist of the apocalypse in America" (Lewicki 14). While many might argue that this work is not literature in its purest sense, most critics agree that such apocalyptic "narratives, sermons, and diaries" (14), written both by and for the Puritan colonists, are as important to early American literature as are the myths, folklore, songs, and other forms of oral tradition in understanding the spiritual beliefs of primitive societies. Therefore, Edwards's powerful sermon, which relies heavily on references to such biblical prophesies as Deuteronomy 32:35, Isaiah 59:18 and 66:15, and Revelation 19:15, reflects apocalypticism in its truest sense. It was intended to strike fear in the hearts of the unconverted members of his congregation, as well as to renew the spiritual commitment of Christians whose flagging faith had become increasingly evident in their daily lives.

The impact of this sermon, delivered in Northampton, Connecticut, on July 8, 1741, was so staggering that contemporaries of Edwards recorded their recollections of the sobbing and distressed breathing of the congregation, so great that it caused the speaker to urge silence in order for the remainder of the sermon to be heard (*Norton Anthology* 245). The essence of this forceful admonition focused on the following words from the book of Deuteronomy: "To me belongeth vengeance, and recompense; their foot shall slide in due time: for the day of their calamity is at hand, and the things that shall come upon them make haste" (245). By using this scriptural reference, Edwards intended to frighten his audience out of its complacency by assuring them that God's wrath was awesome, justified, and imminent.

The specifics of the sermon itself reflect Edwards's understanding of effective literary techniques such as the use of simile, metaphor, and symbolism. For example, he likens sinners' spiritual apathy to the precarious nature of standing upon the slippery cliffs of a mountain. Further, he describes Satan and his demonic minions as "greedy, hungry lions" (248) who are waiting for their "prey" to fall into their eager grasp. More importantly, he vividly portrays hell as a "fiery oven, or a furnace of fire and brimstone" (248) that will voraciously consume unregenerate souls for eternity unless the hearers of his sermon repent of their wicked ways and ask Jesus Christ to save them from such an infernal fate. The crux of his sermon, however, lies in the central metaphor that humans, by their very nature, are sinful creatures whose souls are precariously poised over the pit of hell. And while they have thus far been spared by the grace of God, who holds them above the abyss in his mighty hands, they should be aware that their "wickedness" makes them "as heavy as lead," pressuring downward "towards hell" (251). Further, Edwards warns that at any moment, "once the day of mercy is past," God will remove his supportive hands, the sinners will experience the full force of God's fury, and that even their "most lamentable and dolorous cries and shrieks will be in vain [since they will be] wholly lost and thrown away of God as to any regard to [their] welfare" (255).

Apparently, the conclusion of his sermon, wherein Edwards informs his congregation of their "extraordinary opportunity" to enter the door that Christ has mercifully opened to them (257), caused many to repent on that day, sending them "flocking to [Christ], and pressing into the kingdom of God" (257). Thus, this sermon, *Sinners in the Hands of an Angry God,* became a paradigm for evangelical messages among countless denominations to be delivered from clerical pulpits for centuries to come. Ultimately, the sermon, when viewed as a work of literature, contains the figurative language, the universality of theme, and a reflection of the human experience that is common to all apocalyptic literature as well as to the collective body of art (Lewicki 1984).

See also Apocalypse: Traditional Judeo-Christian; Apocalyptic Literature; Daniel, Book of; *The Day of Doom;* Edwards, Jonathan; Isaiah, Book of; Revelation, Book of.

SLAUGHTERHOUSE-FIVE; OR THE CHILDREN'S CRUSADE: A DUTY-DANCE WITH DEATH

This satirical novel, written by Kurt Vonnegut, Jr. (1969), deals with apocalyptic themes in the form of the science fiction genre. One of the more compelling facts about this novel is that it is based upon the author's historical observations and personal experiences as a prisoner of war during the Allied firebombing of Dresden, Germany, in 1945.

The novel is set during World War II. The protagonist, an optometrist named Billy Pilgrim, returns from duty to Illium, New York. While he is preparing for his daughter's wedding, Billy becomes "unstuck in time" as a result of his being kidnapped by aliens from a planet named Tralfamadore. In this process, Billy travels back and forth between the past and the future, spreading the news that is revealed to him by the omniscient Tralfamadorians. The word itself is apocalyptic in that it predicts the inevitable death of the universe. Armed with this terrible truth, Billy is doomed to be the reluctant prophet who resides in the Tralfamadorian fourth dimension, thereby causing him to live in an eternal present, forced to continually relive his horrible wartime experiences. In the end, he survives both this terrible knowledge and his fate by accepting the fatalism espoused in the Tralfamadorian philosophy. Regardless of the horror of the past, present, or future, all one can hope to do to keep from going mad is to resign oneself by saying, "So it goes."

See also Apocalypse: Secular; Apocalypticism; *Cat's Cradle;* Pilgrim, Billy; Science Fiction.

SLOTHROP, LIEUTENANT TYRONE

Lieutenant Slothrop is the paranoid protagonist of Thomas Pynchon's modern masterpiece, *Gravity's Rainbow* (1973). At the outset of the novel, Slothrop is a young army lieutenant who is stationed in Europe to work with the Allied Intelligence unit. This unit's purpose is to determine the origins and destinations of the Nazi's V-2 rocket attacks at a time near the end of World War II. While he pursues his work in earnest, he is initially unaware that he is the subject of a complex conspiracy that links him with Nazi rocket strikes.

He begins to suspect such a link as a result of an uncanny coincidence. Slothrop's erections seem to occur at the same geographic locations throughout London on which the Nazi bombs are dropped, usually four and a half days following each of his priapic episodes. As a result of this coincidence, Slothrop deserts the army in search of information connecting him with these bombings and, more importantly, in search of meaning for his own unfulfilling life. In his search, he learns about a possible connection with the bomb: apparently, as a child, Slothrop had been the subject of some experiments conducted by a Harvard professor who eventually went to work building bombs for the Nazis. His search for individual meaning, however, is for naught. In an attempt to make human connections, he finds only meaningless sex rather than the love he so greatly craves. Further, in his attempt to escape the entanglements of the political, industrial, and technological forces that threaten his life, he unwittingly enters a decadent underworld known as "the Zone." Instead, what he finds is merely a different type of complicity in which dope dealers and extortioners threaten to undermine the fabric of society just as the bureaucracies from which he has fearfully fled. Ultimately, as a result of separating himself from the systems "that both victimized him and provided him with a context and a history," Slothrop loses both his freedom and his identity as he "is gradually reduced to his final emblem: the Fool in the Tarot deck, the only card without a number, lacking a place in the systems of the world" (Mendelson 1986, 19).

See also Allegory; Apocalypse: Secular; Apocalyptic Literature; Archetype; Entropy; *Gravity's Rainbow;* Myth; Science Fiction; Symbol.

SMITH, FATHER RINALDO

Father Smith is the elderly, alcoholic, and somewhat addled priest, confessor, mentor, and friend to Walker Percy's protagonist, psychiatrist Dr. Tom More, in two apocalyptic novels: *Love in the Ruins: The Adventures of a Bad Catholic at a Time Near the End of the World* (1971) and *The Thanatos Syndrome* (1987). In *Love in the Ruins*, Father Smith supplements his paltry earnings as a cleric by serving as a watchman whose job it is to maintain a lonely vigil in a watchtower for the department of forestry. His vocation has the same duality of the novel itself: (1) He literally watches in an attempt to suppress the fires that are periodically set by lunatics or frustrated societal rebels, and (2) he figuratively watches out for and warns his world-weary flock while serving as a seer or a reluctant prophet who, in his solitude, laments the spiritual ills of the modern world as it perches precariously on the verge of inevitable doom.

In many ways, his sensitivity to an imminent cataclysm is not unlike that of Dr. Tom More's. But Father Smith, unlike his friend More, the novel's messianic madman, remains silent in his watchtower in order to receive God's messages that he prays will save his pitiable flock. In addition to waiting for spiritual messages, Smith is also a conveyor of earthly information as an amateur ham radio operator. These two roles collide in a disturbing display of chaos as he becomes eerily silent while delivering a sermon during his performance of a Roman Catholic Mass. While members of the congregation wait uncomfortably in their seats, they are even more deeply concerned when Father Smith announces that his message, delivered via a divine signal, has been interrupted by a demonic jamming of the system or frequency through which God usually delivers His word.

Although his public breakdown is viewed by the congregation as either a sign of drunkenness or senile dementia, his revelation is actually a precise reflection of the chaotic influences and demonic forces that have infiltrated and have already begun to destroy the church and consume society. He can no longer clearly hear God's words because they have either been drowned out or have become scrambled by diabolical effusions of such secular con-men as the duplicitous Art Immelmann, who ultimately succeeds in tempting the protagonist and thereby precipitating the apocalypse that the unrepentant Dr. More has long feared.

At the close of the novel, and particularly when the world does not end, contrary to Dr. More's fears, the psychiatrist seeks closure to his frightening vigil, and so returns to the church in an effort to find his spiritual and moral way home. He attempts to follow up on Father Smith's suggestion that he confess his sins, but during the course of this exercise, the reluctant penitent acknowledges his sinful activities only to find himself unable to feel genuinely sorry for having committed them. Only temporarily daunted by this predictable impasse, Father Smith's wisdom surfaces when he recommends that Tom begin his return to faith in slow but important increments, such as becoming a more dedicated physician and more loving family man. Tom readily accepts the compassionate secular suggestion as something of a compromise for a backslidden believer who must learn to live righteously amidst the decadence of the modern world. In fact, his first step toward spiritual recovery and his reconciliation with God comes with his surprising demonstration of ancient scriptural penitence: he willingly dons a sackcloth garment while proudly dusting his hair with ashes.

Although his presence is greeted with a curious disdain from his doubtful Presbyterian wife, both eventually are pleased with the results of Tom's gradual spiritual regeneration. Clearly, for Tom, Father Smith's advice is constructive in that it has provided a way for a lapsed Catholic to find inner peace through faith, family, and friends. And while this advice may be less stringent than devout followers would expect, it is appropriate in that it enables More's sinner-saint to become spiritually healed by Father Smith's genuine example of God's unconditional love.

In *The Thanatos Syndrome,* Percy's sequel to *Love in the Ruins,* Father Smith is once again instrumental in assisting his friend, Dr. Tom More. During the time that has passed between the two novels, the author reveals that Tom More has managed to escape the problems of the modern world by getting himself arrested for peddling illegal drugs to road-weary truck drivers. For the two years in which he enjoys his correctional solitude and muses over the wisdom of Father Smith's words, his personality reflects a gradual yet remarkable calm that differs greatly from his earlier cataclysmic paranoia. It is no surprise, however, that just two weeks after his release from prison, the protagonist's renewed commitment to both his wife and his work lead him, once again, to make mental connections between the mysterious behaviors demonstrated by both his patients and his wife.

What disturbs him most about his recent observations is that the affected individuals share the following puzzling characteristics: (1) their language has been reduced to terse phrases or monosyllables; (2) their previous psychological disorders have diminished noticeably and have been replaced by a complacent loss of self; (3) they each demonstrate a savant's uncanny ability for recall and will gladly provide answers to complex out-of-context questions without concern for the implications of such ability; but most notably, (4) the affected individuals have become less inhibited and frequently initiate inappropriately assertive sexual behaviors that mimic the random couplings commonly observed among animals.

These specific findings remind the psychiatrist of the angelism-bestialism syndrome he diagnosed with his invention in *Love in the Ruins*. Fearing a resurgence of the syndrome initiated by high levels of sodium radiation, Dr. More enlists the help of epidemiologist Dr. Lucy Lipscomb, and thereby uncovers an insidious plot known as Project Blue Boy. In this secret pilot project, zealous researchers attempt to control the drug problem, rampant crime, and the spread of AIDS by surreptitiously tainting the area's water supply with excessive doses of sodium ions. While such a project might have originally been undertaken for altruistic purposes, such as the betterment of society, More makes additional discoveries, such as uncontrolled genocide and pedofilia, which cause him to renew his commitment against those who would perpetuate the spiritual ills of the world.

In an effort to develop a strategy and a holistic perspective about his findings, he again enlists the help of Father Rinaldo Smith. This time, however, he finds the old man withering away in a nearly catatonic state in which he has refused to sleep, eat, or speak. For a time, Tom forgets his own troubles and reaches out to help Father Smith. What he learns, paradoxically, is that Father Smith can speak, but because he finds modern man's use of words increasingly devoid of meaning, he chooses to be mute. The cleric is so tormented by the plots that threaten to destroy the moral fabric of society that he becomes literally speechless. However, when Tom genuinely presents the sordid details of his findings at the Belle Ame Academy, where children are being secretly drugged and subjected to repeated sexual exploitation, Father Smith revives somewhat, and in a seemingly unrelated request, he asks More to hear the Father's confession.

The content of this confession is a disturbing one. In this long passage, the reverend recounts images from his boyhood and draws associations with the Nazi's methods of exterminating undesirable factions in order to produce a pure race. These recollections, while specifically related to Father Smith's private memory, present a horrifying parallel to the involuntary chemical manipulation of the local community. In fact, during this confession, Smith and More wonder for a moment whether they too, like the idealistic followers of Hitler, might have been willing to re-create society if their efforts could result in its dramatic improvement. Near the close of the interview, however, he confides his suspicion of any group of idealists such as doctors, priests, or scientists who initiate such well intended social experiments. Thus, with both men feeling convicted of their own idealistic urges, Smith ultimately warns Tom to remember that "tenderness is the first disguise of the murderer" (Ciuba 1991, 275).

Armed with this information, More carefully charts his course for the cessation of all unethical activities that permeate the Belle Ame Academy. With the assistance of several other minor characters, and inspired by Father Smith's muddled but prophetic message, Tom succeeds in closing the facility. In the end, each of the perpetrators is sentenced to perform their respective professional talents in safe and appropriate settings. Fortunately, this also includes justice for Father Smith, who is finally given the opportunity to become whole as a result of More's efforts. Although he had previously been maddened by the Qualitarian centers that specialized in euthanizing the aged, the handicapped, and the infirm, both his sanity and his vocation are restored as a result of his reclamation of the community's Hospice. In the Hospice, where he treats mostly terminally ill AIDS patients, he is happy because he now feels free to be completely honest with his patients, and unlike the rest of the sick society in which they live, his patients are appreciatively honest with him. Thus, in this environment in which "he simply t[ells] the truth to his . . . patients, stay[s] with them, and fe[els] at home with them, only mentioning religion if asked. . . . Father Smith discover[s] the renewal of [the force that opposes Thanatos, or death-in-life]: agape" (276). Therefore, the central moral of the novel, the balm for Father Smith's madness, and the ultimate cure for Dr. More's Thanatos Syndrome is revealed to be difficult but not impossible: it is simply the complete expression of unconditional Christian love (276).

See also Apocalypse: Secular; Apocalypse: Traditional Judeo-Christian; Apocalyptic Literature; *Faust;* Immelmann, Art; *Love in the Ruins: The Adventures of a Bad Catholic at a Time Near the End of the World;* Mephistophiles; More, Sir Thomas; Thanatos; *The Thanatos Syndrome.*

SPENSER, EDMUND

This English Elizabethan poet (c. 1552–1599) is best known for his epic allegorical poem, *The Faerie Queene.* For a time, Spenser was considered to be the greatest living poet since Chaucer, who had died nearly two hundred years earlier. Although he was born in London to an impoverished family, his classical education was arranged and paid for by a wealthy patron named Robert Nowell. According to official records, Spenser first attended the Merchant Taylors' School in London, but then transferred to Pembroke College in Cambridge, where he received both his bachelor's and master's degrees, respectively, in 1573 and 1576.

By 1579, Spenser had anonymously published his first suite of twelve pastoral poems, one for each month of the year, entitled *The Shepheardes Calender.* During that time, he had also continued to foster his favorable relationship with a former schoolmate named Gabriel Harvey, who had good friends in high places. As a result, Spenser soon became employed by the Earl of Leicester, where he met and befriended the Earl's nephew, fellow poet Sir Philip Sydney. This fortuitous association opened the door to a world of literati and artists with whom he shared a love of the arts, and to specific opportunities for future publication.

After unknown events intervened to strain his relationship with Leicester, in 1580, Spenser sailed to Dublin and took a job as the secretary to Arthur, Lord Grey of Wilton, a high-ranking official in the Irish government. Under Lord

Sir Edmund Spenser

Grey's brief rule, Spenser was awarded several impressive positions and was provided with a property in excess of 3,000 acres. Although Grey eventually returned to England, Spenser felt settled in Ireland after having been given the property of Kilcolman Castle, located between Cork and Limerick.

While attending to his duties in Ireland, Spenser continued working on his poems, particularly on a work he had begun while he was working in the Leicester House. In the midst of his efforts, he was visited by an old acquaintance, Sir Walter Raleigh, who read some of the work and encouraged Spenser to return to London in order to publish the completed books of *The Faerie Queene.* Over the next several years, Spenser published other poems, including *Amoretti* and *Epithalamion,* which were published jointly in 1595 in honor of his marriage to Elizabeth Boyle. In the following year, Spenser also published works entitled *Four Hymns, Daphnaida,* and *Prothalamion* while continuing his work on subsequent editions of *The Faerie Queene.*

After these successes, however, both his personal and professional fortunes took a turn for the worse during a violent Irish uprising in 1598. During this rebellion his Castle at Kilcolman was burned, and according to some accounts Spenser also lost one of his children in the conflagration. Spenser's duties required him to return to England with a report of the situation. Although the English privy council planned to send him back to Ireland with an even higher office than he had previously held, Edmund Spencer died in 1599 and was buried in Westminster Abbey.

See also Allegory; Apocalypse: Traditional Judeo-Christian; Arthur, King; *The Faerie Queene;* Gloriana; Revelation, Book of; Una.

SUTPEN, THOMAS

Thomas Sutpen is the demonic antagonist in William Faulkner's apocalyptic novel, *Absalom, Absalom!* (1936). Tormented by the indignities of an impoverished childhood in the West Virginian mountains, he is driven to create a dynasty for himself and his progeny in the highest Southern aristocratic tradition. Following his obsessive lifelong plan, or "grand design," he arrives in Faulkner's Yoknapatawpha County in 1833, accompanied by a wild band of black Haitians, wagon loads of tools, and a reluctant French architect, prepared to forge his one-hundred acre plantation, as well as his future, from the improbable terrain of a Mississippi swamp. Thus, "Sutpen's Hundred" is born.

The dream of "Sutpen's Hundred," however, began with a childhood humiliation in which he was turned away from a rich man's home. From that moment, Thomas Sutpen became obsessed with re-creating his life through the powers of indomitable will and brute force. His strategic plan involves gaining a substantial land dowry by marrying the daughter of a Caribbean planter. He soon learns that the child they bear carries black blood, a reality that runs counter to his design. This revelation also convinces him that his marriage contract has been violated by deceit, and he leaves the wife and child, feeling justified in building his future home on her father's property.

Arriving in Jefferson, Mississippi, he wastes no time consorting with the local aristocracy and finding a suitable wife, Ellen Coldfield, with whom he promptly has two more children: Judith and Henry. Through the years of their loveless, utilitarian marriage, Ellen learns the truth about her husband's ruthlessness, yet she keeps up appearances until her death.

Meanwhile, the children have grown. Henry, the son whose temperament is so contrary to his fiery father's, attends the university in Oxford, Mississippi, where he befriends a rich planter's grandson, Charles Bon. This becomes a fatal friendship: it happens that Charles is the same son that Thomas had abandoned at the end of his first marriage. Unaware of this fact, Henry introduces Charles to his sister, Judith, and eventually the two become engaged. The engagement, however, is suddenly interrupted by the Civil War. Charles and Henry serve together, while Thomas Sutpen serves as a confederate colonel.

During the four-year postponement of their marriage, Thomas's daughter Judith has waited for her lover's return. As she eagerly works on her wedding dress for his imminent arrival, her dreams are dashed by the announcement that Charles Bon has been killed by Henry. It becomes apparent that Thomas has told Henry that Judith was about to marry her racially mixed half-brother, and Henry is charged with eliminating the problem that would obviously interfere with the senior Sutpen's grand design.

Thomas's monomania continues over the years. His diabolical determination to fulfill his plan next results in an indecent proposal to Rosa, his sister-in-law, who had long given up her own dreams to care for her spinster niece, Judith. Desperate to continue his family line, Sutpen proposes that he and Rosa mate in the hope that this union will produce a son. This reckless disregard for morality, custom, and decency confirms Rosa's view that Sutpen is indeed a demon. Shaken by this knowledge, Rosa returns to her father's ruined home and spends the rest of her life contemplating the evil nature of Thomas Sutpen.

The legend of Sutpen is continued as Miss Rosa, before her death, insists on relating the story to Quentin Compson, a Harvard student and descendent of a distinguished family in the town. In this tale, Rosa recalls the remaining details of Thomas Sutpen's life, which include the grisly details of his death. Apparently, even at the age of sixty-five, Sutpen is driven to complete his design by impregnating Milly Jones, the fifteen-year-old daughter of his old acquaintance, Wash Jones. Yet another insult to Sutpen is that the child is a girl; however, this misfortune is ultimately overshadowed by Wash Jones's desire for retribution, which prompts him to kill Sutpen in a rage.

Nevertheless, even after his death, Sutpen's evil legacy continues, and this story is told by Quentin Compson to his Harvard roommate, Shreve McCannon, in an effort to explain the complexities of living in the South. The remaining details include the fact that Henry, disconsolate over killing his friend, Charles Bon, returns to the ruined Sutpen plantation to await his own death. Ultimately, this comes to pass as a distraught relative sets fire to the ruined plantation, killing both herself and Henry. In the end, the only survivor of the tainted Sutpen line is an idiot black son, the child of Charles Bon and his black wife, who was never found after the destruction of "Sutpen's Hundred."

Shortly after revealing the entire lurid saga, Rosa Coldfield dies. However, her portrait of the demonic Thomas Sutpen, a man whose dreams would inevitably destroy the lives of all those he touched, serves as a legacy for those who wish to recount the egoism, decadence, disillusionment, and, finally, the destruction of the old American South.

See also *Absalom, Absalom!*; Apocalypse: Traditional Judeo-Christian; Coldfield, Rosa; Compson, Quentin.

SYMBOL

By definition, a symbol is something that represents itself, as well as a concept, idea, person, or object other than itself. The use of symbols is apparently synonymous with humanity itself, and evidence of this attempt to attach internal order to the external world is represented in artifacts existing since the Neolithic age. Because the use of symbols as a multifarious method of communication is best illustrated through literature, the following discussion will concentrate primarily on that aspect. Perhaps one of the most qualified scholars to discuss the use of symbols within literature is the renowned literary critic, Northrop Frye, who suggests that whenever individuals read anything, they find their minds moving in two directions at once. "One direction is outward or centrifugal" in which the mind moves outside the written word toward outward meanings or "conventional associations." The other direction, however, "is inward or centripetal" in which readers "try to develop from the words a sense of the larger verbal pattern they make" (Frye 1971, 73).

In addition, although symbols can be used within the development of imagery, myth, and allegory, they are distinctly different. Unlike myth and allegory in particular, symbols generally have more than one meaning, a characteristic that makes them invaluable to authors who use them to embed multiple levels of meaning within a text. For example, one of the most recognizable forms of symbolism is numbers. One reason for the popularity of this form is its familiarity within one of the most widely read works of literature in history: the Bible. Throughout both the Old and the New Testaments, numbers have had a significant connotative impact on the readers in that they not only reveal historic or prophetic detail, but they also carry additional meanings in regard to divine revelation. For example, within the Book of Revelation alone, numbers abound to enable readers to expand their understanding of the message. The numbers four, six, seven, and ten, in particular, reveal much about the underlying theme within the book. First, the number four is "symbolic of the earth, of terrestrial space, of the human situation, of the external, natural limits of the 'minimum' awareness of totality, and finally of rational organization" (Cirlot 1972, 232). Therefore, when the "Four Horsemen of the Apocalypse"—conquest, slaughter, famine, and death— appear, they suggest tangible plagues that will descend upon the earth preceding the day of final judgment. Similarly, the number six is "symbolic of ambivalence and equilibrium, six comprises the union of the two triangles (of fire and water) and hence signifies the human soul" or the essence of man (233). Thus, the "repetition of the number stresses its quantitative power

[and] detracts from its spiritual dignity" (235). Therefore, the number 666, otherwise known as the sign of the Antichrist, or the mark of the "Beast," emphasizes the symbolic impact of the personification of evil that will appear on the earth, in human form, in order to deceive weak believers and damn the unrighteous during the end times.

In contrast to these terrestrial numbers, however, are the symbolic numbers of seven and ten. Specifically, seven is "symbolic of perfect order, a complete period or cycle. It comprises the union of the ternary and the quaternary, and hence is endowed with exceptional value" (233). Given this significance, therefore, it is understandable that the number seven is a predominant symbol throughout the Book of Revelation. For example, within the last book of the New Testament, the prophet makes mention of this specific numerical symbol: (1) in the letters to the seven churches of Asia, (2) in the seven sealed books along with their corresponding earthly events, (3) in the judgments heralded by the seven trumpets, and (4) in the seven vials containing the wrath of God that will be poured upon the last unfortunate inhabitants of the world prior to the creation of a new heaven and a new earth.

In a similar vein, the number ten represents "the return to unity" and is "symbolic . . . of spiritual achievement" as well as "the totality of the universe—both metaphysical and material—since it raises all things to unity." Moreover, "from ancient oriental thought through the Pythagorean school and right up to St. Jerome, it was known as the number of perfection" (234). Ten features prominently in the thousand-year millennial concept, which exists at the core of the extant body of apocalyptic literature. Dante Alighieri, in particular, focused heavily on this numerical structure in the development of his magnum opus, *The Divine Comedy*. However, he, like most other authors, also relied upon a myriad of symbols that would lend additional significance to his literary work.

Clearly, the works of the medieval period are punctuated with the use of what have become known as religious symbols. Yet symbols in modern literature also provide important insights into the critical analysis of a particular work. For example, in William Butler Yeats's apocalyptic poem, "The Second Coming," he uses the symbol of the gyre or a spiral to illustrate the cyclic inversion of the human experience. This symbol paved the way for the use of other symbols that similarly reflect the feeling of alienation and chaos that pervades the body of modern literature. Another example exists in the stuffed effigies portrayed in T. S. Eliot's poem, *The Hollow Men*. In this work, although the figures clearly portray the spiritual decimation of modern man, they also cause insightful readers to grasp the subtle irony related to the author's inversion of ancient fertility rituals.

Perhaps one of the more notable examples of the use of symbols within a modern work is F. Scott Fitzgerald's novel, *The Great Gatsby:* a billboard containing a giant set of eyeglasses looms over the ash heaps or wasteland of human refuse. In this instance, not only do they stand for the services of the optometrist as advertised on the sign, but they also symbolize the myopic nature of a divinity that seems blind to the injustices inherent in modern society. In this way, Fitzgerald, like many authors before and after him, have learned to avail themselves of a universal understanding shared within the human spirit, and they continue to attempt to make meaning out of life through the use of the symbol as a vital ingredient of the dynamic narrative form.

See also Allegory; *Anatomy of Criticism: Four Essays;* Apocalyptic Literature; Archetype; *The Divine Comedy; The Hollow Men;* Jung, Carl Gustav; Myth; Revelation, Book of.

TARWATER, FRANCIS MARION

This fourteen-year-old orphan is poised at the heart of a spiritual battle between two principal characters in Flannery O'Connor's apocalyptic novel, *The Violent Bear It Away* (1955). Prior to the beginning of the novel, Tarwater's life is controlled by a series of willful actions by his Uncle Rayber, an agnostic schoolteacher bent on shaping the boy into his own mental image, and his great-uncle Mason, the fire-and-brimstone prophet who has raised the boy in the service of God to become a prophet in his own right. As a result of the divisive influence of the two characters, Tarwater is torn between their opposing philosophies. While he is eager to avoid the detached scholastic life of Rayber, he is equally reluctant to follow Mason's evangelical plans for his future. In short, as a fourteen-year-old boy on the verge of manhood, he wishes to be accountable for his own decisions, to act according to his own volition, and, ultimately, to find his own salvation in the pursuit of his individual destiny.

He gets the chance to become independent after Mason's death. The boy's first action is one that comes from a strange voice inside himself. This voice urges him to violate his great-uncle's wish for a Christian burial, with a cross-marked grave on hallowed ground, by setting fire to the house and entombing his dead uncle in flames while still seated, as he had died, at the kitchen table. As the title implies, it is this first act of violent, sacrilegious rebellion that marks the beginning of Tarwater's quest to find himself.

As he flees the fiery scene, the strange voice soon compels him toward the sin-filled city where Rayber, the agnostic schoolteacher, dwells. In his reunion with Rayber, Tarwater is stunned by the disturbing appearance of the schoolteacher's idiot son, Bishop. Before his death, the old man had been obsessed with baptizing Rayber's son and had charged Tarwater with this duty in the case of his demise. This admonition comes back to haunt him with Bishop's uncanny likeness to the dead prophet. However, he is determined to reject the old man's plan for his life. Tarwater tries desperately to avoid the young boy, Bishop. Nevertheless, Bishop's continual presence, as well as his inexplicable attraction toward water, lead Tarwater to an inevitable act of violence and will in which he unwittingly accepts his prophetic call. Tarwater baptizes the boy, and in a deliberate action of defiance and mercy, drowns the ignorant child in the process.

At this point, Tarwater, unaware that he has moved closer to his great-uncle's vision for his life, has now symbolically rejected the influence of Rayber, and, in doing so, sets out to find his own fate. Soon enough, however, Tarwater finds that his future holds the same violence with which he has tried to close the door on his past. After fleeing the scene of the baptism/drowning, Tarwater hitch-hikes out of the city, and, in the process, is picked up by a mysterious stranger, in a "lavender and cream car" dressed in a "lavender shirt . . . [and] a Panama hat" (May 1972, 438), who offers him a ride. Together, they drive toward the black forest where Tarwater ultimately embraces his fate. At this point it should be noted that Flannery O'Connor's works center around violence as a precursor to revelation, and such is the case in this novel. It is through a violent encounter with this driver, a homosexual who rapes him in the forest, that Tarwater's future becomes clear. Now, after having experienced a full awareness of the force of evil in the world, Tarwater feels compelled to go forth, as a prophet heeding the Lord's command, and "Go warn the children of God . . . of the terrible speed of justice" (339). This decision is confirmed when he returns to his great-uncle's home and finds out the truth about the old man's burial. Although Tarwater had attempted to reject his fate by burning the old man instead of burying him, he learns upon his return that a neighbor had taken the old man from the emblazoned house and had buried Mason properly. According to noted critic John R. May, the cross that marks the old man's grave "brings with it a confirming grace of realization that his [Tarwater's] efforts have been frustrated from the beginning[, and that t]he ultimate judgment is that man is most human when he is open to the rhythm of revelation" (137).

See also Apocalypse: Traditional Judeo-Christian; Grotesque; *The Violent Bear It Away.*

THE TEMPEST

William Shakespeare's final play (c. 1611) is a tragicomedy, dealing primarily with the themes of revenge and ultimately reconciliation, identifying it as an apocalyptic work in the truest sense. While the theme is certainly a weighty one, the story itself is simple. It begins on a remote island where Prospero, the deposed Duke of Milan and the protagonist of the play, has spent the past twelve years with his beautiful and innocent daughter, Miranda. The occasion for his arrival on this island was a nefarious plot that was engendered by his younger and more ambitious brother, Antonio, who was assisted by a rival named Alonso, the King of Naples.

Prior to the beginning of the action of the play, it seems that Prospero, who preferred the company of books to people, had allowed his younger brother to take over more than his share of the government of Milan. As a result of this inattention to duty, Antonio instigated a revolt that resulted in his sending Prospero and his infant daughter, Miranda, out to sea on a decayed vessel in the hope that they would perish and he could usurp Prospero's rule. In spite of Antonio's plot, however, one of Prospero's faithful counselors, Gonzalo, had secretly outfitted the frail vessel with sufficient provisions for survival, including valuable tomes from Prospero's library. This act of kindness enabled the two to live satisfactorily for twelve years on the island, where they had been washed ashore after their inevitable wreckage.

During those twelve years, Prospero delighted in raising his wonderful daughter and became even more deeply involved in studying his books, particularly those relating to magic. With this powerful knowledge, as well as the assistance of a mystical air-sprite named Ariel, Prospero developed a plan that would help him to avenge his loss and regain his rightful position in Milan. The plan ultimately culminated in Prospero's conjuring a great storm or tempest, during which his betraying brother Antonio, the duplicitous King of Naples Alonso, his altruistic son Ferdinand, and their crew would accidentally wash ashore on Prospero's island, and the matter would finally be settled face to face.

Everyone is recovered on the island according to the plan, with the exception of the pure-hearted son of the King of Naples, Ferdinand. Alonso is heartbroken at the possible loss of his son, unaware that the youth has washed ashore on another part of the island. At this point one of Shakespeare's most tenderly portrayed love stories ensues. Miranda, Prospero's ingenuous and virtuous daughter, who has never known a man other than her father, is immediately smitten by Ferdinand, just as he is immediately taken by her. Because of her innocence and lack of guile, she expresses her feelings candidly, which encourages Ferdinand to do the same. Their love blooms under the approving eye of her father, whose magic has rendered him invisible as he observes their promising courtship. Clearly, their favorable union foreshadows a reconciliation between the former Duke of Milan (Prospero) and his rival, the King of Naples (Alonso). In the meantime, Prospero's magic and Ariel's spiritual intervention cause the parties responsible for his exile to suffer mild torments, anxieties, inconveniences, a sense of loss, and, finally, a direct confrontation by their victim before all can be made right.

In the end—in spite of the serious injustices done to him—Prospero, the godlike protagonist, does not kill his enemies. Under a magical disguise of invisibility, he more justly leads the party, with Ariel's assistance, on a search for the lost Ferdinand. When at the end of their search Prospero finally reveals himself in their midst, and reports that Ferdinand is alive and well, he also demands that the guilty parties repent for their wrongs. Consequently, while his brother, Antonio, is shocked to find Prospero alive but is temperamentally disinclined to a genuine apology, Alonso, the King of Naples, has become so soft-hearted as a result of his son's loss and return that he restores Prospero's former nobility and gladly welcomes the symbolic and literal union of their houses through the marriage of Ferdinand and Miranda. Finally, having reconciled his feelings for his wayward brother and former rival, and having seen the happiness of his daughter, Miranda, Prospero releases Ariel from his binding spell, renounces magic forever, and presumably returns to Milan with his family and his respect intact. Therefore, as happens in most apocalyptic fiction, the guilty are punished, the righteous are rewarded, and the forces of justice and mercy ultimately prevail to mark the beginning of a new and better world.

See also Apocalypse: Traditional Judeo-Christian; Apocalypticism; Archetype; Ariel; Caliban; *King Lear;* Miranda; Myth; Prospero.

TERRA NOSTRA

Literally translated as "Our World," this novel is a magnum opus dealing with major apocalyptic themes written by the internationally acclaimed Mexican novelist, dramatist, literary critic, and diplomat, Carlos Fuentes, and published in 1975. This expansive, approximately eight-hundred-page epic is the culmination of Fuentes's diligent independent study of the world's finest authors, his observations as an international diplomat, and his concern for preserving the historical contributions leading to the complex national identity of Mexico. Like many modern Latin American writers, Fuentes's work is a fanciful fusion of history, theology, philosophy, art, myth, eroticism, and politics; i.e., it is a study of humanity on its most essential levels. In *Terra Nostra,* Fuentes attempts to translate the influence of these universal elements as they relate to the continual deaths and rebirths that seem destined to recur within the politics, religion, and culture of his native country and its people.

Because the multilayered meanings of *Terra Nostra* are as broadly drawn as is the history of the ancient world itself, it is perhaps best to examine the work in regard to its scope, its structure, and its style. The scope, in what is perhaps a futile attempt to plot it in linear terms, is set at a future time that ranges beyond the time acknowledged within the text of the story. Specifically, the inciting action of the tale begins at 4:00 A.M. on June 14, 1999, and it ends at midnight on the millennial date of January 1, 2000. Although only six months actually pass between the opening and closing scenes, the contents of this sweeping historical novel deal with the problems facing Spain during the time of its pervasive sixteenth-century Catholic rule. Although the sixteenth century, in general, is the point of the novel's pivotal perspective, the work specifically identifies other countries: France, Rome, and North America, and also "uses the events of 1492, 1521, and 1598 to symbolize the unification, centralization, and homogenization which ended a 700 year alliance of three cultures in Spain—the Christian, Jewish, and the Moorish" (Zamora 1989, 153).

In regard to the specific significance of each of these historical dates, 1492 represented several events of significance to the development of Spanish culture. First, it was the year in which the country's conquest of Granada established a formal Spanish society or *"civitas española."* During that same year, an edict was issued that resulted in the expulsion of Jews from Spain, which, according to literary critic Lois Parkinson Zamora, "deprived Spanish society of those members most able to move Spain into modernity." And finally, an event that is most familiar to European audiences was Columbus's landing on "territory that he [had initially] labeled Hispaniola" (153).

Similarly, the year 1521 marked an important time in Spanish history. It was the year in which Carlos V, the first Hapsburg in Spain, defeated a national uprising in Castille, "an event which signals for Fuentes the defeat of nascent democratic tendencies in Spain and a victory for medievalism . . . for the preservation of the ideal of a monolithic and centralized Holy Roman Empire" (154). Fuentes further notes the significance of 1521 as the year in which Cortes "conquered Tenochtitlan, the great capital of the Aztec empire in the New World," an event that ensured, the author believes, that "Hispanic America" would be consumed by the "totalitarian world of the Spanish Catholic monarchy" (154). Finally, according to Fuentes, the year 1598 is significant in the development of the novel because it marks the year of the death of Felipe II. The grave concern Fuentes has for Felipe's legacy is summarized by Zamora as follows:

> [Felipe] . . . leaves behind him the mechanisms to maintain the political structure of medieval empire and the mechanisms to impose religious and intellectual blinders on Spain and Spanish America. The expulsion of the Moslems from Spain in 1609, the Counter-Reformation and Inquisition by which Spain established itself as *defensor fides* [defender of the faith] and the reactionary center of Europe, are Felipe's legacy (154).

The inclusion of these dates provides readers with the grand historical scope that emerges prominently within the development of the plot. Moreover, because these dates represent both the highest and lowest points of Spanish politics, religion, and culture, they provide the work's ubiquitous cyclical framework of discovery and loss, victory and defeat, and damnation and resurrection that typifies Fuentes's national heritage and thereby enriches both the narrative structure and the expansive experimental style of *Terra Nostra.*

In regard to the structure of the novel, it too is divided into three primary segments, which Fuentes categorizes as "The Old World," "The New World," and "The Next World." The first segment, or "The Old World," is ushered in symbolically on July 14—Bastille Day—in Paris in the year 1999. Within this apocalyptic section of the novel, the focus is on the inevitable destruction resulting from the predominant medievalism of the period. By presenting the opening chapter of the work wherein the protagonist, Pollo Phoibe, wanders amidst the spewing smoke that fills the Parisian streets and portends "catastrophe" (Fuentes 26), the author draws the reader's attention to

> the fog in *Nuit et brouillard,* Alain Renais's powerful film about the Nazi's "final solution." [Further, a] group of naked flagellants, in the style of the Brethern of the Free Spirit, a medieval heretical group which becomes a crucial symbol in Fuentes' novel, announces the coming of a new kingdom and a new concept of history (158).

The second segment of the novel, "The New World," is a short section that focuses mainly on the exploits of a "pilgrim and his companion, an old man named Pedro, who survive 'a whirlpool of the night' . . . and are cast up on a beach covered with pearls" (Faris 1983, 154). Clearly, the beach represents the shores of paradise for the pilgrim, a paradise soon spoiled by human folly. Pedro makes a futile attempt to stake a claim on the island and is killed by natives for his efforts. Pedro's symbolic death is explained to the pilgrim in the following section of Fuentes's narrative: "He defiled us. He raised a temple for himself alone. He wished to make himself owner of a piece of the earth. But the earth is divine and cannot be possessed by any man. It is she who possesses us" (qtd. in Faris 154). Another narrative thread that pervades this second segment of the novel deals with the pilgrim's acceptance by the natives as though he had been expected by them as one of their original princes. Such fulfillment of societal prophesy clearly "recalls the Aztecs' belief that the arrival of Cortes constituted the long-awaited appearance of the plumed serpent god Quetzalcoatl. In each case, the conquest of the new world by the old is facilitated by the incorporation of an old world explorer into the new world religion" (154). Further, as is specifically stated within the fictional narrative itself, it is the destiny of the pilgrim "to be pursued. To struggle. To be defeated. To be reborn from [his] defeat. To return. To speak. To remind men of what they have forgotten. . . . [Essentially, f]reedom is the name of [his] task" (Fuentes 1976, 475).

Ironically, it is such a cyclic view of universal time that ushers in the third and final portion of the novel, "The Next World." At the beginning of this section, after the change-resistant El Señor (from section 1 of the novel) learns of the pilgrim's exploits, the monarch, fearing publicly that "he would go mad if the world [were] extended one inch beyond [its present] confines" (319), issues a decree to suppress "the rumor" of the existence of a new world (491). His edict, however, is little more than a futile attempt to quiet the persistent voices of those who yearn for progress and for freedom from El Señor's antiquated form of oppressive rule. His failure to suppress the inevitable forces of change leads the weary monarch to ascend the stairs of his magnificent fortress, the Escorial, where he awaits his death and "never ventur[es] to explore his new domains across the sea" (Faris 157).

If the beginning of "The Next World" marks Fuentes's observation of governmental resistance to change, then the final chapter of the entire work, entitled "The Last City," not only celebrates the cyclic reunion of a nation divided, but it also reveals the prophetic significance of the postapocalyptic return to a new earth. Ultimately, through the symbolic reunion of the novel's earlier characters, Pollo and Celestina, Fuentes posits that it is the power of love and acceptance that eliminates the need for power struggles, and it is figuratively the act of love that "abolishes the difference between self and other" (157). Such a return to the Edenic ideal reflects Fuentes's hopes for the beginning of a new world in which people are finally free to live "without sin" and can eternally celebrate this freedom through the pursuit of "pleasure" (Fuentes 778).

This powerful reference, both to the androgynous myth of Uroboros and the Western concept of the Millennial Kingdom, is only one of the symbols that pervades the novel and helps readers to interpret the rich revelations within *Terra Nostra*. Other specific symbols appear within the distinct narrative voices of key characters within the novel, and as Fuentes himself admits, these characters have their own origins in other fictional sources such as *La Celestina* and *Don Quixote* (Zamora 155). *La Celestina*, the work of a Jewish convert who remained in Spain after the Jewish expulsion by the forces of Catholicism, is considered by Fuentes to be "a literary as well as a cultural turning point . . . that marks the end of medieval Spanish literature and the beginning of Renaissance literature" (155). In the novel, the sensual and magical character named Celestina, who appears at the outset of the work, serves as a "go between" who "looks backward to the dawn of history and also forward, to its end" (155). Further, according to the author, Celestina's "sacred function" is that of a "secret sibyl," or a medieval prophetess, whose "apocalyptic utterances . . . eluded Felipe II's centralizing policies" (155).

Felipe II also has a symbolic literary parallel: that of the fanciful idealist, Don Quixote. Like Cervantes's delusional protagonist, "Fuentes's monarch lives in a dream whose illusory fabric keeps tearing. He burns heretics, but it is often [as] problematic to tell a heretic from a saint as to tell a windmill from a giant" (157). Although the symbolic relationship between the fictional knight, Don Quixote, and the fictional monarch, Felipe II, reveals as much about government as it does about humanity itself, it is the author of the former work, Cervantes himself, who serves as yet another significant symbol within *Terra Nostra*—Pollo Phoibe—who helps to unify Fuentes's cyclic narrative in both the opening and closing scenes of his apocalyptic novel. Pollo, the beautiful, dark-eyed, blonde-haired seeker of truth, is clearly identifiable as a one-armed man; in this way, he represents Cervantes, himself a natural quester, who "lost an arm in the Battle of Leptano in 1571" (159). In spite of this obvious human flaw, Pollo's pragmatic optimism (much like Cervantes's own) causes him to return in an ecstatic and highly symbolic sexual reunion with Celestina, his more mysterious and ethereal half. This union, which marks the end of the novel "at a privileged instant between the second and third millennia which is *both* end *and* beginning," has also been critically acclaimed as a "hierogamy"—wedding of sky father and earth mother—that confirms Fuentes's ultimate belief in the ancient apocalyptic myth that such an "androgynous form will exist at the end of time as it did at the beginning" (160). Such an image of the ultimate reunion, the reconciliation of opposing forces, and the final reign of order over chaos is the hallmark of apocalyptic fiction, and as one of its emissaries, Carlos Fuentes beautifully celebrates the return of the creative force in the universe throughout his artistic masterpiece, *Terra Nostra*.

See also Apocalypse: Traditional Judeo-Christian; Apocalypse: Traditional Primitive; Apocalyptic Literature; Archetype; Fuentes, Carlos; Jung, Carl Gustav; Myth; Symbol.

THANATOS

Thanatos is the god of death according to Greek mythology. As the mythological grandson of the primeval Chaos and the son of the underworld deities Erebus (god of darkness) and his sister Nyx (goddess of night), Thanatos is also known classically for his close relationship to his twin brother Hypnos, also known as Somnus, the god of sleep. As indicated within the details of the myth, it is the sole responsibility of Thanatos, the personification of death, to guide every living soul either to the blissful eternity of Elysium (heaven) or to the interminable torment of Tartarus (hell) at the conclusion of their earthly lives.

As archetypically reflected in the literature of Western cultures, Thanatos also maintains similar characteristics within various forms of Eastern mythology. For example, in the Chinese myth of *Bodhisattva*, specifically within the legend of the Temptation under the Bo Tree,

> the antagonist of [*Bodhisattva,*] the future Buddha [,] was known as *Kama-Mara,* literally "Desire-Hostility," or "Love and Death," the magician of Delusion. He was a personification of the Threefold Fire and of the difficulties of

> the last test, a final threshold guardian to be passed by the universal hero on his supreme adventure to Nirvana (Campbell 1949, *Hero* 163).

Given this Western and Eastern preoccupation, either with death and salvation or cyclic regeneration, it is reasonable that much of the world's literature has evolved into a historical amalgam of myth, metaphysics, and psychology (164). This combination of contributing factors became a focal point within the psychoanalytical studies of Dr. Sigmund Freud, who proposed that humanity's "life-wish (*eros* or *libido,* correspon[ds] to the Buddhist *Kama,* 'desire') and the death-wish (*thanatos* or *destudo,* which is identical with the Buddhist *Mara,* 'hostility or death') are the two drives that not only move the individual from within but also animate for him the surrounding world" (164).

Attempts to resolve this internal conflict between humanity's collective death wish versus its life wish have proven to be a continual source of considerable inspiration to modern writers. For example, it has inspired apocalyptic author Walker Percy, whose protagonists, such as psychiatrist Dr. Tom More in both *Love in the Ruins* (1971) and *The Thanatos Syndrome* (1987), consider themselves "old fashioned physicians of the soul" whose mission it is to identify the symptoms of spiritual morbidity and ultimately read these symptoms as signs of imminent apocalypse (Ciuba 1972, 253). Within such fictions, Percy's reluctant secular saviors are often represented according to the Faustian archetype, or the analytical and ambitious scientist who willingly contends with the temptations of a Mephistophilean deceiver. Accordingly, Percy's characters personify the universal struggle between good and evil, or the loss of self, which he sees as a form of death-in-life. This struggle, which is diagnosed by Dr. Tom More as the *thanatos syndrome,* names the modern disease "that heralds the spiritual doom of the twentieth century, like the rider on a pale horse that John beholds in . . . [Revelation] 6:8" (261). In doing so, Percy, like countless other apocalyptic and science fiction authors, fulfills the "spiritual goal of his art [as] defined in [his work entitled] *Novel Writing in an Apocalyptic Time* [which proposes that] before life can be affirmed for the novelist or his readers, death-in-life must be named" (261). Percy succeeds in this attempt at naming death, both in *Love in the Ruins* and particularly in *The Thanatos Syndrome,* thereby resurrecting centuries of classical myth, providing corresponding psychoanalytical theories, and ultimately serving as a modern-day prophet of humanity's inevitable confrontation with personal, if not global, apocalypse.

See also Apocalypse: Traditional Judeo-Christian; Apocalypse: Traditional Primitive; Apocalyptic Literature; *Faust;* Freud, Sigmund; Immelmann, Art; *Love in the Ruins: The Adventures of a Bad Catholic at a Time Near the End of the World;* Mephistophiles; More, Dr. Tom; More, Sir Thomas; Revelation, Book of; *The Thanatos Syndrome.*

THE THANATOS SYNDROME

This apocalyptic novel (1987) raises serious questions about humanity's hubris, morality, and destructive tendencies, which threaten the future of the modern world. As a classical scholar, student of theology and devout Roman Catholic, and a physician with a specialty in psychology, author Walker Percy was well aware of the diverse implications of his novel's title. Specifically, the term *thanatos* has various connotations. In the classical sense, the Greek god Thanatos, or the personification of death, was the grandson of the god Chaos, as well as the son of both Erebus, the god of darkness, and Nyx, the goddess of night, and twin to Hypnos, the god of sleep. It was Thanatos's destiny to serve as an underworld guide for the newly departed and to escort them to their rightful eternal homes: heaven or hell.

This classical concept of death, or "death-in-life," was further explored in scientific terms by the renowned psychoanalyst, Dr. Sigmund Freud. According to Freud, humanity has two basic forces that continually fight for supremacy within the subconscious mind. The first force, the sex/procreative drive, or *libido,* is controlled by Eros, the Greek god of love, whose influence promotes human self-preservation, whereas Thanatos, the god of death, is the opposing force that encourages negative behaviors that reflect man's "death wish" or subconscious drive toward self-destruction. Struggling for survival amidst this perpetual human conflict is the *psyche* or soul. Walker Percy ponders the future viability of modern man's soul in his complex, cataclysmic satire of human nature, *The Thanatos Syndrome.*

According to the novel's protagonist, lapsed Catholic and formerly alcoholic psychiatrist Dr. Tom More, the most important aspect regarding humanity is the survival of the soul, in spite of the internal and sociological conflicts that threaten to destroy it. Dr. More's position on this subject is clearly, and often absurdly, presented in Percy's earlier apocalyptic novel, *Love in the Ruins: The Adventures of a Bad Catholic at a Time Near the End of the World.* In that novel, Dr. More determines that environmental exposure to excessive doses of sodium radiation is causing people to develop disturbing psychological disorders. Further, he believes that scientists and physicians have mistakenly misdiagnosed affected patients and have unwittingly recommended the unnecessary institutionalization and/or legalized euthanasia of countless innocent people.

Disturbed by this possibility, More applies his scientific skills to the development of a device that will prevent the inevitable decline of the civilized world. His work in this area leads to his claim that he can successfully diagnose various mental disorders by identifying the areas of the brain that have been damaged by toxins. This is achieved by using his invention, More's Qualitative-Quantitative Ontological Lapsometer. In essence, he proffers that this instrument can measure levels of damage to a human's "being" (i.e., psyche or soul), and once this information has been provided, scientists can then proceed with more precise plans for psychiatric treatment that will return the afflicted to their former selves. In spite of the skepticism of his colleagues, he proceeds with his assertion because he sees signs of progressive mental and spiritual degradation in specific individuals, and fears for the cataclysmic ruin of society as a whole due to the virulent conditions of the modern world.

Although More's predictions for the end of the world are never realized in *Love in the Ruins,* his suspicions about humanity's loss of its essential self are confirmed, with catastrophic consequences, in Percy's apocalyptic sequel, *The Thanatos Syndrome.* In this follow-up novel, Dr. More has changed significantly from his earlier fictional appearance. While it is true that he still worries about the future of the world, he no longer feels compelled to save it single-handedly. His personal change from paranoia to complacency has apparently come as a result of his being jailed for two years after writing illegal prescriptions for fatigued truckers. When his cousin, respected epidemiologist Dr. Lucy Lipscomb, suggests that Tom had committed his crime because he wanted to get caught, More does not protest. Clearly, at the time, he had been in dire need of a long rest—one that would separate him from his personal problems as well as render him powerless to continue in his demanding role as a modern messiah. Whether his motives were intentional or subconscious, Tom concludes the results of his jailhouse rejuvenation by stating, "[P]rison does wonders for megalomania" (Percy *TS* 72).

Nevertheless, only two weeks after his release from jail, a series of unusual events causes Dr. More to make connections that will lead him to the same conclusions that he held before his arrest. On the home front, his wife and former nurse Ellen Oglethorpe has become known as something of a savant in the competitive world of professional bridge. Although Tom is happy that his wife has developed this talent during his absence, he is puzzled by the computerlike skill that makes her virtually unbeatable at the game. In addition, he notices that she has become more assertive, particularly in their lovemaking. In fact, in their first encounter following his return, he is surprised by her bold sexual posturing and the lascivious efficiency with which she concludes their physical reunion. On the same night, as he watches his wife sleep, Tom notices Ellen's utterance of strange words, monosyllables, and seemingly nonsensical phrases such as "Schenken," "Blackwood shmackwood," "Mud," and "Azalea" (56). Although he later finds that these terms are in some way related to the game of bridge, he is concerned when he suspects that she might have been thinking of a term called the Azazel convention when she said the word Azalea. This term, Tom learns, has a nefarious origin and can be used as a double entendre, which makes him concerned about the other changes she may have undergone in his absence.

In addition to his wife's unusual behavior, he makes note of similar changes in some of his patients. Although he has only a few new cases, he recognizes troublesome similarities that accelerate his suspicions. First, he notes that some patients who were formerly tormented by anxiety and phobias are now seemingly free of their neuroses. In their place, however, Tom acknowledges a "curious flatness of tone" (73) that makes him wonder if they are genuinely cured of their problems. Next, there is a marked similarity in their sexual behavior that indicates a more casual, promiscuous, and, in some cases, more bestial approach to the act. Additionally, some of his patients have begun to reflect the same deconstruction of speech: they use three-word sentences, gesture more frequently, communicate information out of context, and in general reflect fragmented and abstract thought. Most significant, however, is their collective demonstration of the same computerlike mental capabilities that his wife has recently shown. Believing that these incidents are more than coincidental, he asks himself, "Is this a syndrome? If so, what is its etiology? Exogenous? Bacterial? Viral? Chemical? In a word, what's going on here?" (74).

The remainder of *The Thanatos Syndrome* chronicles Tom's efforts to respond to these questions. In doing so, he enlists the assistance of Dr. Lipscomb, his old friend and confessor, the beleaguered yet devout Father Rinaldo Smith, and several minor characters who seem willing to help their old friend in a time of trouble. At this point, there is a resurgence of the Faustian legend that served as a sustained metaphor throughout *Love in the Ruins*. Specifically, after Dr. More finds out what is causing his community's strange behavior—the deliberate contamination of the water supply with the dreaded sodium radiation ion—he uses his skills, his wits, and the special assistance of others to expose this diabolical plot.

His investigation leads him to discover a covert initiative known as Project Blue Boy. This project bears a disturbing resemblance to the rarefied intentions of the Third Reich: the fittest are allowed to survive, crime is curtailed, and the sick or the useless are exterminated. Although the project, much like that of the Nazis, was ideally conceived as a noble social experiment intended to improve society, subdue violent criminals, suppress homosexuality, and deter the spread of the AIDS virus, its focus changes when the scientists begin to participate in the experiment, an irresponsible act that ultimately results in diabolical consequences. Therefore, as in the original Faust legend, these prideful scientists, having grown dissatisfied with the limitations of their current knowledge, figuratively sell their souls to the devil in exchange for the alchemical revelations they hope to gain from the project. Inevitably, their collective hubris blinds them to their own psychological deterioration as well as to the chaos they have recklessly unleashed upon the world.

The most chaotic scene that Dr. More discovers, however, is worse than he could have imagined. Through his determined efforts, Tom witnesses the heinous crime of repeated sexual abuse that occurs in a once-respected child care facility called the Belle Ame Academy. Clearly, the children's water supply has been deliberately contaminated, and some even claim to have been given "special vitamins" in order to reduce their physical inhibitions, allay their emotional fears, and make them willing prey that will satisfy the aberrant sexual appetites of bestial project administrators.

Armed with this devastating knowledge, and sickened in spirit by the potential of such an experiment, Dr. More visits Father Rinaldo Smith in hope of finding some answers. During his visit, the Father asks if Tom will hear a confession of something that has cursed the reverend with a soul-sickness of his own. What he confesses is his mute observation of similar atrocities that had occurred during his stay in Nazi Germany. He acknowledges that he too had been seduced by the promises of a perfect society, and would have at the time agreed with a similar solution to the problems of the country.

While the details of his confession are disturbing, both for Father Smith and for Dr. More, the experience has a cathartic impact that will change the two forever. What it specifically does for Tom, however, is to help him to conjure the strength needed to expose Project Blue Boy, while at the same time avoiding the various temptations presented to him by the Mephistophelean perpetrators. This time, unlike a similar situation in *Love in the Ruins,* Tom successfully resists temptation and refuses to sign a lucrative contract that might fill his pockets, but would certainly cost him his soul.

Ennobled by his righteous decision, Tom and his accomplices successfully expose the criminal activity along with the contamination of the water supply.

In reparation for their sins, and once they have been treated for the damage done by the insidious chemicals, several of the project leaders are required to use their knowledge and skill for good, not evil, in various health care facilities. In addition, the once troubled Father Smith is both spiritually and physically renewed by his vow to spend the rest of his life ministering to the sick and the poor in a hospice for the terminally ill. But, most importantly, the once restless and egotistical Dr. Tom More is finally satisfied with his life. With his wife's return to normal and his renewed commitment to his work and his family, Tom's formerly lapsed faith is restored. By putting others' interests before his own, Tom finally understands the concept of grace; consequently, he accepts the salvation from his terrified former existence and learns to appreciate the gift of living in peace.

See also Apocalypse: Traditional Judeo-Christian; Apocalypse: Traditional Primitive; Apocalyptic Literature; *Faust;* Freud, Sigmund; Immelmann, Art; *Love in the Ruins: The Adventures of a Bad Catholic at a Time Near the End of the World;* Mephistophiles; More, Dr. Tom; More, Sir Thomas; Percy, Walker; Revelation, Book of; Thanatos.

THAT HIDEOUS STRENGTH

This novel concludes an apocalyptic science fiction trilogy written by the renowned scholar, teacher, and theologian, C. S. Lewis. Although this novel, set in England and published in 1945, is a self-contained work that sustains its own literary merit, Lewis intended that it be read subsequent to the first two novels in the series, *Out of the Silent Planet* (1938) and *Perelandra* (1944). The common thread that weaves throughout the trilogy is the life and experience of the protagonist/observer/narrator, Dr. Elwin Ransom, a philologist or scholar of linguistics whose career is marked by a particular emphasis on the study of ancient languages.

In *Out of the Silent Planet,* Ransom is kidnapped by two fellow earthlings, Devine and Weston, whose nefarious purpose it is to use Ransom as a human sacrifice to appease the frightening life-forms on the planet Mars, known throughout the novel as Malacandra. Fortunately, Ransom's facility with linguistics enables him to communicate, at least on a basic level, with several of the species on the mysterious and often threatening planet. The essence of Ransom's role in the first novel is to see Earth, or Thulcandra—the "silent planet"—through the eyes of the Martian life-forms. From their perspective, Thulcandra has been under siege by a "bent" or corrupt Oyarsa, a spiritual force that has caused the wayward planet to be disconnected from communication with Maledil, the supreme being who reigns throughout the other planets within the solar system—the Field of Arbol. Through a series of adventures and dangerous escapades, Ransom returns to Earth with the knowledge that individuals must learn to overcome fear if they are ever to experience the joy of faith. Additionally, he learns that the pervasive savagery and materialism of Thulcandra, his home planet, must cease, and repentance must take place if it is ever to be reunited with its more benevolent creative force as well as with its more obedient and moral fellow planets.

In *Perelandra,* Dr. Ransom is again required to make an extraterrestrial voyage. This time, however, because of the lessons he has learned, he faces his journey fearlessly and with complete trust that his mission, whatever it may be, will be successfully executed as long as he obeys the orders of Maledil (the universal God) and respects the protection of the cadre of eldila—powerful angels who escort him on his trip. Soon after his arrival on the lush paradise of Perelandra, or Venus, he learns that his mission is to prepare the planet for the inhabitants of its humanlike species that will eventually be born from the first female, or queen "mother" on the planet, the Green Woman (Eve) and her intended king or "father," whom she has yet to meet. According to the will of Maledil, the Green Woman must overcome the same temptation that faced her earthly counterpart at the beginning of all human life on Thulcandra. Given his knowledge of the sins of the "silent planet," Ransom has been selected to help her make the appropriate choices, to keep her from dealing directly with the forces of evil that are already prowling the planet, and, ultimately, to endure a physical fight with Satan in order to preserve the pristine future of the Perelandrean paradise he has come to know and love.

Fortunately, Ransom's encounter with Satan, who has possessed the physical body of his former nemesis from the earlier novel, the evil physicist Dr. Weston, ends in victory. As a result of his bravery and faithful obedience, the future of Perelandra is secured. The king and queen are united according to the divine plan, and before he is sent safely back to Thulcandra, Ransom is told that his planet will eventually be given one final opportunity to restore communication with the other planets united under Maledil. At the close of *Perelandra,* therefore, Ransom returns with a message not unlike that which was relayed to St. John in the Book of Revelation: at some appointed time before the death of his planet, great plagues, death, and strife will occur as a precursor to one final conflagration between good and evil. And now having experienced living on a planetary paradise, he is certain that if given another chance, and sustained by the help of the eldila, humanity will ultimately choose obedience and find the strength to fight for the force of good as opposed to the evil forces that have terrorized Thulcandra throughout the ages.

Although prior to *That Hideous Strength* Dr. Ransom was portrayed as a middle-aged man, in the final novel of the trilogy he is more physically robust. In addition, he is referred to by another name—Mr. Fisher-King—a symbolic device that links him with the mythical quest for the Holy Grail. Another difference between this and the former novels in the series is that he is no longer the central figure who propels the plot. Instead, and perhaps because of the Achilles-like wound that he received on his heel during his Perelandrean battle, he is more a peripheral character within the novel than its primary participant. His intrinsic mysticism and communication with the eldila enable him to serve as a guide for the action that occurs.

To take the place of Ransom, Lewis introduces two new characters: a married couple named Mark and Jane Studdock. As a couple, they illustrate the basic duality intrinsic to the human race. Jane is a long-suffering, lonely, and spiritually unfulfilled wife. Her husband Mark, conversely, is an ambitious, egocentric social scientist who is involved in the development of a corrupt organization, ironically referred to as N.I.C.E.—the National Institute for Coordinated Experiments. Given their basic differences, Jane's benevolent nature inevitably draws her toward the peaceful Dr. Ransom and his spiritual colleagues, while her husband, because of his evil nature, is drawn more toward the demonic bureaucracy of N.I.C.E. that worships knowledge and power above all else. In the organization's quest for knowledge, they anticipate the scheduled awakening of the ancient necromancer from the Arthurian legend, Merlin, in the hope that his magic will further their self-deifying cause. Their efforts to win his support, however, are thwarted when it becomes apparent that he has chosen to align himself with Dr. Ransom and his associates instead.

With Merlin as the advocate for the force of good, he is placed in direct opposition against the planet's evil force as represented by John Wither, the deputy director of the demonic N.I.C.E. Under his unethical direction, the institute embarks on a quest to pervert language, to control all forms of media, and to selectively distort the dissemination of information. Moreover, he is directly responsible for the mistreatment of animals through their use as objects for cruel scientific experimentation.

Clearly, these abominable actions call for drastic counteractive methods, which come in the form of supernatural intervention. Because the evil Weston from the earlier novels has previously broken the barrier between Earth (Thulcandra) and the other God-fearing planets—Mars (Malacandra) and Venus (Perelandra)—the way has been made for the heavenly forces in the solar system to assist Merlin and Ransom in their fight for the good on their terrestrial plane. Through this powerful divine intervention, the corrupt scientists unwittingly contribute to their own downfall. In scenes reminiscent of Sodom and Gomorrah, N.I.C.E.'s attempt to confound language for their own evil purpose results in the ultimate attainment of their goal: the permanent devaluation of their social scientific language. However, in all of their projected outcomes, they never envisioned that they would become their own victims of the linguistic confusion that descends upon their gathering and reflects the chaos visited upon the biblical Tower of Babel. In another biblical twist, their previous mistreatment of animals in their experiments, merely for the pursuit of knowledge, also results in a commensurate punishment. On the night of a celebratory banquet in which the leaders of N.I.C.E. plan to congratulate themselves for their efforts, their accolades are silenced by a fierce retaliatory rampage of the escaped experimental animals who arrive on the scene, inspired by their celestial assistants, and devour the guests in an apocalyptic orgy.

Clearly, this final novel in the trilogy is powerful in its own right, but as Lewis himself suggested, its message is even more poignant when readers are reminded of humanity's initial state of grace, its devastating fall, and, ultimately, the eternal reward that will result from its final acceptance of the universal divine will. In regard to its artistic form, this novel is also remarkable in its blending of Christian myth, the Arthurian legend, and the fanciful fabric of wonder that was woven by one of the world's finest wordsmiths, C. S. Lewis.

See also Apocalypse: Traditional Judeo-Christian; Archetype; Arthur, King; Lewis, C. S.; Merlin; Myth; *Out of the Silent Planet; Perelandra;* Ransom, Dr. Elwin; Revelation, Book of; Satan; Weston, Edward Rolles.

THINGS FALL APART

This is the first novel by the Nigerian author, Chinua Achebe. Because this novel was written in 1958, two years prior to Nigeria's independence, which was won in 1960, it received popular as well as critical acclaim because it fictionally chronicles the apocalyptic consequences of the Igbo culture's near decimation as a result of over fifty years of colonial rule. In fact, Achebe intends for this novel to be something of a declaration of cultural independence; further, within the work, he seeks to remind his fellow Nigerians of their country's intrinsic value. He states his purpose for writing this novel as follows:

> As far as I am concerned the fundamental theme . . . is that African people did not hear of culture for the first time from Europeans; that their societies were not mindless but frequently had a philosophy of great depth and value and beauty, that they had poetry and, above all, they had dignity. It is this dignity that African people all but lost during the colonial period, and it is this that they must now regain (*DLB* 117:16).

Given this statement of artistic intent, the plot of the novel is more readily understood by the reader. Essentially, *Things Fall Apart* is a work based on the concept of entropic cycles as is symbolically represented in the dramatic lines of William Butler Yeats's powerful apocalyptic poem, "The Second Coming" (1921). It similarly relates the story of one man, named Okonkwo, the leader of the Igbo community in the village of Umuofia. And because it is written according to the entropic cycle, it chronicles the details of his unfortunate banishment, his forced exile, and his eventual return to his community.

At the opening of the novel, Okonkwo, the protagonist, is immediately presented as a local hero who is "well-known throughout the nine villages and even beyond . . . for his solid personal achievements . . . [through which] he had brought honor to his village" (Achebe 7). As a result of a series of impressive feats, he achieves considerable fame and wealth, wives, children, and the power of authority as a high-ranking councilman in his clan. In spite of his personal success, however, Okonkwo is haunted by the embarrassing reputation of his father, Unocal, who is known in the village as a weak and wanton man: the antithesis of his son, who determinedly rejects his father's values in every possible way.

While European readers might wonder how such a weak father could have spawned such a capable son, Achebe explains the phenomenon in accordance with a central belief of the Igbo clan. He explains that Okonkwo's personal strength and dignity come as a result of a favorable "*chi*" or personal "deity that makes each man's unique personality or being" (*DLB* 117: 20). The concept of *chi* is at the center of Okonkwo's personal odyssey, which includes his rise, fall, and eventual return to his original cultural nobility.

If the theme is represented in a triadic form, so too is the narrative cycle in which Okonkwo's story is told. Thus, part 1 of the novel establishes the rituals, traditions, and interpersonal relationships between clan members within the Umuofian agrarian community. Within this setting another clan, that of the Ikemefuna, is introduced as a means of setting up the conflict that ultimately leads to the protagonist's accidental killing of one of his own clansmen and, as a result, his banishment from his village.

Part 2 of the novel chronicles Okonkwo's seven-year exile in Mbanta, his mother's home village, where he first becomes exposed to colonial intrusion and the white man's religious practices. Within this portion of the work, Achebe focuses on the dramatic changes that came about within Africa as the result of the late nineteenth-century influence of the Christian missionaries, as well as the materialism that served as the basis of the European judicial and political systems. Okonkwo observes the concomitant changes in the community, and more importantly, the many ways in which the new systems have begun to distort the traditional customs and practices of his world.

Clearly unsettled by these changes, Okonkwo's return to Umuofia is marked by the beginning of part 3 of the novel. The climactic event that pits the two cultures against one another—a Christian's killing of a sacred python—results in the villagers' torching of the Christian church, and the inevitable incarceration of Okonkwo and his fellow representative clansmen. In an ensuing confrontation, Okonkwo, embodying the wrath of his marred cultural heritage, uses his machete to decapitate a messenger from the opposing colonial force. Ironically, in this symbolic act of cultural salvation, Okonkwo ultimately realizes that he will not be supported by his clansmen, who have been permanently changed by the white man's influence. Overwhelmed by the awareness of the imminent death of his heritage, he despairs by hanging himself from a tree—an act that is "an abomination" (Achebe 190) against his clan's custom. Ultimately, just as the brilliant traditions of the Igbo community fade in the light of colonial rule, so too does the protagonist's former greatness become buried, along with his pitiful remains, in the undignified grave of his "desecrated land" (190).

See also Achebe, Chinua; Allegory; Apocalypse: Traditional Primitive; Apocalypse: Traditional Judeo-Christian; Myth; "The Second Coming"; Symbol.

THOMAS, BIGGER

Bigger Thomas is the defiant, larger-than-life, twenty-year-old black protagonist of Richard Wright's 1940 naturalistic novel, *Native Son*. The character's name, "Bigger," reflects society's view of him: it is a derogatory amalgam of his threatening physical and emotional presence and the negative racial epithet, "nigger." His ubiquitous anger, which results from his oppressive life in a run-down tenement on Chicago's south side, becomes immediately evident in the novel. At the outset, he is violence itself without reason or direction; in his perpetual rebellion, he lashes out at family, friends—and most notably, at neighbors—in the form of recurrent petty crimes.

Clearly, Bigger's problem is that he both fears and is frustrated by the promise of the white world that will never be his. His frustration is fueled by a continual awareness of his poverty and ignorance; he not only reviles himself for these conditions, but he also rages at friends for similar traits, as well as for their passivity in the face of life's blatant inequities. Nevertheless, as the novel progresses, Bigger takes a live-in job with a white family named the Daltons. Here he becomes exposed to many facets of white society, and, eventually, both his political and sexual passions become stirred by his new experiences. In spite of an increasing sense of freedom, these events lead to an ironic twist of fate. His overriding fear causes Bigger to accidentally kill his new friend Mary Dalton, the beautiful young daughter of his white employers and benefactors.

After this, Bigger must rely on his instincts to survive. In the process, he commits yet another murder. Locked in a downward spiral of fear and isolation, Bigger desperately flees police, but he is eventually captured. At this point, he is inconsolable; his friends are of no use to him, his family is economically powerless, and he finds no peace in the symbols of his mother's religious faith. Although it is too little and too late, Bigger's most profound personal growth comes through his relationship with a white Communist lawyer who capably defends him in court. Through this lawyer, Bigger learns much about personal sacrifice and individual integrity, and although he is eventually condemned to death, he finally releases the fear that bound him throughout his young life by ultimately accepting his death as a man.

See also Apocalypse: Traditional Judeo-Christian; *The Divine Comedy;* Harlem Renaissance; *Native Son;* Naturalism.

TRANSCENDENTALISM

A nineteenth-century movement originating in New England, Transcendentalism had a significant impact on both American philosophy and its resultant literature. The seminal ideas for this idealistic movement began, essentially, with the writings and lectures of Ralph Waldo Emerson. This prolific reader and writer had been influenced by the thoughts of Plato and other classicists whose ideas further shaped Immanuel Kant's *Critique of Practical Reason*, which was a strong reaction against John Locke's philosophical reliance upon reason and logic.

During a time when Emerson was clearly examining his own life, he questioned the paradox of passion versus reason. As the result of reading Kant's work, Emerson seized upon the belief that humanity's instinct, creativity, and intuition have long been undervalued by society. Moreover, while humanity seems to extol the virtues of physical labor and believe fundamentally in the material world, he posited that humanity must transcend material boundaries of thought and be able to embrace both the world's spiritual truths and natural lessons that are linked with all creations under the supreme influence of the "Over Soul."

The concept of the Over Soul can be found among some of Emerson's early notes for his lecture series. Although these ideas are developed more completely in his essays "Nature" and "The Transcendentalist," the foundational outline for what was later to become a formal movement originated in one of Emerson's journals, as follows:

> There is one soul. It is related to the world. Art is its action thereon. Science finds its methods. Literature is its record. Religion is the emotion of reverence

> that it inspires. Ethics is the soul illustrated in human life. Society is the finding of this soul by individuals in each other. Trades are the learning of the soul in nature by labor. Politics is the activity of the soul illustrated in power. Manners are silent and mediate expressions of the soul (Emerson xix).

Soon after these ideas were presented formally, they received a considerable following, particularly among the literati of the time. In 1836, others who espoused this view, among them Henry David Thoreau, Margaret Fuller, and Bronson Alcott, formed a loosely structured group known as the Transcendental Club that met regularly under the leadership of the Reverend George Ripley. This group later became known for attempting to demonstrate these principles in the development of a social community called Brook Farm (1841–1847). While this unique social experiment eventually faded, the fervor of its initial days is captured in the literary record by Nathaniel Hawthorne's apocalyptic novel, *The Blithedale Romance* (1852).

See also *The Blithedale Romance;* Brook Farm; Coverdale, Miles; Emerson, Ralph Waldo; Hawthorne, Nathaniel; Hollingsworth; Moodie, Zenobia.

TWAIN, MARK

Mark Twain was the pseudonym of Samuel Langhorne Clemens (1835–1910). Twain is considered by many to be America's greatest literary humorist, and overall one of its most engaging writers and beloved lecturers. Best known for the boyhood experiences depicted in *Tom Sawyer* (1876), *Life on the Mississippi* (1883), and *Huckleberry Finn* (1884), he will long be remembered for his colloquial recollections of his youth spent on the Mississippi River in Hannibal, Missouri.

His earliest association with the field of writing occurred at age thirteen when Samuel became a printer's apprentice to his older brother, Orion, who had established the *Hannibal Journal*. By the time he turned eighteen years of age, Clemens was already immersed in the first stages of his humorous writing career; an early burlesque sketch had been published in a New York periodical, *The Carpet Bag*. Although writing was his primary goal, from 1853 to 1862, Clemens was involved in a variety of other interests. For a time, he served as a licensed pilot for Mississippi steamboats. This career terminated with the outbreak of the Civil War. Clemens briefly served in the Confederate Army but quickly became disillusioned with the experience, deserting within just two weeks. His decision to do so subsequently led Clemens to indulge in an understandable wanderlust; he decided to accompany his brother in the Western migration to the Nevada territory in hopes of securing a fortune prospecting for silver. As it happened, more practical opportunities presented themselves when, in 1862, Clemens took a position as a writer for the Virginia City *Territorial Enterprise*. In the year following his employment, on February 3, 1863, Clemens published his first humorous travelogue under the self-selected pseudonym "Mark Twain," which is a known nautical term meaning "two fathoms deep." His writing flourished under the protection of his pseudonym, until an escalating literary rivalry with another journalist resulted in the ultimate physical threat of a gunfight. Thus, in

1864, Clemens was once again on the move, this time to San Francisco, California. There he lived with a friend in a mining camp, an experience that inspired his first famous work, *The Celebrated Jumping Frog of Calaveras County.* With the publication of this work in the New York *Saturday Press* in the autumn of 1865, Mark Twain had made his first significant literary mark on America's East Coast.

With the arrival of almost overnight success, Twain successfully launched his full-time career as a writer. He composed countless humorous sketches while also conducting other journalistic activities, including a variety of assignments as a travel correspondent. During his travels, such as his visit to Hawaii in 1866 on assignment for the *Sacramento Union*, Twain published his observations and embarked on a fulfilling career as a lecturer. His work for this periodical soon brought him to the attention of California's largest newspaper, the *Alta California*, which subsequently hired him to conduct a world tour. The letters published during his tour were eventually reprinted in Horace Greeley's renowned *New York Tribune*, and because of their remarkable popularity, the collection was revised for publication in 1869 as *The Innocents Abroad*, a work that sealed his fate as one of the country's most popular chroniclers of Americana.

As Twain's professional life began to flourish, so too did his personal life. After a protracted period of making proposals and writing convincing love letters, he convinced a young woman named Olivia Langdon, from Elmira, New York, to assist him in his editorial work. Thus, Olivia became the woman who would serve as his most respected literary critic, and most importantly, she would become his wife of thirty-four years. Although their family union was a happy one, it was not without challenges; his wife was frequently ill, and his capricious ambition often resulted in unsuccessful financial dealings. Fortunately, however, Twain enjoyed considerable success in his writing and lecturing career, which produced such works as *Tom Sawyer* (1876), *A Tramp Abroad* (1880), *The Prince and the Pauper* (1881), and his autobiographical opus, *Life on the Mississippi* (1883).

However, his most successful novel, and one that is considered to be the ultimate American literary masterpiece, was *Huckleberry Finn*, published in 1884. Although this novel in particular fueled his already thriving lecturing career, he continued his writing and again received critical acclaim in 1889 for his comical time-travel adventure, *A Connecticut Yankee in King Arthur's Court.*

Just when it seemed that Twain was enjoying the fruits of a lifetime of literary labor, a series of events marked a sharp reversal of fortune for the popular humorist. First, as a result of an ill-advised investment in his own publishing firm, Twain was rendered bankrupt. He was saved from disaster, however, by signing his copyrights over to his wife for their financial protection. At the same time that his professional life was threatened, so too was the happiness of his personal life. In 1893, after noticing considerable changes in the vivacious personality of his youngest daughter Jean, Twain was distraught to learn that she had been diagnosed with epilepsy, a condition that would eventually claim her life. As a result of the emotional strain of his daughter's illness, as well as his diminishing fortunes, his own health took a dramatic downturn, during which he suffered from repeated bouts of bronchitis and painful episodes of rheumatoid arthritis. In spite of these setbacks, Twain resolved to restore his tenuous fortunes with the publication of another popular novel, *The Tragedy of Pudd'nhead Wilson* in 1894.

The success of this novel precipitated an extensive European lecture tour to promote his work, on which he was accompanied by his wife and one of his daughters. It was during this yearlong tour, however, that Twain experienced his most devastating personal loss; while he was away, he learned that his oldest and favorite daughter, Susy, who had remained in America, had contracted and subsequently died from meningitis. The child's death also had a grave impact on his wife, who became progressively ill as a result of the news and eventually declined during a protracted period of invalidism, which led to her death in 1904.

These catastrophic events also mark a significant change in the tone of Twain's remaining works. The formerly controlled, acerbic wit of America's most beloved humorist began to evolve into a perpetually bitter cynicism. This tone continued to be evident in a frustrated compilation of drafts as his mental and physical condition declined through grief and isolation. The work that captures his subsequent sense of despair is a cathartic effort over which he agonized for many years. Ultimately, although he failed to complete the work during his lifetime, his colleagues and editors Albert Bigelow Paine and Frederick A. Duneka completed and published the misanthropic fragments of his immoral apocalyptic work. Finally published in 1916, six years after his death, the novella entitled *The Mysterious Stranger* remains as the last literary legacy of one of America's greatest social observers, Samuel Clemens, who will remain affectionately known as Mark Twain.

See also Apocalypse: Secular; Apocalypticism; Arthur, King; *A Connecticut Yankee in King Arthur's Court; The Mysterious Stranger;* Science Fiction.

UNA

A beautiful and virtuous virgin, Una is the object of Prince Arthur's affection in Sir Edmund Spenser's romantic epic dedicated to Queen Elizabeth I, *The Faerie Queene* (c. 1590–1609). True to her character, Una is symbolized throughout the work as a gentle maiden of noble lineage, who rides a snow-white horse and who is invulnerable to moral temptation. Her beauty, generosity, and purity of spirit are also represented in her ability to tame wild animals and to win the heart of the valiant Arthur, the Red Crosse Knight of Holiness, as portrayed in Spenser's apocalyptic vision revealed in book 1 of *The Faerie Queene*.

See also Allegory; Apocalypse: Traditional Judeo-Christian; Arthur, King; *The Faerie Queene;* Gloriana; Revelation, Book of.

THE VIOLENT BEAR IT AWAY

This 1955 work represents the culmination of seven years' work for Flannery O'Connor, one of America's greatest Southern gothic writers. The novel's riveting title is based upon the following scriptural passage in the New Testament Gospel, Matthew 11:12: "From the days of John the Baptist until now, the Kingdom of Heaven suffereth violence, and the violent bear it away." Clearly, as in most of O'Connor's works, purgative acts of violence, and often death, mark the moments of spiritual revelation for characters engaged in life's apocalyptic battle between good and evil. Such is undeniably the case for the protagonist, a fourteen-year-old orphan, Francis Marion Tarwater, in *The Violent Bear It Away.*

Specifically, the novel begins with the death of Francis's elderly great-uncle, Mason Tarwater. In the opening scene, the youth is digging a grave for the old man, who has just died. Although the boy tries to complete the task according to the old man's detailed instructions, Francis's efforts soon become distracted by the reality that his great-uncle is dead. Consequently, for the first time in his young life, Francis is able to hear his own internal voice, but this voice is one that differs dramatically from the evangelical pontifications of Mason Tarwater. Thus, the death of the old man marks the birth of the spiritual battle for Francis's eternal soul.

The boy's internal conflicts have long been mirrored by the ongoing conflict between his uncle and great-uncle over the boy's custody. Because Francis was orphaned after a grisly accident, both men immediately staked their claims on the boy's future. In the novel, Rayber, Francis's uncle—a schoolteacher who espouses secular humanism—symbolizes the voice of reason, which to O'Connor is the force of evil. In contrast, the boy's great-uncle, Mason Tarwater, a fanatical fundamentalist and self-proclaimed prophet, embodies the formidable force of righteousness as revealed in his unwavering faith. Although initially Rayber, a childless intellectual with Pygmalion intentions, claims to have taken in the child in the name of charity, the old man fears the agnostic influence that Rayber will use to corrupt the young boy. As a result, Mason zealously responds to a "rage of vision" that compels him to abduct young Francis from Rayber's home and "to fly with the orphan boy to the farthest part of the backwoods [a secluded plot of land called Powderhead] and raise him up to justify his Redemption" (306). More importantly, however, in that action, the prophet also commits himself to raising "the boy to expect the Lord's call himself and to be prepared for the day he would hear it" (306). Thus, the boy is raised with a biased fundamental education in "Figures, Reading, and History beginning with Adam expelled from the Garden . . . [and moving through time to] the Day of Judgment" (305).

One reason the struggle between Rayber and the elderly Tarwater is so poignant is that theirs is an old battle. As a youngster, Rayber himself had lived with the old man; over a period of years he had been baptized and exposed to the power of the prophet's apocalyptic vision. But soon his father rescued him from the old man's ways, and the nephew became entrenched in a lifelong philosophical rejection of spiritual redemption. Thus, Rayber's early experience, and the subsequent confusion that shaped his existence, galvanized his intention to save his nephew from the "crazy" old man. Rayber's determination, which is supported by the efforts of a "welfare-woman" (307) who later becomes his wife, causes him to invade the property of the old man in an attempt to abduct the youth. This effort is thwarted when the elderly Tarwater fires a shotgun at Rayber's head. One bullet tears through Rayber's ear, causing him permanent hearing loss.

This violent confrontation results in the elderly Tarwater warning his great-nephew of Rayber's intrinsic evil. After the attempted kidnapping, he emphasizes to the boy that Rayber neither believes in Christ's resurrection nor in the consequences that will face him on Judgment Day. For these reasons, Mason issues two demands of Francis. First, upon the old man's death, Francis should not allow Rayber to cremate Mason's body. Second, and most significantly, he charges the youth with continuing the evangelical tradition by baptizing Rayber's idiot son, Bishop. Immediately after the old man's death, however, these censures fall prey to the temptations uttered by "the stranger" within Francis's mind. As a result, the youth gets drunk and soon tires of digging his great-uncle's grave. Instead of burying the prophet in hallowed ground marked by a cross as instructed, Francis symbolically begins a new life by burning down the old man's home in an attempt to incinerate both the man and the legacy he intended would be carried on by Francis.

The symbolic inferno not only breaks the physical bonds with his great-uncle, but it also serves as a revelation to the youth of the awesome potential of his free will. Soon Francis is drawn to the sin-filled city, and specifically to his Uncle Rayber's house. This act of will sets several things in motion. First, upon seeing his nephew, Rayber renews his obsession with rehabilitating, or more specifically, re-creating Francis in his own image. Similarly, Francis becomes determined to avoid the ubiquitous gaze of Rayber's idiot son, Bishop. This child disturbs Francis for a number of reasons. Primarily the child haunts him by his resemblance to the dead Mason Tarwater. Most importantly, however, the child is inexplicably drawn to water and serves as a daily reminder for Francis to take up the ways of the prophet and begin his own ministry by baptizing the child.

Because Francis is reluctant to become like his great-uncle, he tentatively opens his mind to the words of Rayber. During their early days together,

Rayber tries to undo Francis's spiritual and mental conditioning with a proliferation of words. These words, however, not only fail to reconstruct the youth, but they also fail to comfort him as he confronts his own ancient spiritual compulsions. Similarly, Francis struggles with his fate. He attempts to resist the injunction to become a prophet and savior of Bishop's soul through baptism. But Francis inevitably succumbs to the violence in his blood. He is compelled to baptize Rayber's child, but he ends up drowning the innocent soul in the process.

Once again, violence becomes a source of revelation to the protagonist. In spite of his will to be free of his legacy, he feels doomed by his great-uncle's prophesy. Consequently, after the baptismal drowning of Bishop, Francis flees from the scene in search of his own life's meaning. It is at this point that he fatefully heads into a black forest where his future is sealed following a violent sexual attack by a stranger who had picked him up on the road. After he returns to his great-uncle's home, he learns that the old man has been buried properly by a neighbor who had anointed both the grave and the land with "the sign of [the old man's] Savior over his head" (446). Seeing the grave marked with the cross, Francis is humbled by the power of the old man's faith, and after experiencing a final fiery vision, Francis accepts his future through a command that comes from his great-uncle's grave: "GO WARN THE CHILDREN OF GOD THE TERRIBLE SPEED OF MERCY" (447). This time, Francis finally fulfills his fate as he moves "toward the dark city, where the children of God lay sleeping" (447).

See also Apocalypse: Traditional Judeo-Christian; Grotesque; O'Connor, Flannery.

VIRGIL

Also known as Puglius Vergilius Maro (70–19 B.C.), Virgil (or Vergil), Rome's greatest poet, was the author of the epic poem, *The Aeneid* (c. 29 B.C.), and the spiritual guide for fellow poet, Dante, throughout two journeys of one of the greatest apocalyptic narratives in Western literature, *The Divine Comedy* (c. 1314). According to historical accounts, Virgil was the son of a successful Roman farmer, and while his early life was somewhat tranquil, the classical education reflected in Virgil's early works reveals that the times of his youth were filled with political strife regarding Roman rule.

As a result of one of the political conflagrations, Virgil came to know an administrator of culture, Asinius Pollio, who urged the poet to polish his writing and prepare it in a publishable form. The result of this prolonged effort was the publication entitled *Bucolica*, a collection that cast a nostalgic glance toward the past with an optimistic look toward the future. Following the success of this work, Virgil began an even more ambitious project, *Georgica*, which was a series of poems dealing with farm life. After the conclusion of this work, he turned his attention to the more serious consideration of the classical literary genre. Consequently, using Homer's *Illiad* and *Odyssey* as patterns for his work, Virgil nearly completed his twelve-book Roman myth, *Aeneid*. Although the author died before he could realize the significance of the work, he is still recognized historically as one of the most closely Christian of all the ancient pagan poets, a distinction that led Dante to portray him as a wise and noble guide.

See also Allegory; Apocalypse: Traditional Judeo-Christian; *The Divine Comedy;* Myth; Symbol.

VONNEGUT, KURT, JR.

A controversial and highly respected novelist, dramatist, and essayist, Kurt Vonnegut, Jr. (1922–), uses fantasy and satire to challenge powerful societal institutions, such as church and government, because of their devaluation of the individual human spirit.

Born in Indianapolis, Indiana, Vonnegut's education included two years of study at Cornell University, one year at Carnegie-Mellon University, and two years at the University of Chicago, from which he received his M.A. in 1971. His early career was similarly sporadic and experimental. His various occupations have included such assignments as a police reporter, a public relations agent, a freelance writer, a professor of English prose, an artist, a professional speaker, a political activist, and a U.S. Army Infantry prisoner of war, for which he earned the Purple Heart.

These myriad experiences enabled the writer to become directly involved with many of the bureaucracies and the attendant technologies that he later chose to satirize in his literary works. His first novel, *Player Piano* (1952), hints at the dehumanizing effects of an increasingly technological society. However, his fears about weapons of war and humanity's progressive moral decay are fully realized in one of the most definitive examples of American apocalyptic literature: *Cat's Cradle* (1963). In this novel, the protagonist ultimately witnesses the accidental events that conspire to initiate the end of the world. The blame is shared by both science and religion. In this story, a self-absorbed physicist creates a molecular substance called "ice-nine" that turns liquids into frozen solids. Before the physicist can complete his work and consider the moral consequences of his discovery, he dies and leaves fragments of his invention with his three dysfunctional children. The result of their irresponsibility, as well as the influence of a man-made religion of negation, "Bokononism," eventually leads to a series of events that leave the protagonist with the weighty responsibility of chronicling the world's end in order to prevent such cataclysmic recurrences in the future.

Although *Cat's Cradle* used tragicomedy and social satire to make an important statement about the destructive potential of technology, Vonnegut is perhaps best known for his observations about the immorality of war, as presented in his time-travel fantasy, *Slaughterhouse-Five* (1969). This novel, which is based on his own experience as a German prisoner of war during World War II, chronicles the similar adventures of an American soldier in a German prison camp and serves as a powerful commentary about the Allied army's firebombing of Dresden and its aftermath.

Although they never received the critical acclaim of *Slaughterhouse-Five,* Vonnegut's other major novels include *The Sirens of Titan* (1959), *Mother Night*

(1962), *God Bless You, Mr. Rosewater* (1965), *Breakfast of Champions* (1973), *Slapstick, or Lonesome No More* (1976), *Jailbird* (1979), *Dead-Eye Dick* (1982), *Galapagos: A Novel*, (1985), *Bluebeard* (1987), and *Hocus Pocus* (1990).

See also Apocalypse: Secular; Apocalyptic Literature; *Cat's Cradle;* Hoenikker, Felix; Ice-Nine; Jonah-John; Pilgrim, Billy; *Slaughterhouse-Five; Or the Children's Crusade: A Duty-Dance with Death.*

Kurt Vonnegut, Jr., in his study

THE WASTE LAND

The best-known poem written by the pioneer poet of the modernist period, T. S. Eliot, *The Waste Land* (1922) reflects an experimental form that was greatly influenced by the innovative style of James Joyce's *Ulysses* and *Finnegan's Wake.* The fragmented style and interrupted narrative of the poem, which is presented in five sections, reflects the confusion experienced by modern man in the wake of religious skepticism and the potential for human annihilation that became evident following World War I.

When examined on is basic critical levels, the plot of *The Waste Land* deals with one man's quest for meaning in the modern world as is represented by his visit to a fortune-teller. This quest, however, provides the central theme of the work wherein the collective soul of modern humanity is suffering from a pervasive spiritual drought. In an effort to convey the various psychological stages through which an individual travels while trying to find meaning within a seemingly soulless society, Eliot invokes the mythological symbol of the Holy Grail as featured in the ancient myth of the Fisher King.

Eliot alludes to this in the reference notes accompanying *The Waste Land,* and he gives particular credit to the work of Miss Jessie L. Weston, whose in-depth analysis of the Grail legend, entitled *From Ritual to Romance,* contributed significantly to the thematic thread that unifies the otherwise fragmented work. Eliot further acknowledges his indebtedness to Sir James Frazer's masterpiece of ancient myths, *The Golden Bough,* in the development of predominant images and symbols that cry for regeneration of a degenerate land.

Although this experimental work was originally written in 1922, Eliot was encouraged by his friend and mentor, Ezra Pound, to edit the body of the text. After Eliot's painstaking effort to reduce the lengthy work to its thematic essence, Pound's hunch proved correct, and the result is a revised masterpiece that was eventually published in 1971. Nevertheless, most of the fragments that were omitted from *The Waste Land* in its original form reemerged within another hauntingly concise treatment of the desolate condition of modern society. This work, which has served as something of a paradigm for the efforts of other writers of the modernist period, is entitled *The Hollow Men*. It was published in 1925, soon after Pound's edition of *The Waste Land* (Cirlot 1972).

See also Apocalypse: Secular; Apocalyptic Literature; Archetype; Eliot, T. S.; Freud, Sigmund; *Heart of Darkness; The Hollow Men;* Jung, Carl Gustav; Myth; "The Second Coming;" Symbol.

WEST, NATHANAEL

Nathanael West is the pen name for Nathan Weinstein (1903–1940), the New York–born son of Jewish-Russian immigrants. Known for his surrealistic style, West eventually became a significant writer of a few black-humored novels that parodied the apocalyptic violence reflected in early twentieth-century America.

As a youth, West did not distinguish himself either as a student or writer. In fact, he abruptly decided to leave high school in 1920 without graduating. This matter, however, was remedied later, via a forged transcript, which facilitated his acceptance into Tufts and subsequent transfer to Brown University, where he finally graduated. After graduation, West spent two happy years in Paris, returning to the United States in 1926 to begin a career in hotel management. It was in this capacity that West became acquainted with established writers such as James T. Farrell and Erskine Caldwell. These associations, along with their resultant introductions, assisted West in the publication of his first novel to appear under his pseudonym. The novel, entitled *The Dream Life of Balso Snell,* was published by a private printer in 1931.

The appearance of this novel—as well as his increasing success with the well-known literati of the day—initiated the publication of subsequent novels, which received varying levels of acclaim. Perhaps the best-known novel, *Miss Lonelyhearts* (1933), was received with critical acclaim. Unfortunately, West was unable to benefit financially from the work since his publisher filed for bankruptcy soon after the initial release of the book. Next, in order to gain a more stable financial footing, West published the novel *A Cool Million* (1934); however, this work also fared poorly as a result of damaging initial reviews.

Perhaps because of this failure, and at the urging of several notable West Coast acquaintances, West moved to Hollywood, California, where he began a career as a scriptwriter. Clearly, this experience served as the basis for his memorable apocalyptic vision of Hollywood's grim realities, entitled *The Day of the Locust* (1939). Although at the time following its writing this novel failed to achieve the expected financial success—partially because of its grotesque portrayals—it has since established its appeal with contemporary audiences.

In 1940, soon after the publication of *The Day of the Locust,* West achieved success in his personal life by marrying a woman named Eileen McKenney, who was the subject of the play *My Sister Eileen.* By all accounts, West and his wife were very happily married. Their union was cut short, however. Upon their return from a trip to Mexico in December of the same year, the couple was involved in a tragic automobile accident in El Centro, California. As a result of West's notoriously poor driving—in this case, he ran a stop sign—there was a fatal collision. Eileen was killed immediately and Nathanael died within the same hour.

See also Apocalypse: Anti-Christian; Apocalypse: Traditional Judeo-Christian; Apocalypse: Traditional Primitive; *The Day of the Locust;* Greener, Faye; Grotesque; Hackett, Tod; *Miss Lonelyhearts;* Shrike; Simpson, Homer.

WESTERVELT

Westervelt is the ominous traveling magician who mysteriously appears during critical scenes in Nathaniel Hawthorne's apocalyptic tale, *The Blithedale Romance* (1852). Clearly based on the evil archetype of the serpent, Westervelt's mystical presence in the Edenic setting of Blithedale foreshadows the corruption and ultimate destruction that pervades the novel. Although at first the reader recognizes that he is exceedingly strange and probably dangerous, it isn't until well into the novel that readers learn that Westervelt's influence has been felt before. Specifically, after Zenobia, who is in love with the charismatic Hollingsworth, meets with Westervelt, it becomes clear that these two have known each other before. It is also evident that they are more familiar, in both their language and gestures. These details confirm the narrator's suspicion that Zenobia is wise in the ways of the world and is not unfamiliar with using evil methods for personal gain. As such, Coverdale draws the conclusion that it is Westervelt who must have seduced, married, and deserted Zenobia in her younger years, and that this experience has left Zenobia both cynical and spiritually tainted by her relationship with him.

It is because she understands his covert style and his malevolent power that she enlists his help in eliminating Priscilla as her rival for Hollingsworth. Accordingly, both their shared past, which can be assumed had corrupt elements, and their shared present—his search for a new "Veiled Lady" in his magic act and Zenobia's desire for Hollingsworth—cause them to conspire for mutual gain at the exclusion of community interests.

Symbolically, Hawthorne allows Zenobia, initially presented as Eve in the paradisiacal garden, to become seduced by Westervelt's tempting possibilities. And as a result, the lives and happiness of everyone in Blithedale, their man-made paradise, are destroyed leaving only the legacy of Westervelt's persistent evil and the novel itself as Hawthorne's warning for humanity to resist similar temptation.

See also Apocalypse: Traditional Primitive; *The Blithedale Romance;* Brook Farm; Coverdale, Miles; Hollingsworth; Moodie, Priscilla; Moodie, Zenobia; Romanticism; Transcendentalism.

WESTON, EDWARD ROLLES

Weston is the fictional physicist featured in the apocalyptic space trilogy written by the renowned British teacher, scholar, and author, C. S. Lewis. Within this trilogy, Weston is first introduced in the initial novel entitled *Out of the Silent Planet* (1938). In this work, Weston is a corrupt and megalomaniacal physicist who consorts with a despicable materialist named Devine to travel to the planet Malacandra (Mars) where they plan to exploit the native landscape and eventually create their own extraterrestrial colony. What is obvious, at the beginning of the novel, is that the two have made this space voyage before, and having encountered the various threatening life-forms that exist on the planet, they decide to kidnap a fellow Englishman, Dr. Elwin Ransom, a linguist by vocation, in an attempt first to learn the language of the indigenous inhabitants and, more importantly, to offer their captive as a human sacrifice for the creatures they mistakenly view as ravenous beasts.

Much to his chagrin, however, Weston soon learns that he is no match for the more curious and less ambitious scholar who succeeds in communicating with the Malacandran creatures through which he learns the universal perspective of Earth, Thulcandra, or as the title of the work implies, the "silent planet." Apparently, as is related to the linguist throughout his stay on Malacandra, the Earth was once part of the solar system (Field of Arbol) that fell under the divine and benevolent leadership of Maledil, the God of the universe. However, when each of the planets was given its own leader or Oyarsa, the one who was sent to the Earth became "bent." This word "bent" is the closest that the Malacandrans can come to defining the force of evil since such a force does not exist on the other planets within the solar system. As such, the Earth after having disobeyed God's laws and having fallen from grace as a result of pride and free will, was placed under universal quarantine, literally a separation from God, which would keep it from corrupting the other planets. This quarantine, however, was eventually broken by the evil force of the physicist, Weston, as he brought the full force of selfishness and corruption to Malacandra. In the end of the novel, however, when his motives are examined by Maledil (God), Weston is sentenced to return to Thulcandra and ordered never to return again.

Nevertheless, and in spite of this dictate, Weston does continue in his attempt to colonize other planets. As such, in the second novel, he is even more determined to get a foothold on the paradisiacal planet, Perelandra (Venus). In fact, his interest in this planet is even greater because only nature has been created; it has not yet been inhabited by creatures of human intelligence. He arrives, however, just at the point when the Green Woman (Eve) is about to meet her predestined mate (Adam) and begin to populate their Perelandrean kingdom. According to Maledil's rules, however, which have clearly been based upon the catastrophe that occurred in the Garden of Eden, the Green Woman must first become familiar with evil and then must actively resist in before she can receive her rightful place as queen "mother" of the planet.

Given this opportunity to colonize a beautiful new world with inhabitants in "his own image," Weston makes an agreement with Satan who would do anything to prevent an eternal paradise such as that which was intended for Earth. As such, given their mutual ambitions, Weston allows himself to become possessed by the spirit of Satan. Maledil (God), however, is aware of this nefarious plot, and as such, sends his eldila (angels) back to Earth in order to summon Ransom to Perelandra in order to intervene in the potential destruction of the planet. After having learned not to fear God's will for his life, Ransom willingly travels to Perelandra whereupon he learns of the pending plan for its fall. What ensues throughout the remainder of the novel, therefore, is the continual pitting of Ransom's good against Weston/Satan's evil as they vie for the future of the planet.

As such, although Weston almost convinces the Green Woman to disobey Maledil's commands for her life, she learns, through her discussions with Ransom, that she must avoid the diabolical creature at all costs. It is also at this point that Ransom realizes that it is he who must physically fight with Satan, in Weston's human body, in order to prevent the recurrence of humanity's fall from eternal grace. Consequently, Weston is endowed with all the physical and intellectual strength possible for him to do battle with Ransom, but in the end, although Weston has left a permanent wound on the hero's heel, the villain is pummeled, strangled, and eventually drowned. As a result of this stunning defeat, Weston/Satan is foiled in his diabolical attempt. Also, before he is sent back to Earth, Ransom, the Christ-figure who was willing to lay down his own life for the future life of Perelandra, is honored and blessed by the union of the Perelandrean king and queen, and his final reward is a promise that someday the beneficent forces of the universe will wage one final battle on Earth and will finally reclaim it as one of the obedient planets in the solar system, which will culminate with a "Great Dance" in the beatific Field of Arbol.

See also Apocalypse: Traditional Judeo-Christian; Archetype; Lewis, C. S.; Myth; *Out of the Silent Planet; Perelandra;* Ransom, Dr. Elwin; Satan; Science Fiction; Symbol.

WIGGLESWORTH, MICHAEL

Michael Wigglesworth (1631–1705), a Puritan American clergyman and poet, is best known for his apocalyptic theological treatise entitled *The Day of Doom.* Although he was born in Yorkshire, England, his parents brought their family to America in 1638 where they settled, in New Haven, Connecticut, and raised their son according to strict Puritan standards. Although little is known about his formal schooling in his early years, Wigglesworth attended and eventually graduated from Harvard University in 1654. While he continued his studies independently, it was not until two years following his graduation that he officially began his preaching career after his ordination as a minister of the Congregational church in 1656.

Although he vigorously pursued his two major areas of interest, specifically, medicine and theology, he was often in poor physical health. It is perhaps this combination of intellectual zeal and physical dissipation that inspired a poem that would become his most famous work. First published in 1662, his long poem entitled *The Day of Doom* provided a horrifyingly vivid portrayal of the Last Judgment, inspired by the biblical book of Revelation, which was indicative of the religious fervor proliferating throughout the early New England community.

Public reaction to this work, which strongly stated Wigglesworth's strict Calvinist beliefs, became an immediate best-seller among the American colonists. Clearly, the popularity of the work, which was carefully composed in ballad meter, came not only from its genuine literary merit but, more importantly, from its theme, which generated fear in its readers and thereby compelled them either to obey God's commands or suffer the apocalyptic and eternal consequences of human pride and disobedience against divine authority.

While the success of the prophetic poem enabled Wigglesworth to marry (he had a series of three wives) and to raise a total of eight children, the author and theologian continued writing about apocalyptic themes in a body of work that appeared as follows: *Meat out of the Eater or Meditations Concerning the Necessity, End, and Usefulness of Afflictions unto God's Children* (1669) and "God's Controversy with New England," which was eventually published in a volume entitled the *Proceedings of the Massachusetts Historical Society* (1883).

See also Apocalypse: Traditional Judeo-Christian; Apocalyptic Literature; *The Day of Doom;* Revelation, Book of; *Sinners in the Hands of an Angry God.*

WRIGHT, RICHARD

The novelist Richard Wright (1908–1960), considered to be one of the pioneers of America's twentieth-century black literature movement, is perhaps best known for his naturalistic/realistic novel, *Native Son* (1940). This critically acclaimed classic exposes the evils of racist oppression, a theme that resulted in the novel's eventual adaptation to feature film in 1986.

Born into a sharecropper's family on a farm near Natchez, Mississippi, Wright's life was filled with poverty, humiliation, and the suffering caused by the relentless blows of racial conflict. The details of this experience are captured in his gripping autobiographical novel, *Black Boy* (1945), which was published soon after his initial literary success.

The chronicle of his early life is grim; he was deserted by his father at the age of six, and, as such, his childhood in the American South was entrusted first to the impersonal care of understaffed institutions, and later to various family members. During his stay with relatives, they continually tried to evangelize him; ironically, their persistence only succeeded in sowing the seeds of an eventual rejection of all formalized religion. Nevertheless, it is precisely this early religious influence that shaped the predominant apocalyptic images and themes that pervade his admirable body of work.

In an effort to escape family pressures as well as the generally restrictive tyranny of his Black Belt origins, Wright eventually began moving north, first to Memphis and later to Chicago, where he had hoped to alleviate minority oppression in the 1930s by joining the Communist Party. To demonstrate his commitment to the cause, in 1937, he went to New York where he served as the Harlem editor of the Communist publication, *The Daily Worker.* However, once he realized that the Party was attempting to take advantage of both his radicalism and his reputation, Wright finally broke with communism but continued developing his fictional efforts, none of which was recognized with the commercial success of his earlier works. These titles include *The Outsider* (1953), *Savage Holiday* (1954), and *The Long Dream* (1958) as well as *Lawd Today* (1960) and *Eight Men* (1961), both of which were published posthumously.

Although Wright's later full-length fictions were less memorable than those of his early career, many of his short stories received critical recognition, and in fact, still frequently appear in contemporary literary anthologies. Nevertheless, in spite of his decades of success, Wright eventually became disillusioned with his life and his work in the United States. Consequently, he made the decision to expatriate to France and ultimately settled in Normandy. During his final years, the author continued to pursue his craft while entertaining such dignitaries as Dr. Martin Luther King, Jr., until his death from a heart attack on November 28, 1960.

See also Harlem Renaissance; *Native Son;* Naturalism; Thomas, Bigger.

Richard Wright

YEATS, WILLIAM BUTLER

Yeats (1865–1939) was the Nobel Prize–winning Irish poet, prose writer, and dramatist who is considered by many to be one of the most significant poets of twentieth-century literature. Born in Dublin, Ireland, of an English mother and Irish father, Yeats's early life consisted of periodic moves between Dublin and London. Although the young writer attended Dublin's Metropolitan School of the Arts, and through his efforts there had his first publications in the *Dublin University Review* when he was just twenty years old, his professional writing career began in earnest after his family's move back to London in 1887.

The essence of Yeats's writing clearly reflects the author's search for symbols that could explain his own personal and professional evolutions as well as the meaning of life in general. Although he had been strongly influenced by his father's profound religious skepticism, Yeats possessed an intrinsic spiritual intensity that caused him to shun orthodox Christian religious practices, yet to incorporate much of its powerful symbolism into an individual amalgam of thought that included Irish folklore, Neoplatonism, mysticism, and theosophy. The result of these influences can be readily recognized within the four distinct periods into which the poet's work falls.

The first period of his professional career reflects the visionary and mystical self-absorption of London's nineteenth-century fin de siècle Romantic poets such as William Blake and Percy Bysshe Shelley. His early works, which appeared in the collection *The Wanderings of Oisin and Other Poems* (1889), reflect the romanticism of the Lake poets as well as the pastoral influence of both the folklore and natural beauty of his ancestral home in County Sligo, Dublin. However, both his ingenuous worldview and his romantic tendencies were blunted somewhat by his unrequited love for an intelligent Irish beauty, Maud Gonne. As a result, these experiences—as well as his continuing search for artistic expression—eventually led to his next observable literary phase.

This second phase of his career is marked less by simple romantic imagery and more by the decadent complexities of the French Symbolist school. While his interest in Blake's work remained, he began to emulate the stylistic tendencies of such English aesthetes as John Ruskin and Walter Pater. The work that most clearly reflects this stylistic shift is his work entitled *The Wind among the Reeds,* which was published in 1899, about the same time that he met an influential

William Butler Yeats in 1908

woman named Isabella Augusta, also known as Lady Gregory, who would forever change the course of his personal and professional life.

Clearly, her passion for gathering information about western Irish lore coincided with Yeats's own latent fascination with pagan rituals and beliefs whose ancient roots still remained within the rarefied soil of Christian symbolism. Their professional alliance resulted in the next phase of Yeats's artistic career, during which he pursued dramatic forms of expression. Such efforts were both encouraged and supported by Yeats's and Lady Gregory's foundation of the Irish Literary Theatre, a venue in which Yeats's first play, *The Countess Cathleen*, was performed on the Dublin stage in 1899. Although Yeats assumed less of an artistic than an administrative role, he retained the position as director of the theater—renamed the Abbey Theater in 1904—until his death. Nevertheless, during the period of 1899 through 1907, Yeats became extremely familiar with the more pedestrian elements of dramatic production such as property maintenance, management of actors' temperaments, and societal pressures that frequently raised censorship issues. In spite of these distractions, however, Yeats continued his individual pursuits as a playwright and had many of his own plays performed in his theater, some of which include *The Land of Heart's Desire* (1894), *The Hour Glass* (1903), *The King's Threshold* (1904), *On Baile's Strand* (1905), and *Deirdre* (1907).

Nevertheless, while these diverse experiences enabled him to mature both as a person and an artist, Yeats's work reached a more practical level in the third stage of his writing. During this time, he experienced a certain cynicism resulting from the responses of what he believed were less-than-sophisticated audiences. In addition, his emergence as a national literary figure placed him in the line of fire from both political and artistic critics. Moreover, his notoriety and personal philosophies brought him in direct conflict with the Irish Catholic middle class. Thus, his work during this time, which is characterized by a sparse realism, reflects his abandonment of both his earlier idealism and his zealous nationalism. The end result of this private and creative crisis was that he moved to England for a time, as an act of personal and professional protest.

Yeats's rejection of Ireland, however, was short-lived. An event known as the Easter Rising, in 1916, caused his former love, Maud Gonne, to encourage the expatriate to return to Ireland. His compliance with her request and his renewed sense of national pride are apparent in his poem entitled "Easter 1916." At this time, Yeats entered the final and most inspirational period of his professional career. This significant artistic transformation was influenced greatly by several factors. First, in 1917, Yeats married a woman who encouraged his earlier visionary and esoteric preoccupation. Further, the new forms of pre–World War I writing and criticism that came from such artists as T. S. Eliot and Ezra Pound encouraged him to expand his existing poetic tastes. In addition, Yeats became involved in a newfound appreciation of the metaphysical elements of John Donne's later works, a combination of factors that ultimately resulted in Yeats's development of a new and distinctive experimental style that would epitomize the zenith of his artistic career.

Some of the more notable works that resulted from this triumphant period include a book entitled *A Vision* (1925, 1937), and two collections entitled *The*

Tower (1928) and *The Winding Stair* (1929). These collections include two of his definitive poetic contributions: "Sailing to Byzantium" and "The Second Coming." The latter is the apocalyptic masterpiece with which he is most closely identified; it also has served as the inspiration for many of the works noted in this encyclopedic volume. Clearly, as an artist, a patriot, and a man, Yeats was committed to the pursuit of creative transcendence. He continued to add to his considerable body of work until his death in 1939. His legacy, however, is one that has stood the test of time in that he continues to be an inspiration to international contemporary authors such as the Nigerian novelist Chinua Achebe and the American novelist Walker Percy, who borrow his original themes in order to re-create the poet's profound concern for the future of humanity amidst the chaos of life in the twentieth century.

See also Achebe, Chinua; Apocalypse: Traditional Judeo-Christian; Apocalypse: Traditional Primitive; Apocalypticism; Eliot, T. S.; *The Hollow Men; Love in the Ruins:The Adventures of a Bad Catholic at a Time Near the End of the World;* "The Second Coming"; *The Thanatos Syndrome; Things Fall Apart.*

ZECHARIAH, BOOK OF

One of the lesser albeit more graphic prophetic books of the Old Testament scriptures, this work, written by Zechariah, whose name in Hebrew means "the Lord remembers," dates from the beginning of the author's ministry between the years of 520 to 518 B.C. The significance of Zechariah, as opposed to several of the other Old Testament apocalyptic works, is that it was written during a time when the prophet's contemporaries were extremely weary from their continually interrupted attempts to restore their Holy City. Within the book, the author suggests that his people had also begun to question whether or not the rebuilding of Jerusalem was actually part of God's plan since they had faced so many obstacles throughout the rebuilding process. The book of Zechariah, therefore, is really something of a wake-up call to his apathetic people and a reminder to them that they are bound by blood, as descendents of their beloved King David, to prepare for their kinsman who will return as their Messiah.

While the early chapters of the work deal primarily with the aforementioned historical perspective, chapters 12 through 14 are considered by scholars to be the most apocalyptic sections of the book. For example, in chapter 12, the prophet reminds his forlorn people that someday soon God will "make Jerusalem a burdensome stone for all people" (Zechariah 12:3) and that He will also "seek to destroy all the nations that come against [it]" (12:9). The prophet further states that the Lord will "pour upon the house of David, and upon the inhabitants of Jerusalem, the spirit of grace and of supplication" (12:10) that will enable them to forgive those who have harmed their people and will encourage them to mourn for those to whom they have brought harm.

Chapter 13 of the book of Zechariah then summarizes some of the apocalyptic elements that they will encounter during the end times, such as a growing apostasy, natural disasters, and the devastation of at least two-thirds of the earth. However, in a symbolic promise that has often been repeated as a consolation for those who have endured great suffering, the prophet reveals God's promise that He "will bring the third part [of the earth] through the fire, and will refine them as silver is refined, and will try them as gold is tried." Consequently, their trust in God's word will bring about the result that "they shall call on [His] name, and [He] will hear them: [He] will say, It *is* my people; and they shall say, The Lord is my God" (13:9).

While the portrayal of the future is bright for the inhabitants of the Holy City, Zechariah's contemporaries must have taken heart from the promises related to their enemies as well. Ultimately, according to prophesy, regarding those who will continue to fight against His chosen people, the words of Zechariah clearly reveal that God will "smite" them thus: "Their flesh shall consume away while they stand upon their feet, and their eyes shall consume away in their holes, and their tongue shall consume away in their mouth" (14:12). One can only assume that, given such a precise picture of the Day of Judgment, Zechariah's people were eager to return to their former zeal (*Open Bible* 1975).

See also Apocalypse: Traditional Judeo-Christian; Apocalyptic Literature; Armageddon; Daniel, Book of; Ezekiel, Book of; Gog and Magog; Isaiah, Book of; Joel, Book of; Revelation, Book of.

ZEITBLOM, SERENUS

Zeitblom is the narrator in German author Thomas Mann's apocalyptic rendition of the Faustian legend, *Doktor Faustus.* As a character who has been close to the ingenious protagonist, Adrian Leverkuhn, since their childhood, he is both familiar with and sympathetic toward the driving ambition of his friend, yet he is removed, as a result of his own placid temperament, from being taken in by the demonic seduction of Nazism.

His function in the novel is one of an ingenuous observer through whom the torment of the Faustian Leverkuhn, as well as the feverish political influences of the novel's historic events, are objectively revealed within the narrative. Specifically, in a critical discussion of Zeitblom's function within the novel, William M. Honsa, Jr., describes the narrator as follows:

> Zeitblom is an onlooker; however much he would like to influence Leverkuhn, he is resigned to the fact that he cannot. He is allowed only to look on, but this is still the most important function of his life. He has a conscience which at times leads him to become something more than an onlooker in respect to his country (he fights for Germany in the First World War, resigns from his profession in protest against Hitler). [Thus, h]e is an onlooker, but not one without character or a position of his own. His Catholic humanism speaks through *Doktor Faustus;* Zeitblom does not hesitate to react against Leverkuhn's demon when it reaches too far toward the powers of darkness, but neither does he ever utterly condemn Leverkuhn. Human understanding in Zeitblom stretches far enough to suggest the possibility of everlasting mercy (Honsa 1986, 224).

As this explanation suggests, therefore, Zeitblom's mercy is the musical counterpoint to Leverkuhn's ruthless ambition. And so, just as the "right hand and the left hand [within a musical performance, as represented by Zeitblom and Leverkuhn] remain unreconciled[,] . . . they are both part of Mann's work in which 'coldness and heat, repose and ecstasy are one and the same'" (226).

See also Apocalypse: Secular; Apocalyptic Literature; Archetype; *Doktor Faustus; Dr. Faustus; Faust;* Freud, Sigmund; Leverkuhn, Adrian; Mann, Thomas; Mephistophiles.

ZOROASTER

Also referred to as Zara-ushtra, Zoroaster (630/618–553/541 B.C.) was the founder of an ancient Iranian religion known as Zoroastrianism, whose scripture—called the *Avesta*—relies heavily on *The Gathas,* or its seventeen scriptural poems, as the basis for the practice of his system of belief. The significance of Zoroaster's writings, however, is that they served as an influential basis upon which a final struggle between good and evil, angels and men, and destruction by fire became essential details portrayed within the subsequent body of Western apocalyptic literature.

Because Zoroastrianism as a religion pertains almost entirely to eschatology, or the study of "last things," its apocalyptic orientation was well suited as an original schema upon which much of the Jewish Old Testament prophesy was obviously built. It is also perhaps as a result of Zoroaster's concept of three historical intervals, wherein three successive saviors or *soshyans* will appear during periods of one-thousand years each, that the concept of millennialism—the anticipation of a savior at the end of a thousand-year period—became a popular conclusion, both for the rehabilitation of the living world and for the redemption of the souls of the dead. Overall, Zoroaster's legacies to the body of apocalyptic literature, in general, include the following characteristics: (1) the omnipotence of God, (2) the role of free will, (3) the belief in a savior, and (4) the eternal restoration of the world to its original paradisiacal form. Clearly, while much has not changed in regard to the elements of apocalyptic fiction, readers can only marvel at the profound insight and native intelligence of a man who inspired centuries of thought regarding the complexities and ultimate fate of human nature (Bierlein 1994).

See also Apocalypse: Persian; Apocalypse: Traditional Primitive; Apocalyptic Literature; Apocalypticism; Myth.

APPENDIX A

AUTHORS FEATURED IN THE TEXT

Achebe, Chinua (1930–)
Alighieri, Dante (1265–1321)
Baldwin, James (1924–1987)
Barth, John (1930–)
Blake, William (1757–1827)
Bradbury, Ray (1920–)
Bunyan, John (1628–1688)
Conrad, Joseph (1857–1924)
Coover, Robert (1932–)
Dickinson, Emily (1830–1886)
Dostoyevsky, Fyodor (1821–1881)
Edwards, Jonathan (1703–1758)
Eliot, Thomas Stearns (1888–1965)
Ellison, Ralph Waldo (1914–1944)
Emerson, Ralph Waldo (1803–1882)
Faulkner, William (1897–1962)
Fitzgerald, Francis Scott (1896–1940)
Fuentes, Carlos (1928–)
García Márquez, Gabriel (1928–)
Goethe, Johann Wolfgang von (1749–1832)
Golding, William Gerald (1911–1993)
Hawthorne, Nathaniel (1804–1864)
Hersey, John (1914–1993)
Hesse, Herman (1877–1962)
Highwater, Jamake (1942–)
Huxley, Aldous (1894–1963)
Ibuse, Masuji (1898–1993)
Lewis, Clive Staples (1890–1963)
Malory, Sir Thomas (c. 1408–1471)
Mann, Thomas (1875–1955)
Melville, Herman (1819–1891)
Milton, John (1608–1674)
O'Connor, Flannery (1925–1964)
Percy, Walker (1916–1990)
Poe, Edgar Allan (1809–1849)
Pynchon, Thomas (1937–)
Shakespeare, William (1564–1616)
Shelley, Mary Wollstonecraft (1797–1851)
Silko, Leslie Marmon (1948–)
Spenser, Sir Edmund (1552–1599)
Twain, Mark (Samuel Clemens) (1835–1910)
Vonnegut, Kurt, Jr. (1922–)
West, Nathaneal (1903–1940)
Wigglesworth, Michael (1631–1705)
Wright, Richard (1908–1960)
Yeats, William Butler (1865–1939)

APPENDIX B

TITLES FEATURED IN THE TEXT

Absalom, Absalom! (1936)
Alas, Babylon (1959)
Almanac of the Dead (1991)
As I Lay Dying (1930)
Black Rain (1969)
The Blithedale Romance (1852)
Brave New World (1932)
The Brothers Karamazov (1878–1880)
Cat's Cradle (1963)
The Confidence Man (1857)
A Connecticut Yankee in King Arthur's Court (1889)
The Day of Doom (1662)
The Day of the Locust (1939)
The Divine Comedy (1310–1314)
Doctor Faustus (1604)
Doktor Faustus (1947)
Fahrenheit 451 (1953)
The Faerie Queene (1590–1609)
Faust (1808; 1832)
Frankenstein (1818)
Giles Goat-Boy (1966)
Go Tell It on the Mountain (1952)
The Great Gatsby (1925)
Gravity's Rainbow (1973)
Heart of Darkness (1910)
Hiroshima (1946)
The Hollow Men (1925)
The Invisible Man (1952)
King Lear (c. 1605–1606)
Kill Hole (1992)
Lord of the Flies (1954)
Love in the Ruins (1971)
Miss Lonelyhearts (1933)
Moby Dick (1851)
Le Morte D'Arthur (c. 1469)
The Mysterious Stranger (1898)
The Narrative of Arthur Gordon Pym, of Nantucket (1838)
Native Son (1940)
One Hundred Years of Solitude (1967)
The Origin of the Brunists (1966)
Out of the Silent Planet (1938)
Paradise Lost (1667)
Perelandra (1943)
The Second Coming (1920)
Siddhartha (1922)
Slaughter-House Five (1968)
The Tempest (1623)
Terra Nostra (1975)
The Thanatos Syndrome (1987)
That Hideous Strength (1945)
Things Fall Apart (1959)
The Waste Land (1922)
The Violent Bear It Away (1955)

APPENDIX C

TITLES FEATURED IN THE TEXT, BY DATE

The Divine Comedy (1310–1314)
Le Morte D'Arthur (c. 1469)
The Faerie Queene (1590–1609)
Doctor Faustus (1604)
King Lear (c. 1605–1606)
The Tempest (1623)
The Day of Doom (1662)
Paradise Lost (1667)
Faust (1808; 1832)
Frankenstein (1818)
The Narrative of Arthur Gordon Pym, of Nantucket (1838)
Moby Dick (1851)
The Blithedale Romance (1852)
The Confidence Man (1857)
The Brothers Karamazov (1878–1880)
A Connecticut Yankee in King Arthur's Court (1889)
Heart of Darkness (1910)
The Second Coming (1920)
Siddhartha (1922)
The Waste Land (1922)
The Great Gatsby (1925)
The Hollow Men (1925)
As I Lay Dying (1930)
Brave New World (1932)
Miss Lonelyhearts (1933)
Absalom, Absalom! (1936)
Out of the Silent Planet (1938)
The Day of the Locust (1939)
Native Son (1940)
Perelandra (1943)
That Hideous Strength (1945)
Hiroshima (1946)
Doktor Faustus (1947)
Go Tell It on the Mountain (1952)
The Invisible Man (1952)
Fahrenheit 451 (1953)
Lord of the Flies (1954)
The Violent Bear It Away (1955)
Alas, Babylon (1959)
Things Fall Apart (1959)
Cat's Cradle (1963)
Giles Goat-Boy (1966)
The Origin of the Brunists (1966)
One Hundred Years of Solitude (1967)
The Mysterious Stranger (1898)
Slaughter-House Five (1968)
Black Rain (1969)
Love in the Ruins (1971)
Gravity's Rainbow (1973)
Terra Nostra (1975)
The Thanatos Syndrome (1987)
Almanac of the Dead (1991)
Kill Hole (1992)

APPENDIX D

FEATURED APOCALYPTIC LITERATURE FROM WORLD SCRIPTURES, MYTHS, AND LEGENDS

Hindu Apocalypse, India (2000–1000 B.C.), Myth of Rudra.

Zoroastrian Apocalypse, Persia (700–600 B.C.), The Gathas.

Buddhist Apocalypse, India (c. 566 B.C.), Maitreya.

Old Testament Apocalypses, Judah (587–400 B.C.), Daniel; Ezekiel 38–39; Issaiah 24–27; Joel 2–3; Zechariah 12–14.

New Testament Apocalypse, Greece (c. 90–96 A.D.), Revelation.

Islamic Apocalypse, Arabia (570–632 A.D.), The Koran.

Norse Apocalypse, Scandinavia (800–1000 A.D.), Myth of Ragnarok.

Noncanonical Apocalypses (not included in text)

Jewish Apocalypses, 4 Ezra; 2 Baruch; 1 Enoch.

Christian Apocalypses, The Apocalypse of Peter; The Shepherd of Hermas; Sibylline Oracles.

PRIMARY SOURCES

Achebe, Chinua. 1959. *Things Fall Apart.* New York: Fawcett Crest.

Alighieri, Dante. 1947. *The Divine Comedy.* Garden City, NY: Doubleday.

Bradbury, Ray. 1953. *Fahrenheit 451.* New York: Ballantine Books.

Conrad, Joseph. 1910. *Heart of Darkness and The Secret Sharer.* Reprint. New York: New American Library (1983).

Coover, Robert. 1978. *The Origin of the Brunists.* New York: Bantam.

Daniel. *Holy Bible.* 1975. Open Bible Edition. Nashville, TN: Thomas Nelson, Publishers, 784–799.

Edwards, Jonathan. 1979. "Sinners in the Hands of an Angry God." In *Norton Anthology of American Literature,* edited by Ronald Gottesman et al. Vol. 1. New York: W. W. Norton & Company, 245–259.

Eliot, T. S. 1986. "The Waste Land." In *Norton Anthology of English Literature,* edited by M. H. Abrams et al. Vol. 2. New York: W. W. Norton & Company, 2180–2196.

———. "The Hollow Men." 1984. In *English and Western Literature.* New York: Macmillan Publishers, 543–545.

Ellison, Ralph. 1953. *The Invisible Man.* New York: New American Library.

Faulkner, William. 1936. *Absalom, Absalom!* New York: Modern Library.

———. 1957. *As I Lay Dying.* New York: Random House.

Fitzgerald, F. Scott. 1925. *The Great Gatsby.* New York: Charles Scribner's Sons.

Frank, Pat. 1959. *Alas, Babylon.* Reprint. New York: Bantam (1983).

Fuentes, Carlos. 1976. *Terra Nostra.* Trans. Margaret Sayers Peden. New York: Farrar, Straus and Giroux.

Hawthorne, Nathaniel. 1958. *The Blithedale Romance.* New York: W. W. Norton & Company.

Hesse, Hermann. 1959. *Siddhartha.* New York: New Directions Publishing.

Highwater, Jamake. 1992. *Kill Hole.* New York: Grove Press.

Huxley, Aldous. 1932. *Brave New World.* Reprint. New York: Bantam (1967).

Ibuse, Masuji. 1985. *Black Rain.* Trans. John Bester. New York: Bantam.

Jonah. *The Holy Bible.* 1975. The Open Bible Edition. Nashville, TN: Thomas Nelson, Publishers, 822–823.

Lewis, C. S. 1965. *Out of the Silent Planet.* New York: Collier.

———. 1944. *Perelandra.* New York: Macmillan.

———. 1946. *That Hideous Strength.* New York. Macmillan.

Mann, Thomas. 1948. *Doktor Faustus.* New York: Vintage International.

Márquez, Gabriel García. 1970. *One Hundred Years of Solitude.* Trans. Gregory Rabassa. New York: Avon Books.

Melville, Herman. 1964. *The Confidence-Man.* New York: New American Library.

———. 1961. *Moby-Dick or the White Whale.* New York: New American Library.

Milton, John. 1986. "Paradise Lost." In *The Norton Anthology of English Literature,* edited by M. H. Abrams et al. Vol. 1. New York: W. W. Norton & Company, 1446–1590.

O'Connor, Flannery. 1955. "The Violent Bear It Away." In *Three.* Reprint. New York: Signet Books (1960).

Open Bible Edition of the Holy Bible. 1975. Nashville, TN: Thomas Nelson, Publishers.

Percy, Walker. 1971. *Love in the Ruins: The Adventures of a Bad Catholic at a Time Near the End of the World.* New York: Ivy Books.

———. "Notes for a Novel about the End of the World." *Katallagete* 3 (Fall 1970), 9; reprinted in Percy's collected essays, *The Message in the Bottle.* New York: Farrar, Straus and Giroux (1979), 101–118.

———. *Sign-Posts in a Strange Land.* New York: The Noonday Press, 1991.

———. *The Thanatos Syndrome.* New York: Bantam Books, 1979.

Poe, Edgar Allan. 1975. *The Narrative of Arthur Gordon Pym of Nantucket,* edited by Harold Beaver. New York: Penguin Books.

Pynchon, Thomas. 1973. *Gravity's Rainbow.* New York: Penguin Books.

The Qu'ran. 1992. New York: Quality Paperback Books.

Revelation. 1975. *The Holy Bible.* Open Bible Edition. Nashville, TN: Thomas Nelson, Publishers, 1182–1198.

Shakespeare, William. 1980. *King Lear.* In *The Complete Works of Shakespeare,* edited by David Bevington. 3d ed. Glenview, IL: Scott, Foresman and Company, 1173–1215.

———. 1980. *The Tempest*. In *The Complete Works of Shakespeare,* edited by David Bevington. 3d ed. Glenview, IL: Scott, Foresman and Company, 1499–1525.

Shelley, Mary Wollstonecraft. *Frankenstein*. 1818. Reprint. New York: Collier (1961).

Silko, Leslie Marmon. 1991. *The Almanac of the Dead*. New York: Simon and Schuster.

Twain, Mark. 1889. *A Connecticut Yankee in King Arthur's Court*. Reprint. New York: Bantam Books (1982).

———. 1962. *The Mysterious Stranger and Other Stories*. New York: New American Library.

Vonnegut, Kurt, Jr. 1963. *Cat's Cradle*. Reprint. New York: Dell (1970).

———. 1968. *Slaughterhouse-Five; or The Children's Crusade: A Duty-Dance with Death*. Reprint. New York: Dell (1981).

West, Nathanael. 1933. *Miss Lonelyhearts and The Day of the Locust*. Reprint. New York: New Directions (1950).

Wigglesworth, Michael. 1662. "The Day of Doom, or A Poetical Description of the Great and Last Judgement." In *The Puritans,* edited by Perry Miller and Thomas H. Johnson. Rev. ed. New York: Harper (1963), Vol. 2, 587–606.

Wright, Richard. 1966. *Native Son*. New York: Harper & Row, Publishers.

Yeats, William Butler. 1991. "The Second Coming." In *Literature: An Introduction to Fiction, Poetry, and Drama,* edited by X. J. Kennedy. 5th ed. New York: HarperCollins, 718.

SECONDARY RESOURCES CITED IN TEXT

Bergsten, Gunilla. 1986. "'Doctor Faustus' as a 'Historical' Novel." In *Modern Critical Views: Thomas Mann.* Ed. Harold Bloom. New York: Chelsea House Publishers, 71–85.

Bierlein, J. F. 1994. *Parallel Myths.* New York: Ballantine Books.

Bloom, Harold. 1988. "Introduction." In *Modern Critical Interpretations: Fyodor Dostoevsky's The Brothers Karamazov.* New York: Chelsea House Publishers, 1.

Browne, Lewis. 1946. *The World's Great Scriptures: An Anthology of the Sacred Books of the Ten Principal Religions.* New York: Macmillan.

Cirlot, J. E. 1971. *A Dictionary of Symbols.* 2d ed. Trans. Jack Sage. New York: Philosophical Library.

Ciuba, Gary M. 1991. *Walker Percy: Books of Revelation.* Athens, GA: University of Georgia Press.

Dewey, Joseph. 1990. *In a Dark Time: The Apocalyptic Temper in the American Novel of the Nuclear Age.* West Lafayette, IN: Purdue University Press.

Ellul, Jacques. 1977. *Apocalypse: The Book of Revelation.* New York: Seabury.

Faris, Wendy B. 1983. *Carlos Fuentes.* New York: Frederick Ungar Publishing Co.

Fjagesund, Peter. 1991. *The Apocalyptic World of D. H. Lawrence.* New York: Oxford University Press.

Frazer, James G. 1981. *The Golden Bough: The Roots of Religion and Folklore.* New York: Avenel Books.

Friedman, Alan J., and Manfred Puetz. 1986. "Gravity's Rainbow: Science as Metaphor." In *Modern Critical Views: Thomas Pynchon.* Ed. Harold Bloom. Chelsea House Publishers, 23–35.

Frye, Northrop. 1971. *Anatomy of Criticism: Four Essays.* Princeton, NJ: Princeton University Press.

———. 1982. *The Great Code: The Bible and Literature.* New York: Harcourt Brace Jovanovich.

Gates, Henry Louis, Jr., and K. A. Appiah, eds. 1993. *Richard Wright: Critical Perspectives Past and Present.* New York: Amistad.

Hamilton, Edith. 1942. *Mythology.* Reprint. New York: Signet (1969).

Henkel, Kathryn. 1973. *The Apocalypse.* College Park, MD: University of Maryland Department of Art.

Hoffman, Daniel G. 1962. "The Confidence-Man: His Masquerade." In *Melville: A Collection of Critical Essays.* Ed. Richard Chase. NJ: Prentice-Hall, Inc., 125–143.

Honsa, William M., Jr. 1986. "Parody and Narrator in Thomas Mann's Doctor Faustus." *Modern Critical Views: Thomas Mann.* Ed. Harold Bloom. New York: Chelsea House Publishers. 219–226.

Kermode, Frank. 1967. *The Sense of an Ending: Studies in the Theory of Fiction.* New York: Oxford University Press.

Ketterer, David. 1974. *New Worlds for Old: The Apocalyptic Imagination, Science Fiction and American Literature.* Garden City, NY: Anchor Press.

Lewicki, Zbigniew. 1984. *The Bang and the Whimper: Apocalypse and Entropy in American Literature.* Contributions in American Studies 71. Westport, CT: Greenwood.

May, John R. 1972. *Toward a New Earth: Apocalypse in the American Novel.* Notre Dame, IN: University of Notre Dame Press.

Mendelson, Edward. 1986. "Pynchon's Gravity." In *Modern Critical Views: Thomas Pynchon.* Ed. Harold Bloom. Chelsea House Publishers, 15–21.

Miller, Perry. 1951. "The End of the World." *William and Mary Quarterly.* 3d ser. 8: 171–191.

Miller, Perry, ed. 1956. *The American Puritans: Their Prose and Poetry.* New York: Doubleday & Company.

Morrell, David. 1976. *John Barth: An Introduction.* University Park: Penn State University Press.

Olderman, Raymond M. 1972. *Beyond the Waste Land: The American Novel in the 1960's.* New Haven, CT: Yale University Press.

Peace, Richard. 1988. "Justice and Punishment." In *Modern Critical Interpretations: Fyodor Dostoevsky's The Brothers Karamazov.* New York: Chelsea House Publishers, 7–37.

Reddish, Mitchell G., ed. 1990. *Apocalyptic Literature: A Reader.* Nashville: Abingdon Press.

Robinson, Douglas. 1985. *American Apocalypses: The Image of the End of the World in American Literature.* Baltimore, MD: Johns Hopkins University Press.

Sandler, Florence. 1984. "The Faerie Queene: An Elizabethan Apocalypse." In *The Apocalypse in English and Renaissance Thought and Literature.* Eds. C. A.

Patrides and Joseph Wittreich. Ithaca, NY: Cornell University Press.

Spiller, Robert E. 1956. *The Cycle of American Literature*. New York: Macmillan.

Tanner, Tony. 1989. "Introduction." In *The Confidence Man: His Masquerade*. By Herman Melville. New York: Oxford University Press.

Telotte, J. P. 1980 "A Symbolic Structure for Walker Percy's Fiction." *Modern Fiction Studies* 26: 227–240.

Tuveson, Ernest Lee. 1949. *Millennium and Utopia: A Study in the Background of the Idea of Progress*. Berkeley and Los Angeles: University of California Press.

Van der Meer. 1978. *Apocalypse: Visions from the Book of Revelation in Western Art*. New York: Alpine Fine Arts Collection, Ltd.

Williams, Raymond L. 1984. *Gabriel Garcia Marquez*. Boston, MA: G.K. Hall and Company.

Wittreich, Joseph Anthony. 1984. *"Image of that Horror": History, Prophesy, and Apocalypse in King Lear*. San Marino, CA: Huntington Library.

SUPPLEMENTARY REFERENCES

Agosta, Lucien L. "Ah-Whoom!: Egotism and Apocalypse in Kurt Vonnegut's Cat's Cradle." *Kansas Quarterly* 14.2 (1982): 127–34.

Barth, John. "The Literature of Exhaustion." *The Atlantic* August 1967: 29–34.

Bass, Thomas Alden. "An Encounter with Robert Coover." *Antioch Review* 40 (1982): 287–302.

Bayer-Berenbaum, Linda. 1982. *The Gothic Imagination: Expansion in Gothic Literature and Art.* Rutherford, NJ: Fairleigh Dickenson University Press.

Beale, G. K. 1984. *The Use of Daniel in Jewish Apocalyptic Literature and in the Revelation of St. John.* Lanham, MD: University Press of America.

Bethea, David M. 1989. *The Shape of Apocalypse in Modern Russian Fiction.* Princeton, NJ: Princeton University Press.

Boyer, Paul. 1985. *By the Bomb's Early Light: American Thought and Culture at the Dawn of the Atomic Age.* New York: Pantheon-Random.

Brians, Paul. 1987. *Nuclear Holocausts: Atomic War in Fiction, 1895–1984.* Kent, OH: Kent State University Press.

Brodtkorb, Paul, Jr. 1969. "The Confidence-Man: The Con-Man as Hero." *Studies in the Novel* 1: 421–35.

Browne, Corinne, and Robert Munro. 1981. *Time Bomb: Understanding the Threat of Nuclear Power.* New York: Morrow.

Buber, Martin. 1957. "Prophecy, Apocalyptic, and the Historical Hour." In his *Pointing the Way: Collected Essays,* translated and edited by Maurice Friedman, 192–207. New York: Harper.

Buck, Lynn. 1975. "Vonnegut's World of Comic Futility." *Studies in American Fiction* 3: 181–198.

Capouya, Emile. 1966. "Real Life in an Unreal World" (review of *The Origin of the Brunists,* by Robert Coover). *Saturday Review* 15 October: 38–40.

Chesnick, Eugene. 1973. "Novel's Ending and World's End: The Fiction of Walker Percy." *Hollins Critic* 10.5: 1–11.

Cohn, Norman. 1970. *The Pursuit of the Millennium.* New York: Oxford University Press.

Coles, Robert. 1978. *Walker Percy: An American Search.* Boston: Little, Brown.

Collins, Adela Yarbro. 1984. *Crisis and Catharsis: The Power of the Apocalypse.* Philadelphia, PA: Westminster.

Comerchero, Victor. 1964. *Nathanael West: The Ironic Prophet,* 1–50, 120–51. Syracuse, NY: Syracuse University Press.

Cope, Jackson I. 1971. "Robert Coover's Fictions." *Iowa Review* 2.4: 94–110.

Cowart, David. 1980. *Thomas Pynchon: The Art of Allusion.* Carbondale: Southern Ilinois University Press.

Daniels, Ted. 1992. *Millennialism: An International Biography.* New York: Garland Publishing.

Davidson, James West. 1977. *The Logic of Millennial Thought: Eighteenth-Century New England.* New Haven, CT: Yale University Press.

Dillard, R. H. W. 1970. "The Wisdom of the Beast: The Fiction of Robert Coover." *Hollins Critic* 7.2: 1–11.

Dorris, Michael, and Louise Erdrich. 1988. "Bangs and Whimpers: Novelists at Armageddon." *New York Times Book Review* 3 March: 1, 24–25.

Ericson, Edward E. 1992. *Fin de Siecle, Fin du Globe: Fears and Fantasies of the Late Nineteenth Century.* New York: St. Martin's Press.

Eubanks, Cecil L. 1980. "Walker Percy: Eschatology and the Politics of Grace." *Southern Quarterly* 18: 121–135.

Festinger, Leon, Henry W. Riecken, and Stanley Schlachter. 1956. *When Prophecy Fails.* Minneapolis, MN: University of Minnesota Press.

Fiedler, Leslie A. 1970. "The Divine Stupidity of Kurt Vonnegut." *Esquire* September: 195–197.

Friedrich, Otto. 1982. *The End of the World: A History.* New York: Coward.

Friedman, Melvin J., and Leris A. Lawson, eds. 1966. *The Added Dimension: The Art and Mind of Flannery O'Connor.* New York: Fordham University Press.

Gitenstern, R. Barbara. 1986. *Apocalyptic Messianism and Contemporary Jewish American Poetry.* Albany: State University Press of New York.

Goldsmith, David H. 1972. *Kurt Vonnegut, Fantasist of Fire and Ice.* Popular Writers Series 2. Bowling Green, OH: Bowling Green State University Popular Press.

Goldsmith, Steven. 1993. *Unbuilding Jerusalem: Apocalypse and Romantic Representation.* Ithaca, NY: Cornell University Press.

Hanson, Paul D. 1975. *The Dawn of Apocalyptic.* Philadelphia, PA: Fortress Press.

Hardy, John Edward. 1980. "Percy and Place: Some Beginnings and Endings." *Southern Quarterly* 18.3: 1–25.

Harris, Charles B. 1971. *Contemporary American Novelists of the Absurd.* New Haven, CT: College and University Press.

Hite, Molly. 1983. *Ideas of Order in the Novels of Thomas Pynchon.* Columbus: Ohio State University Press, 1983.

Hodder, Alan D. 1989. *Emerson's Rhetoric of Revelation: "Nature," the Reader, and the Apocalypse Within.* University Park: Penn State University Press.

Howe, Irving. 1968. "James Baldwin: At Ease in Apocalypse." *Harper's* September: 92–100.

Jaher, Frederic Cople. 1964. *Doubters and Dissenters. Cataclysmic Thought in America, 1885–1918.* New York: Free Press of Glencoe.

Jaspers, Karl. 1958. *The Future of Mankind.* Trans. E. B. Ashton. Chicago: University of Chicago Press (1961).

Kessler, Edward. 1986. *Flannery O'Connor and the Language of the Apocalypse.* Princeton, NJ: Princeton University Press.

Langer, Lawrence L. 1978. *The Age of Anxiety: Death in Modern Literature.* Boston, MA: Beacon.

Light, James F. 1961. *Nathanael West: An Interpretive Study.* Reprint. Evanston, IL: Northwestern University Press (1971).

Lundquist, James. 1977. *Kurt Vonnegut.* New York: Ungar.

McConnell, Frank D. 1977. *Four Postwar American Novelists: Bellow, Mailer, Barth, and Pynchon.* Chicago: University of Chicago Press.

McGinn, Bernard. 1979. *Visions of the End: Apocalyptic Traditions in the Middle Ages,* 1–36. New York: Columbia University Press.

McGuane, Thomas. 1971. "This Is the Way the World Will End" (review of *Love in the Ruins* by Walker Percy). *New York Times Book Review* 23 May: 7, 37.

Mani, Lakshimi. 1981. *The Apocalyptic Vision in Nineteenth Century American Fiction: A Study of Cooper, Hawthorne, and Melville.* Washington, DC: University Press of America.

Martin, Carter W. 1968. *The True Country: Themes in the Fiction of Flannery O'Connor.* Nashville, TN: Vanderbilt University Press.

Martin, Jay. 1970. *Nathanael West: The Art of His Life.* New York: Hayden.

Mendel, Arthur P. 1985. *Nineteen Eighty-Four and the Apocalyptic Imagination in America.* Amsterdam: Free University Press.

Mumford, Lewis. 1954. "Mirrors of a Violent Half-Century." In *In the Name of Sanity.* New York: Harcourt, 100–110.

O'Leary, Stephen D. 1994. *Arguing the Apocalypse: A Theory of Millennial Rhetoric.* New York: Oxford University Press.

Reid, Randall. 1967. *The Fiction of Nathanael West: No Redeemer, No Promised Land.* Chicago: University of Chicago Press, 1–12, 116–163.

Rovit, Earl. 1968. "On the Contemporary Apocalyptic Imagination." *American Scholar* 37: 453–468.

Ryken, Leland. 1970. *The Apocalyptic Vision in Paradise Lost.* Ithaca, NY: Cornell University Press.

Salmon, Arthur Edward. 1983. *Poets of the Apocalypse.* Boston: Twayne Publishers.

Schley, James, ed. 1983. "Writers in the Nuclear Age." *New England Review and Bread Loaf Quarterly* 5.

Schmithals, Walter. 1973. *The Apocalyptic Movement: Introduction and Interpretation.* Translated by John E. Seely. Nashville, TN: Abington (1975).

Shea, Robert, and Robert Anton Wilson. 1975. *The Illuminatus! Trilogy: The Eye in the Pyramid, The Golden Apple, and Leviathan.* New York: Dell Publishing.

Shroeder, John W. 1951. "Sources and Symbols for Melville's Confidence-Man." *PMLA* 66: 364–380.

Stone, Jon R. 1993. *A Guide to the End of the World: Popular Eschatology in America.* New York: Garland Publishing.

Thompson, Lawrence. 1952. *Melville's Quarrel with God.* Princeton, NJ: Princeton University Press.

Tilton, John W. 1977. "Slaughterhouse-Five: Life against Death-In-Life." In *Cosmic Satire in the Contemporary Novel*, 69–103. Lewisburg, PA: Bucknell University Press.

Wagar, Warren W. 1982. *Terminal Visions: The Literature of Last Things.* Bloomington: Indiana University Press.

Weisenburger, Steven. 1979. "The End of History?: Thomas Pynchon and the Uses of the Past." *Twentieth Century Literature* 25: 54–72.

Wilder, Amos N. 1971. "The Rhetoric of Ancient and Modern Apocalyptic." *Interpretation* 25: 436–453.

Wright, Nathalia. 1949. *Melville's Use of the Bible.* Reprint. New York: Octagon (1969).

Zuckerman, Edward. 1984. *The Day after World War III.* New York: Viking.

ILLUSTRATION CREDITS

3 AP/Wide World Photos

5 Springer/Bettmann Film Archive

10 Apocalypse, England (probably Abbey of St. Albans), Ms 524, f 7 v. Pierpont Morgan Library/Art Resource

17 Scala/Art Resource

30 National Archives

32 Alex Gottfryd. CORBIS-Bettmann

35 Bettmann Archive

52 Photofest

65 UPI/Bettmann

74 "Dante e il suo poema," Domenico di Michelino, Duomo, Florence. Art Resource

80 Bettmann Archive

84 Bettmann Archive

91 S.S. Joceyln. Bettmann Archive

93 UPI/Bettmann

95 Library of Congress LC-USZ62-44456

100 Scala/Art Resource

106 The Nobel Foundation

122 Reuters/Bettmann

130 Tate Gallery, London, Art Resource

133 Staedelsches Kunstinstitut, Frankfurt am Main, Germany. Kavaler/Art Resource

142 UPI/Bettmann

150 Library of Congress LC-USZ62-45741
155 Scala/Art Resource
157 UPI/Bettmann
158 Bettmann Archive
160 UPI/Bettmann
165 CORBIS-Bettmann
181 Bettmann Archive
184 Photofest
189 Photofest
197 Bettmann Archive
207 Bettmann Archive
217 Rare Book and Manuscript Division, Library of Congress
239 Springer/CORBIS-Bettmann
249 Bettmann Archive
262 UPI/Bettmann
269 Photofest
271 Library of Congress LC-USZ62-10610
282 Rare Book and Manuscript Collection, Library of Congress
283 Foto Marburg/Art Resource
292 Victoria and Albert Museum/Art Resource
294 UPI/Bettmann
297 Folger, Library of Congress
300 Bettmann Archive
313 Library of Congress LC-USZ61-229
345 Bettmann Archive
353 Photograph by Gordon Parks, Library of Congress LC-USW3-30283
356 Bettmann Archive

INDEX

Note: Page numbers in **boldface** denote entry headings.